A Union Like Ours

OTHER BOOKS FROM BRIGHT LEAF

House Stories: The Meanings of Home in a New England Town
BETH LUEY

Bricklayer Bill: The Untold Story of the Workingman's Boston Marathon
PATRICK L. KENNEDY AND LAWRENCE W. KENNEDY

Concrete Changes: Architecture, Politics, and the Design of Boston City Hall
BRIAN M. SIRMAN

Williamstown and Williams College: Explorations in Local History
DUSTIN GRIFFIN

Massachusetts Treasures: A Guide to Marvelous, Must-See Museums
CHUCK D'IMPERIO

Boston's Twentieth-Century Bicycling Renaissance: Cultural Change on Two Wheels
LORENZ J. FINISON

Went to the Devil: A Yankee Whaler in the Slave Trade
ANTHONY J. CONNORS

At Home: Historic Houses of Eastern Massachusetts
BETH LUEY

Black Lives, Native Lands, White Worlds: A History of Slavery in New England
JARED ROSS HARDESTY

At Home: Historic Houses of Central and Western Massachusetts
BETH LUEY

Flight Calls: Exploring Massachusetts through Birds
JOHN R. NELSON

Lost Wonderland: The Brief and Brilliant Life of Boston's Million Dollar Amusement Park
STEPHEN R. WILK

I Believe I'll Go Back Home: Roots and Revival in New England Folk Music
THOMAS S. CURREN

Legends of the Common Stream
JOHN HANSON MITCHELL

Mind and Hearts: The Story of James Otis Jr. and Mercy Otis Warren
JEFFREY H. HACKER

The Combat Zone: Murder, Race, and Boston's Struggle for Justice
JAN BROGAN

Letters from Red Farm: The Untold Story of the Friendship between Helen Keller and Journalist Joseph Edgar Chamberlin
ELIZABETH EMERSON

A Union Like Ours

The Love Story of
F. O. Matthiessen and Russell Cheney

Scott Bane

BRIGHT LEAF
BOOKS THAT ILLUMINATE
Amherst and Boston
An imprint of University of Massachusetts Press

A *Union Like Ours* has been supported by the Regional Books Fund, established by donors in 2019 to support the University of Massachusetts Press's Bright Leaf imprint.

Bright Leaf, an imprint of the University of Massachusetts Press, publishes accessible and entertaining books about New England. Highlighting the history, culture, diversity, and environment of the region, Bright Leaf offers readers the tools and inspiration to explore its landmarks and traditions, famous personalities, and distinctive flora and fauna.

ISBN 978-1-62534-637-7 (paper); 638-4 (hardcover)

Designed by Sally Nichols
Set in Alegreya
Printed and bound by Books International, Inc.
Cover design by Sally Nichols
Cover art: photographer unknown, *F. O. "Matty" Matthiessen, and Russell Cheney, Normandy, summer 1925*. F. O. Matthiessen Papers/Beinecke 10560792. Wikimedia CC 1.0.

Library of Congress Cataloging-in-Publication Data

Names: Bane, Scott Leslie, 1967– author.
Title: A union like ours : the love story of F. O. Matthiessen and Russell Cheney / Scott Bane.
Description: Amherst : Bright Leaf, an imprint of University of Massachusetts Press, 2022. | Includes bibliographical references and index.
Identifiers: LCCN 2021054624 (print) | LCCN 2021054625 (ebook) | ISBN 9781625346377 (paperback) | ISBN 9781625346384 (hardcover) | ISBN 9781613769119 (ebook) | ISBN 9781613769126 (ebook)
Subjects: LCSH: Matthiessen, F. O. (Francis Otto), 1902–1950. | Cheney, Russell, 1881–1945. | Critics—United States—Biography. | Scholars—United States—Biography. | Painters—United States—Biography. | Gay men—United States—History—20th century. | Homosexuality and literature—United States—History—20th century. | United States—Intellectual life—20th century.
Classification: LCC PS29.M35 B36 2022 (print) | LCC PS29.M35 (ebook) | DDC 810.9 [B] —dc23/eng/20220204
LC record available at https://lccn.loc.gov/2021054624
LC ebook record available at https://lccn.loc.gov/2021054625

British Library Cataloguing-in-Publication Data
A catalog record for this book is available from the British Library.

Portions of the manuscript were previously published as "F. O. Matthiessen and Russell Cheney: A Focus on New England and America," *New England Journal of History*; "In the Footsteps of F. O. Matthiessen," *Gay & Lesbian Review* (November–December 2018); and "Russell Cheney: An Artist in His Own Right," *Gay & Lesbian Review* (July–August 2019). Reprinted with permission. Portions of the epilogue were previously published as "In Sickness and in Health," in *Memoir Magazine* (November 2020), and "A Union Like Ours," in *Hippocampus Magazine* (March/April 2021).

For David

Contents

Acknowledgments   ix

Prologue: Do the Dead Choose Their Biographers?   1

1   The Search for Companionship   7

2   "Between the Old and the New"   26

3   Falling in Love: The Exuberant Years   48

4   A Star Is Born   65

5   Making a Home in Kittery   89

6   Shining in a Dark Time: Politics and Painting
    in the Depression   107

7   In Sickness and in Health: The Hartford Retreat,
    McLean Hospital, and Baldpate Hospital   127

8   The Green Light across the Piscataqua   145

9   Losing Touch: Life without Cheney   174

10 Aftermath and Afterglow   202

    Epilogue: Getting Married After All   213

    Notes   225

    Index   283

Acknowledgments

First and foremost, I am grateful to Richard Candee, professor emeritus, American and New England studies, Boston University, and Carol L. Cheney, Russell Cheney's great niece, for fielding a steady stream of questions from me concerning Russell Cheney's life and work, which together they have explored for more than a dozen years. They have developed a catalogue raisonné of more than 1,150 presently known works, about half of which have now been located, and they cohost an evolving website, russellcheney. com, which illustrates many of these works. They welcome others to submit inquiries with photographs for identification or verification. Russell Cheney sprang to life for me through his painting. I also appreciate Richard Candee and Robert Chase allowing me to reproduce images of Cheney's paintings *Depot Square* (1927) and *Facing East, Kittery, Maine* (1944).

Yale University was helpful in supplying high-quality digital images of Matthiessen's and Cheney's college graduation photographs. I am thankful to Harvard University, Eliot House, F. O. Matthiessen Room; the Manchester Historical Society; and the Wadsworth Atheneum Museum of Art for allowing me to reproduce images of Cheney's paintings. I appreciate the Amon Carter Museum of American Art permitting me to reproduce *Swimming* (1885) by Thomas Eakins, which Matthiessen had used in his most important book, *American Renaissance: Art and Expression in the Age of Emerson and Whitman*.

Throughout my research, my motto has been: Engaged and curious scholars, librarians, and archivists are a researcher's best friends. There have been many people who lived up to and exceeded this high standard, starting with Sachiko Clayton, Paul Friedman, Mary Jones, Clayton Kirking, Angel Pagan, and Ray Pun of the New York Public Library, who have all been enormously helpful. Similarly, Dave Smith of the Manchester Historical Society was generous with his time and resources on Russell Cheney and Cheney Brothers Silk Manufacturing Company. Jeff Roth of the *New York Times* and Andy Lanset of New York Public Radio helped me track down a sound recording of Matthiessen's seconding speech for Henry Wallace in 1948 held by the Library of Congress, so I finally heard Matthiessen's voice for the first time. Maggie Humberston at the Springfield History Library and Archives and Laura Smith, Archives & Special Collections, University of Connecticut Library, both made invaluable scans of materials for me. Donna M. Cassidy, professor of art history and American and New England studies, University of Southern Maine, and Gail R. Scott, independent art historian, Marsden Hartley Legacy Project with Bates College Museum of Art, helped me better understand the art historical context for Russell Cheney's painting. Similarly, staff at libraries, archives, and history societies have been indefatigable, including those at the Beinecke Library, Yale University; Houghton Library, Harvard University; Harvard University Archives; Connecticut Historical Society; Massachusetts Historical Society; Massachusetts Archives; Boston Public Library, New England Historic Genealogical Society; and Portsmouth (NH) Public Library.

Several friends and former professors helped me keep faith in this project, when my energy and spirits flagged. I'm grateful to the late Louise DeSalvo, Ann Lauinger, Diane Stevenson, and S. Kirk Walsh for their wisdom and counsel. Similarly, Malaga Baldi believed in the book until it found a home at Bright Leaf, an imprint of the University of Massachusetts Press.

I was very fortunate when I started my research that a number of Matthiessen's students were available to speak with me, including Daniel Aaron, Warner Berthoff, Vittorio Gabrieli, Eileen Finletter, Justin Kaplan, J. C. Levenson, Leo Marx, Adeline Naiman, Eric Solomon, and Barbara Wasserman. I also talked with several of Cheney's relatives, including Elizabeth (Betsy) Knapp Packard and Donald Pitkin. Everyone's personal recollections brought Matthiessen and Cheney into sharper focus. Several of these people have since died, and I'm thankful to their relatives and literary executors for granting me permission to quote from my conversations with them.

During this project, I had the good fortune to work with the incomparable writing teacher William Zinsser before he died in the spring of 2015. Bill was losing his eyesight in the last years of his life, so I read the entire manuscript aloud to him. He would say things to me along the lines of, "This chapter needs to be 10 percent shorter." But he was also generous with his praise: "It's so damn good." I'm grateful for friends and colleagues who read early drafts of the manuscript, including Peter Antony, Dave Barbor, Martin Duberman, Barbara Fisher, Nicole A. Gordon, James Hatch, Jeffrey Hoover, Barney Karpfinger, and Kevin O'Connor. Their insights, observations, and questions helped me make the manuscript stronger.

As a first-time author, I appreciate the editorial and production staff at Bright Leaf/University of Massachusetts Press, especially Brian Halley, senior editor; Rachael DeShano, managing editor; and Courtney Andree, marketing and sales director. Their questions helped make the book stronger, and their guidance has been invaluable to me. Nancy Raynor's expert copyediting saved me from myself many times.

Thanks to the *New England Journal of History*, *The Gay & Lesbian Review*, *Memoir Magazine*, and *Hippocampus Magazine* for publishing early excerpts from the book and for permission to reprint them here.

As described in the book, Matthiessen had a sometimes-rocky relationship with Harvard, but Harvard professors and staff have been helpful, generous, and welcoming to me, including Michael Bronski, professor of the practice in media and activism in studies of women, gender, and sexuality; Kevin van Anglen, then keeper of the F. O. Matthiessen Room; then masters of Eliot House, Doug A. Melton and Gail A. O'Keefe; and Eliot House administrator, Sue Weltman.

And lastly, I want to thank David W. Dunlap, to whom this book is dedicated. David also read an early draft of the manuscript, and our life together helped me appreciate Matthiessen and Cheney's commitment to each other. He is a part of this book from the first page to the last.

A Union Like Ours

Prologue

Do the Dead Choose Their Biographers?

One morning in 2003, sitting at my partner David's breakfast table, I was thumbing through the paper—David was a reporter at the *New York Times*, so it was a regular feature in our mornings—when I read a review of *The Crimson Letter* by Douglas Shand-Tucci, a book about gay men at Harvard. The review highlighted the relationship between scholar F. O. (Francis Otto) Matthiessen and his partner, Russell Cheney, a painter. Matthiessen had been a professor at Harvard from 1929 to 1950 in the history and literature department; he was also a gay man. Shand-Tucci claimed—not unreasonably, as I later learned—that Matthiessen's landmark study of American literature, *American Renaissance: Art and Expression in the Age of Emerson and Whitman* (1941), was an outgrowth of and a testament to his twenty-year relationship with Cheney. The idea piqued my interest in part because it seemed so far-fetched, a book of literary scholarship as a gay love letter.

I checked out Matthiessen's book from the library the first chance I got. On opening *American Renaissance*, I scanned the author's acknowledgments page until my eye came to the place-stamp at the bottom of the page: "Kittery, Maine." I was dumb-founded. Kittery is a small town on the extreme southern coast of Maine, just over the New Hampshire border. My parents' first home was in Kittery, the town right next door to York, where I later grew up. They were just starting out and rented a bungalow in Kittery. I have no memories of the house, since I was a baby. I only have a photo of me strapped around the waist into a wash-basin in the kitchen sink, taking an early bath and chewing on a facecloth, a favorite activity at the time. What did this signature work of twentieth-century scholarship on American literature have to do with Kittery, Maine? And who were the two men, two gay men, involved in a relationship that looked a whole lot like a marriage that Shand-Tucci claimed the book memorialized? Were they models and exemplars? Or was theirs a cautionary tale? Perhaps a little bit of both? As I dived into *American Renaissance*, I loved it. Matthiessen wrote the kind of cultural history that I had liked so much during college, analyzing literature as art but also considering it as a historical index that can reveal something about the time and place in which it was created.

The following summer, David and I made our annual pilgrimage north to visit my family in York and then planned to go on to Provincetown, Massachusetts, at the tip of Cape Cod. While we were in Maine, we drove to the library in nearby Portsmouth, New Hampshire. I knew about Russell Cheney from the review in the *Times*, but I was only about halfway through *American Renaissance*. (Even though I was enjoying the book, full-time work and full-time graduate school relegated reading books for pleasure to my morning and evening subway commutes.) But in Portsmouth I discovered *Rat &the Devil: The Journal Letters of F. O. Matthiessen and Russell Cheney* (1978), a selection of the some thirty-one hundred letters that Matthiessen and Cheney exchanged. The book also contained Matthiessen's evocative, touching, and well-written story of his coming out to Cheney in 1924 aboard the ocean liner *Paris*. I scanned Cheney's obituary in the *Portsmouth Herald* and thumbed through *Russell Cheney: A Record of His Work* (1946), Matthiessen's monograph about Cheney's painting. Then I saw my first photograph of Cheney and one of his paintings, *Howard Lathrop* (1937), which the library owns. Somewhere in all this I started to focus on the twenty-year age difference between Matthiessen and Cheney; Cheney was the elder. It got my attention because fifteen years separate David and me; David is the elder. Now that we had the address of Matthiessen and Cheney's house in Kittery, we found it on a map and drove by. The modesty, understatement, and restraint of the house compared with ever-grander houses that had started to spring up along the Maine coast in the era of income inequality immediately appealed to us. It was so simple and so perfect.

Later, as I read *Rat & the Devil*, I was especially drawn to Matthiessen's and Cheney's letters. I felt as though I were watching Matthiessen, in particular, mature. Between Matthiessen's time at Oxford University, which he attended on a Rhodes Scholarship, and beginning graduate school at Harvard, he leapt forward in his maturity. I could hear it in his voice. The I-love-you-more-than-the-sunrise quality to both Matthiessen's and Cheney's letters receded, as the first blush of romance ebbed. I also witnessed in the letters Matthiessen's development as a scholar, which was fascinating. His reading was voracious. I kept seeing Matthiessen and Cheney's life together as a movie, and their story made me want to write about them. Matthiessen and Cheney's story hooked me; history had been hiding in my own backyard.

As I plunged into Matthiessen's work and life, he appealed to me intellectually and politically. I felt a kinship with him; I related to his mind in a way that transcended time. Matthiessen spoke to me, and I started to believe that I spoke to him and Cheney, in turn. Both the resonances and the differences between my own life and Matthiessen's and Cheney's lives were uncanny enough that I thought: Do the dead choose their biographers?

F. O. Matthiessen was one of the most important US literary scholars of the first half of the twentieth century. He helped solidify the canon of American classics, notably works by the writers he included in *American Renaissance*: Emerson, Thoreau, Hawthorne, Melville, and Whitman. Beyond *American Renaissance*,

Matthiessen often sought out figures he considered underappreciated but deserving of more attention, such as Sarah Orne Jewett, T. S. Eliot, and Henry James. Although all three writers are today well-recognized members of the literary firmament— Jewett less so than the other two—Matthiessen existed at a time when they were not. He helped affix their stars. Matthiessen is also credited as a founder of American studies, which draws on and integrates different fields, such as literature, history, film, anthropology, and sociology, among others. The magnitude of Matthiessen's achievement stands tall; few people can claim to have helped create a new field. In response, there have been numerous scholarly articles about Matthiessen and his legacy, as well as three books: Giles Gunn, *F. O. Matthiessen: The Critical Achievement* (1975); Frederick C. Stern, *F. O. Matthiessen: Christian Socialist as Critic* (1981); and William E. Cain, *F. O. Matthiessen and the Politics of Criticism* (1988). In more recent years, Matthiessen's influence has ebbed, as the very notion of a canon, much less whose works get included, has been subject to needed debate and reexamination.

Matthiessen appealed to me, too, because he worked to bring the values he held dear in the aesthetic world of literature to fruition in the real world. Living as we do in a new Gilded Age at the beginning of the twenty-first century, Matthiessen remains relevant for his sharp focus on economic inequality. This book contextualizes Matthiessen's political activism within the history of organized labor, the principal vehicle by which Matthiessen expressed his commitment to greater socioeconomic fairness and equality. The book also considers Matthiessen's personal motivations for his political activism, which to date have largely been overlooked. Matthiessen made strides in the right direction on a number of important issues beyond economic inequality, such as advocating for greater racial justice, although not all of his political activities were equally successful. His judgment of political causes wavered toward the end of his too-short life. But his activism did have one important by-product: it further opened up his view of literature to include writers such as Theodore Dreiser, the subject of his last book.

Matthiessen's 1950 death by suicide capped and sealed his mystique, so much so that his life and work have also inspired fiction, including May Sarton, *Faithful Are the Wounds* (1955), and Mark Merlis, *American Studies* (1994). As one scholar noted more recently, "Whether we think of Matthiessen as a naive lefty internationalist, a stuffy formalist, or some other imperfect vessel, something in his life and scholarship still resonates."

Matthiessen and Cheney's relationship and their love for each other were the foundation on which they built their life together and which anchored their endeavors. Given the time when they lived, it's surprising that they did not struggle more with their homosexuality. Part of what fascinates me about both men, but particularly Matthiessen, is that they articulated or tried to articulate a near-contemporary definition of "gay" as an organizing principle to a sense of self. That Matthiessen did so without the aid of LGBTQ rights, the civil rights movement, or the sexual revolution leads to the intriguing question: How does someone reach for representation or rights when they have no language for them? During their lives, both Matthiessen and Cheney saw being gay as a private matter. For Matthiessen, it was not until the last few years of his life that he was able to imagine a world in which a person's sexuality could be part of his or her public identity. Paradoxically, while Matthiessen would support just about any progressive political cause, he never broached the one that would have touched his life most directly. To better understand where Matthiessen's conception of his sexuality was groundbreaking and where he was more conservative, I have situated his and Cheney's personal stories within the larger frame of gay history during the first half of the twentieth century.

Of the two men, Cheney has been the more difficult to research and write about: although his work was well known during the

1920s and 1930s, his painting did not have the far-reaching effects that Matthiessen's scholarship has had. Consequently, much less has been written about him. To date, the most extended examination of Cheney's work remains Matthiessen's monograph, *Russell Cheney: A Record of His Work*. Cheney started off as an impressionist, moved into postimpressionism, and ended his career as an astute regionalist of northern New England. A thorough assessment of Cheney's painting and his career has yet to be written, but *A Union Like Ours* tells Cheney's story in greater detail and breadth than anyone to date has told it, including Matthiessen.

In many ways, Cheney was the emotional center of his and Matthiessen's relationship, and his close connection to his wealthy, successful family of silk manufacturers shaped how the couple's life together unfolded. In Cheney's painting, his connection to the history of New England and America, his roots in Maine, and his friendships with working-class men, Cheney lived or practiced much of what Matthiessen considered intellectually. How thrilling this must have been for Matthiessen to be so close to someone who brought his ideas to life, and how devastating it must have been when Cheney died in 1945.

Chapter 1

The Search for Companionship

Francis Otto Matthiessen was born February 2, 1902, in Pasadena, California. He was named after a paternal great-uncle, who had died a year earlier. Matthiessen had three older siblings: Frederick William III; George Dwight (known as Dwight); and Lucy Orne. Matthiessen's father, Frederick William Matthiessen Jr., was heir to the company fortune of Westclox, makers of the well-known Big Ben alarm clock. Unusual for the time, Matthiessen's parents divorced while he was still a teenager. Matthiessen blamed his father for the breakup, claiming that there was "an empty space where my father should have been." Conversely, Matthiessen idealized his mother, Lucy Orne Pratt, who had originally come from Springfield, Massachusetts, where her family had lived for several generations.

Many years later, based on Matthiessen's own claims about his family's lineage, his friends reported that his mother was "a distant relative of the novelist Sarah Orne Jewett." This claim has not been substantiated because Sarah Orne Jewett's lineage on the Orne side is rather murky. But Matthiessen's connection to the Orne clan generally was quite solid and traceable to the first generation of Ornes in America. Intimately bound up with the Orne family's history was its connection to the early days of Unitarianism in New England. When the Ornes, who had been Congregationalists, first put down roots in Springfield, an upheaval was taking place within Congregationalism over whether one believed in the Trinity that defines one God in three persons, the Father, the Son, and the Holy Spirit, or whether one believed in the essential "oneness" of God. In the early nineteenth century this debate provoked votes in many Congregational churches across New England. Often a minority of parishioners who did not support belief in the Trinity withdrew to form a separate Unitarian Congregational Church. The Ornes were central to this debate in Springfield.

The young woman who later became F. O. Matthiessen's mother, Lucy Orne Pratt, attended the Howard School for Girls in Springfield throughout her youth and young adulthood in the 1870s and 1880s. On Mondays, the girls and young women regularly wrote summaries of the sermons that they had heard in church the day before. Lucy Orne Pratt followed in her family's footsteps, worshipping at the Church of the Unity, and Unitarian beliefs came to have a lasting effect on her and her son. Unitarianism had evolved into a tolerant faith that resisted a formalized creed. As with many liberal Christian sects, in general Unitarians do not believe in predestination or eternal damnation. Love is the basic tenet of Unitarianism: God's love of men and women, and human love as a force for good in the world.

As an adult, Lucy Orne Pratt was neither beautiful nor unattractive; she had a round face and kept her dark hair neatly braided in a bun. Kindness and warmth played over her features, around her mouth and in her eyes, as though the Unitarian teachings of her youth had made their mark on her personality and character. She met F. W. Matthiessen Jr. at a resort in California, and in 1893 they were married at the Church of the Unity in a big ceremony that was the talk of Springfield. F. W. Matthiessen Sr. gave the newlyweds a check for $5,000 (approximately $146,000 in 2020 dollars), an astronomical sum at the time.

The young couple initially lived in LaSalle, Illinois, where Westclox was based. F. O. Matthiessen's eldest brother Frederick

William III was born in Chicago in 1894. A few years later, the young couple moved to southern California, where they set up house on the eight-thousand-acre Potrero ranch in Ventura County—roughly the size of ten Central Parks—that had been purchased by F. W. Matthiessen Sr. On the ranch, Matthiessen's father assumed the role of gentleman farmer, raising cattle, horses, and other livestock. From the late 1890s into the new century, George Dwight, Lucy Orne, and Francis Otto were born in succession a few years apart.

But all was not newly wedded bliss for the Matthiessens in the Golden State. Just a few years after Francis Otto was born, the family returned to LaSalle to live with Matthiessen's grandparents. F. W. Matthiessen Jr., was reckless or careless or both, shooting himself in the arm while cleaning his gun, and he liked to spend money. In 1906, F. W. Matthiessen Sr., announced publicly that he was no longer going to pay the debts that his son and his family incurred. Then, in November 1908, Matthiessen's parents separated. Lucy Orne Matthiessen said that her husband would disappear for weeks at a time and she would not know his whereabouts. When Matthiessen wrote privately about his father, he elaborated further, claiming that his father would live in hotels under assumed names during these weeks away from his family. In 1910, F. W. Matthiessen Jr. told a US Census enumerator that he was "divorced," which may have been wishful thinking on his part, since he would not legally gain that status for another six years.

In Matthiessen's later public writings, he was circumspect about this time in his life, claiming only that he was a "'small-town boy' and 'from the mid-west.'" This dramatically downplayed his paternal family's wealth and influence. Matthiessen's paternal grandfather, Frederick William Matthiessen Sr., made a stronger impression on the young Francis Otto, perhaps more so than his father. Matthiessen described his grandfather as "a man of extreme vigour and energy and great ability." Like Matthiessen's great-uncle for whom he was named, his grandfather came to the United States at the age of seventeen from Denmark. He started a firm that became one of the largest zinc producers in the United States and then purchased the company that became Westclox. F. W. Matthiessen Sr. served three terms as LaSalle's mayor, from 1886 to 1896. In 1943—many years after F. W. Matthiessen Sr.'s death—the grounds of the Matthiessen family summerhouse, Deer Park, became a state park named in honor of the family patriarch.

Following his parents' separation, Lucy Orne Matthiessen was peripatetic for several years, living near Philadelphia and then in Poughkeepsie, New York. After the divorce proceedings, the older boys were at college in Colorado, whereas the younger two children, Francis Otto and his older sister, remained with their mother. Adding to the stress, F. W. Matthiessen Jr. only partially provided alimony for his estranged wife, who had to appeal to her own family for financial support. Notwithstanding, Lucy Orne Matthiessen claimed that if her husband would have taken her back, she would have gone gladly.

By 1914, Tarrytown, New York, about an hour north of New York City, became home for Lucy Orne Matthiessen and her two youngest children. Underlining the shame and stigma of divorce at the time, she apparently didn't feel compelled to correct Tarrytown directories that listed her as a widow. Christ Church in Tarrytown, an Episcopal congregation, which had been Washington Irving's parish, became the family's preferred church. Presumably, like many women at the time, Lucy Orne Matthiessen did not drive, making travel to one of the Unitarian churches in Westchester County impractical, whereas Christ Church was walking distance from her home at 25 Neperan Road. Matthiessen and his elder sister were baptized at Christ Church on May 20, 1917, and confirmed five days later.

It may have been Lucy Orne Matthiessen's Unitarian background that led her to place her son at the Hackley School, a

Unitarian boarding school for boys, also located in Tarrytown. In Matthiessen's student days, Hackley offered only a full boarding option to its students, so he lived on campus from 1914 to 1918, even though his mother's house sat just over a mile away. During those years Hackley aimed to place boys from well-to-do families at Harvard, Yale, and Princeton. In this regard, the school did its duty by Matthiessen, when he later was accepted at Yale after graduation.

At Hackley, Matthiessen did well in mathematics and thought that he might choose it as a major. But as with many teenagers, Matthiessen's interactions with his classmates took precedence over academics, and through these Matthiessen began to discover his attraction to members of his own sex. Matthiessen's first sexual and romantic longings expressed themselves as "hero worship"—as he described it—of older boys, especially athletes. Matthiessen went on to add that "a boy of nineteen was my particular idol . . . I would do anything to attract his attention. My life centered in his presence." Matthiessen was short—like his brothers—and as the youngest member of his class, he "came in for a great deal of good natured 'rough-housing.'" This thrilled and excited him. As Matthiessen wrote, he "loved to be 'mauled' by an older and stronger boy." One day in gym class, while wrestling with another boy, Matthiessen got an erection. He also liked watching the "extremely well developed" thirty-five-year-old athletic director shower and wrote him two anonymous letters "passionately begging him to allow me to take his penis in my mouth." At first Matthiessen thought that another boy had spurred him on in his attraction to other boys and men, but over time, he began to realize that his sexual impulses were a "generic trait." It comforted Matthiessen to think of his sexuality as an in-born trait that was brought out by his experiences at school with other boys.

During the early twentieth century, several thinkers articulated progressive theories of homosexuality. The British sexologist,

Havelock Ellis, whose work on sexuality Matthiessen would read a few years later, believed that sexuality resembled color blindness—that it was a congenital predisposition. This was a nearly revolutionary position, because only thirty years before Ellis's *Sexual Inversion* appeared, homosexuality was punishable by death in England. Similarly, the German sexologist Magnus Hirschfeld also felt that homosexuality was like eye color or handedness. Both Ellis and Hirschfeld believed that the majority of people existed on a continuum of sexuality. Notwithstanding the forward thinking of Ellis and Hirschfeld, inversion or sexual perversion, as same-sex physical intimacy was also called, was not something discussed publicly.

During the first half of the twentieth century—a time that coincides nearly exactly with Matthiessen's life from 1902 to 1950—the conceptual backdrop against which his same-sex physical intimacies played out, the lines between homosexual and heterosexual were much more permeable but would become more sharply defined as the century wore on. People were thought to have gender identities rather than sexual identities. Homosexual men and women inhabited a zone of an intermediate or third sex. The intermediate sex was also closely related to the notion of inversion, in which homosexuals were women inside of men's bodies in the case of gay men, or men inside of women's bodies in the case of lesbians. Some men sexually attracted to other men adopted a feminized, "fairy" persona. As if underscoring their feminine characteristics, fairies sometimes used feminine names and pronouns to address one another. In working-class venues, fairies were often part of the sexual economy, when women were unavailable; some could be equated with female prostitutes. In the early twentieth century, choice in sexual partners was more fluid, and men had less anxiety of being labeled homosexual. If a "normal" man let a fairy perform oral sex on him, and then went home to his wife, that was simply a man's prerogative to seek and enjoy sexual pleasure wherever he might find it.

It took time for men to develop homosexual identities, which was primarily a middle-class phenomenon. These were men who loved and desired other men and understood themselves as men, not women inside men's bodies. (Matthiessen and Cheney would be classified in this group.) Many such men would have used the term "queer" to describe themselves. Doctors and the medical community helped categorize homosexual men as either "fairies" or "queers." Many doctors harbored a special animosity for queer men. In general, many doctors at the time couldn't conceptualize men loving and desiring other men. Because fairies were women inside of men's bodies, the reasoning of some in the medical community went, same-sex attraction was easier to grasp. Fairies were often younger and poorer and therefore cornered into giving up the privileges associated with manhood in exchange for sexual self-expression, whereas middle-class men had too much to lose, notably their jobs, for public display of their homosexuality. Queerness aligned well with the middle-class values of privacy, self-restraint, and lack of self-disclosure.

Gay socializing in public could be dangerous owing to fear of arrest by police or harassment from antigay vigilantes. During the 1910s, the police arrested more than fifty men for sodomy and "crimes against nature" in New York City. In 1917, when Matthiessen was a junior at the Hackley School, this number had climbed to over one hundred men. In 1923, the year before Matthiessen and Cheney met, the New York State Legislature revised its disorderly conduct statute to specifically target men who solicited sex with other men. During the 1920s and 1930s, approximately 650 men were arrested each year in Manhattan on charges of degeneracy. Men had to be especially careful to avoid being arrested under the elevated trains along New York City's Third and Sixth Avenues and in parks—both popular cruising grounds for men seeking sex with other men. In 1927, the New York State Legislature continued its efforts to regulate homosexuality when it passed a statute that prohibited theaters from "depicting or dealing with sex degeneracy, or sex perversion." In subsequent decades, New York City widened this ban to include nightclubs. During the 1930s, the New York State Liquor Authority promulgated a licensing requirement that a bar not "suffer or permit such premises to become disorderly," which it used to close hundreds of bars that served gay men and lesbians. Professionally successful men and women stayed away from gay bars for fear of being caught in a raid, in which they would have to reveal their names, addresses, and employers. By the 1940s, over three thousand men were arrested per year in Manhattan alone for homosexual solicitation.

During his years at Hackley, Matthiessen spent a lot of time going into New York City, where he "began to develop homosexual practises rapidly." He pursued anonymous sexual encounters first by pressing his leg up against those of strangers in movie theaters, and then, after a man of twenty-four or twenty-five responded, Matthiessen felt emboldened. He quickly began seeking other chance sexual contacts with men that he met in hotels, public washrooms, and on trains. He pursued these encounters furtively but with an almost preternatural boldness that would come to characterize much of his later life. Matthiessen knew what he wanted, and he went after it. Still, it was a confusing time for Matthiessen, as he struggled to make sense of these experiences, desiring other men's bodies and unable to control his own body, but also desiring more affectionate activities: "What I delighted in most was mutual embracing, passionate kissing, and then an emission in whatever way my companion desired." In Matthiessen's mind, none of these activities and feelings precluded the possibility of his eventual marriage to a woman.

In the early twentieth century, Matthiessen was stepping into a world in which gay men managed to find one another, especially in New York City—notwithstanding the growing legal risks. During the 1910s and 1920s, gay men met one another at movie theaters, especially in the standing room section or balcony. The same was true of public washrooms, notably in the subway. And Matthiessen was hardly alone in these encounters. At the same time that Matthiessen was coming into Manhattan and meeting men in such places, one of Hackley's teachers, the composer Charles Griffes, also ventured into Manhattan to seek sexual liaisons with other men. Griffes frequented the Lafayette Baths, where he met a number of men with whom he had sex, socialized, and became good friends. One day in 1916, Griffes reported to his diary that he spent seven hours at the baths, and on another occasion he met the new manager of the Lafayette Baths, Ira Gershwin.

After graduation from Hackley in 1918, Matthiessen took a year off in which he spent a brief stint in the Canadian Royal Air Force, after which he took a road trip across the United States with two school friends, keeping a journal about the experience. In the fall of 1919, Matthiessen followed an uncle and several cousins to Yale, from which he graduated in 1923.

The Yale College that Matthiessen entered was mostly a bastion of wealthy, white, Protestant men, although a small number of intelligent outsiders—Jews and Catholics—were tolerated. For many young men, Yale was simply a stepping-stone to a career, and it was a frosty place for those of an idiosyncratic bent. Because Matthiessen fit neatly into a number of Yale's unspoken prerequisites, he did well at college, and many years later, he wrote lovingly about his formative years at Yale—enough to warm the heart of any college administrator. But even in these early days there were glimpses of a contrarian streak in Matthiessen's personality. He may have fit Yale's mold on the outside, but internally, he wasn't quite so sure. And his growing sense of his homosexuality played a role in this intellectual and emotional stance.

Matthiessen's favorite professor was Robert (Bob) Dudley French, who was an expert on Chaucer. Students adored Bob French and his warm and mischievous disposition. French was a strong supporter of Yale's honors program and instruction in small groups—both of which appealed to Matthiessen. As with so many men in Matthiessen's life, French himself had gone to

Yale and was a member of Skull and Bones, the most prestigious "secret" society for seniors. One day, Matthiessen overheard French explain to another student that the student didn't know how to speak the English language properly and that his purpose at college was to learn how. Although patronizing-sounding by today's standards, at the time the directness of French's words thrilled Matthiessen. He had rarely heard an adult in a position of authority speak so candidly. The promise that communication could lead to more honest, forthright relationships captured Matthiessen's heart and mind in his early days at Yale.

Matthiessen took a broad range of liberal arts courses, including English, Greek, Latin, philosophy, mathematics, and economics; he graduated with honors in English with exceptional distinction. In addition to his academic studies, Matthiessen participated in a full complement of activities and societies while in college. He was elected into Phi Beta Kappa, was managing editor of the *Yale Daily News,* and was editor of the *Yale Literary Magazine.* Perhaps growing out of his mother's religious beliefs and his early religious training, while at college Matthiessen remained religious, which likely had an important emotional dimension for him. Although Matthiessen's senior class voted in 1923 to do away with compulsory religious observance, in his day Sunday services and daily chapel for prayers and announcements were compulsory for most students. He was elected class deacon and served as chair of the Bible Study Committee. In his role as class deacon, Matthiessen became involved in community service, which at the time often meant teaching English to recent immigrants. In Matthiessen's understanding of his faith, it wasn't enough to profess the universal camaraderie or other Christian values—he had to work to bring those values to fruition. He felt compelled to try to make the world a better place.

Matthiessen came alive at Yale, emotionally and intellectually. For an economics course his junior year, Matthiessen read *The Acquisitive Society* by English economic historian and social critic R. H. Tawney (1880–1962). For a young man already influenced by religious notions of social responsibility, the main ideas from *The Acquisitive Society* that appealed to Matthiessen and shaped his later thinking were the importance of fellowship; that economic activity should provide a valuable service to the broader community; and that men and women develop stronger social bonds as a result of their joint efforts in service. If making money is the only goal in a person's life, Tawney argued that such a person could be interested only in what was in it for himself or herself, which wasn't enough to produce a vibrant society. Tawney believed that economic activity must have a social function; it cannot exist solely for private gain. Economic activity should also promote the ends of society, not the other way around. Society is not simply the backdrop for private economic gain. The real economic cleavage in a capitalistic system, per Tawney, is not between employers and employed but between those who do constructive work, such as scientists or laborers, and those who exist off of proprietary rights to property (and the income attached to it)—"functionless property"—regardless of whether they contribute to society. Discussing "functionless property," Tawney elaborated further: "Thus functionless property grows, and as it grows it undermines the creative energy which produced property and which in earlier ages it protected. It cannot unite men, for what unities them is the bond of service to a common purpose, and that bond it repudiates, since its very essence is the maintenance of rights irrespective of service. It cannot create; it can only spend." Matthiessen, too, was coming to believe that fellowship, comradeship, and fraternity were salutary antidotes to "the wolfish world"—as Melville wrote in *Moby Dick*—and Tawney helped point him in this direction.

Tawney posited that a society ordered by function would be united and moral. This idea also appealed to Matthiessen, who was already interested in moral questions from his religious background. Tawney showed Matthiessen how the economic organization of societies helped shape the lives of the men and women in those societies. Literature responded to people's spiritual needs in part by raising and pondering such moral questions. Matthiessen later wrote that "Tawney's ideas about equality have remained more living for me than anything else, except Shakespeare, that I read at college." Matthiessen didn't so much read as "internalize" many of the authors he studied, especially Tawney during his undergraduate days.

Matthiessen's initial exposure to organized labor occurred during his Yale years, when he became involved with the Yale Liberal Club, to which he was elected vice president in 1922. In the early days of the Liberal Club, figures from organized labor addressed many meetings, and the club got labeled as "socialist" and "radical"—not compliments. For Matthiessen, this was just a taste of what was to come in the years ahead. Although his religious community service helped set the emotional tone for his later progressive political activism, the Liberal Club gave Matthiessen the conceptual framework to make his ideals a reality. According to Henry Demarest Lloyd, a progressive journalist of the era, organized labor sought "to extend into industry the brotherhood already recognized in politics and religion, and to teach men as workers the love and equality which they profess as citizens and worshippers." This quotation succinctly expresses Matthiessen's almost religious zeal with respect to organized labor. Throughout his life, he would always be searching and yearning for greater fellowship.

The organized labor movement of Matthiessen's day must be understood within the larger social, economic, and political developments of the early twentieth century. In the post–World War I economy, layoffs rose and spread. The Clayton Antitrust Act of 1914 freed unions from the threat of antitrust actions and permitted peaceful strikes, picketing, and secondary boycotts until a series of damaging US Supreme Court decisions weakened it. Meanwhile, labor unrest continued to grow. In 1914, there had been 1,200 labor stoppages, but in 1918 and 1919, this number increased to 3,500 each year. In response, union membership grew dramatically. At the beginning of World War I, union membership stood at 2.7 million, but by Armistice in November 1918, that number had grown to 4.2 million. In 1923, organized labor membership had fallen, but there were still over three and half million union members.

In the spring of 1922, Matthiessen was tapped for Skull and Bones. Matthiessen's life became richly veined with friendships that he formed through the secret society. Against the backdrop of his fractured family, Matthiessen claimed Skull and Bones was the first family that he ever had. Matthiessen's dedication to Skull and Bones ran so deep that many years later he wrote a history of the secret society in honor of its one-hundredth anniversary.

In the society's headquarters, known as the Tomb, Matthiessen was called Little Devil, a name that is given to the shortest member of the entering class of fifteen seniors. In the initiation into Skull and Bones, the Little Devil is carried upside down in a devil's costume by the four strongest members of his class, known as "shakers." In the era of Matthiessen's initiation, it was possible that the shakers would have been clad only in jock straps and sneakers during the ceremony. Following his homoerotic experiences at Hackley, Matthiessen must have been thrilled. For the remainder of senior year, the Little Devil was charged with collecting fines from other members for transgressions, such as tardiness, absences from biweekly meetings, or the use of a Skull and Bones nickname outside of the Tomb. Members went through elaborate rituals to help them get acquainted and strengthen their bonds. These activities included relating one's sexual and life history in a session that could last up to three hours. During the session, other members were free to ask questions, request further elaboration, and offer analysis of the speaker's account of himself. It was understood that what was said in the Tomb stayed in the Tomb.

Participating in Skull and Bones initiation exercises went beyond elaborate, collegial high jinks for Matthiessen. The experience of camaraderie and bonding with other men struck a chord in Matthiessen that he followed, amplified, and developed throughout much of his life. Matthiessen never said whether he spoke honestly during his initiation about his teenage sexual experiences with other men in New York City. But his enduring loyalty to his fraternity brothers suggests that he at least alluded to them. For Matthiessen, his initiation into Skull and Bones took the meaning of communication to a new level.

But Matthiessen's notions of camaraderie at Yale didn't stop with Skull and Bones. Growing out of his duties teaching English to Hungarian immigrants in New Haven, near the end of the course to thank him, the men took Matthiessen down into the basement of the Hungarian Club to enjoy some prohibition wine they had been secretly fermenting. "I had felt in the natural and hearty comradeship of these men a quality that I was just beginning to suspect might be bleached out of middle-class college graduates. It was a kind of comradeship I wanted never to lose," Matthiessen later wrote.

The juxtaposition of Skull and Bones to the Hungarian Club signals an important facet of Matthiessen's personality. All through his life, Matthiessen traveled in and was at home in some of the most elite institutions and organizations in higher education, and in the country for that matter. As was common with many people of Matthiessen's generation and socioeconomic class, he took for granted a social order that hewed closely to privileged, white, Protestant, and male lines. Yet from his early student days, more egalitarian and democratic groups and organizations captured Matthiessen's time, attention, and heart. Matthiessen was a complicated man, and the evidence was apparent in his life from these college days.

During his years at Yale, Matthiessen made the college his own. As such, he felt perfectly justified in turning a self-critical appraisal back on the institution that housed him, and this would not be the last time that he did so. In his senior year, Matthiessen decided he wanted to teach, and that winter he won a prize for public speaking, delivering a speech entitled "Servants of the

Devil" about the failings of a Yale undergraduate education. Matthiessen took issue with the men who oversaw the university allying themselves more closely with the interests of big business rather than with the needs of undergraduates. In Matthiessen's view, few undergraduates at Yale knew why they had come to college; most came to make friends or because their families sent them. And few graduates left college with a trained mind or a sense of public purpose. As Matthiessen wrote of his fellow Yale undergraduates, "It seems never to have occurred to him that the very acceptance of an education might involve an obligation— the tremendous obligation of realizing one's highest self and of contributing that self to the advancement of light and truth." More than a little youthful sanctimoniousness rings in Matthiessen's words, but his willingness to stake out a strong, against-the-grain position speaks to his idealism and boldness.

By the end of his senior year in college, Matthiessen's intellectual and emotional experiences had even coaxed him to the edge of the political pool. Earlier in his Yale career, Matthiessen expressed amazement when Bob French supported Eugene V. Debs, the Socialist candidate for president, who in 1920 received over one million votes, while in prison. Just before graduation Matthiessen heard Debs speak at Yale and decided that he agreed with the politician's Socialist views. Matthiessen would later come to identify himself as a Socialist, which given his family's wealth and conservatism was surprising. But the seeds of Socialism were planted in Matthiessen's mind at Yale during the impressionable days of his youth. In his Yale senior album, Matthiessen listed himself as an "Independent." He graduated from Yale in the spring of 1923, winning a Rhodes Scholarship.

But the joy was short lived. In September 1923, soon after her last child had completed college, Lucy Orne Matthiessen died at age fifty-seven of pernicious anemia, a condition in which the body cannot make enough healthy red blood cells, because of a vitamin deficiency. At the time, Matthiessen speculated that his mother's anemia had been brought on by "overexertion in domestic duties."

FIGURE 1. F. O. Matthiessen, 1923 Yale graduation. History of the Class of Nineteen Hundred and Twenty-Three, Yale College (New Haven, CT: Printed under the direction of the Class Secretaries Bureau, 1923), 193.

She left him a nest egg of $25,000 (approximately $391,000 in 2021 dollars). But this was small consolation. Matthiessen was devastated; he had adored his mother.

After the death of his mother, Matthiessen's father did not step in to fill the parental void. In May 1917, F. W. Matthiessen Jr. had remarried in Chicago, a little over a year after his official divorce from Lucy Orne Matthiessen. Nine months later, F. W. Matthiessen Sr.—the family patriarch—had died. He left an estate valued at approximately $9.5 million (a little over $180 million in 2021 dollars), of which F. W. Matthiessen Jr. inherited over

$2 million dollars (approximately $45 million in 2021 dollars). Matthiessen's father and his new wife promptly moved back to the Potrero Ranch, which he had also inherited, and he continued to raise thoroughbred horses. In 1921, F. W. Matthiessen Jr. purchased a ranch in Santa Barbara County, described by the *Los Angeles Times* as a "veritable mountain empire, embracing 47,500 acres of hills, ranges, and valleys." At roughly the same time that Matthiessen set off for Oxford, his father's second marriage began to break up. F. W. Matthiessen Jr.'s second wife claimed that her husband gave too many parties, refused to speak with her unless he criticized her, and spent all of his time in the barn with his horses. Her reports echoed Lucy Orne Matthiessen's accounts of ill treatment several years earlier.

If Matthiessen hadn't known it before, he certainly knew after his mother's death that at age twenty-one he was alone and out on his own in the world. But with his Rhodes Scholarship and money of his own, Matthiessen set out for England.

Matthiessen described his Rhodes Scholarship as "the greatest present that he had ever received . . . because it allowed him to do nothing but sit in Oxford and read for two years." During the fall of his first year at New College, Oxford, Matthiessen wrote several articles for the *Yale Daily News* describing his experiences at the English university. Perhaps foreshadowing his interest in teaching college, Matthiessen still wrestled with the notion of making higher education vital and engaging. In one of his dispatches, he wrote: "If, on the contrary, you feel that you have already had too much instruction and too little education; if you want to prove the strength and development of your mind by obtaining your intellectual stimulation almost entirely from your books, with no instructor's aid or commentary; if you want to immerse yourself in a society where many of your companions are immature, but where you have the quiet and charming atmosphere, that is in many ways ideal for work, why then Oxford will truly be your Utopia."

But as Matthiessen wrote publicly about his experiences at Oxford, he also wrote privately. That spring, Matthiessen read the volume on sexual inversion by Havelock Ellis and John Addington Symonds in *Studies in the Psychology of Sex* series. The book captivated him. Throughout it Matthiessen came across revolutionary statements and ideas about homosexuality. Ellis and Symonds wrote: "However shameful, disgusting, personally immoral, and indirectly anti-social it may be for two adult persons of the same sex, men or women, to consent together to perform an act of sexual intimacy in private, there is no sound or adequate ground for constituting such act a penal offense by law." Ellis and Symonds's ideas had a profound impact on Matthiessen, strengthening his belief that there was nothing innately wrong with his homosexuality. Again, the distant echoes of Matthiessen's early religious training and schooling may well have prepared the ground for these ideas to put down roots.

But perhaps just as important as Ellis and Symonds's pronouncements on the amorality of same-sex desire and love were their numerous case histories of homosexual men and women in the book. Ellis and Symonds followed a regular template: in each case history they noted a subject's general physical characteristics, such as age, height, hair color, and muscular development. The authors then detailed their subjects' sexual histories and also wrote about their family backgrounds and personality characteristics.

These case histories made a strong impression on Matthiessen, and he sought to emulate them. Sometime after reading Ellis and Symonds's work, Matthiessen wrote a personal essay about his own sexual awakening. Referred to by scholars as the "Oxford Letter," the piece is quite revealing and a splendid minor work of autobiography. It's not clear whether Matthiessen intended for anyone else to read the essay or he simply wrote it for himself. If the Skull and Bones initiation ritual of relating one's sexual history introduced Matthiessen to the idea that sex could be discussed, Havelock Ellis and John Addington Symonds gave Matthiessen the form which emboldened him to commit his own experiences to paper.

In the Oxford Letter, Matthiessen described his physical attributes: "I am only five feet six inches in height, but well-developed, and weigh about 150"; family history; abilities and aptitudes as a student: "Intellectually I am quick, noted for my power of clear analysis, and for my memory"; goals: "I am now studying English Literature at New College, Oxford, with the intention of returning to Yale and becoming a Professor"; and sexual awakening at the Hackley School and his sexual practices in New York City. Throughout much of the essay, working with then-contemporary ideas regarding sexuality, Matthiessen wrestles with notions of masculine, feminine, and inversion. He is constantly on the alert for any trait or behavior within himself that could be deemed feminine and therefore mark him as an invert, a woman inside a man's body: "In temperament I have much of the feminine." The essay is written in a straightforward, matter-of-fact style. Matthiessen did not blanch in his willingness to shine the light of his prose on all facets of his history. Despite its subject matter, the essay is not pornographic or salacious. Like several of the American writers Matthiessen would come to study and admire so deeply, he wanted to understand *all* of himself, and he seemed to trust implicitly that by his writing he could make sense of his disparate, seemingly contradictory experiences, feelings, and impulses and set his course for the future.

In many respects, Matthiessen was right.

Chapter 2

"Between the Old and the New"

In September 1924, Francis Otto Matthiessen, boundless as a dynamo, was on his way back to New College, Oxford, on the second year of his Rhodes Scholarship. Simultaneously, a handsome, worldly, and rich painter named Russell Cheney had also booked passage aboard the ocean liner *Paris*. Cheney was traveling back to Venice and Florence to keep the momentum going in his painting career after his initial ascent in the New York art world a few years earlier at the age of forty.

Russell Cheney was born October 16, 1881, at home in South Manchester, Connecticut, approximately ten miles east of Hartford, all but a company town for Cheney Brothers Silk Manufacturing Company. He was the youngest of eleven children of Knight Dexter Cheney and Ednah Dow Smith Cheney. His father served as president of Cheney Brothers until his death in 1907, while on his annual extended summer holiday in York Harbor, Maine. Cheney's mother, to whom he was close, grew up in Exeter, New Hampshire, but had been born in South Berwick, Maine, very close to Kittery, where Matthiessen and Cheney eventually settled.

Cheney and his siblings were a tight-knit family known as the "KDs" by other members in the extended Cheney clan. They lived in an ornate forty-five-room, four-story house—known as the "KD House"—sited majestically atop a large hill alongside the other Cheney family homes in South Manchester. Unusually for many New England textile mill owners at the time, the Cheneys lived on the grounds of their mills with smokestacks visible over the gables of their homes.

To understand how being a Cheney influenced Russell Cheney's sense of himself—and by extension how Matthiessen and Cheney's life together developed—it is necessary to understand Cheney Brothers Silk Manufacturing Company and its extraordinary success between the Civil War and the Depression. On the most practical level, money from Cheney Brothers financed Russell Cheney's painting career for much of his adult life. If he ever contemplated following his grandfather, father, uncles, brothers, and many other male cousins into the family business, he kept those musings to himself. Nonetheless, Cheney was keenly aware of and relished his family's influence and importance, which Cheney Brothers had made possible. Russell Cheney had history at his back, and he gravitated to his family's history again and again as a personal and artistic touchstone throughout his life.

The Cheneys originally had come to the Massachusetts Bay Colony in 1635 and settled in Rowley before moving to Connecticut in the eighteenth century. They were clockmakers, among the first to substitute wooden movements, the moving parts of a clock, for the more expensive imported brass parts. Clocks with wooden parts were cheaper, and more people could afford them; as a result, the Cheneys were said to have "Americanized" clockmaking.

In the nineteenth century, the industrious Cheneys focused their collective gifts on mechanizing silk manufacturing. Cheney Brothers was founded in 1838 by Russell Cheney's grandfather Charles, his four brothers, and an outside business partner. Charles's brother Frank was the mechanical genius of the seventh generation of Cheneys. In 1847 he developed and patented a machine that would double, twist, and wind silk, an operation that had previously been done by hand. His inventiveness was complemented by the business acumen of Ward, another founding brother. By 1860, Cheney Brothers employed six hundred people.

In the generation following the founders, the family fortified its position as one of the leaders in the silk industry. Frank Woodbridge Cheney—one of Russell Cheney's uncles, who lived next door to the KDs—spent two years in China and Japan securing supplies of raw silk. Cheney Brothers developed a training program for the men of the family, in which they would rotate through all departments of the business and then select a specialty. Russell Cheney's father, for example, made a specialty of overseeing the weaving department, and his brother Clifford, to whom he was especially close, oversaw the velvet mill. By 1872 Cheney Brothers had built large new mills for spinning silk from damaged cocoons that previously had been thrown away, allowing the company to offer a range of less expensive silks to a broader public—as an earlier generation of Cheneys had done with clocks.

Cheney Brothers produced dress and millinery silks, plushes, velvets, satins, pongees (a soft, unbleached Chinese or Indian fabric made of raw silk), yarns, printed silks, ribbons and sashes, flags, and crepes. The company also made a large line of tapestries and decorative upholstery fabrics. In 1920, the firm employed 4,670 workers, roughly a quarter of the Town of Manchester's entire population. Sixty percent were foreign born. In the company's peak year, 1923, the mills of Cheney Brothers covered thirty-six acres in South Manchester, and its sales were $23 million (a little over $368 million in 2021 dollars). Cheney Brothers had additional mills in Hartford and offices and showrooms in New York City. Some of its products were works of art. In 1925 the firm exhibited its fabrics in a show of silks at the Louvre.

The Cheneys were proud of their mills, homes, and surrounding property in South Manchester, often referring to it as a "park," which contributed to Russell Cheney's sense of his family's influence and importance. The firm and the family were strongly connected to South Manchester and the people who lived there and worked for them. The historian William E. Buckley noted that Cheney Brothers decided "it had a deep responsibility to the community and that in fulfilling that responsibility it would create conditions of small labor turnover and employee loyalty which were important factors in achieving business success." But Buckley went a step further and linked the success of the Cheneys to their collective character: "There seems to have been something in the character of the individuals composing the Cheney firm, which went beyond self-interest and economic theory . . . They believed that business and community rose and declined together." Farwell Knapp, the husband of Russell Cheney's niece Helen, sounded a similar note in his diary: "The Cheneys occupy a curious predominating position in this little town, whose economic prosperity depends so largely on the Cheneys. It is almost a feudal position, and the family feels the responsibility. All its various branches are equally public-spirited; they spend much time + trouble + money on running the town."

The Cheneys built a number of ancillary businesses to support the production of silk and its workforce. To accommodate the need for large amounts of water in the manufacturing of silk, Cheney Brothers built several reservoirs and created the South Manchester Water Company. The reservoirs also provided water for fire protection, and men and boys swam in them during the summer. Electricity and gas came from a plant built by Cheney Brothers, which also developed the sanitary and sewer systems in South Manchester. Cheney Brothers built the two-and-a-half-mile-long South Manchester Railroad, which connected the silk mills to the main line in Manchester. At the time the railroad was built in 1869, it was the longest private railroad in the United States. In 1881 there were eighteen trains daily. The railroad was also used by students to travel back and forth between Manchester and Hartford public schools, at least until the Cheneys built schools in South Manchester. The company also constructed housing for its workers and supervisors to rent and employed a housing department to maintain its property.

But all was not benevolent paternalism however, and the Cheneys remained firmly in control of the terms by which it interacted with workers. Management charged fines for poor quality of work. In 1902, when the company instituted a system by which weavers were assigned to work two looms instead of one, the workers went on strike. With close to 350 workers sitting idle, Cheney Brothers called in additional deputies from Hartford County and constables to escort and protect nonstriking workers. The company also obtained a court injunction to prevent striking workers from picketing its mills and trains. In the end, the two-loom arrangement prevailed. The family refused to negotiate with strike committees or unions, opposing any effort to organize its workforce. Frank Woodbridge Cheney declared in 1902: "We will not submit to dictation from our employees and reserve the right to hire whom we please and to discharge for cause." Two more strikes occurred, in 1923 and 1934, and it was not until 1934, when the National Industrial Recovery Act increased the power of unions and collective bargaining, that the workers at Cheney Brothers organized. John Sutherland, a historian of local history, noted that the work stoppages were brief, and none left "searing bitterness." Rather than blame the Cheneys, he wrote, "strikers seem to have taken out their grievances on individual supervisors or the system." Overall, Cheney Brothers workers were well paid—approximately 10 percent higher than in comparable textile mills at the time—and the company provided a very stable place to work. A survey of the workers in the early 1920s estimated that 60 percent of more than twenty-six hundred employees had been at the company five years or longer.

The Cheneys developed traditions and rituals that helped reinforce their identity. Thanksgiving was an especially important holiday to the family. After World War I, there were nearly 120 members of the Cheney family living in the vicinity of the mills in South Manchester. At some Thanksgiving meals held at Cheney Hall, there would be over one hundred family members at dinner. Theatrical skits presented at the Cheney Homestead would dramatize family stories or events. And the young Russell Cheney played an important role at Thanksgiving theatricals, which must have made him feel valuable within his extended family: he designed and drew the posters "advertising" the theatricals to the rest of the family.

The Cheneys made a big impact on Russell Cheney's development, and being a Cheney was an essential part of his personality. The family personified Yankee ingenuity, practicality, and doggedness. But it was more than just money. Around a highly successful business, the Cheneys built a culture within its workforce and within the Town of Manchester. This decision was not a bighearted, misty-eyed populism; it made good business sense. The Cheneys exhibited the combination of idealism and sharp-penciled practicality that has often been synonymous with both New England and America and helped write history in their corner of the country.

Russell Cheney graduated from Hartford public high school in 1899. That spring he saw a show of paintings at the high school organized by the Hartford Art Society, including work by Walter Griffin and William Merritt Chase. Griffin's paintings must have made a strong impression on Cheney, because soon thereafter, he became Cheney's first painting teacher. Griffin was a minor American impressionist painter, well known for his landscapes and paintings of trees, both of which interested Cheney. Griffin was also recognized as a "master draftsman" and "great colorist." Cheney, too, would become known for his use of color, and his drawing was often fluid and quick if occasionally a little shaky. Overall, the two artists shared a sensibility but differed in their styles. Griffin favored an impressionistic style, in which he used a heavy palette, whereas Cheney began painting in an impressionistic manner and later developed a flatter, postimpressionistic style. But there was another side to Griffin which attracted Cheney's interest.

Although Griffin was not gay in the contemporary sense, he developed a number of close relationships with other men. Griffin's marriage to Lillian Baynes ended in divorce in 1908, and he never remarried. After his divorce, Griffin spent several summers painting in Maine and Europe with William Henry Singer Jr., the son of a Carnegie Steel executive. While a student at the Museum of Fine Arts School in Boston, Griffin had maintained an "intimate friendship" with Walt Whitman. He described their meeting: "One evening when I was working alone the door opened and a strange gentleman, a patriarch with long white beard came in saying: 'Hello boy, this is a fine place to work,' he came over to me, put his arm around my shoulder and examined my drawing." Griffin helped Cheney develop as a painter, but just as important, Cheney presumably recognized a kindred spirit in terms of sexuality. Cheney and Griffin's initial teacher-student relationship grew into a long-standing friendship.

Russell Cheney followed his four brothers to Yale and into Skull and Bones. During these years Cheney picked up the nickname "Rat," which he used throughout his life. He was popular at college but also known for being very quiet. Cheney enjoyed both Yale and Skull and Bones, yet neither institution dominated his life: in his sense of self, being a Cheney ranked higher than either Yale or Skull and Bones. After graduation, Cheney's path diverged from those of his brothers, all of whom went into management positions within Cheney Brothers. Their choice may have caused Cheney to feel a twinge of guilt or shame, as though he was not quite up to family standards. Nonetheless, when Cheney graduated in 1904, he decided to continue to study painting, which was already his secret resolve, even though he spoke about becoming an architect.

When Cheney approached his parents about studying painting, they did not refuse to support him financially, yet they probably didn't enthusiastically endorse his choice either but rather tolerated it. The desire to become an artist or an architect was not unheard of within the extended Cheney family. Two of Cheney's great-uncles, John Cheney and Seth Wells Cheney, had been painters and engravers. A few years later in the mid-1920s, Cheney gave a talk on Seth and John Cheney at the Wadsworth Atheneum Museum in Hartford. Also, Cheney's cousin Charles Adams Platt went on to become a renowned residential and landscape architect. Cheney wanted to paint, but juxtaposed against the paths of his brothers and many male cousins, this decision was both bold and anxiety producing: What if he wasn't any good?

As a grown man, Cheney was five feet nine and a half inches tall, had a dark complexion, was slight of build, and had a "rich vibrant Connecticut voice," which, given his family background, probably meant the breezy, vaguely patrician intonations often associated with the Eastern Establishment. But it was Cheney's eyes that people commented on more than any of his other features. Officially listed as "hazel" on his passport applications, one friend later wrote that Cheney had "unusually large brown eyes that could take in and hold, without cunning or anxiety, whatever they looked at" —a useful attribute for a painter.

In terms of personality and temperament, Cheney had a "lively mind" and was highly sensitive, but he was not particularly self-reflective. Helen Knapp, Cheney's niece, later astutely added that he had the ability "to imbibe culture through his nerve ends rather than his brain."

Given his fortuitous meeting with Griffin, Cheney's painting career seemed to get off to a good start. But it would be over a decade before his first major exhibitions of paintings, which followed years of schooling and an extended bout with tuberculosis. Born to many advantages, Cheney was nonetheless unsure of himself, perhaps as a result of the lack of emotional support

FIGURE 2. Russell Cheney, 1904 Yale graduation. *Yale College Class Book*, 1904, 32.

from his family for his artistic ambitions as well as his homosexuality. Cheney had talent, liked painting, and was good at it. But he found it difficult to articulate or hold to his inner vision of his chosen pursuit so as to make the kinds of choices in teachers, living situations, and familial connections that would have aligned his life with his chosen ambition. Cheney moved forward with his painting, but he did so haltingly.

After graduation from Yale, Cheney began to take himself more seriously as a painter—or at least a student of painting. He went to New York to study at the Art Students League, during which time he lived mostly with his brother Thomas, who worked for Cheney Brothers in Manhattan. Cheney was at the Art Students League from 1904 until 1906. At the time the league had a mix of academic and innovative teachers and students. Cheney studied with Kenyon Cox, George Bridgman, and Frank Vincent DuMond among others. Cox was an academic painter who was also well known for his criticism, particularly against modernism. Presumably, Cheney studied with Cox to fortify the foundations of his artistic training and his drawing in particular, one of Cox's strengths. Being unsure of his own vision for painting, Cheney made the "right" decision in selecting Cox as a teacher. The small social world in which Cheney existed reinforced this conventional choice. Cox dedicated his book *Concerning Painting* to Cheney's cousin Charles Adams Platt, who had also studied at the Art Students League. If Cheney didn't know about Cox by reputation, he probably learned about Cox through Platt.

In the early years of the twentieth century, Picasso, Braque, and others were transforming the art world in Paris. And although Cheney did not much share an aesthetic with these painters, the allure of Paris led him across the Atlantic from about 1906 to 1909 to study at the Académie Julian. Several of Cheney's teachers, relatives, and friends had studied at the Parisian painting school, which was popular with foreigners and open to all students who applied, unlike the more formal École des Beaux-Arts. At the Académie Julian, Cheney continued to study with academic teachers, notably Jean-Paul Laurens. It's unlikely that Cheney had a great intellectual or creative affinity with Laurens, a realistic history painter. But again, Cheney probably felt that studying with Laurens further reinforced his artistic foundations. As with coming to New York, perhaps the real value of studying at the Académie Julian was meeting other painters and living in France for an extended period of time.

When Cheney returned to the United States in 1909, he again studied at the New York Art Students League: with Cox and privately with William Merritt Chase for two years. Despite Cheney's mostly conventional choices of painting teachers up until this point, with Chase, Cheney began working with a teacher who helped him move toward finding his own style. Chase was recognized as a great artist and a charismatic teacher. His pet peeves were overconscientiousness and conventional prettiness. Cheney had no fear of being labeled overconscientious, but his painting would sometimes be described as "decorative." Like Cox, Chase was opposed to modernism, and students who were inclined to modernism soon went in a different direction from their teacher. Along these lines, Cheney didn't swallow all of Chase's lessons completely, particularly regarding Paul Cézanne. Chase did not believe that Cézanne was a great painter, whereas Cézanne had become more important to Cheney since his years living in Paris.

Chase pushed his students' work toward originality, encouraging them to develop their own style and gather their impressions from a subject, but not belabor the execution of it. Cheney would often try to convey the feeling that a scene created in him rather than simply a pictorial record of it. In paintings of landscapes, interiors, and still lifes, Chase stressed that his students should seek to imbue the commonplace vista or everyday object with beauty and grace, another principle that Cheney gravitated to throughout his career. Chase advocated that his students complete a work in one sitting so as not to overwork their paintings. This practice fit well with Cheney's developing aesthetic philosophy to quickly convey a fleeting impression of a subject or scene before analyzing it too closely. It also helped Cheney dodge the cramping effects of self-doubt and self-consciousness with which he wrestled.

Still, Cheney couldn't quite pull away from being an art student. In 1912 at age thirty-one, he began to study with Charles H. Woodbury at his summer painting school in Ogunquit, Maine. The proximity of York Harbor, the summer outpost of the KDs, probably led Cheney to Ogunquit, which is the next town to the north of York along the Maine coast and had developed into an arts colony in the early twentieth century. The KDs spent summers in York Harbor, as did several other members of the extended Cheney family. In York Harbor, Cheney had a painting studio, perhaps his first. After Cheney's parents had died, he and several other KDs continued to spend summers at York Harbor. They stayed frequently at Kincroft, the large summer "cottage" of their cousin Ethel Cheney Thorne.

Once again, when faced with a choice between a more traditional teacher, Woodbury, and a more avant-garde instructor, Hamilton Easter Field, who also ran a painting school in Ogunquit, Cheney chose Woodbury. Field was a cosmopolitan painter based in New York who encouraged his students to experiment, whereas Woodbury was more in the Yankee mold. Based out of Boston, Woodbury favored technical rigor and representation, which appealed to Cheney. Given the contrast between the two teachers, Woodbury's students tended to be "older, quieter, and more sedate."

Still, Woodbury was not so wedded to tradition, as was a teacher like Cox, and Cheney's studying with Woodbury further helped him develop his style and philosophy of painting, beyond where he had progressed under Chase. Woodbury also underscored Cheney's connection to northern, coastal New England. Woodbury emphasized interpretation of the image, and the emotion it created in the artist, over technique: "Art is not based on the way things are, but on things as you see and feel them." Woodbury went on to tell his students: "Be as artistic as you want to be, but always on the basis of truth ... Drawing is not imitation, not following outlines, but mental, the summarizing and selection of important things, masses and essential lines." Woodbury was also known to paint outside in good weather and in bad, even when it snowed. Later, Cheney said that Woodbury "taught him how to paint out of doors and helped him loosen up his style."

In the fall of 1915, Cheney's beloved mother, Ednah, died.

When Cheney's father, Knight Dexter, died in 1907, he had left his estate in trust to his wife for use during her lifetime, but upon her death, his property and holdings were to be distributed equally among his eleven children. By far, the largest part of the estate consisted of stock in Cheney Brothers Silk Manufacturing Company. Ednah Cheney left 7,539 shares of company stock to Cheney and his siblings, with each receiving approximately 685 shares. Valued at $125 per share, Cheney's allocation would have come to approximately $85,000 ($2.3 million in 2021 dollars). That fall, Russell Cheney became independently rich.

But roughly a year later at age thirty-five, Cheney's development as an artist was further delayed when he was diagnosed with tuberculosis and departed for Cragmor Sanatorium in Colorado Springs for a lengthy stay of several years. As advances in medicine and science have since shown, the sanatorium cure worked best for people whose illness had advanced only to a limited extent. Given that Cheney ultimately recovered, he likely had only a minimal tuberculosis infection when he went to Colorado Springs, but he had no way of knowing this at the time. In his decision to go to Cragmor, Cheney was presumably—and rightly—erring on the side of caution. He had already lost his sister Elizabeth and brother Knight Dexter Jr. to tuberculosis, and a second brother Thomas with whom he had lived in New York was gravely ill in a Colorado Springs sanatorium and died just a week after Cheney arrived in town. Cheney must have felt deeply grieved by his brother's death, but reflecting the upper-class conservatism of his family that frowned on displays of emotion, he probably kept his sadness to himself.

In the early part of the twentieth century, the number of tuberculosis sanatoria across the United States grew dramatically. Before antibiotics became more widely available during the 1940s, treatment of tuberculosis consisted primarily of rest, plenty of outdoor air, and a healthy diet. It was in this context that Dr. Edwin Solly envisioned Cragmor. Dr. Solly was an English physician who had suffered from tuberculosis himself and extolled the virtues of the dry climate of Colorado Springs for treatment of the disease. He advocated a combination of traditional medicine, climate, and nutrition and built an institution that came to be known as the "Sun Palace." The Sun Palace's main building, a large four-story structure built in the Mission style with turrets, porches, and many windows, was completed in 1914—just two years before Cheney's arrival. In an early form of economic development, Colorado Springs tried to lure well-to-do consumptives to the area, making Cheney an ideal patient.

Cragmor would admit only those patients whose doctors felt their pulmonary tuberculosis could be cured. Cheney was silent on the subject, but typically patients with general symptoms of pulmonary tuberculosis suffered from loss of appetite, weight loss, night sweats, fevers, and fatigue or weakness. To ensure that patients got plenty of fresh air, doctors at Cragmor prescribed "heliotropy," or sun treatment. This consisted of lying in the sun with a loin cloth or in the nude—likely an enjoyable practice for Russell Cheney, as a budding sensualist. Patients often slept on a screened-in, unheated porch for continued exposure to fresh air. Cragmor provided its patients with spacious quarters, large enough to allow patients to have their families or hired help with them. The sanatorium sought to create a homelike atmosphere. Cheney's room at Cragmor had a large oriental rug, a well-stocked bookcase, a writing table, several chairs for visitors, and fresh flowers.

Cheney's doctor at Cragmor, Gerald Webb, was a rising star in the medical world. Dr. Webb was a physician-scholar who had written a biography of the inventor of the stethoscope. He was a proponent of patients using their time well while at Cragmor to expand their minds and encouraged reading of serious literature. Serious reading was an aspect of his treatment that

Cheney had no trouble following. He read constantly, widely, and in several foreign languages, including French. He read the works of antiquity, memoirs, poetry, and, of course, art books. Sherwood Anderson's stories, the poetry of T. S. Eliot, Robert Frost's *North of Boston* and *Mountain Interval*, and Joyce's *Portrait of an Artist as a Young Man* most affected him during his stay. Cheney read these authors before they were the well-known writers they are today. If Cheney hewed close to convention in some of his painting education choices, in his reading he gravitated toward more avant-garde choices typical of many artists.

In the spring of 1917, Cheney had recovered enough that he could get out and paint. While at Cragmor, he bought himself a new Ford. Cheney was a Ford man, and he fondly referred to the cars as "Fordies" throughout his life. If Cheney put down stakes in a new locale for an extended time, he often bought a new car. He had to get around somehow, didn't he? Showing some of the mechanical inventiveness of his forebears, Cheney had his Fords specially outfitted with slots built into the running boards to carry his paintings. While at Cragmor, Cheney toured the surrounding countryside painting the landscapes. In 1918, he completed *Garden of the Gods*, named for the nearby park in Colorado Springs known for its unique formations of red rock. Cheney's eye feasted on the otherworldly landscape at Garden of the Gods. As during much of his career, Cheney responded strongly to his environment.

During Cheney's time at Cragmor, he "assimilated" Cézanne more deeply. Cézanne's importance to Cheney dated back to at least 1910, if not before. In 1911, Cheney painted the portrait *Professor A. Canolle*, which features a bearded Professor Canolle sitting in a chair reading the French newspaper *Le Figaro*. The composition of Cheney's painting is strikingly similar to Cézanne's painting "Portrait du père de Cézanne," which art historians believe is the painting that became known as *The Artist's Father, Reading "L'Événement"* (1866). The painting depicts Louis-Auguste Cézanne reading the Parisian newspaper *L'Événement* while sitting in an armchair. Cheney either saw Cézanne's painting as an illustration to a 1911 *Art Journal* article on the French artist or at an exhibition at Galerie Vollard in Paris from June 27 to July 23, 1910, in which this painting may have been included. After Cheney's return to New York from his years at the Académie Julian, he made a number of trips back and forth to Paris. In 1910, for example, Cheney listed a Paris location as his business address. Given Cheney's presence in Paris during the Vollard exhibition, he most likely saw Cézanne's painting in person.

Cézanne's balance between realism and a stylized interpretative vision, together with his biography, attracted Cheney. At 14,115 feet, Pike's Peak dominates the skyline from Cragmor and many other vantage points in Colorado Springs. Cézanne's many paintings of Mont Sainte Victoire may well have inspired Cheney to focus so closely on the mountain and its surrounding landscapes in a series of paintings from this time. Cheney did not follow Cézanne's strongly geometric patterns of Mont Sainte Victoire, but he adopted and experimented with Cézanne's composition, in which the mountain sits in the distance as a backdrop to a more traditional landscape in the foreground. This arrangement conveys some of the size and mass of the mountain and also communicates the effect of its presence. But if natural features loom large in the Pike's Peak paintings, human beings are nearly nonexistent. The majority of Cheney's landscapes do not have people in them, another trait that he shared with Cézanne. Art historians have noted how the absence of figures in Cézanne's landscapes invites the viewer to contemplate the composition aesthetically, and many of Cheney's Pike's Peak landscapes attract the viewer in a similar manner.

Beginning in June 1917, Cheney's friend, the poet Howard Phelps "Put" Putnam joined him at Cragmor. In a scenario worthy of *The Magic Mountain*, in which the protagonist is treated for tuberculosis at the sanatorium where he had gone simply to visit his cousin, Putnam found himself admitted to Cragmor for his asthma by Dr. Webb while on a visit to Cheney. The incident also highlights the degree to which patients were expected to surrender completely to the orders of their physicians at sanatoriums. Putnam's originally planned stay of one month turned into approximately ten months, paid for by the ever gracious and magnanimous Cheney. For Cheney, paying for Putnam's visit was a mere formality to secure some lively and enjoyable company for himself.

Cheney and Putnam had met at Yale the year before, when Putnam was still an undergraduate and Cheney was visiting the campus. Cheney was handsome, rich, and effervescent, and Putnam—famously handsome himself—was drawn to him. Like Cheney, Putnam was also in Skull and Bones. A friendship sparked between the two men and continued until Cheney's death. Although Cheney was already quite clear on his attraction to other men, Putnam's sexuality seemed to exist in more ambiguous territory. At the time Cheney and Putnam were at Cragmor, Putnam was twenty-two and Cheney was thirty-five. In general, Cheney had an affinity for younger people.

Cheney's ongoing breathing difficulties prevented him from serving in World War I, which likely caused another pang of guilt, because it was one more way in which he stood in contrast to his two elder brothers Philip and Clifford, who had served in the war. But feelings of guilt or shame didn't slow Cheney down for long. Throughout much of 1918, Cheney was well enough that he traveled back and forth from Cragmor to the East Coast and then to the West Coast to visit his sister Harriet.

On one trip back to Connecticut, in the spring of 1918, Cheney's local doctor, perhaps fearing a relapse, sent him off to the mountains in Vermont. As usual, wherever Cheney was, he simply set up his easel and continued to paint. Cheney had begun painting the landscapes of Vermont before he went to Cragmor, but after his time in Colorado Springs and his focus on mountains there, he returned to landscapes with renewed vigor. Cheney concentrated on Red Echo Farm in Topsham, owned by Charles Macdonald, the handsome brother of his friend Evelyn Macdonald, from the Art

Students League of New York. Many of the Vermont paintings contained one of Cheney's signature combinations of landscape and architecture set against a backdrop of "Jehovah Skies," as Putnam termed Cheney's expansive skies with hues of blue, green, and pink.

At the end of his time at Cragmor, Cheney's tuberculosis had gone into remission. With the broadening of his literary horizons, the evolution of his painting, and the strengthening of his friendship with Putnam, Cheney came to see his "enforced idleness" at Cragmor as a stroke of good fortune. Perhaps most important, having graduated from Yale over twelve years ago and "having been a student too long," Cheney felt that his long apprenticeship had finally ended.

When the art world gave a nod of recognition to Cheney's painting, he was thirty-five years old and relished the attention. His first major exhibition in January 1917 was close to home at the Wadsworth Atheneum Museum in Hartford. It elicited favorable reviews in both the *Hartford Courant* and *Hartford Times*. Out of the seventy paintings in this show, Cheney sold at least four and maybe many more. For a 1919 show at the Atheneum, which included over eighty paintings, the Sunday *Hartford Courant* gave Cheney a big illustrated spread and trumpeted his name under the headline, "Connecticut As a Field for the Artist's Brush." In this article, Cheney made plain his aesthetic theory: he tried "to convey through the canvas the mood the scene creates within himself."

But if Cheney's family history made him feel the need to measure up, it also served to strengthen his painting. One work included in these exhibitions, that of Gideon Welles's house in nearby Glastonbury, Connecticut, speaks to the rich cultural heritage of Cheney's family and its effect on his painting. Gideon Welles was secretary of the navy under President Abraham Lincoln. He was also a good friend of Cheney's grandfather

Charles. On behalf of the navy, Welles purchased seven hundred Spencer repeating rifles, in which the Cheneys had invested heavily. When the army could not be persuaded to purchase the rifles, Charles Cheney arranged a meeting with senior officials in the War Department and influential legislators to overcome its bias against repeating rifles. After Lincoln himself tested the Spencer, the army purchased twenty-five hundred rifles.

Russell Cheney may not have been aware of all the details of the rich, complicated history between his grandfather, Gideon Welles, Cheney Brothers, and American history when he decided to paint Welles's house. But he likely knew in a general way of Welles's historical significance and his family's close association with him. Cheney didn't so much set out to capture historical narrative in his paintings; rather, he expressed it in an unselfconscious way of someone who had been born into a considerable historical legacy. In other paintings of interiors, landscapes, and still lifes, distant family associations flowed almost endlessly from Cheney's paintbrush. Given the Cheneys' central role in New England culture and history, Russell Cheney was able to tap into this rich cultural inheritance in his artwork, and he kept coming back to it again and again. It was the solid foundation on which his aesthetic sensibility was set.

The show that established Cheney's presence in the art world opened at the Babcock Galleries in New York in late 1921 before traveling to the Rhode Island School of Design. Cheney had begun "to employ color, form, and design for their own sake," Christian Brinton, the well-regarded critic and advocate of modernism, wrote in the catalogue. Not long after this exhibit, Brinton made a studio visit in South Manchester. He was an important ally in championing Cheney's paintings, and many New York reviewers of Cheney's show simply quoted from Brinton's foreword in the catalogue.

The exhibition arrested viewers, too, because Cheney not only hung his paintings but also created an environment, arranging "old furniture, tables, chairs, and soft toned pottery" alongside his art. Was this interior decoration or an early art installation? Cheney didn't articulate his exact motivations in arranging his show, but his overall aim seems clear: creating a beautiful environment that invited viewers into an aesthetic experience. Because it launched him into the New York art world, the Babcock exhibition was arguably the single most important show in Cheney's career. At age forty, almost overnight, he was at long last being recognized.

The assessment of the Babcock show was the lead story in the December 17, 1921, issue of *American Art News* and featured an image of Cheney's painting *Woodstock* (1916) on page one. The reviewer picked up on the competing forces within Cheney between realistic presentation and a push toward greater expressiveness and even abstraction. "It is the struggle going on within Mr. Cheney, between the old and the new, that makes his exhibition the most interesting and significant of the week." The *New York Herald* declared, "Of the new people Russell Cheney exhibiting in the Babcock Galleries is the most likely candidate of the week for fame."

The reviews in the *New York Times*, the *Brooklyn Daily Eagle*, and the *New York Tribune*, however, were mixed. The *New York Times* coolly condescended, saying that "the flower paintings are decorative and vases, idols and strips of fabric are brought together with that logic which is the fortune of interior decoration." Hamilton Easter Field in the *Brooklyn Daily Eagle* and Royal Cortissoz, the influential critic at the *New York Tribune* sounded more substantive notes of caution. Despite Field's promotion of an avant-garde aesthetic in his Ogunquit art school in contrast to Charles H. Woodbury, Cheney's teacher, Field thought that Cheney "feels surfaces well and masses of color. He has a strong feeling for rhythm." But Field added, "His foundation, his drawing, his sense of form are still a bit shaky." Cortissoz, who was generally opposed to modernism, also credited Cheney with talent but noted that the painter "needs only to be on his guard against too great haste."

Cheney had another show at the Babcock Galleries in November 1922, which was again reviewed favorably on page one by *American Art News*, followed by his third show at the Wadsworth Atheneum. In these exhibitions, Cheney included *Vitrine* (1921), which depicts vases of flowers along a windowsill overlooking a garden and other buildings in Santa Barbara, combining still life and landscape. What does Cheney mean by the title? Does the window serve as a border around the landscape, as though the image were in a vitrine? If so, Cheney is inviting viewers to consider aesthetic contemplation of the landscape, similar to his paintings of Pike's Peak. Or perhaps the painter and viewer alike are within the vitrine overlooking the landscape—did Cheney feel "on view" as a painter? In his correspondence, Cheney did not hint at either of these interpretations, but he would go on to further develop this technique of mixing still lifes and landscapes, as well as portraiture and landscapes, suggesting that combining genres and layering images held meaning for him.

At the 1922 Babcock and Wadsworth Atheneum shows, Cheney sold thirteen paintings, which brought in just over $6,000 (approximately $96,000 in 2021 dollars). The exhibitions, positive press, and sales no doubt buoyed Cheney's feeling that he had arrived. The high point of his artistic expression would not follow for another decade and a half, but in terms of his painting career, during the early 1920s, the art world touched its scepter to Cheney's shoulder, and it must have thrilled him.

That the exhibitions of those several years were so close to home, too, helped justify Cheney's standing as an artist to his family and to himself. Cheney's long desire to paint and be recognized as an artist was finally corroborated by the world. And the Wadsworth Atheneum couldn't have come up with a more fitting way to emphasize this fact, when the trustees agreed to acquire

Skungimaug—Morning, included in the 1922 exhibit, for its permanent collection. Cheney's painting series of the Skungimaug River, meandering through a snowy Connecticut landscape of denuded trees, began in 1915 and lasted through 1922. In these paintings, Cheney showed his natural feel for New England landscapes, conveying the quiet, serene, although somewhat lonely and desolate feeling of New England in winter. Cheney successfully put into practice those lessons learned from Chase and Woodbury. "The thing is to get the motive impulse down in concrete form," Cheney said. He had succeeded in that ambition; he was a real painter after all.

FIGURE 3. Russell Cheney, *Skungimaug—Morning*, ca. 1922, oil on canvas, 39 ½ x 49 ¾ in. (100.4 x 126.4 cm), Wadsworth Atheneum Museum of Art, Hartford, CT. Gift of Philip and Clifford D. Cheney in memory of their mother, Ednah Dow Cheney, 1922.401. Allen Phillips/Wadsworth Atheneum.

Chapter 3

Falling in Love
The Exuberant Years

The morning of September 24, 1924, each man made his way through the tough, industrial precincts of Manhattan's West Side to Pier 55 on the Hudson River, at the foot of West 15th Street. Cheney would have arrived in New York a day or two earlier from the KD house and stayed with his sister Ellen Lambert and her husband, Alex, on the East Side. Cheney frequently stayed with the Lamberts when he was exhibiting his paintings in New York. Matthiessen had come to Manhattan a few weeks earlier himself and was in good spirits, because he had served as best man in the wedding of his Skull and Bones brother Louis Hyde, who married Penelope Overton on September 9. It's possible that Matthiessen even specifically booked passage aboard the *Paris* to accommodate his friend's wedding. The *Paris* set sail at ten o'clock in the morning, as the Woolworth Building—the tallest skyscraper in the world—disappeared into the overcast sky. Had either Matthiessen or Cheney flipped through that day's *New York Times*, he would have been greeted by advertisements heralding the opening of Saks Fifth Avenue.

The *Paris* was the three-year-old flagship of the French fleet with room for roughly two thousand passengers and abundant touches of luxe—such as square windows in the first-class cabins instead of portholes—of which the Compagnie Générale Transatlantique was capable. Aboard the *Paris* that trip, Matthiessen and Cheney traveled with an elite crowd including the writer Ring Lardner; tennis player René Lacoste; and railroad heir and horseman Reginald C. Vanderbilt, Gloria Vanderbilt's father. Matthiessen probably spotted Cheney at meals in the first-class dining room; everyone always noticed Cheney with his hazel eyes and dark hair. The two men also may have already been acquainted through Yale or Skull and Bones. But now, they "fell into easy intimacy," as Matthiessen talked freely about his family and religion. And Cheney showed the younger man his most treasured possession: a small leather case containing a photograph of his mother.

On the fourth day of the voyage, Matthiessen decided to speak more candidly about sex. Presumably, Matthiessen felt a spark of attraction to Cheney, and their shared Skull and Bones membership made it easier to reveal such confidences. Besides, Matthiessen knew from his Skull and Bones experiences that an act of confidence might yield greater openness and fraternity, qualities he cherished in his friendships. Matthiessen brought up Havelock Ellis, whose writing on homosexuality he had read the previous spring, but then backed away. Later, after an evening of stargazing on deck, Matthiessen brought Cheney into his cabin to give him a good-night snack of a pear. Then he summoned all of his courage and jumped in: "I know it won't make any difference to our friendship, but there's one thing I've got to tell you," he said by way of awkward preface. Referring to his days at the Hackley School, Matthiessen declared: "I was sexually inverted. Of course, I've controlled it since."

Matthiessen described the miraculous moment that followed: "The munching of the pear died away. There was perhaps half a minute of the most heavily freighted silence I have ever felt. Then in a faraway voice I had never heard came the answer: 'My God, feller, you've turned me upside down. I'm that way too.'"

Matthiessen and Cheney sat for several minutes in stunned silence: They were no longer alone. Each man had found another—someone whom he viewed as an equal and a peer. Until then, both Matthiessen and Cheney had largely cordoned off their lives with friendships on one side and chance, clandestine sexual encounters on the other side. But that night aboard the *Paris* in the middle of the Atlantic Ocean, a different world in which love and sex could come together suddenly blossomed. This moment of emotional communion, however, did not lead to sex. Instead, Matthiessen and Cheney stayed up until four o'clock in the morning, talking about their respective sexual histories and experiences, as each man had done as part of his induction into Skull and Bones. When Cheney said good-night before returning to his own cabin, he affectionately tousled Matthiessen's hair and thanked him for his courage in speaking so candidly.

The remainder of the voyage passed quickly, as Cheney and Matthiessen talked and talked. On the last night, they rested on the couch in Cheney's cabin, with Cheney's head in Matthiessen's lap. Later, they changed positions, with both men simply lying next to the other, fully dressed. Their shoulders and knees occasionally touched. Words ebbed, as each man savored the presence of the other. And then Cheney turned and kissed Matthiessen squarely on the lips, and Matthiessen ran his fingers through Cheney's wondrously thick hair. In a more contemporary era, *this* might have been prelude to sex. But not for Matthiessen and Cheney. As Matthiessen later wrote about the experience: "That was all. The next morning we shook hands and I got off the boat at Plymouth. I knew I had a new, unbelievably rich friendship." He and Cheney made plans to meet in Italy over Matthiessen's Christmas holiday and pledged to write often.

At Oxford, Matthiessen lived the life of the twenty-two-year-old student that he was. He explored London, met friends, visited the British Museum, and went to nightclubs, but mostly he continued to read and read, as he had done a year earlier. In light of his budding relationship with the highly literate Cheney,

Matthiessen read with newfound energy many gay or proto-gay writers, such as Walt Whitman and Edward Carpenter. At the time, Matthiessen was stunned, as he wrote to Cheney, that literature was not just about reading but also about living: "I carried Walt Whitman in my pocket. That's another thing you've started me doing, reading Whitman. Not solely because it gives me an intellectual kick the way it did last year, but because I'm living it."

As with many people in their twenties, urges, longings, and musings about sex punctuated Matthiessen's rigorous reading schedule. Once, around the Marble Arch on the edge of Hyde Park in London, a well-known "cruising" area at the time for men seeking sexual contact with other men, a man caught Matthiessen's eye. As historian George Chauncey has pointed out, parks "provided a useful cover" for men seeking out sex with other men, because most people come to parks to linger, loiter, and stroll, and such men would not necessarily attract much notice. As a teenager, Matthiessen had been fearless about meeting other men in New York City, but now he paused. "Hard faces. One, Red-hair. White flower in his button hole. Compelling eye. I look—the blood rushes hot into my face—and what then? I swing right past the whole damn bunch of them . . . Of course I could have stopped in that gesturing crowd. I could have drunk in a lot of luscious slime through my eyes," he wrote to Cheney. Though they had not yet had sex, Matthiessen also took it for granted that they had begun a great love affair, akin to a marriage. Right from the beginning in a letter from September 1924, Matthiessen even used the word "marriage" to describe their relationship: "Marriage! What a strange word to be applied to two men!" Because of this belief, Matthiessen tried to spurn his desires for other men and save himself for Cheney. Matthiessen assumed that the addition of intellectual and emotional connection that he felt with Cheney would raise his sexual impulses to a higher plane, above sheer physical desire.

In Matthiessen's exuberance over his relationship with Cheney, he felt physically different about himself. One night he went to the nightclub Forty-Three and danced provocatively with a young woman. Matthiessen felt that Cheney's attention both on the ship and in his subsequent letters had given him "confidence," so that "even painted whores fall for me now!! These girls give me all this sensuous movement. I hold them as I never held a girl before. I dance in a way that would ordinarily land me in jail!! The acme of vulgar. Body glued to body." For Matthiessen, feeling desired by Cheney made him feel more generally desirable, including to women. Despite Matthiessen's sexual activities with other men up to this point and his budding love for Cheney, he still felt that he would one day get married to a woman. Heterosexual marriage was the societal expectation of both men and women at the time, and Matthiessen continued to believe that he would follow such a path.

Cheney, who had gone on to Paris and then Venice after Matthiessen departed from the ship, was having none of Matthiessen's condescension about dancing with "painted whores." The young woman at the nightclub, Cheney reminded Matthiessen, probably knew "more about life than you or I will know if we live to be a hundred." In Venice, Cheney installed himself at the famously luxurious Hotel Danieli, with its pink facade, Murano glass chandeliers, and interior pink marble columns, and met up with his cousin Howell and his wife, Anne. Cheney set out to paint, as he did no matter where in the world he traveled. Throughout many of his early travels in Europe, the main tourist attractions captured his attention. This trip Cheney painted *San Marco/St. Mark's* (1924) and *Colleone* (1924) based on an equestrian sculpture. Cheney modeled *Colleone* on *Old Venetian Houses* (1913) by his former teacher William Merritt Chase. In Cheney's painting, he orients the view along a north-west axis in order to incorporate the ornate facade of the Scuola Grande di San Marco into the scene. Throughout his life, Cheney liked painting architecture; it spoke to him. Although Cheney could be both freewheeling and wild, he liked architecture's solidity and practicality.

All the while, letters sped back and forth between the two men. Matthiessen wrote in a steady, regular, almost flowing hand. Cheney's handwriting was highly erratic, bordering on illegible much of the time. He himself described it as "hentracks across eternity." But right from the beginning, through their practice of nearly daily letter writing, Matthiessen and Cheney's intimacy grew.

Over Matthiessen's Christmas break from Oxford, he met Cheney in Florence, from where they traveled through the Italian hill towns north to Genoa and as far south as Taormina in Sicily. Cheney documented the southern leg of their trip in *Taormina* (1924–25), in which he depicted the Greek Theatre with Mount Etna in the background, a site that had long been on the grand tour of continental Europe taken by young English gentlemen and later well-to-do American young men and women. At the time, the photographer Wilhelm von Gloeden had a studio in Sicily and was known for his photographs of Sicilian boys and young men arranged in nude or seminude classical poses. Gloeden's allusions to classical Greece and Rome gave his work the patina of respectability, so much so that the Royal Photographic Society of Great Britain awarded him a gold medal. European royalty and rich American tourists visited Gloeden's studio. But the homoerotic sexual undercurrent of Gloeden's work also attracted a wide gay audience, including Oscar Wilde, who signed Gloeden's studio guest book. Given Cheney's travels in artistic circles in New York and Paris, he very likely knew Gloeden's photography. So Cheney may have led the two men to do some early proto-gay tourism.

During this trip, Matthiessen and Cheney probably had sex for the first time. For Matthiessen, sex with Cheney thrilled him; that someone so handsome, from a similar social background—in essence, that one of the boys after whom he had been pining since his student days at Hackley—should in turn desire him enchanted Matthiessen. For Cheney, he, too, reacted strongly, but differently, to sex with Matthiessen. Sex with Matthiessen did not fulfill his fantasies—Cheney had more of a penchant for tough, thuglike boxers. But Matthiessen's willing submission of himself to Cheney, the sweetness and tenderness with which he yielded to Cheney physically and emotionally, drew Cheney to Matthiessen. And that Matthiessen was so obviously brilliant clinched the deal. With physical expression, the emotional temperature between the two men reached a near spiritual state. Each man was in love, and both saw this experience as permeating every aspect of their lives.

At the end of their vacation, Matthiessen returned to Oxford, and Cheney went on to Cassis, France—one of his favorite places in the world. Ambitious young man that Matthiessen was, he immediately cast his love for Cheney in terms of his literary studies. "My union with you during those seven weeks brought me to a state where I thought that for the first time I knew the meaning of love, and perhaps felt some ability to express this white sacred flame in my life and work," he wrote. Matthiessen's predilection for thinking in historical terms can also be seen. "We stand in the middle of an uncharted, uninhabited country," he wrote. "That there have been unions like ours is obvious, but we are unable to draw on their experience. We must create everything for ourselves." Whether it was being an American, his nascent readings in American literature, his ambition, his wealth and privilege, or more likely a combination of all these factors, Matthiessen took it for granted that he and Cheney could figure out for themselves the terms and tenor of their relationship, in which they had almost no role models. That Matthiessen made this claim just before his twenty-third birthday speaks to his preternatural self-confidence and self-assurance.

Soon after their winter break together, Matthiessen decided that he had to tell his Skull and Bones brothers about his relationship with Cheney. Matthiessen was impassioned, direct, and young; he wanted to share the good news that he was in love. Given the Skull and Bones initiation ritual of confiding one's sexual history, Matthiessen's desire wasn't completely outlandish. Still,

Cheney did not like this development at all, and the considerable age difference between the two men showed itself in their debate.

For Cheney, homosexuality was very much "the love that dare not speak its name." From an older generation, Cheney, far more so than Matthiessen, could conceivably have married a woman and had a family, while seeking out sexual liaisons with other men quietly on the side. Matthiessen's desire to tell his friends about their relationship led Cheney to propose that they stop having sex altogether. "The base of our love is not physical but intense under-standing of a mutual problem," Cheney wrote referring to their homosexuality. Summoning Walt Whitman's poem "I Sing the Body Electric" to his aid, Matthiessen protested: "You say that our love is not based on the physical, but on our mutual understanding, and sympathy, and tenderness. And of course that is right. But we both have bodies: 'if the body is not the soul, what then is the soul?'"

Matthiessen's relationship with Cheney was about love in the modern sense of romantic love and quickly became a critical factor around which he organized his sense of himself and the world. "For it is obvious that the only conceivable sexual expression for either of us is with the other," Matthiessen wrote. Because of their emotional connection, Matthiessen viewed his sexual experiences with Cheney as distinctly different from his early sexual experi-ences as a teenager at the Hackley School or in Manhattan. Sex with Cheney helped Matthiessen discover himself as a person, and this discovery intoxicated him. In this sense, Matthiessen reached for a contemporary definition of "gay," in which sexuality becomes an organizing principle to a sense of self. That he did so without benefit of having been born after the sexual revolution or contem-porary gay liberation movement speaks to Matthiessen's conceptual sophistication—he was a Rhodes scholar after all—combined with the power of his romantic and sexual feelings for Cheney.

Still, Cheney disagreed, and his response illustrated their diverging points of view. Cheney wrote about sex: "It is a much smaller thing for me than that. Nor would I find other expression necessarily impure or ugly—merely unwise." Not surprisingly, Cheney was well aware of the legal consequences of homosexuality, including arrest, fines, and imprisonment, and he had grown accustomed to and comfortable with having love and sex divided starkly by the law. Sex with Matthiessen, pleasurable though it was, challenged Cheney's worldview. For all of Matthiessen and Cheney's compatibility, Cheney's worldliness and conservatism stood in sharp contrast to Matthiessen's inexperience and idealism.

In the end, Matthiessen told his friends all about his and Cheney's relationship, which was strikingly frank for a young man in the mid-1920s. Somewhat surprisingly, several of Matthiessen's friends, including Russell Davenport, a Skull and Bones brother, who went on to become the managing editor at *Fortune*, were resoundingly supportive. Davenport wrote: "Thank God you found it! . . . Vision—love—sympathy . . . I only know that you have found what you needed—what we all need—what we are put on the earth to find." Reluctantly, Cheney told his friend Howard Phelps Putnam, who simply urged Cheney to be discreet.

Cheney and Matthiessen met—for a third time—in Paris in March 1925. The details of how they resolved the question of continuing sexual intimacy are lost to history, but their enduring partnership would suggest that they managed to find a mutually agreeable solution. Cheney sailed back to the United States later that month to prepare for two exhibitions.

In the spring of 1925, the Babcock Galleries in New York exhibited another show by Cheney, followed again by one at the Wadsworth Atheneum. Cheney sold eighteen paintings, mostly to family and friends, with some commanding prices as high as $750 (nearly $12,000 in 2021 dollars). Cheney brimmed with enthusiasm about the shows, but in his correspondence with Matthiessen, he also gave voice to insecurities, which gnawed at him and which until then he had kept largely to himself. On a visit to the Atheneum in

Hartford, he described seeing his Skungimaug River painting, which hung in the same gallery as works by John Singleton Copley and Sir Joshua Reynolds: "I got near knuckled flat with my big canvas hanging there—same room as Copley & Reynolds . . . I am ashamed way down inside—I jumped the pistol. I thought I was better than I was."

Cheney was correct on some level: Although abundantly talented, he did not have the same level of technical ability as Reynolds or Copley, but perhaps more interesting was his use of them as his yardstick. In his mature style, Cheney was after a much different aesthetic effect from the realist painters to whom he compared himself. But the difficulty for Cheney was having confidence in charting out his own direction. Still, Cheney's telling Matthiessen about his self-doubt comforted him and helped draw him closer to his younger partner.

Cheney's other balm for his insecurities was drinking. Early on, within the first months of their relationship, Cheney's drinking was a subject of discussion between him and Matthiessen. Matthiessen urged Cheney to read or write to him instead of having his "tenth cognac." When Cheney confessed to sneaking a drink in the morning, Matthiessen responded with exuberance and naiveté about the early warning signs of alcohol dependence: "The remark about sneaking a few drinks mornings and brushing your teeth so I wouldn't know was like a whip lash across my face, and then I laughed at its absurdity. I remember picking my nose when I thought you wouldn't see me! It's funny how human beings can't escape from occasional pettiness even when living in the richest harmony. For God's sake, Mr. Cheney, have your drink as well as bread in the morning." Complications from Cheney's drinking would grow in the future, but in the spring of 1925, they caused only the faintest ripples in two men's relationship.

Matthiessen's brightness and buoyancy countered Cheney's darker moments. That same spring back at Oxford, Matthiessen felt enormous excitement and joy over his relationship with

Cheney, and his happiness quickened his pulse. On a visit to Dorset on England's southern coast, he bicycled through the English countryside: "Being alone, I could feel my heart swelling like the seeds in the ground, and I kept shouting over and over to the wind: 'Rat, Rat, my God feller how I love you.'" On another occasion, visiting a cathedral, Matthiessen stood in the choir and caught the eye of a "husky, broad-shouldered" man of about forty, "the perfect Chaucerian yeoman." The man approached Matthiessen. "Fine old building, sir," he said. The man's voice was unusually gentle and his eyes were "dark full brown." On leaving, Matthiessen let his elbow graze the man's stomach, and this encounter gave him an erection. Cheney wrote back to Matthiessen: "I get the whole scene in the cathedral . . . You are sure, darn it, he must have had the same sense. He wouldn't have stopped to speak to you if you didn't attract him." Once again, Cheney, as the voice of worldly wisdom and experience, coached his younger partner through the encounter.

Soon into Matthiessen's correspondence with Cheney, he bought a strongbox in which to keep Cheney's letters—and perhaps to safeguard them from prying eyes. Matthiessen sent Cheney a picture of himself as a well-muscled fourteen-year-old at the Hackley School wearing only a jock strap, standing before a measuring grid. It was a photo that appeared to have been taken by the school, a visual record to go along with the student's height and weight. A few weeks before, Cheney told Matthiessen that he had done a painting of a handsome man and would send him a snapshot. Whether relaying stories of fraught, pent-up sexual feelings in cathedrals or trading seminude photographs, Matthiessen and Cheney grew closer through their correspondence.

Reflecting a deepening intimacy and their aesthetic impulses, Matthiessen and Cheney quickly developed their own private language, verbal and visual. It started with their Skull and Bones nicknames, used in their correspondence. But Cheney took this playfulness to another level by alluding visually to the Little Devil in the painting *F. O. Matthiessen at Vieux-Port* (1925), in which he placed a small figurine of a devil on the table next to Matthiessen, who, not surprisingly, is depicted sitting in a chair reading. Their nicknames for each other quickly expanded. In a restaurant in Venice, Cheney had overheard a busboy referred to as "Il Piccolo"—the small one—and decided that the diminutive suited Matthiessen. This quickly became "Pic" for short. Matthiessen called Cheney "Pictor," Latin for painter. They used the term "moby" to refer to sex or maybe even more suggestively to their penises, and they egged each other on like two teenage boys. Cheney wrote: "I'm afraid Mr. Matthiessen, I'm afraid my guard is down if Moby isn't." As with nearly all of Matthiessen's and Cheney's writing about sex, their underlying intimacy, companionship, play, and exuberance with the other was the real subject of their private language. It was as though the ability and opportunity to share their desires, feelings, and thoughts was the truly important matter. All through Matthiessen and Cheney's lives together, frank, regular communication was of primary importance. And these early years set the tone of much joy and intimacy for the twenty years that followed.

In August 1925, Matthiessen and Cheney met again in Paris, and that fall they returned to the United States. Cheney settled at his family home in South Manchester, and Matthiessen began graduate school at Harvard. Before beginning school, Matthiessen visited Cheney in South Manchester, where he played the overly solicitous host, wanting to ensure that everything about Pic's visit went smoothly. They spent most of their time in Cheney's palatial painting studio, keeping to themselves and trying to dodge Cheney's new brother-in-law, who according to family rumor was secretly homosexual.

Many years earlier in South Manchester, Cheney had created an artistic haven for himself, when he converted a barn on the Cheney family compound into his painting studio. The architects of the renovation were his cousin Charles Adams Platt and John Watkinson Huntington of Hartford. It may have been that Cheney's exposure to William Merritt Chase's famous painting studio gave him the idea to create an oasis of art and culture in his own backyard. Tall pine trees and a pathway of fallen needles lined the approach to the studio, and thick-growing vines covered the entrance into the building. It was like a doorway into another world.

The main room of the studio was enormous, nearly forty feet long and over twenty feet wide with fifteen-foot ceilings and a north-facing, twelve- by ten-foot window. Next to the window was a large fireplace with a six-foot mantle of cast plaster, looking as though it were from a European manor, with an elegantly tapered flue. The studio also featured shelves lined with leather-bound books, an oriental rug, pieces of porcelain and china that Cheney had collected, and paintings everywhere—on the walls or resting in racks about the room. A balcony at one end of the studio gave Cheney an excellent vantage from which to survey his paintings.

Throughout his adult life, Cheney was an accomplished gardener, and on the north side of his studio, just outside the large window, he created a walled garden, in which he planted violets, pansies, lilies of the valley, fuchsia, calendulas, and zinnias, many of which frequently appeared in his paintings. In the garden, Cheney also placed two Chinese guardian lions. The lions stand as protectors or guards of Buddhist temples and other places of importance, flanking each side of the entrance. Typically, the lion on the right is male, while that on the left is female. The male lion is sometimes depicted with his left paw on an ornamental ball, and the expression "The lion throws the embroidered ball" is a euphemism for sex. Cheney used the male lion in a number of his paintings, and knowing his wit and playfulness, he probably purposefully alluded to this sexual innuendo. Both decor and landscaping heightened the sense that Cheney's studio and garden were a world in which beauty reigned supreme, and the

Chinese lions protected this artistic oasis. For Cheney, his studio and garden were the perfect spot to host his new young lover.

Early in 1926 Cheney traveled to the West Coast to visit his sister Harriet in Santa Barbara. While out west, he had an exhibit at the Santa Barbara Arts Club and worked on *Desert Pool* (1926), a serene depiction of an oasis surrounded by palms, reflecting tranquilly in the water. Cheney also completed *Calla Lilies* (1926), which he described in a letter to Matthiessen as "a sea green pale background, white bowl, twisting, aspiring, very sexually inclined white lilies, each with a darting yellow pricker. A damn good job, if I do say so."

Until he was forty-five, Cheney had never permanently lived anywhere but the KD House, which his sister Helen had managed after their parents died. In the spring of 1926, the KDs decided to sell the house to their brother Philip, who was well-off enough to buy and extensively remodel it. Had Cheney wanted, he could have purchased or rented a house just about anywhere else in the world, since Cheney Brothers dividends provided him an income. But he was conflicted about the sale of his family home, which made a more decisive course of action difficult. As a result, Cheney was adrift for the next couple of years—traveling to Europe, staying with his brother Clifford in South Manchester, living in New York City, and spending summers in Kittery before he and Matthiessen settled there permanently.

In his diary, Farwell Knapp captured Cheney's attachment to his family home. Perceptively, Knapp understood how the KD House symbolized Cheney's internal conflict between his attachment to his family and his desire to paint. "He is so steeped in homely and New England tradition that they are a vital part of him. He wouldn't be himself without a home—this very home," Knapp wrote referring to the KD House. "True, this is largely unconscious. His conscious part often wants to run away, so he can paint undisturbed. He would be a far better painter if he would do that, and would deny himself some of his charming sociability."

Matthiessen, too, saw Cheney's separation from his family as a great opportunity for his painting. On April 26, he wrote: "I have not been blind to the feeling of what a family can mean. I saw it in the gay happy way you all talked about the past at the dinner table. Its quiet dignified spirit caught me as we sat those times in your mother's room. I say this because I want you to know that when I seem hard-boiled about your giving up the house and freeing yourself from inessential claims, it is not because I am blind to certain things, but that I see other things [as] more important. To be an achieved artist, you must be responsible to nothing except those things which your painting demands." Matthiessen's powerful need to see Cheney as a professional painter was perhaps even greater than Cheney's own need to see himself in that light. A few days later, Matthiessen encouraged Cheney to "get out" of his family home. Matthiessen's stridency may have stemmed in part from his own lack of deep family connections, as well as the importance that he placed on achievement. But for all of Matthiessen's support for Cheney's painting, he and others failed to see that Cheney's family was not good *or* bad for his art: they were good *and* bad. In the near term, Cheney's family often distracted him, but going back a generation or two, Cheney family contributions to New England and American history lay behind Cheney's intuitive grasp of New England life in his paintings.

In late spring of 1926, Matthiessen received his master's degree from Harvard, and later that summer, he and Cheney returned to Europe. Cheney stayed in Venice through the fall, while Matthiessen returned to Harvard to begin his work on his PhD. Around this time, a transition is apparent in Cheney's work, as though the intensity and vibrancy of his relationship with Matthiessen helped him produce bolder, more stylized views of the world. During these years, Cheney himself made the connection between love and painting soon after he and Matthiessen had sex. He wrote: "God, feller, how I feel this last year has enriched and deepened me . . . To have really deeply felt Giotto and stood with you there before the windows at Chartres, to have at once reached the full expression of my physical life, and to have seen the new vision of Beauty, to know that to love and to create are the same."

Some of Cheney's strongest, most dynamic combination flower-landscape paintings date from his sojourn in Venice during the summer and fall of 1926. These include *Lilies and Salute* (1926), in which a large vase of flowers partially blocks a view of the basilica of Santa Maria Della Salute, and *Flowers in Venice* (1926), which also depicts flowers in a window looking out over the church of San Giorgio Maggiore. Cheney partially obscures the famous tourist sites of Venice, which had been the primary focus of his paintings just a few years earlier. Now, flowers and architecture stand in a more surprising juxtaposition. It was as though the flowering of Cheney's love for Matthiessen now radiated throughout his life, and the paintings done during this period capture some of the freshness with which Cheney was seeing Venice. The change was not lost on the critics who reviewed this crop of Cheney's paintings.

Cheney used a similar technique in a strong portrait of Matthiessen done around this time. A handsome, twenty-four-year-old Francis Otto Matthiessen stands on a balcony in shirt-sleeves and stares strongly at the viewer. Given the architecture behind him, Matthiessen is almost assuredly standing on a balcony at the Hotel Royal Grande Bretagne. (The hotel was later destroyed in World War II.) Similar to Cheney's paintings of Venice, the emphasis is on the figure in the foreground, but the architecture in the background balances out the composition. Matthiessen looks self-confident and direct, as though he's every bit a match for Western culture and history, as symbolized by the basilica of Santo Spirito over his shoulder. This particular example of Cheney's mixing genres, portraiture and landscape, also invites the question as to whether this technique captured his experience as a gay man, in which the personal, private image that the painter wants to focus on stands before the traditional, tourist backdrop that the painter knows he is supposed to be interested in, a kind of visual double-consciousness?

FIGURE 4. Russell Cheney, *F. O. Matthiessen on Balcony* (1902–1950), 1926, oil on canvas, 36 x 29 in. (91.4 x 73.7 cm), Harvard Art Museums, H848. Gift from Barney and Lucy Bowron, Minneapolis, on the occasion of Harvard University's 350th anniversary, 1986.

Late in the fall of 1926, Cheney rented an apartment and studio in New York City at 134 West 4th Street to concentrate on portrait painting. The Florentine portrait of Matthiessen was featured in a May 1927 show at the Wadsworth Atheneum and reproduced in the *Hartford Courant*. The painting may have seemed like a graduation present of sorts for Matthiessen, who completed his doctorate degree in English at Harvard around this same time. It was the perfect gift really, their love for each other given concrete expression in a painting.

Chapter 4

A Star Is Born

Had Matthiessen and Cheney's relationship consisted primarily of vacationing in Europe together, their story might have been that of a passionate and romantic love affair. But necessitated by Cheney's need for a home after the sale of the KD House, the couple found their way to Kittery, where they began spending summers together in the late 1920s.

For Cheney, Maine's evocative landscapes helped him reconnect with his family's roots and his own history. It was the New England world to which Cheney had been born. At the time, as Matthiessen said, Cheney was "filled with an increasing desire also to paint New England, and yet not be swamped by too much family." This statement also supported Matthiessen's own assessment of the negative effect Cheney's family had on his ability to concentrate on his painting. Kittery quickly won Matthiessen's heart too. He loved the ocean and old buildings of nearby Portsmouth, New Hampshire. But perhaps even more important, Kittery was a place where the normally intense young man could lighten up, relax, and even play.

During the summer of 1927, Matthiessen and Cheney rented the Ditty Box cottage in Kittery Point. The name had symbolic meaning for them: It was in a ditty box that "the sailorman locks all his love letters and monograph notepaper, ink, pen, and photographs of loved ones," the *Marine Review* explained. On a ship in which everything else was common property, a ditty box was the one place in which a sailor kept those items that were his alone. For Matthiessen and Cheney, inside the privacy of their cottage—their ditty box—they were free to love each other and share their lives.

Cheney's instinctive connection to Kittery and its environs showed itself in his paintings of the area. These settings gave Cheney a chance to explore the bleaker side of New England that was already suffering even before the Great Depression hit with such force. Cheney's darker paintings are often among his best. In *Depot Square* (1927), for instance, Cheney successfully conveys a sense of desolation that hangs in the atmosphere of the train station in Portsmouth. There are hints that the scene supports life—or had once supported life—such as the parked car, but the balance of images suggests the absence of people. There is no one in the car, no smoke rises from the chimneys of the buildings, and the telephone poles look like denuded trees. The composition works well, because Cheney has successfully depicted at least seven different diagonal roof planes broken up

FIGURE 5. Russell Cheney, *Depot Square*, 1927. Collection of Richard Candee and Robert Chase.

by the evenly spaced repetition of vertical lines of chimneys and telephone poles, so that the painting captures the hodgepodge of New England architecture but coalesces into a unified vision.

It is also somewhat surprising that a scion of a wealthy and prominent manufacturing family should prove to be a sensitive chronicler of New England noir. But in 1927, just two months before Cheney was working on *Depot Square*, Cheney Brothers announced a "whale of a cut" —roughly 40 percent—in dividends it paid to family members due to declining demand for silk. This was Cheney's primary income, so even before the stock market crash of 1929, his antennae must have been especially sensitive to socioeconomic changes going on in the country. These decrepit landscapes gave Cheney ample opportunity to express these conditions visually.

But for Matthiessen and Cheney personally, the summer of 1927 was a very happy one. Two photographs survive that tell a lot about their first summer in Kittery. In one, Matthiessen stands naked in the surf, facing the ocean with his arms outstretched in a jubilant gesture; in the other, he is once again at the surf's edge and faces the camera with a large piece of seaweed draped around him like a feather boa, providing just enough modesty. (Over a decade later, Matthiessen considered "Man in the Open Air" as the title of his landmark study of American literature, and these photographs from Kittery more or less embody that idea.) The photographs are provocative and sexy but not vulgar. To see Matthiessen so playful is to witness something of the light-heartedness and joy that characterized his life with Cheney in Kittery. The photographs contradict the later assertion by a former student of Matthiessen's that he "seldom overflowed with pure upsurge of spirits." When Matthiessen was with Cheney at Kittery, he could tap into a lighter, more joyful side to his personality.

In the fall of 1927, Matthiessen began teaching as an instructor at Yale—just as he had planned during his student days—and Cheney returned to South Manchester and lived in his studio, which he had remodeled to make room for living space.

Matthiessen and Cheney went back and forth between New Haven and South Manchester but soon learned that although their growing relationship provided great joy and emotional sustenance for them personally, it attracted the notice of other Cheney family members for both good and ill. Cheney's brother Clifford and his wife, Cass, told him that they liked Matty the best of all of his friends. (Matthiessen did not like his first name, Francis, so as an adult he most often went by Matty among his friends.) But a few months later, Cheney learned through a Skull and Bones friend that Hugh Aiken Bayne, his former brother-in-law, had hired a detective who had watched him and Matthiessen in Paris the previous summer of 1926. He wrote to Matthiessen: "Feller I am writing this all down more as a record of what I feel—I don't reach any conclusion until your more level head helps me—this is what I feel now—but I tell you what Bill Lusk said: 'Bayne had you and Matty watched by detectives while you were in Paris.'" Presumably, Bayne did not want his daughter Helen Bayne Knapp—Cheney's niece, of whom he was especially fond—to become overly attached to two known homosexuals. It was dawning on some members of Cheney's family that his friendship with Matthiessen was more than close. And they were not happy.

During that winter and the spring of 1928, Matthiessen and Cheney saw each other mostly on weekends, except for one week when Cheney went off to Charleston, South Carolina, after announcing that he was "sick of Manchester." Without the usual constraints of finances, the downturn in dividends from Cheney Brothers notwithstanding, or family responsibilities, Cheney could be impulsive. If he had an idea to do something—or not do something—he acted on it and with brio. While in Charleston, Cheney attended a friend's exhibition at the Charleston Museum, and as usual, he painted. Charleston is known as "the Holy City," and Cheney painted a number of well-known houses of worship, as well as more humble structures. Similar to Cheney's pattern in Europe, his paintings of the offbeat structures and scenes were often more original than those of the better-known sites. It was as though he felt freer and less constrained by conventional views of the more famous sites.

In early April 1928, Cheney's first painting teacher and friend Walter Griffin visited him back in South Manchester and encouraged Cheney to "paint less and 'dream' more." Griffin was known to work very, very slowly, sometimes spending many weeks finishing a canvas, whereas Cheney now worked so quickly that he sometimes completed two canvases a day—one in the morning and one in the afternoon. A few years earlier, Matthiessen had made the same recommendation to Cheney, encouraging him not to produce so many "half day masterpieces."

But slowing down was difficult for Cheney, as though he was often trying to stay one step ahead of self-consciousness—the lack thereof being a state he prized in his painting. In 1928, Knapp wrote much the same thing about Cheney: "He has all the technical skill, the opportunity, the keen perception, sense of color, feeling for line and mass and design, all the temperament, the enthusiasm necessary, but although he tries desperately hard not to think, yet at bottom in his queer elusive way he is a skeptic." If self-consciousness could not be outrun, then Cheney occasionally sought to blot it out some nights with one drink too many.

Matthiessen and Cheney returned to Kittery over the summer of 1928 and were again joined by Farwell and Helen Bayne Knapp, who also had rented a house in Kittery Point that summer. Cheney spent his days painting local scenes, while Matthiessen had begun work on his literary biography of Sarah Orne Jewett. Matthiessen had by this time developed his practice of working in the mornings after breakfast—a pattern from which he rarely strayed throughout his life. The conviviality of Matthiessen and Cheney's life together at Kittery almost never seduced Matthiessen to relax the drive to achieve his long-range ambitions.

Later that fall, Cheney had his first exhibition at New York's

Montross Gallery, to which he had switched from Babcock. This was his first large exhibition that didn't feature any paintings with European subjects. Cheney now focused his efforts on America in general and New England in particular. He included many of the portraits that he had been painting over the last year, including those of Matthiessen, Farwell Knapp, and Louis Hyde. And he also exhibited the paintings of the Jewett house that Matthiessen later used in *Sarah Orne Jewett*. The *New York Times* rewarded him, noting the "full richness of Mr. Cheney's palate" in the landscapes.

In focusing on New England, Cheney tapped into the regionalist movement in American art. In response to the social disruption and dislocation that came about during the 1920s and especially in the 1930s, precipitated by the Depression, a number of painters and writers sought the stability, security, and certainty of rural communities. In painting, the movement was especially associated with painters of the Midwest in the work of Thomas Hart Benton, John Steuart Curry, and Grant Wood (a painter whose style Cheney later characterized as "cheap"). But as art historians have persuasively demonstrated, New England gave birth to regionalism as well with painters such as Marsden Hartley, who chose Maine as his subject, and whose lifespan (1877–1943) closely paralleled Cheney's (1881–1945). An important characteristic of regionalism was the belief that the rural landscapes and folk art portraits expressed America writ large. The tricky thing with Cheney is that he did not specifically carve out an identity for himself as a regionalist; rather, he painted those landscapes, interiors, still lifes, and portraits that appealed to him. By contrast, Hartley deliberately and consciously set out to establish himself as "the Painter from Maine." But given Cheney's close connection to New England and American history through his family, he expressed a stronger link to regionalism than has been appreciated.

Soon after the Montross show closed, Cheney rented an apartment at 4 Beekman Place in New York, and at age forty-seven began another thread of his career: trying to paint more portraits on commission. Although several critics didn't approve of his portraits, these works give greater insight into Cheney, his painting, and the dynamics of his career.

It's curious that at this juncture Cheney did not begin teaching. Having spent roughly sixteen years as an art student in one form or another, Cheney may not have wanted to go back to the atelier under any condition, even though teaching had been such an integral part of the careers of most of his own painting teachers. And although Cheney would take on a student here and there in the years to come, in retrospect his decision not to teach made his career more difficult, because he did not have a particular school or institution to serve as his home base to help mold the next generation of painters and with which he could later be affiliated and identified.

But Cheney could get paid for portraiture—at least some of the time. Since Cheney Brothers had cut dividends, Cheney presumably wanted to supplement his income, at least in part. Considering Cheney's portraits from this time, a split showed itself in his art, divided up most strongly along pecuniary lines. For better or worse, Cheney seemed unable to summon his talent for money alone. Cheney needed some connection with his sitters—friendly, emotional, or sexual—to raise the level of his expressiveness. Such a connection enabled him to get beyond the public personas of his sitters and communicate something of their inner lives. Having a connection with a sitter probably also allowed Cheney to relax. Not coincidentally, nearly all Cheney's most successful portraits were of men and tended to be less wooden and more spontaneous.

Cheney was less successful with portraits of society women, which were often stiff. While in New York, Cheney painted Katharine Hepburn (a love interest of Cheney's great friend Phelps Putnam in the late 1920s); Elizabeth Foster (whose husband was in Skull and Bones); Virginia Biddle; and Marcia Clarke (whose soon-to-be husband was also in Skull and Bones). The drawing in these portraits was acceptable; the women no doubt recognized themselves, as did their families. But in general, these portraits are rudimentary and mediocre—not Cheney's best work.

As Knapp had suggested, Cheney's skepticism about the whole exercise of portrait painting on commission seemed to cramp his style. Cheney may have felt compelled to give the women and their families faithful, realistic images of themselves, so that he could not strive for a stronger, bolder interpretation or vision. Still, Cheney yearned for self-expressiveness, and in an attempt to assert this desire, he added self-referential images of his own paintings to some of these portraits. In *Mrs. Marcia Clarke*, for example, Cheney reproduced his painting *Flowers in Venice* (1926), hanging on the wall behind Clarke's figure. Cheney did not plumb the metaphorical depths of adding his own work to his paintings the way his hero Cézanne did in *The Artist's Father, Reading "L'Événement,"* in which art, as symbolized by the reproduction of Cézanne's own painting, and commerce, as symbolized by his father reading the newspaper, compete for the viewer's attention. But within the confines of painting on commission, adding self-referential images to these works enabled Cheney to expand his creative range.

Even if expressiveness and conventionality competed for control of his paintbrush, in life Cheney had a streak of adventurousness in him. While living in New York, Cheney saw Malcolm Forbes—not *the* Malcolm Forbes but a friend and early sexual partner who predated Cheney and Matthiessen's relationship. Although Forbes ultimately married and had a family—as Cheney predicted he would—as a younger man he seemed to be willing to engage in sexual activity or experimentation of some kind with other men. As described earlier, the lines between homosexual and heterosexual were more permeable in the earlier part of the twentieth century than they became later. In January 1929, Forbes visited Cheney at his apartment. The cordial catching-up with each other quickly gave way to sexual tension. Cheney wrote: "Well, all of a sudden after having been just casual and friendly[,] the air got very tense. I don't know whether it was more him or me. Anyhow he took my hand and I held and kissed him full." Before either of them knew it, they had fallen into bed and had sex. The following morning, Cheney made breakfast for them both, and neither man mentioned what had happened the previous afternoon.

As usual, Cheney discussed his extracurricular sexual liaisons with Matthiessen, even comparing the sex that he had with Forbes to that he had with Matthiessen. Cheney viewed his relationship with Matthiessen as set apart from all of his "whoring" (Cheney's word). With Matthiessen it was sex *and* emotional intimacy, and this made their relationship and sex life more substantial in Cheney's mind.

If Cheney's sexual activity outside of their relationship shook Matthiessen's trust or hurt his feelings, he didn't let on. By this time, Matthiessen trusted Cheney deeply enough to reveal many, many emotional states to him, but Matthiessen hid hurt feelings from everyone—even Cheney. On another occasion, Cheney wrote to Matthiessen about a sexual encounter with a doctor of Matthiessen's in New York, who liked both male and female partners: "He [the doctor] has a friend he sees here every week that way, and also two girls, seems to be absolutely double, as well as extremely matter of fact. Says he knew us from the way you held yourself away from him when he was examining you." In response, Matthiessen gave the impression that he enjoyed the stories of Cheney's escapades. Early in 1929 Matthiessen was still teaching at Yale and working on proofs of *Sarah Orne Jewett*. He contrasted his life in New Haven with Cheney's in New York. "This time, after the freshness and vitality of our life in New York, I have felt more strongly than ever the arid remoteness from actuality of academic life," he wrote. "My God, why have most people connected with a university given up all desire to live?" Perhaps as a consolation prize, early on Matthiessen warmed himself by the fires of Cheney's adventures. For years Matthiessen simply viewed Cheney's adventuresome spirit, drinking, and seeking out sex as part of his overall vitality and effervescent personality. Weren't all artists attracted to sensual pleasures? In any case, the excitement of Manhattan did not last too long for Cheney. As Matthiessen later wrote, "New York always stimulated him to the point that he finally burst."

In early 1929 Cheney landed back in Cragmor Sanatorium in Colorado Springs for six months with a recurrence of tuberculosis. During his first stay at Cragmor in 1916, Cheney had smoothly acclimated himself to sanatorium life. But this second stay sounded the same note but in a different key. Cragmor was a legitimate retreat from the world, which Cheney welcomed with a sense of relief. While there, he wouldn't have to worry whether his portraiture business of the late 1920s was a success or a failure. At Cragmor, all would be well behind the heavily fortified walls of luxurious sanatorium life.

From the beginning of his career, Matthiessen sought out underappreciated literary figures. He was, for example, Sarah Orne Jewett's first biographer. In a canon that recognizes T. S. Eliot and Henry James as literary masters, it can be hard to remember that Matthiessen existed in a world in which they were less well known. Matthiessen's book about T. S. Eliot's poetry was among the first to bring attention to the poet's work in the United States. Similarly, Matthiessen was one of James's early champions.

Matthiessen's homosexuality must have played a role in several of his pioneering choices. As writer David Bergman has observed, "Matthiessen and Cheney constructed much of their sexual identities from what they read." Matthiessen discusses the importance of reading to formation of identity in his book *Translation: An Elizabethan Art*. Repeatedly he selects writers who gravitated toward same-sex intimacy and love, such as Jewett or Whitman, or writers whose sexuality existed in more ambiguous territory, such as Melville or James. In other instances, such as in his book on T. S. Eliot, Matthiessen's homosexuality helps animate the poet's ideas and work. Matthiessen also explores works or scenes within novels, in which a definite gay or homosocial subtext can be read. In *American Renaissance*, Matthiessen discusses work with a definite homosexual theme, notably Melville's late story *Billy Budd*. In *Henry James: The Major Phase*, same-sex desire shapes the scenes he analyzes. Finally, in *Theodore Dreiser*, Matthiessen's posthumous literary biography, Dreiser's position as an outsider helps Matthiessen envision a more public stance for homosexuality. Consciously or not, Matthiessen's homosocial or gay sensibility shaped his canon of American literary classics.

Just after Cheney returned to Cragmor in April 1929, Houghton Mifflin published Matthiessen's first book, *Sarah Orne Jewett*, which mixes biography, criticism, and history to tell the story of the Maine writer and her work. In his notes to the book, Matthiessen writes: "My friend Russell Cheney not only gave me the idea of the book, and its three best pages, but also introduced me to Miss Mary Rice Jewett," Sarah Orne Jewett's sister. By "three best pages," Matthiessen was referring to three paintings of the Jewett house that Cheney contributed to the book as illustrations. Cheney liked Jewett's literary work and had long been acquainted with her family home in South Berwick. *Sarah Orne Jewett* marked Matthiessen's only official, public collaboration with Cheney. At the time, Matthiessen was twenty-seven, and Cheney was forty-eight.

Cheney contributed *Miss Jewett's Staircase* (1927); *Jewett House* (1927?); and *Jewett Doorway* (1927?) to the book. Cheney was continuing to strive for a more stylized representation in his paintings at the time, to which he came closest in *Miss Jewett's Staircase*. His painting teacher from Ogunquit, Charles H. Woodbury, likely had given Cheney the idea for the composition of *Miss Jewett's Staircase*, as his painting entitled *The Hall* had been included in *Deephaven*, an illustrated version of Sarah Orne Jewett's collection of short stories and sketches that appeared in 1894. Still, in Cheney's painting, he makes the scene his own by infusing his New England sensibility with sharper angles and brighter colors. It is a pleasing balance for him. The brightness offsets the conventionality of the scene, so the painting is not stiff, and the quirkier angles of the composition move the painting beyond "picturesque," another word that was on occasion applied pejoratively to some of Cheney's work.

As for Matthiessen's book, he connected to Jewett and her work for personal reasons, as he did with most literature that inspired him: Russell Cheney suggested the idea; the project summoned Matthiessen's Orne family roots of his beloved mother to whom the book is dedicated; Jewett's most intimate and important relationships were with members of her own sex, a fact not lost on Matthiessen; and Jewett's work beautifully evoked the Maine coast, where he and Cheney had already passed many happy days together. As David Bergman notes, *Sarah Orne Jewett* is "a covert celebration of the homosexual artist."

Throughout *Sarah Orne Jewett*, Matthiessen strove to identify with Jewett. He put himself in Jewett's mind and tried to evoke Jewett's relationship with her father, a country doctor, and the rest of her family; the backdrop of the Civil War; and the passing of pastoral New England and growth of industrialism in the late nineteenth century along the southern Maine coast. Matthiessen drew heavily on Jewett's letters and discussed the publication of her early stories, as well as the network of professional and personal contacts and relationships that helped Jewett establish herself as a writer. As Matthiessen got into Jewett's more substantial work, he examined how her stories and sketches connected to the worlds she knew so well in the towns surrounding South Berwick, her literary influences, and how her sense of detachment strengthened her most acclaimed work, *The Country of the Pointed Firs*.

In *Sarah Orne Jewett*, Matthiessen discussed Jewett's long-term, obviously loving relationship with Annie Fields and hinted at their Boston marriage. He reproduced in the book a photograph of Fields and Jewett sitting together in Fields's drawing room in Boston. Annie Fields was the widow of noted publisher, James T. Fields, whom Jewett had known professionally. After his death in 1881, the two women became close friends. They were together constantly, even traveling to Europe together. Their pet names were "Pinny" for Jewett and "Fuffy" for Fields. The intimacy and affection of these names couldn't have been lost on Matthiessen. The fifteen years that separated Jewett and Fields may also have resonated with Matthiessen, given the twenty years that separated him from Cheney. Matthiessen wrote of Jewett and Fields that "when they were separated, daily letters sped between them, hardly letters, but jotted notes of love." He could have been describing his correspondence with Cheney.

Matthiessen made no explicit reference to same-sex relationships in *Sarah Orne Jewett*. But in his discussion of Fields and Jewett's relationship, he cited the character of Nan Prince in Jewett's novel *A Country Doctor* as evidence that Jewett did not believe in the necessity of marriage. Indicative of the mutually exclusive choices that American women faced in the nineteenth century, Jewett portrayed Nan as needing to decide between marriage or becoming a doctor. Matthiessen quoted Nan's guardian, Dr. John Leslie, who acknowledges that "Nan is not the sort of girl who will be likely to marry." Although Matthiessen's discussion of *A Country Doctor* is about marriage, in the context of Fields and Jewett's union, he seems to imply that there are reasons besides wanting a career that a woman may not want to marry. These oblique allusions to the possibility of same-sex love were probably as direct as Matthiessen thought that he could be at the time. But his reading of same-sex relationships formed a critical part of his examination of Sarah Orne Jewett and her work.

At the time of publication, most reviews of *Sarah Orne Jewett* praised the book and singled out Matthiessen as a critic who "deserves to be read." One of Jewett's later biographers credits Matthiessen (and Willa Cather) with helping resuscitate interest in her fiction. That Matthiessen wrote the book and published it in his late twenties makes it even more impressive.

But more contemporary critics have been less forgiving, and the general consensus now is that *Sarah Orne Jewett* is not a very good book. As Giles Gunn, who wrote the first critical book about Matthiessen's work, pointed out, Matthiessen had a tendency to empathize with his subjects too much, and this seems true of Jewett. Matthiessen assesses Jewett's work only in the final chapter, where he points out her "inability to portray passion in her books" and her attraction to the "gentler emotions." He also observes that Jewett depicted only the sunny, warm, and cheerful side of New England and did not show a New England that was "sordid, bleak, and mean of spirit." But in *Sarah Orne Jewett*, Matthiessen also put into words for the first time an idea that he later developed throughout his readings of T. S. Eliot and Henry James, among others: the necessity of marrying form and content. He wrote of Jewett: "She has withstood the onslaught of time, and is secure within her limits, because she achieved a style. Style means that the author has fused his material and his technique with the distinctive quality of personality. No art lasts without this fusion."

Looking at Matthiessen's book in the context of his relationship with Cheney, there is a striking parallel between Matthiessen's words about Jewett with Cheney's own description of his painting. Several months earlier, before Cheney went back to Cragmor, the *Portland Press Herald* profiled him. Throughout the article, Cheney came across as his ever ebullient and effusive self. When asked if he had always wanted to be a painter, he replied: "Not at all. I never did anything at it until my graduation from Yale. It was almost as if painting chose me rather than myself choosing the art." His candor and straightforwardness are appealing. Cheney also indicated the importance he placed on self-expression in his art, the importance of getting something of himself onto a canvas. When asked "What gives a painting artistic merit?" he replied:

"Personality. The undescribable [*sic*] something that the artist puts on the canvas with his paint. I can't say for sure if I have it but I do know that I can recognize it in others. Personality is the difference between a painter and an artist. There are plenty of good painters but their paintings might as easily been done by one of them as another. Personality is what makes the older masters what they are, and personality is the driving germ of any branch of art."

This quotation shows how Cheney had internalized the lessons from former teachers, especially Chase and Woodbury. It also closely parallels Matthiessen's notions of literary expression as a fusion of form and content inflected with the author's unique personality. Both Matthiessen and Cheney were interested in how authors and artists communicated their personalities in their works. This is not to say that they set out to develop a joint aesthetic theory. Rather, Cheney frequently lived or put into practice that which Matthiessen considered in a more scholarly and analytic way. The relationship between Cheney's practice and Matthiessen's theory is a strong theme in their story and lives together, one that cemented their bond of sexual attraction and emotional intimacy. *Sarah Orne Jewett* with Cheney's accompanying paintings ratcheted up the two men's growing intimacy.

At the end of Cheney's stay at Cragmor in the early fall of 1929, Matthiessen joined him out west, and they went on to Santa Fe. Cheney rented a house, and after Matthiessen returned east, Phelps Putnam joined Cheney, just as he had done at Cragmor back in 1917.

By the time he joined Cheney, Putnam had become a complicated figure in Cheney's life. Their correspondence was voluminous, especially through these early years; it is exceeded only by Cheney's correspondence with Matthiessen. Matthiessen later described Putnam as Cheney's artistic conscience and a source of intellectual challenge for Cheney. Certainly, Putnam and Cheney had lively, oftentimes playful visits and exchanges over the years, but they were serious too. The parallels in their lives went beyond a shared sensibility. Cheney was a minor painter, whereas Putnam was a minor poet. Both men suffered from breathing problems. Over the years, they developed a symbiotic relationship, often compounded by heavy drinking. If Matthiessen frequently played the angel in Cheney's life, recalling him to his painting and restraint from drinking, Putnam played the real devil. He egged Cheney on not so much with words but by serving as a willing party to Cheney's pleasure-seeking. Perhaps it was all of these factors—good and bad—in Cheney and Putnam's friendship that led Farwell Knapp to observe trenchantly: "Much as he loves him, Rat has come to see that Put is poisonous to him—as indeed he is, sooner or later, to everyone. Put, as Rat truly says, is a toxic person; the poison which has been draining into his system for years has created his genius—without that poison he would have been just an ordinary fellow in an insurance company—but with it his strange gnarled toxic intellect has developed."

Putnam brought out a ribald earthiness in Cheney. In one letter Cheney addressed Putnam as Madame Sosostris, the fortune-teller in Eliot's *The Waste Land*. And in another letter Cheney wrote: "Dear Baby Doll: —I got to let loose a little because today I've been painting like a hell cat." In a third letter, Cheney gives his Old Ferry Lane address in Kittery as "Old Fairies Lane." Cheney's correspondence with Matthiessen had a similar lightness, but there was often a line of seriousness with Matthiessen over which Cheney would not step. With Putnam, however, the field was wide open. As Cheney later wrote to Putnam, "I feel the need of communication—and know none better than you to communicate with."

In Santa Fe, Cheney and Putnam quickly became part of a wealthy and artistic circle of mostly men. Other members of their crowd included Bronson Cutting, a Republican US senator from

New Mexico and owner of the influential *Santa Fe New Mexican*; Witter Bynner, a poet; Frederick Manning, a history professor at Swarthmore College; Andrew Michael Dasburg, a painter; and Clifford McCarthy, who started out as Bynner's companion and secretary and became Cutting's. Some of these men—like Bynner and McCarthy—were gay; others—such as Putnam and Manning—were married but maintained close, intense relationships with other men.

There was, of course, almost no overt mention in the late 1920s and early 1930s of the group's homosocial overtones. But subtle clues abounded. In late 1929, Larry Tighe, a Skull and Bones friend of Matthiessen's and Cheney's and a partner at the investment bank Brown Brothers & Company, sent a telegram to Putnam. Using a euphemism for homosexuals, he asked to be remembered to "Cheney and his little boys." Cheney replied: "I wrote 'inexcusable' across it and am sending it back to Larry. At least I leave it here on the table to [sic] Put to mail if he thinks best. It plain broke me—such indecency." Tighe's sentiment bothered Cheney less than the quasi-public form in which he expressed it, before the eyes of Western Union clerks, who relayed the message. But the homosocial tone and tenor of Cheney and Putnam's circle in Santa Fe was such that even President Franklin Delano Roosevelt, speaking posthumously of Cutting a few years later, referred disparagingly to "that crowd that he traveled with in New Mexico."

Although Cheney moved in a wealthy and artistic circle in Santa Fe, he could get along with ordinary people when he wanted to. In the fall of 1929, Cheney befriended Paul Hoen and his wife. Paul Hoen and his brother Fred ran a garage and an adjoining shop, where Cheney had gotten "Fordy" repaired. As was typical of the ever-genial Cheney, if he liked a new acquaintance, he quickly adopted him into his life. Cheney spent much time with the Hoens. When Paul Hoen's wife became ill and went into the hospital, Cheney took over running the shop so that Hoen could visit her. During his stint as a shopkeeper, Hoen gave Cheney a loaded gun to keep under the counter; this both thrilled and horrified him. The couple's unkempt home offended Cheney's sensibility, so in the Hoens' absence, Cheney scrubbed the sink and hoped no one would notice.

Cheney painted two portraits from his time with the Hoens, *Fred Reading* (1929) and *Paul Hoen* (1930). In contrast with Cheney's portraits of society figures, he invested those of the Hoens with genuine feeling. But unlike the society portraits, Cheney almost certainly did not get paid for either one but painted them because he wanted to. Cheney's painting was often at its best when he divorced it from the demands, expectations, and tensions of his career.

In the portrait of Paul Hoen, Cheney managed to achieve something similar to his landscapes that capture the bleaker side of New England life. Hoen's face is careworn—rough and ravaged. He does not make eye contact with the viewer. Cheney communicates all of this straightforwardly, but with compassion. In April 1930, Cheney wrote enthusiastically to Matthiessen, telling him: "I am certain this picture of Paul Hoen is my most direct achievement. My complete indifference to its technical quality is what I'll stand by or fall by. It's as natural as breathing, and here's the cross-roads. Should you trust yourself and just be yourself, as this picture is, or should you consider your job a craftsman's job and be miserable because there are spots in the background and dull drawing of the fingers . . . No consideration, no careful preparation, and God damn, it lives and breathes . . . Showing this group of things to Knapp yesterday did it, removed me enough to suddenly see what it all meant—a direct expression of myself, painting no longer something to try, but crossed the border line *into being me*" (Cheney's emphasis). The change in Cheney's attitude toward his own work was strikingly different from those instances when he described himself as "a damn bourgeois imitation of an artist." As Cheney's connection with his subjects relaxed, he likewise relaxed about his technical proficiency and concentrated more on expressing what he felt and saw.

And that resonated powerfully with Matthiessen, who replied

to Cheney's letter about *Paul Hoen*: "Your extraordinary poignant letter about your painting and your new feeling towards it has been throbbing through me all day. How you can invigorate me feller when you write like that. It's just as though you poured new hot blood into my veins." Matthiessen's reply points to the fusion of intellectual, creative, and sexual energy that so captivated him with Cheney. Through their shared life, Cheney helped Matthiessen better appreciate beauty in art, literature, and the world more generally. Then over the years and strengthened by Matthiessen's own scholarship, aesthetic experiences became a critical part—if not the crucial part—to Matthiessen's definition of reality. Exchanges like this one over *Paul Hoen* illustrate how and why this dynamic developed between the two men.

After Matthiessen returned from his visit with Cheney in the Southwest in 1929, he left Yale for Harvard, where he had been hired as an instructor. Harvard set the stage for Matthiessen's most important professional and intellectual achievements. But the environment there was stressful, and Matthiessen was keenly aware that although he could officially "pass" in terms of education, socioeconomic background, and scholarly ambition as a member of Harvard's professional community, at heart he felt like an outsider because of the need to hide his homosexuality. In response, he worked harder yet. And as luck would have it, these developments for Matthiessen occurred as Cheney's career stalled on the New York art scene. Cheney, too, chose another classic method of escape: he drank more.

The Harvard that Matthiessen arrived at in many ways resembled the Yale that he had left. Harvard College of the early 1930s was a locus of white, male Protestantism which catered to the social and economic elite, primarily of the Northeast. There were few Catholics, and Jews were restricted. Women attended Radcliffe College. Matthiessen came to Harvard to help establish the History and Literature Program with the scholar Perry Miller and others.

History and Literature was a selective undergraduate program that took approximately fifty students per year. Matthiessen was also a strong supporter of the tutorial system, which Harvard's then-president, Abbott Lawrence Lowell, had instituted.

From Matthiessen's earliest days at Harvard until the late 1930s, he lived at Eliot House, one of twelve residential houses at Harvard College. He became head tutor there and was sincerely devoted to its students. Matthiessen did all he could to nurture a sense of community among faculty and students at Eliot House, such as shepherding the production of the annual holiday play.

Alfred Kazin and others later noted that Matthiessen was "essentially a teacher, and a very good one." Over the years, American literature, criticism of poetry, Shakespeare, and forms of drama became Matthiessen's main courses. Matthiessen was not a slick lecturer, and several of his students described his lectures as halting and tortured, because he often thought out ideas in real time. Many of Matthiessen's students felt that his gifts as a highly sensitive reader of literature shone more brightly in tutorials, in which he could have freer, less structured conversations with students. Matthiessen also liked to prompt his students to talk and formulate their own views. He was often at his best when he developed a one-on-one rapport with a student, as though he sought to give what he had most wanted for himself—inspired and meaningful relationships with other people.

Many of Matthiessen's students, though not all, grew to love him, and he loved them in return. The poet Richard Wilbur said years later that Matthiessen "knew more students, and cared more about them than any teacher of his time at Harvard." Matthiessen's teaching at Harvard also provided a solid perch from which he could influence the next generation of professional scholars and writers, as well as a few activists, notably social justice lawyer Arthur Kinoy, who famously filed the last appeal on behalf of Julius and Ethel Rosenberg before they were executed for conspiracy to commit espionage in 1953. Over the years, Matthiessen's students would grow to include Leo Marx, J. C. Levenson, Warner Berthoff, Harry Levin, C. L. "Joe" Barber, Justin Kaplan, Bernard Bowron, Rufus W. Mathewson Jr., Arthur Schlesinger Jr., Richard Wilbur, Pearl Kazin Bell, Daniel J. Boorstin, and many others. J. C. Levenson went so far as to characterize Matthiessen as a kind of surrogate father to many of his students. Among his students and friends, Matthiessen developed a reputation for being warm, friendly, and humorous. But he was also hardworking, ambitious, intense, and fiercely competitive.

Matthiessen was now well launched on his professional career. It was both anxiety producing and exhilarating. By the fall of 1929 he had sold almost fourteen hundred copies of *Sarah Orne Jewett*, a respectable number for a first-time, unknown author. He also received a favorable note from Edmund Wilson, then an editor at the *New Republic*, for his review of Newton Arvin's book *Hawthorne*. It must have pleased Matthiessen to have one of the leading gatekeepers of American letters recognize him and his work. Matthiessen's intellectual development matched his professional achievements. An essay in the *Yale Review* about two books by the literary scholar and critic Norman Foerster started with the kind of bold statement that people in their twenties make: "It is time for the history of American literature to be rewritten." Matthiessen said that literature must be read and studied in a broader cultural context, looking at factors like religion, education, travel, the Ford—which, no doubt, prompted thoughts of Cheney—movies, and technological innovations in communications, among other things. Matthiessen was, in essence, laying out the boundaries of the field that became American studies.

If Matthiessen's esteem for his own abilities skirted arrogance, true to his admonitions to his fellow undergraduates back at Yale, he used his gifts in the service of higher social good. That same fall, Matthiessen got involved in the case of the Watch and Ward, a censorship organization that entrapped Al DeLacey, the owner of the Dunster House Bookshop in Cambridge, into selling a copy of

Lady Chatterley's Lover by D. H. Lawrence, which had been banned under US law. Matthiessen worked to rally influential professors and Harvard publications to support DeLacey. As one of his students later wrote, Matthiessen was "a natural fighter, he liked a scrap." His defense of Al DeLacey marked the transformation of his community service while a student into greater involvement in academic, local, and national politics over many years to come.

Yet, if Matthiessen's first year at Harvard was a professional triumph, privately it came at a high cost. Unthinkingly, Matthiessen had made a Faustian deal. In 1929 he could not have secured a job at America's preeminent university—or any other university for that matter—and been open about his homosexuality. Conversely, Matthiessen could have lived more openly in artistic or bohemian enclaves in Greenwich Village or Paris, but this would have meant giving up his professional ambitions. In this regard, Matthiessen's drive and the professional expectations of his social class worked against him. Matthiessen probably never even considered that he couldn't or wouldn't reach his professional goals because of his sexuality. He simply assumed that he would keep his sexuality in the shadows. What he did in his bedroom with Cheney was a private matter anyhow. Matthiessen was unwilling to view himself or be viewed by others solely through the lens of his sexuality. But he underestimated the powerful combination of love and sex. The Matthiessen who stood naked in the surf at Seapoint Beach two summers ago could not be pushed back underground without the sense he was being buried alive.

Matthiessen described his depression in the context of his new and expanded professional horizons: "I have been lost in loneliness that I can't seem to get out of. There seems to be film between me and everything. Nothing seems really vital: books are just a procession of words, and I can't find any real significance in my work." Feeling ashamed of his sexuality contributed to this state. Trying to hone his public speaking skills, Matthiessen visited a "professor of public speaking" at Harvard, who told him that his speech was "blurred and soft." In response, Matthiessen wondered in a letter to Cheney if he was "just like any fairy." Matthiessen's remark was especially poignant, given the public speaking prize that he had won as an undergraduate. But it also shows how "fairies" stood at the feminized end of popular understanding of homosexuality. Matthiessen looked to Cheney for love and support. He wrote: "My sex bothers me, feller, sometimes when it makes me aware of the falseness of my position in the world. And consciousness of that falseness seems to sap my confidence of power. Have I any right in a community that would so utterly disapprove of me if it knew the facts? I ask myself that, and then I laugh; for I know I would never ask it at all if isolation from you didn't make me search into myself. I need you, feller; for together we can confront whatever there is."

The recent reappearance of Cheney's tuberculosis and his return to Cragmor compounded Matthiessen's depression. When Cheney's health was threatened, it shook the foundation on which Matthiessen had built his rich personal and professional worlds. Matthiessen wrote: "Dear feller, unless I know that you are building up for our future, I don't see how I'll get through this winter. I have a horrible feeling of being shut in. I need your support more than I ever imagined I would. Be good to me, feller."

As Matthiessen worried about Cheney's health, he also fell into another pattern that shaped his later life: he threw himself into work. During this time of depression, Matthiessen began to turn his doctoral dissertation into a book. Over the winter of 1930, Matthiessen worked on his "contemptible manuscript" for his "regulation seven or eight hours" a day. But the more he dived into work, the more the world responded favorably. In March 1930, Matthiessen was promoted from instructor to assistant professor. His colleague and friend Kenneth Murdock told him that he had made a great impression in his first year at Harvard.

As Matthiessen's star brightened, Cheney's dimmed. Cheney's largest one-man show from this period was at the Montross

Gallery in May 1930. Most of the reviews were mixed, but *Art News* verged on the cruel. "There are other equally disturbing contrasts in the exhibition between personal phantasy and worn out conventions. A man who can deal successfully with macabre skeletons does not need to revamp the tired old Chinese sages into acceptable accessories for interior decorators. Perhaps Mr. Cheney doesn't realize he is bored with nature and flowers and still life." Just as the art world had so quickly taken up Cheney as a fresh, new painter in 1923, it threatened to drop him just as quickly for his presumed failure to live up to his early promise. The critical response to the show disappointed Cheney.

It was at this time that Knapp made the connection between Cheney's difficulty with his art and his tendency to drink too much. Knapp wrote in his diary that Cheney "drinks because he is unhappy (as does most everyone who hits it hard). He has always dodged life's problem. Of course it is particularly bad for him to drink right now, just as he is barely over T.B. And, of course, Rat denies this is why he drinks, says he's just dull without it, but with it his gorgeous imagination is let loose . . . He wants to be a good painter, but isn't and can't be until he can summon resolution to cut away from home ties and sociability." It was almost as if Matthiessen and Cheney were playing parts in *A Star Is Born*, in which the career of the young ingenue Vicki Lester eclipses that of her increasingly drunken husband, Norman Maine.

Chapter 5

Making a Home in Kittery

The economic downturn that hit the textile mills of New England in the mid- to late 1920s soon spread to nearly all other industries and throughout the country. Ahead of the stock market crash in October 1929, the number of unemployed had stood at 492,000. By March 1934, the number had growth dramatically to over fifteen million unemployed people. Overall, 1929 to 1933, the gross national product fell 29 percent, manufacturing was down 54 percent, and construction dropped 78 percent.

The resulting social disruption was similarly dramatic. Many unemployed people—especially men—just wandered. In 1932 the Southern Pacific Railroad removed almost 700,000 people from its trains. At the end of this same year, an estimated 200,000 boys wandered, many of whom traded sexual favors for a meal. Tent cities sprung up from New York to Oakland. In the spring of 1932, thousands of homeless, unemployed ex-servicemen arrived in Washington, DC, to demand that their bonuses for service in World War I be paid ahead of schedule. With no place to go, the men set up camp in the Anacostia neighborhood. Eventually, President Hoover called in the army, which burned the camp to the ground. The historian Irving Bernstein reported that Hoover could see the fire's glow from his comfortable perch at the White House.

In response to unemployment and social disruption, many in government and organized labor devised public policy solutions to address the multiple and varied economic and social problems facing the country. Franklin Delano Roosevelt, while still governor of New York, advocated for New York and other states to adopt unemployment insurance, an idea later endorsed by the Democrats in the summer of 1932 at their national convention. After the election of 1932, organized labor worked with the Democrats to pass the National Industrial Recovery Act, which President Roosevelt signed into law on June 16, 1933. Section 7(a) of the legislation established the right of employees to organize and participate in collective bargaining without restraint, interference, or coercion from employers. Also, the federal government created the National Labor Relations Board to resolve disputes between employees and employers. Still, progress was slow, and many people grew disillusioned and impatient, turning to either Socialism or Communism for answers. The Communist Party USA created unemployment councils, which designated National Unemployment Day as March 6, 1930, and held rallies in cities across the country. At the New York City rally, William Foster, head of the Communist Party USA, addressed a crowd estimated at thirty-five thousand in Union Square.

Because of Matthiessen's job, he and Cheney were insulated from the worst consequences of the Depression. But it was against this bleak backdrop that the two men established themselves more permanently in Maine. Matthiessen grew up in Illinois and Tarrytown, New York, without his father and spent his professional life in Massachusetts. Cheney was born and raised in a big, happy home in Connecticut. But as a couple, they had only one true home: Kittery, Maine. Beginning in 1930, when the two men purchased a house in the town, the importance of Kittery cannot be overstated in appreciating how their lives together unfolded. At the time Kittery was a small town with a population of roughly forty-four hundred.

Though modest, the house at 12 Old Ferry Lane is one of the most beautifully situated in the town. Built in 1790, the two-story boat builder's home sits on a peninsula of land, where the Spruce Creek estuary empties into the Piscataqua River at the mouth of Portsmouth Harbor. The house faces the water, and several old apple trees dot the lawn leading down to the rocky shore. The view of the harbor from the house includes the then-active US Coast Guard Station on Wood Island; the Portsmouth Harbor Lighthouse in New Castle, New Hampshire; and several barren outcroppings of ledge known as Hicks Rocks. The house is of typical New England proportions with small rooms and low ceilings. Matthiessen used one of the upstairs bedrooms as his study. A square chimney sits squatly on the roof. For Matthiessen, the house was simply the "most beautiful house in America," as Bernard Bowron, one of Matthiessen's students, later reported. Cheney completed many paintings of the house, including *Facing East, Kittery, Maine*.

Matthiessen and Cheney first rented the house from its owner, Alice Shurtleff, whom they had met through her husband, Harold, who was working on his doctoral dissertation at Harvard. Matthiessen and Cheney then purchased the house when Alice decided to put it up for sale. After Harold's death in the late 1930s, Matthiessen and Cheney stayed in touch with Alice, who painted a watercolor of Matthiessen at the house.

Over the summer of 1930, Cheney Brothers announced that it would stop paying dividends altogether. This directly affected Cheney, who depended on the family business for much of his livelihood. As a result, Matthiessen purchased the Kittery house but put ownership in both their names. The cut in dividends also meant that the forty-nine-year-old Cheney became financially dependent on twenty-eight-year-old Matthiessen.

The end of Cheney Brothers dividends paid to family members also raises a thought-provoking question about Matthiessen and Cheney's relationship in terms of Matthiessen's early intellectual hero, R. H. Tawney. Did Matthiessen ever apply Tawney's ideas about "functionless property" to Cheney? And if so, how did he reconcile himself to them? Cheney had never worked at anything other than his painting, because the dividends paid to family members had provided him with an independent income—or "functionless property," in Tawney's words. What did Matthiessen make of this, if anything? Perhaps the Cheney family's connection to their workers and progressive interest in their welfare—however imperfect by present-day standards—influenced Matthiessen's thinking on the subject, but there are no references in Matthiessen's professional or personal writing to indicate that he knew about the realities or was particularly interested in the conditions of workers at Cheney Brothers. More likely, Matthiessen felt that Cheney's job in society was to paint, so if dividends from Cheney Brothers enabled him to do that, Matthiessen overlooked the nuances of the situation.

But Matthiessen probably didn't care about the theoretical implications of his purchase of the Kittery house, because he loved Cheney dearly and for the first time in his life, he had something to which he had never before been able to lay claim: a home. As Farwell Knapp observed in his diary, "Matty has no experience of happy home life, no memories, no roots, while Rat is more so that way than most men." Bernard Bowron later echoed the same thought, claiming that Kittery was Matthiessen's "only real home."

And it was Cheney who made the Kittery house a home. Cheney imported family possessions and traditions into life at Kittery. From his South Manchester studio, Cheney brought furniture, china, glass, and fabrics—appropriately enough for the son of silk manufacturers. He also brought books from family members to Kittery, many of which had been inscribed and passed down through the generations. Cheney planted flowers around the house, including pink and white phlox, tiger and plantain lilies, lilacs, and many others. No place would have been a home for Cheney without a painting studio, so he renovated a barn on the property to serve as one, just as he had done in South Manchester. Although the Kittery studio was not as opulent as the one in South Manchester, it did have plenty of room and a large north-facing window. The two men had found a handsome

FIGURE 6. Russell Cheney, *Facing East, Kittery, Maine*, 1944. Collection of Richard Candee and Robert Chase. Photograph by Jeremy Fogg.

house in a beautiful setting, and they had each other. Why would they want for anything more?

Thanksgivings in the Matthiessen-Cheney home were especially important, just as they had been for the Cheneys in South Manchester. Guests, including graduate students and colleagues of Matthiessen's, would arrive in Kittery on Wednesday afternoon. Thanksgiving would begin with a walk, as Matthiessen put aside his usual morning work regimen. The dinner table was happy and peaceful, which C. L. Barber later ascribed to the fact that the group "was not a family, and yet its members were making together, especially at Thanksgiving, something like a family without the dead weight of arbitrary and routine association." It's doubtful that Matthiessen and Cheney thought about the holiday in these terms, but they were forming a nontraditional family, the way so many gay men and women have done before and after them. Thanksgiving became as important to Matthiessen and Cheney as it had been for the Cheney family, but the two men redefined traditions for themselves at Kittery.

By the time that Matthiessen and Cheney had settled in Kittery, several more nicknames had arisen between them, including "Deezie," which they used interchangeably for one another. "Weeds," "Creature," and "Branchy" all surfaced with some regularity. In his effervescence, Cheney coined most of these nicknames, and their playfulness and lightheartedness further extended Matthiessen and Cheney's private language.

Cats completed the domestic scene in Kittery. Matthiessen and Cheney loved their cats, and they would have many of them over the years, including Miss Pansy Littlefield, Pawsey, Pretzel, Barney (also known as Terza Rima), and Baby (also known as Zuzu). Cheney featured Matthiessen sitting with various cats in several of his paintings. Matthiessen and Cheney also developed a "special language," which built on their private language of nicknames, to talk about their cats, as Louis Hyde noted. Conceiving of themselves as cats in their letters, the two men often said things to each other that they might not ordinarily have found the words to say. To an extent, their cats served as alter egos. After visiting Cheney in the hospital, for example, Matthiessen wrote: "I only hope that I managed to relax you rather than gearing you up, I'm not sure. Strange cats don't make ideal guests. Anyhow, I didn't climb the curtains." As usual Cheney pulled their language into visual expression, and doodles of cats decorated many of his letters to Matthiessen. In an early letter, Cheney wrote, "I think that I probably need a whipping" and then seemed to confess to a sexual or drinking indiscretion, although he did not go into details. In closing his letter, he placed a halo over a cat. Through Matthiessen and Cheney's love of their cats and their special language surrounding them, symbolic expression and playfulness reigned supreme at Kittery, which further strengthened and solidified Matthiessen and Cheney's connection to the place and one to the other.

Kittery was the great—almost "gay"—oasis for Matthiessen and Cheney. On the one hand, the small northern New England town was in keeping with some of the other comparably conservative decisions that each man had made throughout his life, such as Cheney's choice of several academic painting teachers or Matthiessen's unwillingness to step off the ladder of professional ambition. But at the same time, as professionals who did not depend on the local economy for their jobs or income, they were accorded a degree of privacy and freedom that made living as a relatively open, same-sex male couple possible. At Kittery, the two men would put down strong roots over the next two decades, Cheney especially, but they never quite shed their identities as well-to-do outsiders. Even after Matthiessen and Cheney bought their house in Kittery, in the annual Town Reports of real estate tax receipts, they were officially listed as "non-residents" until 1946, the year after Cheney's death. At Kittery, the two men carved out a near-idyllic, proto-gay niche for themselves, but the niche rested on Matthiessen and Cheney's unique social and economic circumstances that were not widely shared by the larger society.

In 1931, Matthiessen's second book, *Translation: An Elizabethan Art*, was published. The book grew out of Matthiessen's doctoral dissertation, and he dedicated it to his much-admired professor from Yale, Bob French. Yet as he worked on the manuscript at Kittery, he watched as Cheney reflexively put some of the book's aesthetic theories into practice. The deeper Cheney's roots grew in Kittery, the more he captured the spirit of the place in his painting. If Cheney didn't stimulate Matthiessen's ideas, then his painting at least reinforced them. This was particularly true of Cheney's snow paintings, one of his favorite subjects.

Translation: An Elizabethan Art focuses on the translations of Sir Thomas Hoby, Thomas North, John Florio, and Philemon Holland, all of whom published during the reign of Elizabeth I in England. In the book Matthiessen introduces many of the themes that he would go on to develop throughout his career: examining the formal qualities of a literary work; the interplay between experience and imagination, especially through reading; and the social role of literary works and other arts in society. In Matthiessen's view, when art and literature are fulfilling their function, they are the living, breathing mechanisms whereby societies can express their collective feelings and values.

In the book Matthiessen stressed the value his translators placed on reading. Hoby believed that a person's reading shaped the course of his or her life. Florio's translation of Montaigne had a lingering effect on Shakespeare. Matthiessen observed that a book's rhetorical style can cling to a reader's mind long after he or she puts the book down. But in discussing Holland's translations, Matthiessen goes one step further, noting that the work of Livy and Suetonius became part of Holland's life, because the content of these books "were flesh and blood" to him.

The importance of reading resonated personally with both Matthiessen and Cheney. A quick scan of their books at Kittery on homophile topics by proto-gay and other sympathetic writers suggest how these books shaped Matthiessen's and Cheney's budding gay identities and life together. These books included *Love's Coming of Age, Towards Democracy, The Intermediate Sex,* and *An Unknown People* by Edward Carpenter; *Studies in the Psychology of Sex* by Havelock Ellis; *Walt Whitman* and *Studies of Greek Poets* by John Addington Symonds; *Leaves of Grass* by Walt Whitman; *Oscar Wilde: His Life and Confessions* by Frank Harris; *Complete Works,* in French, by Arthur Rimbaud; and *À la Recherche du Temps Perdu/Remembrance of Things Past,* in both French and English, by Marcel Proust and translated by C. K. Scott Moncrieff. In addition to helping Matthiessen and Cheney construct gay identities, these seminal works also helped them to situate themselves within a gay historical and cultural context.

In *Translation*, Matthiessen's notions of aesthetic vibrancy also reinforced his interest in the connection between literature and society. Matthiessen's Elizabethan translators, for example, had purposefully made their writing racy and vivid, while remaining true to their sources. They used the "slang of the streets," direct speech, strong images, and metaphors that would be recognizable to ordinary people. Although the ideas that the translators sought to convey may have been sophisticated, their means of communication were well grounded in common usage. Writing about Hoby, Matthiessen pointed out that his book did not have a "literary finish" that would have removed it from everyday speech and that he employed a colloquial tone. Matthiessen liked that his translators were generalists and for the most part not scholars, with the exception of Holland. North, about whom Matthiessen ventured the assessment that he was the greatest artist of his survey, had commanded more than three hundred men in the English Armada. For Matthiessen, such experiential breadth helped the translators keep their works rooted in the societies of which they were a part.

Cheney's influence on *Translation* lingers in the background in a general way. At Kittery Cheney was beginning to embody Matthiessen's ideals about the writers—or artists—expressing the feelings, values, and concerns of the community of which they are a part. Beginning in the early 1930s, Cheney became deeply rooted in coastal Maine and New Hampshire—just as the Cheney family was deeply rooted in South Manchester, Connecticut—even if his status as comparably affluent newcomer kept him slightly apart. Throughout much of that decade, Cheney was productive, and many of his best paintings grew out of his connection to the area and its people. The painter and his easel became a regular fixture on the streets of Kittery and nearby Portsmouth and Newcastle. Cheney got to know local people, and several of them became subjects for his paintings. Reflecting on his connection to Kittery one evening, while sitting near the ocean, Cheney described how he "sat there a long while with the tide swishing and swirling and gurgling, and the moon so bright and light on the house, and pear blossoms—a wonderfully rich and poignant moment somehow. The sense of really belonging, of being fused with the surroundings and part of it, a sort of wide peace." Referring to Kittery, Cheney felt "fixed here for life," Matthiessen said.

In the early 1930s, local subjects bubbled out of Cheney, including a strong group of snow paintings. "Make hay while the snow lasts" was one of Cheney's mottoes, and several photographs exist that show him painting outdoors during winters, steam rising from his breath as he contemplates a canvas. As with so much of Cheney's oeuvre, he expressed two definite sensibilities in his snow paintings: sunny and cheerful, and bleak and desolate. The darker snow paintings tend to be the stronger of the two subgenres, but even the brighter paintings have a confident sophistication to them. Artistically, Cheney was proud of his snow paintings, they were among his most original works. But for personal reasons, too, Cheney liked these works, even if he could not have put why into words. They struck a chord with the "skeptic" in him, to use Farwell Knapp's word, that sounded beneath his effervescence, playfulness, and occasional wildness.

One of Cheney's most compelling paintings from this time, *Water Front*, hints at the impact of the Depression. The painting depicts the industrial waterfront of Portsmouth. Cheney makes strong use of the diagonal planes of the roofs, which are especially arresting covered in white. A single telephone pole stands in the middle of the painting, which breaks up the planes, while at the same time providing a central focal point, which unifies the whole. Beyond this, although there are tire tracks in the foreground of the scene, the snow is largely undisturbed. The inactivity is unsettling. Yet the hushed quality to the streetscape also gives the scene its beauty. Cheney was able to import the quiet and serene qualities from his pastoral snow paintings into an urban, industrial setting, producing more complex effects.

Cheney also conveyed the brighter, sunnier side of New England within his snow oeuvre. These paintings often captured the hearty determination to form communities against an austere and desolate backdrop of winter in New England. This quality was captured in *Piscataqua Lane* (ca. 1933–36), which depicts a lane in New Castle, New Hampshire, after a recent

FIGURE 7. Russell Cheney, *Piscataqua Lane*, ca. 1933–36, oil on canvas, 24 x 30 in. Courtesy of the Manchester Historical Society, Manchester, CT.

snowfall. The houses are tightly packed together and sit directly on the street, as is typical in older New England towns and villages. Unusual for Cheney, he depicts a man outside shoveling. In other winter town scenes, including *Pepperell's Cove* (1933) and *Bolt Hill Road (Eliot, Maine)* (1933), buildings punctuate the landscapes, so that New England community stands in contrast to the severe natural elements. Given Cheney's intuitive grasp of New England life, he was a faithful recorder of life in the place where he and Matthiessen made their home.

When Cheney included the snow paintings in exhibits in New York and Andover, Massachusetts, several reviewers singled them out for praise. A *New York Evening Post* reviewer wrote: "These wintry landscapes are good paintings, carried out in easy suavity of handling, nicely adjusted nuances of color in the lower registers of the palette, unexpectedly intensified by sharp notes of green in hardy pines or the almost acid blue of the clear wintry sky." Writing about the show in Andover, Dorothy Adlow, the sharp-eyed critic of the *Christian Science Monitor*, who had followed Cheney's work for over a decade, also praised his snow paintings. "Those who know New England will feel the wintery chill, the threatening skies, the loneliness of old roads, the tranquil beauty of Mr. Cheney's pictures."

In the early 1930s, Matthiessen and Cheney's life together at Kittery was largely warm and harmonious. Despite some early danger signs because of Cheney's drinking and the stress that Matthiessen faced at Harvard, the two men gradually transformed their early exuberance and excitement in their relationship into a kind of marriage-like solidity, a quality that, along with the books, paintings, and physical beauty of the Maine coast, made Kittery such an appealing place.

Early in 1931, on the advice of his doctors, Cheney prepared to spend the winter on the French Riviera because of his breathing difficulties. On his way to New York, from which he would sail, he stopped in Providence to visit the artist Hope Smith, who also had been a student of both Woodbury and Chase. Cheney reported that Smith "yearned" after him, which threw him off-balance emotionally. In response, alcohol offered an easy escape from those uncomfortable emotions. When Cheney got to New York, he and Putnam went on an all-night drinking binge, the two men draining Cheney's flask "in the early morning light." The incident unnerved Matthiessen when Cheney told him about it. Matthiessen wrote back poignantly: "I wish I could describe how it makes me feel. Acting in that perfectly reckless uncontrolled fashion, absolutely heedless of consequences, just as though we didn't have the extraordinary blessing of our union, is like spitting on a crucifix. Someday you'll do it once too often, crush yourself and me too." Coming from his excesses in New York, Cheney caught pneumonia aboard the *Lafayette*, and when he arrived in Europe, he went to a hospital in Nice to recover. This trip marked the last time that Cheney would paint in Europe.

Such drinking binges may have led Cheney to purchase *The Common Sense of Drinking* by Richard Rogers Peabody, first published in 1931. In all likelihood, it was Cheney who purchased the book, since he had begun wrestling with his drinking during the early 1930s. Although the book is not inscribed and dated on the front flyleaf, as Cheney did with so many of his other books, he may not have wanted to memorialize his ownership of this particular volume. Moreover, although Matthiessen had started to worry about Cheney's drinking by this time, it was not yet so severe that he would have purchased a book on alcoholism. By the end of the decade, it would be a different matter.

The Common Sense of Drinking identifies characteristics of the alcoholic and prescribes "steps" to promote recovery. Cheney fit Peabody's description of those prone to alcoholism in several key ways, noting that alcoholics often came from the ranks of only children and youngest sons, were self-conscious, and suffered from inferiority complexes. Peabody advocates that alcoholics should try to completely abstain from drinking, suggesting that once a person becomes an alcoholic, it was unlikely that he or she could resume drinking in a normal manner. It would be many years before Cheney followed this suggestion, but it may have been Peabody who first planted the idea in the back of his mind.

The summer of 1931, Matthiessen joined Cheney in Europe. They traveled in the Netherlands seeking out Vermeer's paintings, then on to Germany and finally to Austria for the Mozart Festival in Salzburg. Their vacation ended in England, where they met up with Putnam and spent their days walking across the downs. Perhaps the most tense moment occurred when Matthiessen booked second-class tickets for their return home, hoping that such a downgrade wouldn't "infuriate" Cheney. Despite the cessation of dividends from Cheney Brothers, economizing did not come easily or naturally to Cheney, who had grown up accustomed to considerable privilege. But the summer was a wonderful respite from the stresses and strains related to Cheney's health problems earlier that year. Matthiessen and Cheney had a stabilizing effect on each other. Looking at paintings, listening to music, walking through the English countryside—sharing their lives—seemed to induce tranquility in each of them.

Early in 1932, Cheney had another show at the Montross Gallery in New York. He worked hard setting up for the show and seemed to have made a conscious effort not to drink too much. Generally positive but subdued reviews dribbled from the newspapers. Cheney no longer commanded the enthusiastic raves that he had received early in his career, but most reviewers acknowledged his talent. *Art News* summed it up: "Russell Cheney's painting progress continues apace, though without any startling transitions. The group of recent canvases now on view at the Montross Gallery show him forging ahead, gaining a little here and there, and solidly intrenching himself at every step of the way." Cheney ended his trip with a day spent at the Metropolitan Museum of Art looking at Cézanne's paintings.

And as usual, Cheney met new people wherever he went. "I walked home along the park & let myself be picked up by a husky young guy whom I took for a beer at . . . 56th & 3rd Ave., a professional boxer! He wanted me to go home with him, but I did not want to." Returning to Kittery from New York, Cheney stopped to pick up a hitchhiker along the New Hampshire seacoast, one of the many men who wandered in search of work. The young man said he was broke, so Cheney brought him home, fed him, let him take a bath, drove him back to Portsmouth, and gave him some pocket money. Cheney reported to Matthiessen, who was in Cambridge at the time, that he enjoyed talking to the young man and took pleasure in watching him revive with a meal and a hot bath. The evening did not feature heavy drinking or sex, nor did Cheney apparently see any danger or risk in bringing a stranger back to his and Matthiessen's home. Perhaps not surprisingly, the young man came back a few days later, and Cheney painted his portrait.

Another place Cheney met men was at the boxing ring. Cheney was an avid boxing fan and went to matches in Kittery, Portsmouth, and Biddeford, Maine. He clipped notices from local newspapers about boxing and sent them to Matthiessen. He enjoyed the physicality of boxing, as well as the sexiness and cockiness of the boxers. Cheney also relished the violence of the sport, noting with near-teenage glee when one boxer made "mince meat" out of another. He knew boxers and recited their names to Matthiessen: "Chili" McCaffery, Rocky Stone, and Babe Lemieux. Cheney was also attuned to the presence of other homosexual men at boxing matches. Writing to Matthiessen about one match, he noted that there were "no special amicis [*sic*]" there. Cheney relished the spectacle and atmosphere of these events. It was a very male world, in which he felt quite at home.

Cheney's zest for life—expansive and adventuresome—could also be scary. One day in December 1932, Cheney headed off to the movies in Portsmouth after "a couple of drinks," as he reported to Knapp, who recorded the incident in his diary. Driving Fordy across the Memorial Bridge from Kittery to Portsmouth, he collided head-on with another car. Cheney was unhurt, had his car towed to a nearby garage, ignored the irate owner of the other car, and proceeded to go to the movies. When he came out of the theater, he couldn't find his car, apparently having no memory of the accident. Cheney's lack of recall suggests that he had been in a "blackout," a state in which alcohol or drugs can cause temporary loss of short-term memory. He then spotted his car in the nearby garage, walked in, and upbraided the owner over what had happened to his car. When the garage owner explained the story and told Cheney that he was wanted by the police, Cheney turned himself in. Cheney could be imperious when he wanted to be, but he also respected the law. The police offered him a choice: pay $1,000 in bail or spend the night in jail. Cheney spent the night in jail. The following day, he got himself a lawyer and worked out a settlement with the other driver, who agreed not to press charges if Cheney would pay for the damages. After settling, Cheney went back to the garage, where another Ford had just been brought in after a rear-end collision. The mechanic took undamaged parts from the second Ford and installed them on Cheney's. So Cheney drove away with a car nearly as good as new. It was almost as if no lessons were learned.

Meanwhile, Matthiessen's professional responsibilities and intellectual development continued to progress at Harvard. He had been appointed chair of the Board of Tutors at Eliot House back in 1931. Nonetheless, he was uneasy with many of the expectations of higher education. "I wholly disapprove of the Ph.D., and yet as an assistant professor I belong to the system that upholds it." Matthiessen had explained his reasoning nearly a year earlier: he disliked small, incremental advances in knowledge. He wrote, "One little piddling article leads to another: Had Bacon read Montaigne? Where was Florio in 1583? And to think that there are thousands of such volumes being manufactured every year. Every time I come into contact with this so-called scholarship it makes me very grave: for with such sand slowly piling up how long is it going to be before the house is entirely covered?" Deeply influenced by his relationship with Cheney, Matthiessen was developing an idiosyncratic and personal method of scholarship, in some respects more akin to an artist than to a scholar. He wanted a scholarship that gave the mind free range to make big, unexpected, and unprecedented connections, and he chafed against anything that fell short of that.

During these years, Matthiessen further developed his ideas about works of literature or art—or writers or artists themselves, for that matter—and their relationship to society. Since his student days at Yale, Matthiessen had constantly questioned the privileges and prerogatives of power, and his homosexuality played a critical part in this point of view. He gravitated to writers and thinkers who also struck intellectual stances as outsiders. In his review from the early 1930s of a book on the literary historian

Moses Coit Tyler by Howard Mumford Jones, a critic who later went on to spend the bulk of his career at Harvard, Matthiessen was drawn to Tyler's unusual background as a minister before becoming a scholar and his extended period of searching for himself. In another review from this period of V. F. Calverton's book *The Liberation of American Literature*, a volume Matthiessen did not like, he wrote that "our most powerful individuals have again and again been dangerously isolated from or opposed to society as a whole." Matthiessen himself was getting more of a taste of this state at Harvard.

There was an emotional price to Matthiessen's increased profile and professional responsibilities. As the Depression deepened, even students at Harvard had difficulty paying some of their expenses: "Yesterday was the culmination of a nasty week. The business of the room prices got badly on my nerves, especially when Roger and I went up to talk to the Treasurer of the University about the whole matter, and got from him . . . the charming answer that nobody except for the house masters thought the prices too high, and that we needn't worry for Eliot House would be full! Whereupon I hit the chandelier, and told him I didn't care whether there was a single room filled in Eliot House, that the only thing I was interested in was a sensible education system, and that Harvard had now finally been made into a rich man's college. I was so thoroughly angry that my voice still shook when I went to lecture on Hawthorne the next hour. If it weren't for Roger, I would have resigned from the House on the spot." Although Matthiessen had many of the unconscious elitist attitudes of the social class into which he had been born, he just as often used his privilege to help others. But Matthiessen could not entirely let go of the tension of this incident and others, and a few months later, he woke up out of a nightmare screaming. As usual, he turned again to Cheney as his emotional safe harbor.

Their closeness was epitomized in the fall of 1932, when Cheney landed in Portsmouth Hospital for a three-week stay after having an appendectomy. One night, Matthiessen visited while Cheney was asleep. Matthiessen left a note, roughly drawing a rat in the salutation and closing with a picture of a devil. For the very verbal Matthiessen, his love for Cheney pulled him into the realm of visual expression, awkward as he was with it. But these simple drawings captured all of Matthiessen's tenderness and affection for Cheney, and they highlight the playfulness that accented their lives together.

That fall T. S. Eliot served as the Charles Eliot Norton Professor of Poetry at Harvard, and early in 1933, Matthiessen recounted to Cheney the beauty and poignancy of hearing Eliot read his poetry aloud after a special dinner one night. Eliot then visited Matthiessen and Cheney in Kittery over the summer of 1933. Cheney described him as a "darn good guest," and Matthiessen recalled Eliot taking a canoe trip in Portsmouth Harbor during that visit dressed in a derby hat and spats, surely a memorable spectacle to the passing lobstermen.

As with Matthiessen's graduate students at Thanksgiving dinner, how did Matthiessen and Cheney portray their relationship to a houseguest like Eliot? They were most likely discreet and formal, because that's who Matthiessen and Cheney were as people. As a scholar and an artist, both men were involved in solitary pursuits, so it was not entirely surprising that they were bachelors, friends, and housemates. Their association through Yale probably fed neatly into this narrative as an explanation for their ongoing companionship. Presumably, they portrayed their decision to share a home in a beautiful setting as a practical way to foster intellectual and creative stimulation and avoid isolation. But Eliot and many others knew and implicitly accepted them as a couple. Even though Eliot had traveled widely in the sexually freewheeling circles of Bloomsbury, if he had any misgivings about receiving the domestic hospitality of a male couple, he was probably quickly won over by Cheney's warmth and charm, as so many other guests were. As C. L. Barber later wrote about Cheney at Kittery, he was the "genius of the place."

Chapter 6

Shining in a Dark Time
Politics and Painting in the Depression

In the mid-1930s, as the Depression wore on, it reverberated strongly in Matthiessen's and Cheney's lives and work. For Matthiessen, the Depression—and by extension organized labor—spurred him politically and intellectually. For Cheney, his portraits and landscapes from this time were especially strong, perhaps marking this period as the high point of his artistic expression, as distinct from the pinnacle of his standing in the art world, which had occurred over a decade ago. All the while, Kittery remained their happy home base.

In response to the massive unemployment caused by the Depression, both strikes and union organizing surged. In 1934 alone, 1,856 work stoppages involving 1,470,000 people erupted across the United States. From 1934 to 1937, unions recruited five million new members. One of these strikes in San Francisco over the summer of 1934 shines direct light on the state of organized labor and introduces Harry Bridges, a labor leader who came to make a strong impression on Matthiessen in the coming years.

As a result of Section 7(a) of National Industrial Recovery Act, the International Longshoremen's Association in San Francisco had grown enough to attract the notice of the Industrial Association, a group of area businessmen devoted to scrubbing labor activism from the San Francisco docks. Waterfront workers chafed under a practice known as the "shape-up," in which men reported for early morning hiring calls along San Francisco's Embarcadero and employers would hand-pick individual workers from the crowd. Before the Depression, roughly 2,500 men would pick up work along the docks when the ships came in, but during the Depression, only 500 to 700 could get work out of 4,000 reporting. The shape-up was brutal and inhumane. The Port of London had done away with the practice in 1891.

Soon, the situation exploded. A splinter group within the International Longshoremen's Association led by Harry Bridges, an Australian-born labor leader, wanted union halls to run the shape-up. When attempts at negotiations failed, the association went out on strike, from Seattle to San Diego. The Industrial Association worked with the San Francisco police to use guarded trucks to reopen the docks. Rioting and skirmishes broke out between the police and strikers. The National Guard was called in, and they used gas that induced vomiting on the strikers, who in turn protected themselves with gas masks similar to those used in World War I. In the end, two men were killed and 115 were injured in the melee. In response, Bridges announced a general strike, and an estimated 125,000 workers went out on sympathy strikes, bringing business to a halt in San Francisco. After four days, the International Longshoremen and employers entered arbitration. The International Longshoremen did not get a union-run hiring hall, but given the its militancy, management paused before trying to saddle its members with other unfair or inequitable practices.

In the fall of 1934, around the tenth anniversary of Matthiessen and Cheney's meeting and beginning their relationship, they spent roughly ten months together in Santa Fe. Matthiessen was on sabbatical and had come to the Southwest to do research on the book that would become his crowning achievement, *American*

Renaissance. After visiting Cheney's sister Harriet and her husband in Santa Barbara, the two men drove to New Mexico. With so many men roaming in search of work, Matthiessen and Cheney picked up one hitchhiker after another along the way. On the trip to Santa Fe, Cheney often drove, and Matthiessen would move into the back to give their guest the front seat. According to Matthiessen, this arrangement enabled them to talk to their passenger and have a strategic advantage if the man should try to attack either of them. The Depression-toughened hitchhikers were often haggard: they included a boxer, a Russian immigrant, and a "blue-eyed, square jawed" roofer from Nebraska among several others. Not surprisingly, Cheney had an immediate rapport with the roofer. Matthiessen and Cheney's passengers talked about their lives, work, and experiences. Matthiessen enjoyed talking to laborers so as to better understand the forces that shaped their lives. So while Cheney's eyes no doubt rested pleasantly on the handsome good looks of the Nebraska roofer and other passengers, Matthiessen was getting an education in what he considered "real life." (About a year later, Cheney might have thought twice about picking up more hitchhikers. While traveling alone in Massachusetts, he gave a ride to two men, one of whom was a prizefighter. They beat up Cheney and stole his car.)

When Matthiessen and Cheney arrived in the Southwest, they rented the adobe Nordfeldt House at 460 Camino de las Animas, or "Path of the Souls." Cheney set about painting the local scenes, people, buildings, and landscapes. Matthiessen confronted first-hand the poverty that hollowed out the lives of coal miners and their families during the Depression.

During the 1930s, the coal industry, like so many other businesses, had collapsed. Production and prices dropped precipitously from 535 million tons at $1.78 per ton in 1929 to 310 million tons at $1.31 per ton in 1932. Roughly a third of coal miners earned just $2.50 (approximately $50.00 in 2021 dollars) per day in 1933. Poverty devastated mining towns across the country. In 1931, a commission headed by Theodore Dreiser led a group of writers to Harlan County, Kentucky, in the southeast corner of the state, to document the lives and struggles of local coal miners and their families in a report later entitled *Harlan Miners Speak: Report on Terrorism in the Kentucky Coal Fields* (1932). Dreiser's group included John Dos Passos and Sherwood Anderson. Given the poverty of miners and their families, landlords let company housing deteriorate into decrepitude. Once when visiting a coal-mining family in Harlan County, Dos Passos leaned against a wall, only to have it collapse under his weight. In general, when a miner lost his job, his lease was automatically terminated. Similar problems played out in coal-mining towns across the country, and Matthiessen soon got involved in a transformative event in his political development that erupted in Gallup, two hundred miles west of Santa Fe.

Gallup was a coal-mining town with a rough history. During a 1917 strike, the Gallup American Coal Company had brought in hundreds of Mexican miners, whom it housed in a 110-acre shantytown of adobe houses and wood shacks. But by 1933, approximately half of the area's two thousand miners were unemployed. In labor-organizing efforts, the Communist-affiliated National Miners' Union was successfully appealing to Mexican workers, and tensions were heightened when its members began receiving federal relief benefits. Over the summer of 1934, local chapters of the Elks, the Veterans of Foreign Wars, and the American Legion organized to protest emergency relief assistance to migrant workers. To make matters worse, in 1934, Gallup American sold the land under its shantytown to New Mexico state senator Clarence F. Vogel, a man with purported ties to the underworld. He quickly offered his tenants a choice: pay $150 for a lot that cost $25 elsewhere in Gallup or face eviction.

On April 1, Vogel evicted his first tenant, Victor Campos, and had his first leaseholder, Exiquio Navarro, arrested. News of the eviction and arrest spread quickly. At the hearing, roughly 125 people gathered outside the courthouse. Apprehensive about the crowd, Sheriff Mack R. Carmichael tried to take Navarro out a back door and into an alley. A crowd of about 75 people was waiting, and someone may have tried to pull Navarro away from the deputies. In response, one of the deputies threw a tear gas bomb into the crowd. Pandemonium and gunshots erupted, leaving Sheriff Carmichael and several of the protesters dead.

It was as though many Gallup residents had been waiting for just such an incident to unleash their fear and built-up animosity toward the migrant workers. Within an hour of the ambulances carrying away the wounded, Deputy Dee Roberts, who had been promoted to sheriff on Carmichael's death, swore in over one hundred special deputies from the American Legion and Veterans of Foreign Wars. Under New Mexican law at this time, if a law officer was killed in a riot, everyone in the mob could be held responsible and charged with murder in the first degree—a capital offense. Sheriff Roberts and his special deputies arrested over one hundred people, many of whom did not speak English. Fifty-five people were charged with murder, and many others were deported on immigration charges.

Working with a group similar to that of Dreiser in Harlan County, Matthiessen joined a crew of reporters and lawyers associated with the then-fledgling Santa Fe chapter of the American Civil Liberties Union who went to Gallup to investigate the riot and offer their services. Scholarship engaged Matthiessen with books and ideas, but these ideas played out slowly and incrementally over time, if they played out at all. Being with the lawyers and journalists investigating the Gallup riot quickened Matthiessen's pulse. It was a chance to make abstract ideals concrete. Matthiessen felt that he and the others were fighting for justice and fairness in real time, for real people, and with real consequences. This thrilled him.

Matthiessen's article about the Gallup riot appeared in the *New Republic*. In the piece, he displayed a good command of the facts, which have squared with the historical record. He also cast institutional and individual actors into a larger cultural context, noting, for example, the "strong-armed frontier refusal to recognize labor unions" among the coal companies. He was particularly hard on Vogel for his role in inciting the conflagration, but cautioned against making the senator a scapegoat. Instead, Matthiessen pinned blame on the larger socioeconomic conditions faced by the miners. "Vogel's action have made him the focus of the workers' dread and hatred of exploitation. Toward Sheriff Carmichael they seem to have held no resentment; he had the reputation of being a good officer. They had simply been goaded beyond endurance, and could not suffer the sight of another of their fellows being led to jail. But there is a danger that too much blame will be attached to the Senator. He makes too convenient a smoke-screen behind which the mine operators can hide their own social irresponsibility; too easy a scapegoat for abuses that are not the product of any individual or group of individuals but of a whole diseased condition of society."

Though Matthiessen's later political activism would come to be criticized for being too strident, idealistic, and naive, at Gallup he demonstrated that he could be incisive and timely. He helped spread the word nationwide about the riot in a small town in New Mexico and the injustices behind it.

Cheney did not participate directly in Matthiessen's political activism and likely regarded it with detachment: What Matty did with his politically minded friends and acquaintances was his own business. But he was perfectly willing to be indirectly supportive, joining Matthiessen at a garden party fundraiser for the Gallup miners in July 1935.

That summer, Cheney focused on a show of his paintings at the Museum of New Mexico in Santa Fe. A warm profile of Cheney by Ina Sizer Cassidy, a poet, journalist, and lecturer, appeared in *New Mexico Magazine*. She called Cheney one of Santa Fe's "best known visiting artists," noting that he was from "an old New England family famous the world over as manufacturers of silks." For outsiders, Cheney's family name was still an important defining characteristic. But what is most telling about this interview was Cheney's statement that "if one gets entirely away from a touch of the illustrative one gets into the realm of the abstract and that is not life. I want to paint the life about me as I see it and feel it." As Cheney wrestled with the tension in his painting between realism and a more stylized, interpretive vision, other American and European painters continued to push the art world toward abstraction.

Later that spring, Matthiessen and Cheney's friend and a member of their social circle in Santa Fe, Republican US Senator Bronson Cutting, died at age forty-six in a plane crash near Kirksville, Missouri, about two hundred miles east of Kanas City, while traveling from Albuquerque to Washington, DC. The *New York Times* hinted at the unusually close relationship between Senator Cutting and Clifford McCarthy, who was reported to have "collapsed on viewing the Senator's body" at the site of the crash. Growing out of Senator Cutting's friendship with Cheney back in 1929, there had been talk a few years earlier of Cheney painting his portrait, but that never seemed to have materialized. On the day before his death, however, Senator Cutting purchased Cheney's painting of Jesus Baca, the longtime sheriff of Santa Fe and a friend of the senator. A lifelong wealthy bachelor, in his will, Senator Cutting was very generous to a number of his friends, close associates, and people who had worked with and for him. He left McCarthy $50,000 (over $975,000 in 2021 dollars), and $25,000 (roughly $488,000 in 2021 dollars) went to Phelps Putnam, thereby ending the poet's chronic money problems.

After Matthiessen and Cheney returned east in the fall, Matthiessen's third book, *The Achievement of T. S. Eliot* was published. Matthiessen dedicated the book to Kenneth and Laurette Murdock. Kenneth Murdock was a literature and history professor who went on to have a long academic and administrative career at Harvard. At the time of Matthiessen's dedication, Murdock was still married to his first wife, Laurette, with whom Matthiessen and Cheney remained close after the Murdocks divorced.

One of the early scholarly books on Eliot, *The Achievement of T. S. Eliot* is more like a standard book of literary criticism than Matthiessen's two earlier books. Contemporary scholars consider it emblematic of Matthiessen's mature critical style. Unlike *Sarah Orne Jewett*, Matthiessen excised Eliot's biography and put it in a note at the beginning of the book. He then surveyed the range of Eliot's poetry, essays, and plays, emphasizing the main ideas from Eliot's work, such as the "objective correlative," the importance of feeling in poetry, the relationship of an artwork—literary, visual, or dramatic—to society, and how unity of personality gives cohesion to a collective body of artistic work. Along the way, Matthiessen touched on other themes that would reappear in his own work over the years, such as a critical connection among Hawthorne, Henry James, and Eliot or the English playwright and critic Harley Granville-Barker's notion that dramatic art is "the working out ... not of the self-realization of the individual, but of society itself."

Eliot's notion of a unified sensibility excited Matthiessen. Eliot developed these ideas from his reading of seventeenth-century English poets and writers, in which he sees an interweaving of thought and emotion: thought helped shape feeling, and feeling helped shape thought for many seventeenth-century authors. Matthiessen quoted Eliot: "When a poet's mind is perfectly equipped for its work, it is constantly amalgamating disparate experience; the ordinary man's experience is chaotic, irregular, fragmentary. The latter falls in love, or reads Spinoza, and these two experiences have nothing to do with each other, or with the noise of the typewriter or the smell of cooking; in the mind of the poet these experiences are always forming new wholes." Having now dipped into Matthiessen's early ecstatic letters to Cheney about the unity between literature and his experiences with Cheney—love was the key that further opened up literature for Matthiessen—it's clear how personally Matthiessen also read and reflected on literature. Matthiessen fell in love and read Walt Whitman and Havelock Ellis (instead of Spinoza), and Eliot gave him words for how those experiences influenced each other and fed into better appreciating and understanding literature. Scholars, such as Richard Ruland and Giles Gunn, have written about Eliot's influence on Matthiessen's thinking. Linking Matthiessen's appreciation of Eliot to his love for Cheney helps answer the question of why he found Eliot so compelling.

As C. L. Barber later wrote, Matthiessen did not have the normal divisions between his personal life and work that most people have, but tried to fashion his life into one seamless whole of literature, art, and ideas. Of course, to many people living after the birth of the LGBTQ rights movement, the divisions between Matthiessen's personal and professional lives seem greater rather than fewer. Although he pushed the envelope in "coming out" to his Skull and Bones brothers and in select, private circles of friends, Matthiessen could never be officially and publicly "out" anywhere in his life, whether at Hackley, Yale, Oxford, or Harvard. How, then, did Matthiessen reconcile his strong attraction to a unified sensibility—being able to bring all of his thought and experience to his scholarship—with his knowledge that he existed in a community that "would so utterly disapprove of me, if it knew the facts"? Through Cheney's contribution of images to *Sarah Orne Jewett* or his more general influence on *Translation: An Elizabethan Art*, Matthiessen probably felt that he was bringing this critical part of himself to his work and life. Matthiessen's love for Cheney was like a drop of ink in a pool of water: it suffused and tinctured the whole. Given the times in which Matthiessen lived, he simply couldn't imagine that the political and cultural landscapes would tolerate—much less support—a more self-assertive voice of same-sex attraction, desire, and love.

Inner conflicts aside, Matthiessen again had pushed literature's boundaries with *The Achievement of T. S. Eliot*. He is credited, along with Cleanth Brooks, as being part of the first generation of scholars who spread Eliot's fame in the United States. More contemporary scholars have criticized Matthiessen for failing to address Eliot's politics, religion, and sexuality. But as late as the 1970s, over thirty-five years after Matthiessen's book was published, there were critics who claimed that some of his readings of Eliot's poems "probably remain ... the best."

As Matthiessen's critical and political engagement grew, Cheney and Kittery were the anchors, as always. During the mid-1930s, Matthiessen and Cheney passed several happy summers of painting, scholarship, and socializing at Kittery with their extended circle of family and friends. Cheney continued to get to know local people and respond to the Depression-scarred landscapes in his paintings. While Matthiessen was advocating politically on behalf of "the people," Cheney was actually getting to know and paint them in coastal Maine and New Hampshire. From the beginning of Cheney's career until its end, he was always capable of producing expressive and arresting canvases. To do so consistently was more difficult for him. But in the mid-1930s, Cheney hit a steady stride, firmly rooted in Kittery.

During the summer of 1936, Matthiessen and Cheney saw much of Farwell and Helen Knapp, who once again spent the summer in Kittery Point, as they had been doing for several years. Other friends and colleagues of Matthiessen's visited the two men throughout the season. Matthiessen wrote each morning, while Cheney painted, gardened, and ran errands, such as going to Portsmouth to pick up lobsters for lunch or dinner. Afternoons usually featured a swim in the frigid Maine water, about which Matthiessen boasted endlessly over his bravery and stamina for enduring the cold. After swimming, deck tennis, a game played with rubber rings and a net, followed on the front lawn. In the evenings, Cheney cooked dinners which required no "fussy preparation," as Barber explained, usually a main dish in some kind of sauce, salad, cheese and crackers, and wine. Fruit from the table's centerpiece served as dessert. After dinner, Matthiessen would read aloud from the early drafts of his manuscript that later became *American Renaissance*.

The respite that Kittery provided was welcome, but Matthiessen had difficulty relaxing. He could not easily suspend his ambition and drive to succeed, which permeated all aspects of his life, even with games. "Matty's attitude toward athletic games, and particularly deck tennis, was one of passionate concentration," Helen Bayne Knapp wrote. "No light recreation this. He cared intensely to win, and he played with a whirlwind ferocity." Farwell Knapp observed much the same thing in his diary: "Matty enters into all games so earnestly that he can't play at them, but works at them."

By 1936, Matthiessen and Cheney were well enough established as a couple in Kittery that the *Kittery Press*, in an article about one of Cheney's exhibits, described them as "partners," which likely meant "life partners" without romantic or sexual undertones. As noted earlier, given that sexual contact between members of the same sex was officially and publicly taboo, in the days before a modern taxonomy of sexuality, the culture granted men and women a degree of same-sex companionship with little or no sexual contact implied—in part because it was so unthinkable. It was under this umbrella of vagueness that Matthiessen and Cheney inched toward a contemporary definition of "gay."

All the while Cheney was painting prolifically and, in the fall of 1936, began showing at the Ferargil Galleries in New York, which dealt largely in American art. His work won praise from the influential critic Royal Cortissoz, who wrote of the exhibition: "In the main room there are oils by Russell Cheney, who is especially proficient in making the portrait of a place." Certainly the *Kittery Press* felt that way too, saying that Cheney had "taken this vicinity to his heart and has permanently preserved the best of it. His landscapes seem to smell like home. The east wind can be felt and, in some of them, even old Whaleback can be heard"—referring to a lighthouse in Portsmouth Harbor.

In 1937, Cheney painted two of the strongest portraits of his career. *Howard Lathrop* depicts a Portsmouth fisherman and friend of Cheney and Matthiessen standing on the waterfront, holding his work gloves in his left hand. The steeple of St. John's Episcopal Church rises over his right shoulder, as Cheney again combines portraiture and landscape painting. Cheney and Lathrop were well acquainted. They went to boxing matches together and took short road trips together along the Maine coast. Cheney's expressiveness in this painting is notably strong. His depiction of Lathrop's high cheekbones and kind, sensitive eyes captures the fisherman's inner poet underneath his rough work clothes and cap. Lathrop's gaze is intent and direct in a way that holds viewers and invites them to question who he could be. There is clearly a sexual undertone, too, in the way Lathrop is holding his gloves. A few years after Cheney's death in 1945, Matthiessen donated the painting to the Portsmouth Public Library, saying that he was fulfilling Cheney's wish. This painting is one of the most reproduced of all Cheney's work.

Figure 8. *Howard Lathrop* (or *A Portsmouth Fisherman*), 1937, oil on canvas, 32 x 42 in. Portsmouth Public Library.

Kenneth Hill (1937) is even more suggestive. With his dark jacket and fisherman's cap rakishly cocked to one side, Hill looks like "rough trade," an early twentieth-century term for a purportedly heterosexual man who will engage in sex with other men for money or physical gratification, if not emotional intimacy. His eyes are knowing, as though he is aware how the viewer is responding to his handsome features. He could be a forerunner to James Dean, handsome, sexually magnetic, and seemingly aloof. In a very contemporary stance, he seems ready to translate these characteristics into personal advancement of some kind.

Cheney exhibited *Howard Lathrop* and *Kenneth Hill* at shows in Boston, New York, and Portland, Maine, in early 1937. Even critics who could not or would not put into words the existence of sexual energy that crackled beneath the surface in these paintings recognized it all the same. Having seen both works, the reviewer for the *Boston Evening Transcript* said that Cheney's "talent emerges as one of the most virile and capable that contemporary New England has to offer."

For Cheney, knowing Lathrop and Hill went beyond sexual magnetism. The paintings are not prurient. Rather, Cheney's attraction helped him appreciate and express the range of factors that shaped the lives of these two men and to communicate these qualities. Cheney holds these factors and emotions in tension with one another. In their complexity, Lathrop and Hill are as representative of northern coastal New England and its people as the crowded old houses along crooked streets that so attracted Cheney's eye. Cheney's growing comfort in being able to express the range of emotions associated with his sitters also points to his ever-deepening connection to Kittery and its people.

Cheney painted a number of strong landscapes during the mid-1930s as well, including two paintings entitled *Portsmouth Waterfront* (1933? and 1937); *Atlantic Gypsum Company* (1934); *Portsmouth Factory* (1935); and *Hauled Up* (1937) among others. Cheney's consistent use of industrial settings in these paintings also illustrates how far his range had expanded beyond more traditional bucolic impressionistic scenes of mountains and trees that had been his primary focus earlier in his career. *Hauled Up* is a particularly complex painting for Cheney. The skyline of Portsmouth is composed of several buildings and the then-distinctive Memorial Bridge, which connected Kittery and Portsmouth, rises in the distance. The focal point of the painting is a boat "hauled up" on pilings. It doesn't look as though the boat has been out to sea recently, nor is there any suggestion that it will be sailing anytime soon. Inactivity clings to the landscape. As usual in so many of Cheney's landscapes, there are no people in *Hauled Up*, which heightens the sense of desolation. In terms of artistic excellence, if not critical acclaim or commercial success, *Howard Lathrop* and *Kenneth Hill*, together with Cheney's other paintings of New England landscapes from the mid-1930s, help establish this period as one of the brightest—if not the brightest—in his career.

Howard Lathrop and *Kenneth Hill* also hint at the difference between Cheney's and Matthiessen's friendships. So long as it was on his own terms, Cheney made friends wherever he went. He befriended Cecil Ladd in Kittery, who helped him with odd jobs around the house and later sat for a portrait, and the local boxer Charles "Chili" McCaffery, who worked at the Portsmouth Naval Shipyard. Though Cheney knew many well-to-do and influential friends, in general and especially at Kittery, Cheney primarily judged people by their "openness to life and the capacity to enjoy." This condition was sometimes fueled with alcohol. But Cheney's affability brought him into contact with many people from various walks of life.

By contrast, Matthiessen's circle of friends was a who's who of American letters in the 1930s and 1940s. Matthiessen described having an intellectual breakfast one morning—"Trotsky and toast"—with Harry Levin, a former student, who went on to become a well-known literary scholar based at Harvard. When in New York, Matthiessen had dinner with Howard Lowry, head of Oxford University Press in the United States (his publisher). Matthiessen listened to the Max Baer–Joe Louis boxing match on the radio with Harvard colleagues. Even Matthiessen's warm friendships with his students can be read as relationships with professionals-in-training. And his new friends in political and labor circles tended to be leaders, rather than rank and file. Matthiessen was primarily attracted to people because of their achievements.

When it came to friendships with working-class men, once again Cheney lived what Matthiessen theorized. Perhaps based on his own insecurities about his masculinity and a perceived need to overcompensate, Matthiessen liked to portray himself as one of the boys, hanging out in working-class bars. Although the concept of comradeship animated Matthiessen's scholarly thinking and lay behind much of his political activity, his actual knowledge of the working class was "spotty, irregular, and sometimes tentative," as his student John Rackliffe wrote. Matthiessen was self-conscious about interacting with working-class men and women. Cheney, however, enjoyed minding Paul Hoen's store in Santa Fe, picking up a hitchhiker from North Carolina, and moving lilac bushes with Henry Fuller in Kittery. How compelling this must have been for Matthiessen. Cheney's openness to many different kinds of people and experiences formed another big part of his attraction for Matthiessen.

Matthiessen's political activism in Gallup energized and emboldened him. After returning to Cambridge, he helped organize the Harvard Teachers' Union. The union sought to ensure that merit was taken into consideration during appointments to faculty positions and aimed more generally to recognize the needs and voices of younger faculty. It had been founded to take a stand against the Teacher's Oath, which required teachers at public and private schools in Massachusetts to take an oath of allegiance to the constitutions of the United States and Commonwealth of Massachusetts. As the British historian M. J. Heale so lucidly describes, the debate in Massachusetts over the Teacher's Oath was more than a little inflected with the overarching themes of socioeconomic class and sexuality. It largely pitted legislators who were Irish, Democrats, urban, lower middle class, and working class against the intelligentsia at the elite universities. Heale quoted an unidentified American Legion member during the Teacher's Oath debates as saying: "You know as well as I do that these long-haired men and short-haired women are a menace to the country." Although the coded references to bias and prejudice against gay men and lesbians are unmistakable to many contemporary ears, at the time Matthiessen gave no hint in his correspondence that he was aware of these dynamics.

From its earliest days, the Harvard Teachers' Union worked to build and strengthen ties to other teachers' unions and the organized labor movement more generally. Soon into its life, the union joined the American Federation of Teachers (AFT) and welcomed new members from the Massachusetts Institute of Technology and Tufts University into its ranks. The union would continue to grow to more than two hundred members right before World War II. Some of Matthiessen's friends and colleagues cautioned him about his participation in the union, fearing that its connection with the AFT was too progressive. Matthiessen rebuffed these cautions. He believed on principle that academic freedom meant being able to stand up in public for one's beliefs, and he saw the union as a way to break down barriers between scholars and the larger world. Matthiessen wrote to Kenneth Murdock: "I simply cannot take the attitude of let-sleeping-dogs-lie toward the society of which I am a part. If academic freedom is simply the freedom not to voice publicly the political and social convictions which you believe important to the well-being of that society, I do not see much value in education." Matthiessen's involvement in the union also brought him into contact with two young economists at Harvard, J. Raymond Walsh and Alan R. Sweezy. Walsh had been president of the Harvard Teachers' Union at its founding, and Sweezy was on its executive board. Matthiessen's engagement with Walsh and Sweezy led to another defining incident in his development as a political activist.

In the spring of 1937, the Harvard administration informed both Walsh and Sweezy that they would receive two-year "concluding appointments." As junior faculty, they did not have tenure and were hired on a year-to-year basis, so receiving a "concluding appointment" was tantamount to being dismissed. Since both men had been popular teachers, many students and several faculty members at Harvard—including Matthiessen—assumed that Walsh and Sweezy were being let go because of their progressive political views. After Harvard president James Bryant Conant asserted that the decision was based "solely on grounds of teaching capacity and scholarly ability," the controversy grew and spread. Many people at Harvard felt that President Conant's statement reflected poorly—and unfairly—on the abilities of the two economists. The story attracted the attention of major newspapers across the country, and even the *Kittery Press* chimed in on the subject, noting Matthiessen's "misgivings" about President's Conant's decision. President Conant defended the decision but relented to the extent that he appointed a committee to study the dismissals.

When the committee recommended a year later that the two men should be reappointed, Conant again fanned the flames of controversy by rejecting the conclusion in less than a week. He said that reinstating Walsh and Sweezy "would be both unwise and impractical." Matthiessen was incensed. He and David Prall, a philosophy professor and then president of the Harvard Teachers' Union, submitted an open letter to President Conant protesting his decision. The letter was published in the *New Republic* and highlighted "how far short" Matthiessen and Prall believed the administration at Harvard had "fallen of any conception of democracy, justice or wise educational policy."

The story of Walsh and Sweezy is an illuminating one for the light it reflects on Matthiessen and his political beliefs. In many ways this was the ideal forum for Matthiessen; one in which he had a measure of political power as a tenured associate professor who knew many of the players involved. Matthiessen's friend and colleague Kenneth Murdock was on the committee reviewing the dismissals. But what emerged was Matthiessen's idealism and naiveté in the face of politics. Beyond writing his open letter, Matthiessen didn't conceive of a plan to try to persuade or pressure President Conant to change his mind. To him, such persuasion and pressure should have been unnecessary, because the committee's recommendations were clearly the right thing to do. How could President Conant not follow the committee's recommendations? Although Matthiessen was now thirty-five, he seemed astounded to learn that people in power sometimes exercise it arbitrarily, blindly, or poorly. It's not clear that Matthiessen would ever come to accept this lesson.

Notwithstanding the protests by some members in the Harvard community and the attention from the national press, President Conant stood by his initial decision, and the Harvard Corporation stood by President Conant. Walsh and Sweezy left Harvard at the end of their two-year appointments.

The Depression also brought about substantial changes at Cheney Brothers. Clifford Cheney was mill manager and spoke about the changes to the local Manchester press, so Cheney must have been aware—at least tangentially—of the severe toll that the Depression took on the company. The effects of these changes were cataclysmic for the Cheney family and might explain why images with distant family associations percolated to the surface in some of Cheney's paintings from 1937.

In 1933 at the nadir of the Depression, the silk business bottomed out for Cheney Brothers with sales of $5 million, an 80 percent decline from a decade earlier. The company's economic situation was exacerbated by its decision not to go into the production of synthetics, which the family viewed as an inferior product. What the family did not anticipate was that in many instances, the public preferred the cheaper fabric.

Throughout the late 1920s and into the early 1930s, Cheney Brothers got out of the business of public utilities and education, reduced the number of carpenters and painters it employed, sold company housing, and forced several family members to retire without pensions. In 1935, the firm filed for permission to reorganize under bankruptcy laws, laid off workers, and then cut the remaining employees' pay between five and ten percent. The company still had to borrow over one million dollars from the Reconstruction Finance Corporation to meet payments to outstanding creditors, such as the town of Manchester for taxes.

Cheney was well known among family and friends for his "collection d'art chinois," which he liked to feature in his paintings. His use of these objects more than likely derived from William Merritt Chase, who also liked putting artifacts and figurines, especially those from the Far East, in his paintings to demonstrate his technical virtuosity. But for Cheney, Asian art objects went beyond associations with his former teacher. Cheney's father Knight Dexter had kept a collection of Asian art objects and bronzes at the KD House, and Cheney's uncle Frank Woodbridge Cheney, who had lived next door, had a special room in the house, known as the "treasure room," devoted to his collection of valuables assembled on trips to China and Japan during the mid-nineteenth century to secure supplies of raw silk for Cheney Brothers mills. For Cheney, these art objects must have held distant childhood associations with his family.

The diminution of the Cheney empire must have been profoundly unsettling to Cheney, given how his innate sense of culture was so tied to his family, its history, and the business. It may not be too great a stretch to imagine him yearning—at least unconsciously—for a time when Asian art and artifacts abounded in Cheney households. These objects made a reappearance in Cheney's work in 1937 in such paintings as *Nicotiana*, which featured an image of a Buddhist lion, similar to those that had flanked the entrance of Cheney's studio garden in South Manchester. These images of Asian art objects reminded an astute viewer that no matter how independently the painter now lived with his same-sex partner, he could never stop being a Cheney.

Chapter 7

In Sickness and in Health
The Hartford Retreat, McLean Hospital, and Baldpate Hospital

Doctors played a key role in legitimizing antigay laws of the 1920s and 1930s passed by state legislatures. Forced sterilization to prevent the spread of "sexual perversion" began in the late nineteenth century. By 1917, fifteen states had eugenic sterilization, and by 1930, thirty states had such laws, which applied to "moral degenerates," including homosexuals, prostitutes, and drug addicts among others. By 1931, over twelve thousand of these operations had been performed. As the 1930s wore on, the general scientific and medical consensus was that homosexuality when expressed publicly or overtly was socially undesirable and psychopathic. Psychoanalysts also became increasingly hostile toward homosexuality. At the time, the medical community propagated the conceit that a "normal" man was exclusively heterosexual.

For Matthiessen and Cheney personally, after the largely productive and content period of the mid-1930s, the late 1930s and early 1940s were a particularly stressful time. Precipitated by life events, difficulties that had been building for some time rose to the surface. For Cheney, those years were marked by increased problems with asthma and drinking. When younger, both men saw Cheney's drinking as part of his broader sensuality, an attraction to drink and flesh, as Cheney himself said. But as the years went by, Cheney's drinking crossed the line into alcoholism. At that time, alcoholism was not seen as a disease or disorder, as it is viewed by the medical community today, but as a state of moral turpitude often linked with homosexuality, which compounded the problem.

As a result, Cheney was in and out of numerous hospitals and sanatoriums, notably the Hartford Retreat in Connecticut and Baldpate Hospital in Georgetown, Massachusetts. These institutions and others like them offered comfortable, homelike respites from the world and tended to cater to wealthy, often emotionally fragile men and women. The names of the institutions differed, but their character was remarkably similar from one to the other and resembled Cragmor, where Cheney had stayed for extended periods during the teens and late twenties because of his bouts with tuberculosis. But unlike Cragmor, where Cheney actually recovered, the hospitals and sanatoriums in which he spent time during the late 1930s and early 1940s were mostly holding stations that temporarily patched up Cheney until his next scrape.

Still, ever the artist, Cheney painted through it all. Although he gave up his freedom and independence in the sanatoriums, he could paint and read at his leisure. And just as the "comfort" of Cragmor enabled Cheney to end his long artistic apprenticeship, Cheney's days and nights in sanatoriums yielded another new development in his painting career: quirky still lifes.

At first Matthiessen offered his steadfast support and served as Cheney's beacon to see him through these experiences—"in sickness and in health." But in late 1938, the situation reversed, and Matthiessen admitted himself to McLean Hospital in Belmont, Massachusetts, another private psychiatric sanatorium. Associated with Harvard Medical School, McLean followed in the same pattern as the institutions in which Cheney spent so much time. But unlike many of Cheney's hospitalizations, Matthiessen benefited from his time at McLean, which relieved him of the stress and strain brought on by researching and writing *American Renaissance*.

As the couple's principal breadwinner, Matthiessen on the surface often seemed the more physically robust and emotionally resilient of the two men. At McLean, however, Matthiessen's fears of Cheney's premature death weighed heavily on him. Just the idea of Cheney's death made Matthiessen wonder if he could go on himself. It was around this time that Matthiessen first eerily envisioned himself jumping out of a window and in retrospect invites the question whether Matthiessen's psychological state was more fragile than Cheney's, despite appearances to the contrary.

If Russell Cheney needed an excuse to drink heavily, fate handed him a double tragedy in the opening months of 1938. First came the sudden death in mid-January of his sister Ellen in New York from a heart attack. Scarcely had the shock of Ellen's death subsided when Cheney's sister Harriet in California died of heart disease in early April. In response, Cheney's drinking at Kittery grew so toxic that at age fifty-six, he checked himself into the Hartford Retreat before the month was out.

Despite the 1935 bankruptcy reorganization of Cheney Brothers, the business held on for two more decades under family control. As a result, the Cheney family's importance and influence in the Manchester-Hartford area did not recede for several decades. So it's not surprising that the Cheneys were responsible in both direct and indirect ways for the character and sustainability of the Hartford Retreat during this period. The family's connection with the institution probably led Cheney to choose it in the first place. He had easy access to one of the finest sanatoriums in the country, why would he have wanted to go anywhere else? But this was an instance in which family associations were suffocating, rather than liberating. Had Cheney decided not to go there, he would have needed to exercise an extraordinary degree of independence, which he seldom mustered when it came to his family.

The Hartford Retreat was founded in 1822 by Dr. Eli Todd, who created "moral treatment," which maintained that mental illnesses were curable diseases rather than moral failings. Similarly, medical care at McLean initially grew out of "moral treatment." At both institutions, treatment consisted largely of rest, as well as occupational, physical, and talk therapies, which included a focus on the patient's family history. Baldpate, too, followed this regimen with a few important supplements.

In 1861, Frederick Law Olmstead, creator of Central Park, redesigned the Retreat's thirty-five-acre campus. (A little over a decade later, Olmsted would also conduct site surveys for McLean Hospital.) In Hartford, he created gently rolling hills and planted them with paper birch, sugar maple, saucer magnolia, northern red oak, and European copper beech among many others. He dotted the grounds with small Tudor cottages for patients. All the institutions—the Hartford Retreat, McLean, and Baldpate—sought to erase as many traces of institutional living as possible and tried to create homelike settings. During Cheney's day, the Retreat had a barbershop for men, a dressmaker and beauty shop for women, a regular afternoon tea, a library, a smoking room, a gym, a pool, tennis courts, and a bowling alley. (Baldpate also had a bowling alley, and Cheney became an avid bowler when he was a patient there a few years later.) Patients' rooms were outfitted with comfortable furniture, writing desks, radios, books, and newspapers. Patients were also provided with fresh fruit, flowers, and, in at least one case, original artwork. A year earlier in 1937, Cheney, in one of those grand, magnanimous gestures that he pulled off with flair, shipped two of his paintings to Phelps Putnam, who was then a patient at the Retreat, to decorate his room during his stay. Putnam nicknamed the paintings "Philippine Pete and Katchina Kate."

Cheney's doctor at the Retreat was C. Charles Burlingame, who had served there as psychiatrist in chief since 1931. Prior to this appointment, Dr. Burlingame had been the head psychiatrist at

Cheney Brothers, a job that chiefly entailed matching a worker's skills to a specific job. During World War I, before coming to Cheney Brothers, Dr. Burlingame had been head of personnel for the American Red Cross hospitals under Cheney's recently widowed brother-in-law, Alex Lambert, who had been married to Ellen. During Cheney's stay there, three family members sat on the Retreat's board of directors, including Howell Cheney, who had recommended Dr. Burlingame for his job as psychiatrist in chief. Dr. Burlingame was instrumental in defining and developing the character of the Retreat during his twenty-year tenure. He transformed the institution from a hospital to a combined hospital, university, and country club, appealing to wealthy clients by offering "a place for education and reeducation under psychiatric guidance based on sound medical practice."

It can be inferred from Matthiessen and Cheney's correspondence that Cheney was not admitted to the Retreat because of his drinking. Rather, it seems that his doctors felt that Cheney suffered from a nervous condition, which was a result of his breathing problems, and that he drank to try and calm himself. Cheney told Matthiessen that his doctors "assure me it was mostly shock" and "only very partly beer and sherry taken hysterically to relieve it." This view that alcoholism was a reflection of other ailments was consistent with general understanding of the addiction in the field of psychiatry at the time. Dr. Robert Fleming, an expert on alcoholism who later treated Cheney, wrote that "the individual takes alcohol in an attempt to obtain relief of the symptoms of some underlying condition which may be physical, psychological, or social, or any combination of these." Cheney and Matthiessen operated on this premise for several years.

At the Retreat, Cheney submitted to a variety of physical and psychological treatments. He got much rest and regularly received massages, which he presumably enjoyed. On one occasion, he did an hour of Rorschach tests and another time answered a battery of questions along the lines of, "Do you ever cross the street to avoid meeting someone?" Cheney likely regarded the psychological tests with a combination of wry amusement and condescension. Why on earth would he meet someone he didn't want to see? Given the effects of his breathing difficulties and chronic drinking, he may also have received "light baths," concentrated exposures to incandescent light that induced patients to perspire and were thought to help rid their bodies of toxins. This was a common treatment for both asthma and alcoholism, which Putnam, who also suffered from both illnesses, had received during his stay at the Retreat the previous spring.

Cheney may also have received some form of "milieu therapy," a kind of talk therapy championed by Dr. Burlingame in which the psychiatrist worked to retrain a person's family about his or her condition in an attempt to mitigate against familial stress. As Dr. Burlingame wrote: "At least half the doctor's battle . . . is the re-education of the patient's family. It does no permanent good to restore a patient to a normal emotional balance and then return him to the conflict-causing situation." While at the Retreat, Cheney's brothers Philip and Clifford visited him, so they may have participated in his "milieu therapy." Philip and Clifford no doubt wanted to help their brother, but at the same time, like Cheney, they probably bristled at any prospect of exposing any family tensions to strangers, even if the strangers were doctors who at one time had been on the family's payroll. After Cheney was released, Dr. Burlingame counseled him not to stop in Manchester on his way home, suggesting that even though Dr. Burlingame was a close confidant of Cheney's family, he perceived them to be a potential source of stress. Yet the person who could have most benefited Cheney in joining his family therapy, Matthiessen, was almost certainly not included.

Cheney worried about the effect of his hospitalization on Matthiessen. "Dear Matty," he wrote on April 15, "I am deeply grieved for this trouble I am bringing on you." At first, he counseled Matthiessen not to visit: "I hated to send you word not to come Tuesday . . . I know if you came in the door I'd probably cry like a fool." But when Matthiessen did come, Cheney's spirits were bolstered. He told Matthiessen, "Your visit did me solid good—no it didn't key me up[,] just gave me the precious source of continuity and confidence in our life."

Cheney left the Retreat after a little over three weeks. When he returned home to Kittery, Matthiessen was hard at work on *American Renaissance*. Cheney's experience at the Retreat had been unsettling for both men, but it did not prevent them from going to Europe that summer, sailing in July 1938. Beginning with a walking trip in Ireland, they then went on to Munich and Berlin for two weeks, followed by three weeks in Moscow. According to Louis Hyde, given Matthiessen's interest in socialism, he was keen to see firsthand the "experiment" of Communism in Moscow. In the years preceding Matthiessen and Cheney's visit to Moscow, however, Stalin had purged the state of those he considered disloyal, as well as conducted show trials, in which political figures—both supporters and detractors—were put on "trial," forced to confess, and either executed or imprisoned. Matthiessen, like many other liberals at the time, remained quiet about the show trials, suggesting that he was not deeply knowledgeable about Communism under Stalin.

Matthiessen and Cheney returned to the United States on September 15, 1938, aboard the *Europa*, just a week before a powerful hurricane pummeled New England. When the hurricane hit, winds around Kittery and Portsmouth reached ninety miles per hour, and waves crashed over the breakwater at the mouth of Portsmouth harbor. After the hurricane, Cheney went to South Manchester to assess the damage to his studio, which he began renting out after settling in Kittery full-time. Throughout Manchester, many trees had blown down; plate glass windows of stores along Main Street through the center of town had been shattered by flying debris; and portions of buildings collapsed from the rain and wind. Cheney's brother Clifford lost nearly ninety old trees on his property.

Although Cheney had stopped drinking after his stay at the Retreat the previous spring, something about the trip to South Manchester and seeing his family prompted him to go on a binge, which Matthiessen later claimed he knew would happen, though he gave no hint as to how or why he knew. But it's quite possible that Dr. Burlingame had been right: much as Cheney loved his family, they stirred up his complicated and conflicting feelings. During the episode, Cheney somehow made it from South Manchester to the Copley Hotel in Boston and then called Matthiessen to come get him.

The following morning back home in Kittery, Cheney lay in his bed, "his hands still shaking desperately from the nervous shock," Matthiessen explained. Cheney said that he wanted to die, which stunned Matthiessen. It is more likely that Cheney's hands were shaking from delirium tremens rather than "nervous shock," suggesting that he was becoming physically addicted to alcohol. The event stoked Matthiessen's fear of Cheney's death. Reflecting on this moment, Matthiessen later wrote: "Having built my life so simply and wholly with Russell's, having had my eyes opened by him to so much beauty, my heart filled by such richness, my pulse beating steadily in time with his in intimate daily companionship, I am shocked at the thought of life without him."

In the fall of 1938 Matthiessen began a one-year sabbatical. He and Cheney were living together full-time at Kittery, which Matthiessen loved. During this time Matthiessen wrote and published several shorter reviews, including of books about Hart Crane and Walt Whitman, poets who touched on same-sex emotional intimacy or exhibited a homophile sensibility in their works and lives.

Newton Arvin, a gay American literature professor at Smith College, who had written *Walt Whitman*, wrote to Matthiessen in early 1939, telling him that he appreciated Matthiessen's generally positive review of his book that had appeared in the *New Republic*. In one of the many tragic events that form the backdrop to the treatment of gay men and lesbians in the days before Stonewall and gay liberation, Arvin was arrested in 1960—ten years after Matthiessen's death—in an antigay sting operation involving his receipt of gay physique magazines through the US mail. He was forced to retire from Smith because of the scandal and died three years later. Matthiessen's former student Daniel Aaron became a friend and colleague of Arvin's at Smith. Aaron described how Matthiessen poked fun at Arvin for his "girlish" affect, while respecting Arvin's intellectual rigor.

But as Matthiessen's sabbatical wore on, the effect of not teaching began to show in his life. Matthiessen's students provided him with intellectual, social, and emotional ballast. Without the structure of school, Matthiessen *really* began to push himself and work obsessively. His work on *American Renaissance* began to overshadow everything else. Throughout the fall, Matthiessen grew more and more strained. Rather than take a break or rest, he drove himself still harder. His work began to ride him, he told Cheney, rather than the other way around. He lost sleep. He questioned his talent, knowledge, and maturity. He started taking Nembutal, a barbiturate, to help him sleep. By early December, as he later described, the stress had built to a point that Matthiessen acknowledged suicidal impulses, noting that he was "hauled out of sleep by the fantasy that it would be better if I jumped out the window. And during the succeeding week in Kittery I was recurrently filled with the desire to kill myself." So at the midpoint of his yearlong sabbatical and roughly seven months after Cheney's stay at the Retreat, at age thirty-six Matthiessen checked himself into McLean Hospital.

Matthiessen entered McLean on the day after Christmas 1938. McLean boasted nearly all the amenities and comforts of the Hartford Retreat and then some. Originally situated on 250 acres—in contrast to the Retreat's 35 acres in downtown Hartford—McLean built beef and dairy farms, vegetable and flower gardens, apple and pear orchards, and even an apiary, all for occupational therapy *par excellence*. During his time at McLean, Matthiessen underwent hydrotherapy, soaking in a bathtub to relax. He took a pottery class as a form of occupational therapy. He exercised and listened to music. Although he loved listening to music, Matthiessen's treatment mostly bored him, but he submitted to it with forbearance. Matthiessen was ill and wanted to get better, so he did his best to follow the advice of his doctors. But as usual, Matthiessen really came to life in his writing. He wrote letters to Cheney, of course, but also wrote several long diary entries about his experience of being ill and hospitalized.

While at McLean, talk of Cheney and fear of his death dominated Matthiessen's thoughts, writings, and conversations with his friends and doctors. He was surprisingly frank for the time, which speaks to the degree to which Matthiessen and Cheney enjoyed acceptance in select private circles at a time homosexuality was condemned in public. A few days before he checked himself into McLean, Matthiessen visited Kenneth Murdock, his Harvard friend to whom he had dedicated his book on T. S. Eliot, and confided in a tearful revelation his fears of Cheney's death. While at McLean Matthiessen wrote about this visit with Murdock: "He [Murdock] also reasoned with me that I was strong, and when the time came would find resources to face Russell's death. He kept urging upon me how many friends I have and how much I meant to them. God knows I am aware of how much they mean to me. At one point in our talk I broke into tears, and said that I loved life, that I had felt myself to be in contact with so many sides of American society and believed there was so much work to be done, absorbing it, helping to direct it intelligently. And now I felt a film of unreality between me and everything that had seemed most real, that I had to find some way to break through it." Matthiessen's willingness to disclose his fears to Murdock speaks to the strength of their friendship, but the stakes were quite high in doing so. Even though Matthiessen was a tenured professor at this point in his career, had Murdock reported him to the Harvard administration—which he did not do—even with tenure Matthiessen could have been dismissed on "moral grounds" for being gay.

While at McLean, Matthiessen saw Dr. Maurice Fremont-Smith for his insomnia. He candidly described to the doctor the upsetting aftermath of Cheney's trip to South Manchester the prior fall after the hurricane. Matthiessen also saw Dr. William Barrett, a psychiatrist with an expertise in human sexuality, who, as Matthiessen wrote, "was quiet and impressive, assumed my relationship with Russell at once." With Dr. Barrett, Matthiessen discussed his search for a father figure in Cheney and others, notably his friends, Harry Dorman and Hanns Caspar Kollar, to both of whom Matthiessen later dedicated *American Renaissance*. Matthiessen had wondered for years if the absence of "paternal affection" in his life contributed to his attraction to older men.

Although Matthiessen continued seeing Dr. Barrett in Boston on and off for several months after he left McLean, not much seemed to come of those sessions. Matthiessen had a disdainful attitude toward psychoanalysis: "I have hated imaginary illnesses in tweed coats and costly sanitariums." He worried that his stay at McLean was self-indulgent. Matthiessen felt that there was nothing really wrong: "I have every reason to live that can be enumerated: work that I believe to be important, an interest, no a zest for understanding and participating in shaping the society of which I am a part, more generous and devoted friends than ordinarily fall to the lot of any man. And none of the more usual pressures: I have money in the bank, a good job, and no physical illness. Where has this fear come from to engulf one who has never even been bothered by anxiety or worry before?" What was the point to psychoanalysis? Of course, Matthiessen's insomnia and suicidal impulses weren't imaginary. But the absence of a rational basis for his illness made Matthiessen want to dismiss it.

It would be interesting to know, too, if Matthiessen's doctors thought that he also had some form of manic-depressive psychiatric illness. He had a number of the classic symptoms: the alternating periods of intense, ceaseless productivity punctuated by troughs of despair and a sense of futility; suicidal impulses; and later heightened anger and irritability. Matthiessen's diagnosis may not have mattered much, because in the days before lithium treatment and other effective medications for treating this illness, many psychiatrists in the United States emphasized psychological and social factors in their treatment of patients.

Despite Matthiessen's surprising degree of openness in private with his friends and doctors, reticence and circumspection shaped his more public interactions with Cheney at McLean. Cheney brought Matthiessen things from Kittery that he knew would be a source of comfort to him: photographs of the Kittery house in the snow and of their beloved cat Pretzel, as well as an album of reproductions of Cheney's paintings. But during those visits, under the watchful eyes of doctors, nurses, and orderlies, Cheney seemed to want nothing more than to cut short his visits.

As usual, Matthiessen and Cheney were at greater liberty in their correspondence, which in turn led to greater intimacy. Cheney once again expressed regret about causing Matthiessen stress since his own hospitalization at the Retreat the prior spring, but he also sounded a note of inner self-resolve. "I fight my own devil who whispers I have drained too much life from you by my constant demand lately for help and backing—and even if it is partly true I am here and solid to back you now," Cheney wrote. "Well, the letters warmed right through just as they used to do when I was at Oxford, or you were in Santa Fe, or whenever we were long apart," Matthiessen replied. "It's one of the real beauties that never once has the freshness of your life lost any trace of its magic for me. Every day is a new discovery of your wealth."

Matthiessen was not simply solemn and serious in his letters but also lively and irreverent. During one visit a friend from Harvard gave Matthiessen a snapshot of Cheney at the beach building a large, complex sandcastle. In the photo Cheney is dressed in long trousers, a long-sleeved shirt, and a tie. A sailor stands at the edge of the scene, leonine and sexy, cap cocked to one side, hands on his hips. Matthiessen sent the snapshot to Cheney and scrawled across the back: "Would you like to have the cap?" Matthiessen's ribald humor implied their great intimacy. Even when confined in a sanatorium, Matthiessen could still make jokes about sex to Cheney. This was a great source of comfort to him. As had long been true, Cheney brought out Matthiessen's lighter side, one that was humorous and fresh (in both senses of the word), qualities that buoyed and sustained Matthiessen during his dark hours.

And in an exhortation from another letter that could have been taken right out of a scene from Henry James's *The Ambassadors*, Matthiessen encouraged Cheney to *"live*, hold on to this rare thing we have, and that will help me find my way back to the light."

Matthiessen left McLean in mid-January 1939. He moved out of Eliot House several weeks later, temporarily renting an apartment at 42 Mount Vernon Street before settling at 87 Pinckney Street on Louisburg Square on Beacon Hill. Matthiessen grew to love the Pinckney Street apartment, where Cheney could now live with him for extended periods of time, as he could not do at Eliot House. Soon into their lives on Pinckney Street, Matthiessen and Cheney began to give a regular party on Christmas Eve, at which graduate students, Harvard colleagues, old friends from Yale, and political acquaintances all mingled. Cheney and Matthiessen also memorialized the holiday with fanciful Christmas letters to their friends. In these Cheney did the exuberantly playful illustrations, and Matthiessen wrote the text in light verse. The Christmas letters focused on the playful high jinks of Matthiessen and Cheney's cats, Pretzel and others, and their fictitious mistress, Lady Vere de Vere, in reference to Alfred, Lord Tennyson's poem, "Lady Clara Vere de Vere." As Thanksgiving was Matthiessen and Cheney's holiday together in Kittery, Christmas became important to them on Beacon Hill, and the annual Christmas letters became another aesthetic expression of their enduring union.

After his successes of the mid-1930s, Cheney's paintings did not evolve appreciably, though he continued to turn out portraits, still lifes, and landscapes of Kittery, Portsmouth, and now Boston. But in the ever-changing art world, the critics' impatience with Cheney hardened. The *New York World Telegram* said of Cheney's April 1939 show at Ferargil Galleries that his work consisted of "lively, fluent, agreeable studies of American landscape, undistinguished by any arresting originality or point of view or technique." At least the *World Telegram* knew who the artist was. A review of a show from the previous year in Boston referred to Cheney throughout as the writer and art historian Sheldon Cheney.

But if Cheney didn't seem to be advancing in his painting, neither was he sinking, despite his health problems. Beginning in the spring of 1940, Cheney entered several more hospitals and sanatoriums in rapid succession: Portsmouth Hospital, followed by Peter Bent Brigham Hospital in Boston, and finally the Baldpate Hospital in Georgetown, Massachusetts. Far from being at Baldpate for a "couple of weeks," as Matthiessen originally hoped, beginning in the fall of 1940 Cheney was in and out of the sanatorium for next three years. Knowing Cheney's sensitivity to history, he was probably keenly aware of the perverse symmetry that his life's path should plant him in Georgetown, a town just a few miles from Rowley, Massachusetts, where the Cheneys originally put down their roots in American soil in the seventeenth century.

Baldpate was opened in 1939 by a consortium of Boston doctors led by Dr. Harry Cesar Solomon. It treated about forty patients at a time for alcohol and drug addictions, personality disorders, neuroses, and psychoses. Baldpate's setting and amenities resembled the Retreat and McLean, but doctors at Baldpate relied in particular on neurological means to cure mental illnesses. Several forms of "shock therapy" were used, including insulin shock therapy, in which a coma was induced in a patient with large doses of insulin, and metrazol and electroshock therapies, in which seizures were induced in patients. Doctors at Baldpate also performed lobotomies. Cheney's doctors at Baldpate included Dr. Robert Fleming and Dr. V. Gerard Ryan.

Dr. Solomon championed pushing mental health treatment out of hospitals and into communities. He was an early proponent of halfway houses. It appears that Baldpate functioned much like a contemporary halfway house for Cheney throughout the early 1940s. He was not there continuously but went back and forth between Baldpate and Kittery. Whenever something traumatic would happen and Cheney resumed drinking, he would retreat to Baldpate for several weeks or months to get sober. At first Cheney lived in a cottage, which he occasionally shared with one or two other men. But later he stayed on a ward with five or six men to save money. It was quite a comedown in the world for the man who had routinely traveled first-class back and forth to Europe.

As historians and scholars have shown, interaction between psychiatry and gay men and lesbians during much of the twentieth century was not easy. During Matthiessen's and Cheney's day, many doctors discerned a strong, causal link between alcoholism and homosexuality, which was then categorized as a form of mental illness. One of Cheney's doctors, Robert Fleming, together with Kenneth J. Tillotson (who had been the chief psychiatrist at McLean when Matthiessen was a patient there), had written an article a few years earlier that appeared in the prestigious *New England Journal of Medicine* entitled "Personality and Sociological Factors in the Prognosis and Treatment of Chronic Alcoholism." They analyzed a cohort of one hundred male and twenty female patients diagnosed with alcoholism and asserted that the majority of patients had emotional instability or feelings of inferiority of some kind and that male patients' attachment to their mothers was about twice that of their attachment to their fathers. Although only a few in Fleming and Tillotson's cohort exhibited "overt" homosexual tendencies, the doctors wrote that heterosexual adjustment was considered "unsatisfactory" in 72 percent of the males and 65 percent of the females.

Doctors Fleming and Tillotson cited a study of one hundred alcoholic male patients by the psychiatrist James Hardin Wall in which he strongly indicated a causal connection between alcoholism and homosexuality. Dr. Wall said of patients that "their lack of masculine security and aggression was obvious." He noted that many had overprotective mothers and were attracted "to rough and tough types of the lower walks of life." In his treatment regimen, Dr. Wall favored "proper" masculine pastimes, such as metal- or woodworking. Given the general stance of the field of psychiatry, it would not be surprising if Cheney's doctors saw his homosexuality as an underlying cause—if not *the* underlying cause—of his alcoholism. Because his doctors must have quickly divined the nature of Cheney's relationship with Matthiessen, they may have simply written him off as incurable.

Undaunted, Cheney continued to respond strongly to visual stimuli and to paint. While at Baldpate, Cheney saw the Disney movie *Fantasia*, which he described to Putnam as "intricacy & beauty of form & rhythm & color that is a new thing." And he completed a wide range of paintings: architectural, portraits, and still lifes of miscellaneous objects. *Meeting House Hill* (1940), for example, depicts the South Ward Meeting House in Portsmouth, which was built in 1866 in Greek Revival style. In Cheney's painting, he faithfully represents the clarity and simplicity of the Greek Revival details, including the portico, classical pediment, pilasters on the clock tower, and entablature above the columns. Cheney's style fit well with his subject, so that the majesty of the building comes through with little interference. A few years later, Matthiessen wrote a review of *Greek Revival Architecture in America* by Talbot Hamlin, entitled, "Our First National Style." Matthiessen was interested not in the "dominance of a few Easterners, nor of a few big cities, but by the simultaneous flowering [of Greek Revival architecture] in hundreds of local centers"—local centers such as Cheney captured in *Meeting House Hill*. Cheney's artistic expression was met and furthered by Matthiessen's critical interpretation.

Cheney also completed a portrait of Nelson Cantave, who was of Jamaican descent and worked as Matthiessen and Cheney's houseman in Kittery and Boston. As with Cheney's portraits of working-class men generally, he captured a greater level of expressiveness and complexity than in his society portraits. In *Nelson Cantave* (1940), Cantave is pictured peeling vegetables while sitting at a kitchen table in a scene that took place in Matthiessen's Pinckney Street apartment, since a multistory building rises outside the nearby window. A cat—Pretzel or Zuzu—sits on the table eating or drinking from a nearby shallow bowl, as Cantave casts a sidelong glance that suggests wariness or apprehension at someone or something outside the frame of the painting.

During this time, Cheney also began painting quirky still lifes. While at Baldpate, Cheney chose from objects that he had near at hand. Once again, the long reach of William Merritt Chase showed itself. Chase liked to paint homely subjects in his still lifes, to show that even commonplace objects could be beautiful when rendered skillfully by the talented artist. Chase also liked to paint images of reflective surfaces, such as copper, brass, and pewter jugs, once again to show off his technical proficiency. Cheney did not follow exactly in his teacher's footsteps in this regard; many of the metallic surfaces that Cheney chose were dull, tarnished, or muted. But it is very likely that Chase's enduring influence prompted Cheney to include metallic objects in these still lifes—watering heads and cans, scythes, rakes, and metal pots, among others.

No matter where he was, Cheney was devoted to his art, and despite his chronically poor health, he painted through it all. But he withdrew from the professional scene during this time, turning down an invitation from the Ferargil Galleries to mount another exhibition of his work in the spring of 1941. The critical response to his last show had simply been too difficult to bear; he didn't have the emotional reserves to withstand more criticism and disappointment. Cheney was content to spend his days painting and bowling, and in the evenings, when he wasn't continuing to paint in the kitchen at Baldpate, he read a couple of chapters of *The Odyssey*. Life at Baldpate might not have been as intellectually and emotionally fulfilling as life with Matthiessen at Kittery or in Boston, but in its own way it was comfortable.

For Matthiessen, Cheney's hospitalizations in the early spring of 1941 certainly were not welcome. But they gave him the chance to work steadily on revising and correcting proofs of *American Renaissance*, his masterpiece.

Chapter 8

The Green Light across the Piscataqua

The early 1940s had a dual personality for Matthiessen and Cheney. *American Renaissance* was published, which is Matthiessen's most significant and enduring achievement. He followed this up a few years later with a book on Henry James. Meanwhile Cheney went back and forth from Baldpate, struggling with his drinking but continuing to paint. During the early 1940s, Matthiessen and Cheney spent more time apart than at any other point in their relationship. Even their wonderful summers and holidays together were curtailed or disrupted entirely. In response, as if seeking to fill a void, Matthiessen's political activism grew.

Nonetheless, Cheney remained the great source of art in Matthiessen's life. From their earliest days together aboard the *Paris* with the famous "incident of the pear" to their private language of nicknames, Cheney helped Matthiessen think—and more important—live a life enriched by creative expression. Literature and Cheney and his painting were the poles that anchored reality for Matthiessen. These invigorated Matthiessen and spurred his scholarship. But as Cheney became sicker and withdrew from the world, Matthiessen questioned the power of literature and art in his life, which also fueled Matthiessen's progressive political activism. As his faith in more aesthetic worlds wavered, he began to believe more and more in direct political action. But none of this stopped Cheney's ready command of aestheticism from being any less compelling. Tormented though he was during much of the early 1940s, Cheney exerted his compelling magic on Matthiessen until his death.

In May 1941, *American Renaissance* was published. The question at the center of the book is fairly straightforward: In the years 1850 to 1855, a number of classic texts by American authors were published, including *The Scarlet Letter* (1850), *The House of Seven Gables* (1851), *Moby Dick* (1851), *Walden* (1854), and *Leaves of Grass* (1855). Matthiessen asks why? What did this moment of cultural expression represent? How did it come about? And why did it happen when it did? Matthiessen was in many ways the consummate insider but one whose homosexuality often made him feel like an outsider. As a result, he contemplated the questions at the heart of *American Renaissance* from a valuable perspective.

American Renaissance is not strictly literary criticism, which is one of its appeals. In the book, Matthiessen taps multiple disciplines: literature, painting, sculpture, and architecture. He moves backward in time, discussing how the authors in his survey drew on writers of the past, and he moves forward in time describing how his subjects influenced later poets and writers. This fluid erudition led another founder of American studies, Henry Nash Smith, to describe *American Renaissance* more like an artistic work than a work of scholarship. On reading the manuscript, Cheney said that he was strongly struck by the "fine intricacy of pattern and thought in the book." Matthiessen's deep engagement with literature and cultural history is evident on almost every page. He is always asking: What makes a piece of literature work as art? What does it express? And what does it tell us about its time and place? Sharpened by his own growing political sense, Matthiessen was especially sensitive to "the spirit of protest and revolution" in the authors he examined.

Matthiessen dedicated *American Renaissance* to Harry Dorman and Hanns Caspar Kollar, as the two men "who have taught me most about the possibilities of life in America." This was not really true. Russell Cheney taught Matthiessen the most about the possibilities of life in America, but Matthiessen knew that he shouldn't dedicate the book to Cheney. Although their close friends understood the nature of their relationship, to more distant acquaintances and colleagues, Matthiessen likely felt compelled to maintain the fiction that he and Cheney were just "friends." A more public avowal would have signaled the depth of his connection with Cheney. Although he could collaborate with Cheney in a workman-like way, as he did on *Sarah Orne Jewett*, anything that touched on deeper feelings—paradoxically, one of the very qualities that Matthiessen and Cheney prized so highly in literature and painting—was strictly to be avoided. Cheney, for his part, didn't object to Matthiessen's overlooking him publicly in the dedication to the book. If he thought about it at all, he probably felt relieved. Cheney knew how close they were, which was all that mattered. He was perfectly content with Matthiessen naming Dorman and Kollar. Cheney—and the Cheneys—informed *American Renaissance* in other, deeper ways.

As Matthiessen had written to Cheney in the early days of their relationship, it thrilled him to be living Whitman's words. By the time he wrote *American Renaissance*, Matthiessen further upheld the value and primacy of experience. In Matthiessen's world-view, experience came before language or analysis, even as it was intimately related to both. As he wrote, "man cannot use words unless he has experienced the facts that they express, unless he has grasped them with his senses." How far did writers live what they advocated? Thoreau, for example, was an American scholar in action, and his chief distinction in Matthiessen's opinion was that he lived what others preached. In Thoreau's view—and Matthiessen's—writers grew "wooden" when they did not speak and write out of their experience. Of Melville, Matthiessen wrote that the weight of his experience "backed up what he wanted to do with words."

Closely related to experience was a writer's use of language. Matthiessen noted that Emerson believed that it was the artist's job to "fasten words again to visible things." He went on to add that Emerson "responded instinctively to 'the vigorous Saxon' of men working in the fields or swapping stories in the barn, men wholly uneducated, but whose words had roots in their own experience." Matthiessen credited Whitman with understanding that "language was not 'an abstract construction' made by the learned, but that it had arisen out of the work and needs, the joys and struggles and desires of long generations of humanity." Whitman believed that ordinary talk of men and women approached meaning not directly, but through the "circuitous routes of lively fancy." If Matthiessen and Cheney's love of nicknames did not serve as his starting point for this strand of analysis, then it reinforced these ideas.

Another outgrowth of experience and language was Matthiessen's analysis of the beauty of the human voice. As a minister, Emerson valued the American tradition of oratory. In his poetry, Whitman also valued the spoken word, and as Matthiessen noted, his "richest feelings were aroused by the sound of the human voice." Matthiessen went on to add that for Whitman, "the lurking yet compelling charm of the voice was the ultimate token of personality. It was not something that could be taught, but was bound up inextricably with the growth of experience." That Whitman was able to put Emerson's theories into practice likely heightened Matthiessen's regard for the poet. And once again, Matthiessen's love of Cheney's voice probably anchored these ideas.

Matthiessen's relationship with Cheney also sensitized him to the process of how knowledge is passed down from generation to generation in the absence of established traditions. This became a powerful idea for Matthiessen, the American willingness to create everything for ourselves. It closely informs Matthiessen's explorations of how the writers of *American Renaissance* developed their crafts in a young nation with few cultural traditions. Matthiessen could imagine American writers making it up as they went along, because he knew what that felt like from his own life with Cheney. Matthiessen explicated Emerson's influence on Thoreau and Whitman. He traced how Hawthorne learned from Milton and then how Melville and later James learned from

Hawthorne. Matthiessen explored how James in turn influenced Eliot and Ezra Pound.

The key mechanism by which writers passed down knowledge to others was through reading. Matthiessen had already examined the importance of reading in *Translation: An Elizabethan Art*. In *American Renaissance*, he went a step further, noting how a writer, such as Thoreau, had been able to "assimilate his reading with his experience and make a fresh combination." Matthiessen was enthralled by Melville's reading of Shakespeare in the winter of 1849. Matthiessen claimed that Shakespeare liberated Melville, expanding his vocabulary and notions of tragedy, in the same way that Havelock Ellis, John Addington Symonds, Walt Whitman, and others extended Matthiessen's and Cheney's notions of sexuality and taught them how to be gay.

No discussion of Matthiessen and Cheney would be complete without an acknowledgment of Matthiessen's indebtedness to the visual arts—*en plein air* painting in particular—in helping him excavate the cultural terrain of *American Renaissance*. Matthiessen noted the importance of sight for Emerson and the development of outdoor painting in the nineteenth century. Sculpture also figured prominently into Matthiessen's analysis.

Although Matthiessen's discussion of painting is an implicit nod to Cheney—*the* open-air painter in his life—his analysis ends up reflecting the homophobia of the world of which he and Cheney were a part. In *American Renaissance*, Matthiessen compared the paintings of Thomas Eakins and others to the work of Walt Whitman. In the Eakins's painting *Swimming*, Matthiessen finds the greatest resonance with Whitman. *Swimming* (1885) depicts a group of young men naked and swimming at Dove Lake outside Philadelphia. The figures are arranged in a pyramidal formation. At the apex of the pyramid, one man stands on a stone pier with his buttocks facing the viewer, while another man dives into the water. Two other men recline on the pier enjoying the sun. A fifth man emerges from the water, climbing onto the pier. In the lower right-hand corner Eakins depicts himself crouched in the water surveying the scene. The men are outside on a sunny day enjoying swimming with one another. Presumably, the homosocial—not to mention the homoerotic—qualities attracted Matthiessen to the painting.

But the repressive atmosphere of Matthiessen's time colored his discussion of the painting from there. It was as though Matthiessen couldn't resist using an image of *Swimming* but then didn't feel at liberty to follow through with writing about the homoerotic qualities of both it and the eleventh section of Whitman's poem "Song of Myself" beginning with the line, "Twenty-eight young men bathe by the shore," to which he compares the painting. Lines such as the following could have given Matthiessen something to work with:

FIGURE 9. Thomas Eakins (1844–1916), *Swimming* (1885), oil on canvas, 27 3/8 x 36 3/8 in. Amon Carter Museum of American Art, Fort Worth, Texas, Purchased by the Friends of Art, Fort Worth Art Association, 1925; acquired by the Amon Carter Museum of American Art, 1990, from the Modern Art Museum of Fort Worth through grants and donations from the Amon G. Carter Foundation, the Sid W. Richardson Foundation, the Anne Burnett and Charles Tandy Foundation, Capital Cities/ABC Foundation, Fort Worth Star-Telegram, The R. D. and Joan Dale Hubbard Foundation and the people of Fort Worth. 1990.19.1.

> The beards of the young men glisten'd with wet, it
> ran from their long hair,
> Little streams pass'd over their bodies.
> An unseen hand also pass'd over their bodies,
> It descended tremblingly from their temples and ribs.

But Matthiessen apparently didn't feel that he could be so bold to linger too long on the subject of same-sex physical attraction. Instead, he fell back on a vague and meandering comparison of *Swimming* to the fourth section of Whitman's "To Think of Time," in which he emphasized the hardships and premature death of a working-class Broadway stagecoach driver. Not exactly the typical first thoughts that come to mind on seeing *Swimming*. Still, it took a proto-gay scholar such as Matthiessen to pick up a homoerotic subtext in *Swimming*, even if he did not follow his analysis all the way to its conclusion.

Matthiessen knew implicitly the invisible boundaries and unspoken expectations of his profession, Harvard, and America. The combination of his ambition and unwillingness to be defined solely through the prism of his sexuality led him to try to push the cultural envelope from the inside, rather than rip it open from the outside. For someone in Matthiessen's position, it was not an unreasonable calculation and decision to make in 1941.

Nonetheless, the homosocial and homoerotic themes that had registered with Matthiessen in his selection of *Swimming* were part of the culture, whether others wanted to acknowledge them or not. Matthiessen didn't know it, but *Swimming* found an astonishing echo in a photograph that Cheney Brothers used in its promotional pamphlet *The Miracle Workers* published in 1916 to attract workers to the company. An uncredited picture appears on page thirty-two of the pamphlet by a photographer who must have been familiar with Eakins's work. It shows a group of male Cheney Brothers employees—we're meant to assume—swimming and diving in the nude, as men did at the time. The figures are arranged in more of a gentle arc, rather than the pyramidal composition that Eakins used. Still, the similarities between the photograph and the painting are striking. One man with his back to the viewer, both hands on his hips, and right knee bent forward is almost a dead ringer for the central figure in *Swimming*. Both painting and photograph also feature another man diving into the water.

But unlike *Swimming*, where the image of men enjoying the outdoors is abstracted as an idealized Arcadian image—Who are these men? And what has brought them to the country to enjoy a day in the sun and water?—in the context of *The Miracle Workers*, the answers are clear. The men swimming are Cheney Brothers employees, and through gainful employment at decent wages and comparatively good working conditions, Cheney Brothers has made it possible for them to experience a relaxing moment in the water and sun. The unknown photographer and the executives at Cheney Brothers recognized the power of such relaxed homosocial images. And evidently, they couldn't—or wouldn't—see them as homoerotic: this was simply how men swam at the time. Once again, Russell Cheney, his family, and their history tapped into and made concrete some of the very cultural forces that Matthiessen considered intellectually and theoretically; these cultural forces were an implicit part of Cheney's rich family legacy.

As the critic William E. Cain has pointed out, *American Renaissance* is an astounding work, but not a perfect work. The most obvious omission is that Matthiessen did not examine slavery in the writers he surveyed, the central issue in the Civil War. Some of this is attributable to the narrowness of Matthiessen's literary judgments. In his opinion, Melville was a superior writer to Harriet Beecher Stowe—end of discussion. But Matthiessen did not explore slavery even in those writers he included in *American Renaissance*. As Cain elaborates, Matthiessen left out a discussion of Melville's story *Benito Cereno*.

But Matthiessen's homosocial literary choices led him to analyze another Melville story in *American Renaissance* with a strong "gay" subtext, *Billy Budd, Sailor*. In this book, same-sex

FIGURE 10. *Swimming Pool for Summer*, in *The Miracle Workers*, Cheney Brothers Silk Manufacturing Company Records, Archives & Special Collections, University of Connecticut Library, Storrs, CT. CC BY-NC 4.0.

attraction is a critical element in the story's action. Matthiessen notes the contrast between Billy Budd's innocence and beauty and master-at-arms John Claggart's pallor, which "seemed to hint of something defective or abnormal in the constitution and blood." Matthiessen describes a scene in which Billy knocks over a can of greasy liquid at Claggart's feet aboard the *Bellipotent*. The normally ill-tempered Claggart responds with the equivocal line, "Handsomely done, my lad! And handsome is as handsome did it, too!" Matthiessen adds, "This is one of the scenes in which the writer of to-day would be fully aware of what may have been only latent for Melville, the sexual element in Claggart's ambivalence." Although the picture of Claggart is not a sympathetic one, and it would be many years before scholars pointedly interpreted *Billy Budd* using a queer lens, Matthiessen was picking up on the power of same-sex desire as a force in American literature and writing about it when he had no explicit language for it.

The critical reception of *American Renaissance* was nearly all laudatory. Clifton Fadiman in the *New Yorker* noted that the book was of "great importance" to understanding American culture, as did George Hellman in the *New York Times*. Robert E. Spiller in the *Saturday Review of Literature* called *American Renaissance* "perhaps the most profound work of literary criticism on historical principles by any modern American." And Stanley Williams, writing in the *Yale Review*, said it was a "dynamic book" and "boldly experimental in method." Matthiessen's reputation had been growing over the years, but *American Renaissance* solidified his standing as one of the preeminent scholars of his generation and helped pave the way to his appointment as a full professor the following year.

Yet for all of the positive press about the book, there were two reviews—one by Alfred Kazin in the *New York Herald Tribune* and the other by Granville Hicks in the *New England Quarterly*—that raised mild complaints and in retrospect provide yet another glimpse of the entrenched homophobia of the day that shaped Matthiessen's scholarship and his and Cheney's world. Both Kazin and Hicks were admiring of *American Renaissance*, but both wanted to know more about Matthiessen's own thoughts about the literature and culture that he examined. Hicks put it most succinctly: "The whole book is based on the proposition that what a writer believes about man, about society, and about the universe has a great deal to do with what he writes; and yet Mr. Matthiessen refuses to be explicit about his own beliefs." Some of what Kazin and Hicks refer to is observable in Matthiessen's discussion of *Swimming* and the related passages from Whitman's poetry.

Many of Matthiessen's friends and colleagues noted his forthright and intensely honest personality in private or semipublic settings, such as college classrooms. In his letters to Cheney, too, he was candid in his opinions about literature: he loved Shakespeare and Melville; he appreciated Henry James but was more ambivalent about him. So accustomed to being circumspect about himself, his life, and his desires and feelings, it may have been harder for Matthiessen as a gay man to translate his closely held personal opinions onto the broader public stage. He could do so indirectly and obliquely, such as in the gay and Cheney-related themes that form a subtext to much of Matthiessen's work. But even a man with as many advantages as Matthiessen had could not entirely overcome the repressive power of his time. Kazin's and Hicks's comments in their own way hinted at this dynamic, even if neither writer hazarded a guess as to why.

In the end, *American Renaissance* helped legitimize American literature and found a discipline. As one American literature scholar pointed out, "*American Renaissance* (1941) has given its name to courses taught at hundreds of institutions." Over eighty years later, this is still true, even if *American Renaissance* is now read primarily as a work to react against. The three contemporary scholarly books noted earlier by Giles Gunn, Frederick C. Stern, and William E. Cain devote ample attention to explicating *American Renaissance*, while exploring the full range of Matthiessen's work. To their credit, all three scholars acknowledge the importance of Cheney in Matthiessen's life.

Matthiessen felt proud of *American Renaissance*. In 1929, he had written in the *Yale Review*: "It is time for the history of American literature to be rewritten." That day arrived in 1941 with the publication of *American Renaissance*. To celebrate the book and its author, Matthiessen's students, colleagues, and friends organized a dinner for him in the dining room at Eliot House at Harvard in May 1941. It was a sweet occasion with spring near its height and apple and cherry trees in blossom in the Eliot House yard. According to Leo Marx, there were about thirty to forty people at dinner, and they celebrated Matthiessen with "a spontaneous eruption of affection" for the success of someone who had been the faculty guide and unofficial hero to many students. Harry Levin went so far as to describe Matthiessen's dinner as the "apogee of his career."

The dinner moved Matthiessen deeply, but Cheney was not there to savor the moment with him. The two men practiced a kind of self-imposed censorship, so that Cheney was not involved in Matthiessen's academic career. Of course, from a post-Stonewall perspective, the lines between self-imposed and externally imposed censorship are far from clear. But even if Matthiessen could have comfortably had Cheney by his side that night, it would have been difficult, because in May 1941 Cheney was back at Baldpate.

And then, as luck would have it, on the day after *American Renaissance* was published, the Federal Bureau of Investigation opened a file on Matthiessen because of his support—however innocuous—for groups considered by the government to be Communist controlled or influenced. To the extent that American literature strengthened Matthiessen's sympathy for organized labor and his insistence on social and economic justice, it might be said that American literature, having shaped Matthiessen as an intellectual, now placed him under the watchful eye of J. Edgar Hoover's FBI.

Over the summer of 1941, while *American Renaissance* was being celebrated nationwide, Cheney's paintings were being shown at Lanier's Tea Garden, a local arts colony in Eliot, Maine. In late October and early November, Cheney showed thirty paintings at Ferargil Galleries. It was to be his last show in New York. The critics were generally far more positive than they had been in recent years. They noted that Cheney had simplified his canvases, pared down his images to essential elements, and made better use of color. In the *New York Journal American*, Margaret Breuning announced a "definite advance" in Cheney's work, adding: "Mr. Cheney is a prolific painter, generally employing much the same range of subject matter—landscapes and still-lifes—but he does not repeat himself or suggest a forced expression. Rather it is the freshness and variety of his canvases that make [a] first impression. He is an artist who continues to live close to the natural forms he depicts and continues to study them with sensitive appreciation of their particular colors and contours, so that each canvas reflects a new experience, a swift response to a pleasurable emotion." Yet for all of the positive reviews, the opening was poorly attended, which threw Cheney into a state of depression. He was soon back at Baldpate again, where he would remain through the spring of 1942.

It was beginning to dawn on Matthiessen that Cheney should not drink at all, that he needed to develop ways to avoid taking the first drink. "I'm sure that you can live here productively and happily if you'll only learn to pay attention to the first danger signals and especially to remember that it's the first drink only that lies in your control," Matthiessen wrote from Kittery in November 1941. Over the next several months, Matthiessen repeated this idea several times: "I do wish I could make it come home to you as irrefutable evidence that when once you have had the first drink, there is no stopping whatever you may wish." Over a year later, Matthiessen again returned to the theme of avoiding the first drink: "For I still believe there must be some checks you can work on to prevent your taking the first drink. After all it isn't as though you simply had to walk into a bar, for your drinking here involves the whole elaborate chain of going into the liquor store, getting a package, putting it in the car, bringing it out here, and hiding it. Surely that gives you plenty of time for your judgment and will to step in. And that's the only point you can work on it—not after you've gotten started."

This sounds like a basic principle of Alcoholics Anonymous (AA) that was being described in the press at the time, that avoiding the first drink precludes setting off a physical reaction and a craving for more and more alcohol. There are no references in Matthiessen and Cheney's correspondence that either of them was ever exposed to AA, which had then been in operation for seven years. Although some of Cheney's doctors were beginning to recognize AA, it's unlikely that he would have been introduced to it at Baldpate. In addition to favoring neurological interventions for mental illness and substance abuse problems, doctors at Baldpate considered organizations such as AA "déclassé." But if Cheney had been exposed to AA, he probably would have hated it. Cheney could be lively and outgoing when he met people on his own terms, but he often recoiled if forced to interact with strangers.

In the late 1930s and early 1940s, however, a number of stories began to appear in newspapers and magazines about Alcoholics Anonymous, most prominently in an article by Jack Alexander which appeared in the *Saturday Evening Post* on March 1, 1941, just eight months before the idea—and exhortations—of avoiding the first drink began to show up in Matthiessen's letters to Cheney. Describing the steady descent of an alcoholic, Alexander wrote: "After a while, he no longer needs rationalization to justify the fatal first drink." Although no specific references exist to Matthiessen having read the Alexander piece, it seems possible given the wide reach of the *Saturday Evening Post*, the sensation that followed its cover story on Alcoholics Anonymous, as well as Matthiessen's hunger for helpful and dispassionate information on the subject.

Cheney's frustration and despair over his continued drinking were so great that in May 1942 he decided to undergo pentylenetetrazol-induced shock therapy at Baldpate. Evidence is circumstantial but compelling, beginning with Cheney's reference to getting "shots," because PTZ (also known as metrazol) was injected for the purpose of causing convulsive seizures. These were believed to restart normal functioning of the nervous system by temporarily disrupting it. As Jennifer Terry has pointed out, a doctor in Atlanta also experimented with metrazol to "cure" homosexuality.

In his correspondence with Matthiessen, Cheney was clearly anxious over the prospect of undergoing shock treatment. But the psychic pain of the vicious cycle of excessive drinking, pledging and trying to stop, failing, and resuming drinking nonetheless nudged him along this unwelcome course. Cheney was ready to try just about anything to lift his compulsion. On May 4, he wrote: "I want to take the drastic step that he [Dr. Robert

Fleming] suggests . . . I don't care how hard it is. I am going to do it." Cheney's term of treatment in the spring of 1942 lasted for about three to four weeks. Dr. V. Gerard Ryan, who treated Cheney at Baldpate, and Dr. Lucie Jessner described in *Shock Treatment in Psychiatry: A Manual* an average course of PTZ therapy as seven doses administered over four weeks. If a patient did not improve after two or more induced seizures, the injections would be administered every other day. If Cheney's sessions followed typical practice, he would have been injected with PTZ, gagged, and been held down by attendants, so as not to harm himself once convulsions began. Seizures generally started within fifteen seconds of an injection and lasted up to a minute. Patients were often grumpy coming out of a PTZ-induced seizure.

The days, weeks, and months following shock therapy were up and down for Cheney. By this time, Matthiessen had become increasingly guarded and skeptical of Cheney's pledges to stop drinking, even when Cheney took so dramatic a step as to undergo convulsive shock therapy. His hopes for Cheney's sobriety had been dashed so many times that Matthiessen couldn't permit himself the luxury of optimism. It appears that Cheney resumed drinking near the end of or directly after finishing his course of treatment. In a weary tone, Matthiessen almost seemed to be washing his hands of the whole affair when he wrote on May 25, saying that Dr. Fleming recommended that Cheney remain at Baldpate "until the alcohol has been out of your system long enough to give you a chance to settle down and to let the psychological effects of your 'cure' also have a chance to hit home" (Matthiessen's single quotation marks). He reiterated to Cheney that it was only the first drink that lay within his control.

In a voice that is heartbreakingly familiar to anyone who has ever known someone struggling with addiction, Cheney replied on June 1 with unwarranted optimism. "More and more I realize that the beneficial experience really has worked . . . You will see feller I am different. I wrote to Fleming I am keeping away from letting myself dwell on the past. Nothing in the world could have pulled me out but your unfailing love for me. And the thing is not to look back to say I'm sorry but to just look ahead to the confident & quiet future of our life together with you not having to worry or dread what you may find when you get home." But again that hope evaporated, when Cheney again began drinking. By December of 1942, he landed in Elm Crest Manor, a private sanatorium in Portland, Connecticut about twenty miles south of Hartford, where Dr. Ryan was an associate psychiatrist.

When shock treatment didn't work, it was as though something snapped for the ever buoyant, effervescent Cheney, and a chasm of despair opened up inside him. It was all useless. He had steeled his nerves to undergo this frightening and disagreeable treatment, which didn't help. Instead, it further drained Matthiessen's patience, as was clear when he told Cheney on December 13 that "it strikes me that you are hardly even trying to resist drinking. You don't want to get into a jam, but you don't do anything positive to avoid it." Reflecting his difficulties in 1942, Cheney completed only three canvases, making it one of the least productive years of his career.

For all the stress and strain, Cheney finally did hit on a method to better control his drinking. He went to live with his sister Theodora and her husband, General Halstead Dorey, at their ranch in Boerne, Texas, not far from San Antonio. In a climate that did not aggravate his breathing difficulties and surrounded by the nominal comforts of family, Cheney resumed painting productively. It took only a few weeks, however, for him to become bored with his relatives: "regular 'family' life makes me realize how much richer we are in ideas and real contentment than most people." As had long been the case, family was often a double-edged proposition for Cheney. Much as Cheney loved his family and being with them reinforced a salient feature of his identity, it came at too high a price. He couldn't go back to being seen as the bachelor Sunday painter.

Cheney was an adult man, a talented painter, who made his home and forged a life with his same-sex partner. He belonged by Matthiessen's side, and Matthiessen belonged by his side. Although Cheney knew this intellectually and felt it deeply, this self-assertive act rattled him. So when he returned to Kittery in the spring of 1943, it wasn't long before his drinking was once again out of control. He landed back at Baldpate, where he remained on and off until returning to Boerne in November.

Cheney's brief stays in Kittery proved to be far from a respite— for either man. Matthiessen often scolded Cheney over his drinking. Not surprisingly, this had an effect opposite to what Matthiessen intended, causing Cheney to drink more rather than less. Matthiessen's admonishments must have made Cheney feel even more pressured, so he drank to soothe himself. But there developed between the two men the pernicious idea that Cheney could stay sober only when he was away from Matthiessen. Cheney's experience in Texas of relative peace and sobriety, followed by his quick relapse to drinking when he returned to New England, buttressed this notion. That summer Matthiessen's voice became increasingly more desperate: "There's nothing whatsoever that I —or anyone else, I guess—can do for you anymore. If you don't want to destroy yourself, you will have to take hold *now*, not later. You have all my love." Several weeks later, he wrote again to Cheney at Baldpate encouraging him to devise a plan on avoiding the first drink: "So please try to work out a defense there, even though you won't do it with me."

Alcoholism was the lonely disease for both Matthiessen and Cheney. It alienated them from the other people in their lives, but perhaps more important, it alienated them from each other. These difficulties contributed to the personality change that Matthiessen's friends noted in him during the early 1940s. They described how he grew irritable, demanding, rude, and even belligerent. Other friends and colleagues of Matthiessen's attributed the increasing strain of the early 1940s to a period of growing estrangement from Harvard and greater political activism. These factors no doubt exacerbated Matthiessen's stress, but the events in his personal life were most likely the primary cause.

Matthiessen had a beloved partner who was seriously ill at a time when traditional medicine offered little help with addiction. And as gay men, Cheney and Matthiessen had an understandably apprehensive relationship with the field of psychiatry, which had done so much to pathologize same-sex love, much as some of their individual doctors seemed open-minded and sympathetic. Jack Alexander had described Matthiessen's predicament in his article on AA in the *Saturday Evening Post*: "The wife or husband of an alcoholic and the children, too, frequently become neurotics from being exposed to drinking excesses over a period of years."

May Sarton, who eventually settled in York, Maine, next door to Kittery, went even further. Her novel *Faithful Are the Wounds* features the central character Edward Cavan, who was based on Matthiessen. Not surprisingly for a novel published in 1955, Sarton, herself a lesbian, dropped only vague hints as to Matthiessen's/ Cavan's sexuality. But describing the personality change that came over Cavan during the course of the novel, one character observes that "it's like some illness he has." Though Sarton could not have guessed the causes of Matthiessen's personality change, it was in keeping with Alexander's description of the alcoholic's effect on the family and loved ones. Donald Pitkin, who had been married to the late Emily Knapp Pitkin, Cheney's great-niece and Matthiessen's godchild, confirmed the stress that Cheney's drinking had on Matthiessen: "Russell's drinking was very hard on Matty."

Despite his personal difficulties in 1943, Matthiessen did not slow down in his scholarly output. He wrote a number of reviews and essays and began teaching a course on Henry James—the subject of his next book—in the winter of 1943–44. He also wrote a thoughtful essay for the 1943 Harvard Album entitled "The Humanities in War Time," a nod to T. S. Eliot's essay "Poetry in Wartime."

The early 1940s marked the beginning of Matthiessen's increasing intellectual distance from the Harvard community. Matthiessen disapproved of the push by Harvard president James Bryant Conant toward greater emphasis on the physical and social sciences and away from the humanities in light of World War II. As George Abbott White wrote, Matthiessen disliked that Conant focused on "how" but not "why" in his approach to pedagogy. Trained as a chemist, Conant is credited with transforming Harvard into a research university; he is also remembered for his role as an adviser to the US government on the development of the atomic bomb.

As if feeling intellectually estranged from his professional community wasn't bad enough, Matthiessen's circle of professional and personal friends at Harvard shrank during the early 1940s. His former student and friend, C. L. Barber, was not promoted and forced to leave Harvard because he had not finished his book. (If this is the book that became *Shakespeare's Festive Comedy: A Study of Dramatic Form and Its Relation to Social Custom*, 1959, the loss was Harvard's.) Matthiessen cast Barber's brush-off from Harvard in the ethos of a changing university, noting that Joe, as Barber was known to his friends, simply didn't "possess the slick competitive knacks that a big business university demands." Matthiessen's sense of separation grew over the next several years, and he summarized his feelings in a later letter to Cheney: "I've got a fairly low view of my conduct lately; much too quick tempered and lashing out at the things and people at Harvard I think poorly of. Too much filled with irritability and distrust, with too little forebearance [*sic*] and too little active sense of cooperative sympathy. One reason is that I've never felt myself with so few fellow spirits there. No one has begun to take the place of the Bakers and the Barbers . . . So, very often, as I catch distant glimpses of Conant's scheme for the higher vocationalism of the future, I feel way out in left field with nobody like Paul Sweezy to turn to. But I like my job, I have plenty of other resources, and I must not let myself be driven into the defensive position of a continual fighter against the administration just for the sake of fighting."

Perhaps seeking greater camaraderie in a different sphere, the forty-year-old Matthiessen did his best to join the Marines after the attack on Pearl Harbor. Matthiessen had initially advocated for nonintervention in World War II. But once the United States entered the war, Matthiessen's socialism didn't hold him back, and he wanted to contribute to the effort. A number of his friends, including Kenneth Murdock, submitted letters of recommendation on his behalf. But as 1942 closed, Matthiessen learned that he had been turned down, because he was a half inch too short and two years too old. As part of his registration with the Selective Service, Matthiessen revealed a remarkably candid bit of evidence as to the nature of his relationship with Cheney: a declaration that Cheney was Matthiessen's dependent, who as an artist by trade was "unable to make a living for himself." Since Matthiessen's purchase of the house in Kittery, he had contributed significantly to Cheney's livelihood, but to make such an assertion further pushed the public boundary of their relationship. It meant little to the Selective Service at the time, if it meant anything at all, but the fact did turn up in Matthiessen's FBI file a few years later.

One of the first national political fights in the early 1940s in which Matthiessen got involved was the campaign to secure naturalization for Harry Bridges, the West Coast labor leader associated with the International Longshoremen's Association, who had been accused of membership in the Communist Party. Matthiessen spent considerable time with Bridges and admired him as a tough-minded, canny, and effective labor organizer. He feared that the US government's heavy-handedness in the Bridges cases set a dangerous precedent for deporting people it deemed undesirable. In response, Matthiessen joined with director Orson Welles and record producer John Henry Hammond to form the Citizens Victory Committee for Harry Bridges, with Matthiessen as its chairman. Matthiessen spoke on behalf of Bridges at various left-leaning political meetings over the years, including a speech in the fall of 1943 for the American Committee for the Protection of the Foreign Born, which was responsible for defending Bridges in his various court battles.

For Matthiessen, there was almost something romantic—as distinct from sexual—in his enthusiasm for Harry Bridges, as though Bridges were a more politically engaged, modern-day Melville. Leaving Melbourne in 1920, Bridges became a sailor for six years after reading Jack London's *Sea Wolf*. He was of medium height with a lean, wiry build. Even after he became successful, Bridges lived modestly, drew only a small salary, and dressed in rumpled clothing. In his free time, he played the mandolin. President Franklin Delano Roosevelt's labor secretary Frances Perkins knew Bridges from his West Coast labor organizing, and from time to time she talked to the president about his naturalization problems. From then on FDR would occasionally ask Perkins about Bridges: "How's your mandolin player getting along?" Broadly speaking, Bridges tried to put into place social and economic justice reforms worthy of Matthiessen's undergraduate intellectual hero R. H. Tawney. Bridges went on the record about wanting to see Americans put their pioneering spirit in the service of their fellow citizens, instead of for personal gain alone.

Matthiessen's turn to political activism may also have been a way to fend off loneliness, in response to feeling increasingly isolated at Harvard and separated from Cheney for long stretches of time. His correspondence with Cheney from this period was filled with much love and tenderness but also with many references to increasing solitude and frustration. In January 1943, Matthiessen wrote: "I feel pretty lonely when I wake up in the morning." Matthiessen could not even revel in his partner's letters, since it became even more difficult to decipher Cheney's handwriting, which had always bordered on illegible. When Cheney started to write in pencil, Matthiessen asked in a voice of exasperation in the same January 1943 letter: "Are you ever going to get a fountain pen again?" Meanwhile, loneliness continued to gnaw at him. That August he added: "I needn't pretend that it hasn't been very difficult here [the Pinckney Street apartment], and that loneliness hasn't left me empty for long stretches of time. But I can get fairly good hold as long as I'm not left absolutely alone."

Because of Cheney's drinking, it was difficult for them to be together, but it was even more difficult for them to be apart. During the early 1940s, Thanksgivings and Christmases were curtailed or disrupted entirely. In 1941, Cheney had been at Baldpate; in 1942 he was in Portsmouth Hospital with pneumonia; and in 1943 he was in Texas, where he remained at Christmas too. In 1943, Matthiessen gave their annual Christmas party on Pinckney Street by himself. The day after Matthiessen wrote to Cheney about the party and told him that "I had a funny sense all Christmas Eve, not of you being away but as though you were right here." It was as though he were addressing a ghost, which in many ways he was.

Ambitious man that Matthiessen was, he always worked hard. But his past performance paled in comparison with his productivity during 1944 and 1945, which may also suggest that he was entering a period of mania. Beginning with a fight for free speech and racial justice in 1944, Matthiessen went on to publish his book on Henry James, edit collections of James's stories and Melville's poems, and write nearly a dozen reviews and other short pieces. During these years, Matthiessen focused his scholarly efforts on Henry James, whose work he considered an acquired taste. Nonetheless, Matthiessen helped spark interest in James's work, and he claimed that his book on James was his contribution to the World War II effort. Henry James's ambiguous sexuality probably also attracted Matthiessen's interest.

Beginning in the spring of 1944, Matthiessen saw the influence of his nemesis, the Watch and Ward Society, behind the ban on the novel *Strange Fruit* by Lillian Smith and its depiction of interracial love. Matthiessen worked with critic and civil rights supporter Bernard DeVoto to protest the ban, which was initiated by the Boston Board of Retail Book Merchants and later upheld by the Supreme Judicial Court of Massachusetts, because of so-called obscene language in the book. Matthiessen denounced the ban as a violation of the free press. Although technically an issue of freedom of the press, Matthiessen made clear in a letter to the *Harvard Crimson* that "it is thoroughly shameful for such a book to be banned in Boston at the very time when we need to examine every phase of our American race problems with something of Lillian Smith's care and wisdom." Matthiessen's movement in the direction of greater racial equality was nearly a decade before the US Supreme Court's decision in *Brown v. Board of Education*, banning segregation in schools, and more than twenty years before the US Supreme Court struck down the Commonwealth of Virginia's law prohibiting interracial marriage in *Loving v. Virginia*. From fighting racial discrimination to explicating Henry James's fiction, Matthiessen tried to encompass it all.

Henry James: The Major Phase surveys the writer's late, great novels: *The Ambassadors*, *The Wings of the Dove*, and *The Golden Bowl*. Matthiessen also included analysis and commentary on James's travelogue through America, *The American Scene*, and his unfinished novel, *The Ivory Tower*. As an appendix in the book, Matthiessen tacked on his essay about James's revisions to *The Portrait of a Lady* between its original publication in the United States in the *Atlantic Monthly* from November 1880 to December 1881 and the 1907 version of the book, known as the New York Edition. Matthiessen rooted James's own interests in painting in the broader nineteenth-century stress on sight. He noted how James used titles to convey imagery, such as in *The Golden Bowl* and *The Ivory Tower*, and made effective use of visual analogies, for example, when he compared the heroine in *The Wings of the Dove*, Milly Theale, to a Bronzino portrait. Presumably it was Cheney's influence that helped Matthiessen see the importance of seeing in Henry James, and Cheney rewarded him with a warm assessment of the book: "Reading the opening sections I love the sense of your growing easiness," Cheney told Matthiessen. "You write so well and give a feller a lovely sense of being in your confidence. You write much more easily now."

Beyond empathizing with the authors about whom he was writing, Matthiessen seems also at times to identify with some of the fictional characters in the books he is examining. As one scholar noted of *Henry James: The Major Phase*, Matthiessen wrote about characters as though they were real people. Throughout the chapter on *The Portrait of a Lady*, Matthiessen concentrates on James's revisions to the scenes in the novel between Isabel Archer and Casper Goodwood; Matthiessen picked up on the sexual energy that crackles between the two characters. And homoeroticism, in turn, infuses Matthiessen's writing. According to Matthiessen, "indomitable energy" characterizes Goodwood; James's readers feel the "overpowering sensation of his physical presence." And, finally, Isabel is "completely overpowered" by Goodwood. But Matthiessen had no language to be more open about how his own same-sex desire might be coloring his reading of Archer and Goodwood. As a result, his analysis seems circumscribed. Perhaps feeling some of Isabel Archer's own attraction to Caspar Goodwood, Matthiessen could not explore such a response fully, being careful not to reveal too much about himself and his own reactions to the book.

Critics of the day also noticed Matthiessen's increasingly political tone in *Henry James*. In *The Kenyon Review*, Philip Rahv cited Matthiessen's discussion of *The Golden Bowl*, writing: "To say that *The Golden Bowl* is morally deficient and decadent is one thing, but to claim that for this reason it is empty of life and, by implication, an inferior work of art is something else again. To my mind, this is an example of moral overreaction at the expense of literary judgment." And Robert Heilman, in his *New England Quarterly* review, felt similarly. Heilman liked Matthiessen's phrase, "religion of consciousness" for James's sensitivity to and awareness of morality in feeling and action. Heilman also agreed with Matthiessen that consciousness can come to carry a sense of social responsibility and therefore have "a kind of socio-political usefulness." But Heilman felt that Matthiessen had gone too far in demanding that the moral worldview in the works of James serve as a barometer of contemporary affairs. Heilman wrote that requiring literature to be "relevant to a crisis is likely to demand of a work of art, or a body of art, a kind of immediacy that it cannot of its nature possess." With Matthiessen's own increasing political activism and Cheney's withdrawal from their shared life, Matthiessen began to demand more from literature. It was not enough that a writer's words hold true in the symbolic world of art; Matthiessen wanted them to hold true in the political realm as well.

Contemporary critics have been mixed on *Henry James: The Major Phase*. In the late 1960s, the somewhat cranky critic and editor Maxwell Geismar felt that Matthiessen was "sentimental, uneasy, apologetic, and evasive" in his discussion of James's late novels. Geismar also criticized Matthiessen for failing to examine sexuality in James's work. Although Geismar picked up on the homoerotic elements in James's fiction, he didn't make the connection—at least in print—about that quality in James's work attracting Matthiessen's interest. Still, Geismar credited Matthiessen for bringing attention to James's work: "Harvard Professor F. O. Matthiessen . . . was largely responsible for the revival of 'the later James' and . . . [his] essay on *The Ambassadors* in particular, in *Henry James: The Major Phase*, set the tone for the received opinion of the novel." Geismar was not alone in this assessment. R. W. B. Lewis, a well-known American studies scholar and writer in the generation succeeding Matthiessen's, similarly praised Matthiessen's assessment of James's three late novels.

Henry James: The Major Phase was widely reviewed, and Oxford University Press honored Matthiessen in New York in November 1944 with a party for the book. Soon thereafter, Vanguard Press offered him a contract to write a book about Melville, and the *New*

York Times invited Matthiessen to speak at a symposium on the nation's current state of book reviewing, which over one thousand people attended. At the event Matthiessen was introduced as one of the leading critics in America. While in New York, he had dinner with the publisher Alfred A. Knopf Sr. to discuss a book about James's American stories and novels. Within the world of arts and letters, Matthiessen was now famous. He could be counted among a select group of scholars, writers, artists, and intellectuals in mid-twentieth-century America who helped shape the cultural discourse of the country.

And Matthiessen just kept working. In 1945, reviews and essays continued to stream from his pen. Matthiessen also began editing a collection of writings by other members of the James family and Henry James's notebooks, a project on which he collaborated with Kenneth Murdock. Matthiessen arranged with Harvard to take off without pay the fall semester of 1945. If he finished all his work in time, he wrote to Cheney, they might be able to make a trip together to the Southwest that winter.

Although Cheney's life was stable and productive in Texas, he once again grew bored with his relatives and missed livelier interactions with people. Rather than risk a reenactment of his ill-fated 1943 return to Kittery, he decided to go to one of his and Matthiessen's favorite places, Santa Fe. But Santa Fe was also not without problems or peril. In May 1944, Cheney could not make it there from his sister's home in Texas without falling in with a railroad man and a French veteran of World War I. The three men went on a drinking spree, which once again landed Cheney in the hospital. As with many alcoholics, Cheney careened between acquiescence and fear. "I don't know whether the relief to my spirits isn't more than the bad of drinking, just as long as I stop," he wrote to Matthiessen in May.

But six months later a new development appeared. Cheney seemed to recognize for himself that his drinking was a problem. As with many people suffering from addictions, seeing his problem as just that, a problem, was his first step toward liberation. He wrote to Matthiessen: "You and I know I just can not [*sic*] drink alcohol." Two months later, he wrote very straightforwardly: "The thing is for me to stop drinking. Without that we are OK, anywhere."

In the midst of this agonizing battle with alcohol, Cheney undertook a painting, *The Lost Cause* (1944), which engaged him as few others had. "It's been very exciting. I never reached an equal intensity in anything I've done before. It's so hard to stick to a high-pitch like that I near vomited once or twice," he wrote to Matthiessen. *The Lost Cause* depicts St. James the Greater on horseback as a carved wooden figurine known as a bulto, popular in the Southwest. There is an inherent paradox in seeing the patron of the conquistadors depicted as a toylike character. But there is great poignancy, as well, knowing that St. James was the first of the Apostles to be martyred. Did Cheney see himself as warrior? Or martyr? Or a little bit of both? Or was Cheney simply attracted to the bulto, as he was to so many other figurines and artifacts that he put in his paintings? Did he see it as an indigenously American expression of a European art form? And why did he choose that title? It is difficult to separate the painting from Cheney's struggles with alcohol—futile, but ennobled by valor. To some degree all of these associations were embodied in *The Lost Cause*, even if Cheney didn't have words for them. On some level, Cheney probably felt that he didn't need words—his paintings expressed everything he had to say.

In January 1945, Cheney returned to his sister's home in Boerne, Texas, before coming back to Kittery in the spring. Matthiessen and Cheney's correspondence during these months is at once both tender and heartbreaking. Matthiessen was by turns excited at the prospect of being reunited with Cheney and wary about his drinking. As always, he gladly acknowledged his indebtedness to Cheney's artistic eye. Matthiessen visited the Metropolitan Museum of Art in March 1945, after which he recalled his travels with Cheney in France, Holland, and England: "The best time of all was by myself at the Metropolitan Saturday morning. There is a [William Sidney] Mount show there, but after that I revisited for the first time in quite a while many of our favorites, and got some new impressions too. All of which made me realize how much you have taught me." Matthiessen hoped that they could have a peaceful and productive summer and fall together in Kittery. He even adopted the voice of their cat, Zuzu, and composed a short, playful poem to celebrate Cheney's impending arrival home:

Here I lie with sheathéd claws
Holding up my nether paws
Cold as haddock though they be,
They are Free from any FLEEA!

As usual, their playful language brought Matthiessen and Cheney closer together. But Matthiessen's warmth and love notwithstanding, he went on to add about their planned summer in Kittery: "I'm counting on our getting settled and am confident that you can establish a happy balance there—if you will only plan ahead to avoid the well known perils. So let's make it a good productive summer and fall." He signed it "My love, Pic."

Cheney, too, eagerly anticipated a "good steady time all summer." He was not drinking in April and May, feeling confident and thrilled to be coming home to Kittery. As if to get himself in the mood for his return to coastal Maine, he was rereading *Deephaven* by Sarah Orne Jewett.

"When the moon is full again, I'll be seeing it across Piscataqua waters with a green light and good smells of salt," Cheney wrote on May 6. In a literal sense, he referred to the green beacon of the lighthouse at Fort Constitution, which signals the entrance to Portsmouth Harbor, across the Piscataqua River, and is visible from the house that he shared with Matthiessen. But the highly literate Cheney was almost certainly alluding to the green light that Jay Gatsby watches longingly at the end of Daisy Buchanan's pier, a light that came to symbolize Gatsby's hope that his love for Daisy would make up for all the sordidness of his past as a bootlegger. Beyond that, the image of the green light is so fertile because it taps into a strong current of American thought: that everything can be made right, that the brightness of the future will make up for all the difficulties of the past.

This was Cheney's genius for living and use of literary allusions at its finest. It's also why Matthiessen loved him so. For Cheney had the ready and easy ability to hold in suspension both senses of the green light across the Piscataqua. Like Henry David Thoreau at Walden or Herman Melville in the belly of a whaling ship, Cheney knew the physical world in which he lived and worked. He intimately knew Kittery, Portsmouth, and the surrounding areas of the Maine and New Hampshire coasts; he had been painting them for years. But Cheney also had a ready command of literature and used it to enrich and broaden the associations that he and Matthiessen had with the green light of Fort Constitution. That Cheney's allusion to the green light was set against what had been a difficult time for them because of his drinking and hospitalizations only deepened the meaning. But it was Cheney's ability to link these different layers of meaning that so captivated Matthiessen. To watch and listen to Cheney correctly and seemingly effortlessly toss off these allusions allowed Matthiessen to experience firsthand some of the very qualities that he had analyzed in literature. Through Cheney, Matthiessen understood that in their relationship, in their life together at Kittery, and in their love for each other, they embodied all that America could promise.

Chapter 9

Losing Touch

Life without Cheney

Cheney had been back in Kittery since the end of May, and on July 12, 1945, the green light across the Piscataqua waters was one of the last scenes on which he closed his eyes. Not long after retiring upstairs that Wednesday night, he was felled by thrombosis, a blood clot in the circulatory system. In the morning Matthiessen looked up the back stairs leading from the kitchen to Cheney's room and saw the painter's feet protruding beyond the door jamb. As Matthiessen described to a reporter for the *Portsmouth Herald*, Cheney was still breathing when Matthiessen found him on the floor of his bedroom but died later that day at Portsmouth Hospital. He was sixty-three. The obituary in the *Portsmouth Herald* said he was best known for a painting in a local market of a chicken and vegetables.

On July 14, Cheney's body was returned to South Manchester. He was buried from the KD House, which was still owned by his brother Philip, the same house into which he had been born. Lavender, gladiolas, lilies, and red roses—all of which would have met with Cheney's approval—decorated the rooms for his funeral. Cheney was laid to rest in the family plot of the East Cemetery in Manchester.

In the end family reasserted itself in Cheney's death—and by extension Matthiessen's life. By this point, several of the Cheneys had developed an uneasy relationship with Matthiessen. The family had liked Matthiessen in the early days, when it seemed that he was just a housemate and good friend of Cheney's. But as the years went by and it became clearer that Matthiessen and Cheney were more than just friends, the family bristled. There were limits to tolerance. Matthiessen's presence at the funeral was an outward and unavoidable acknowledgment of Cheney's homosexuality, a fact that the family—not to mention the larger culture—preferred not to recognize. Moreover, the family resented that Matthiessen occupied a special place in Cheney's heart, as Helen Knapp reported in her written recollection of her uncle's death. As a result, at Cheney's funeral the family was outwardly courteous, but subterranean hostility flowed strongly toward Matthiessen. In his will, Cheney bequeathed his studio, adjacent buildings, and land in South Manchester to his brother Clifford. The house on Old Ferry Lane and two hundred unsold paintings were left to Matthiessen. But these were no consolation.

After Cheney's death Matthiessen's grief was nearly unbearable, and history is replete with stories of marriages in which one spouse barely survives the loss of the other. Matthiessen acknowledged that being at the house in Kittery was painful, but he opted to stay there instead of going away because, as he described to a friend, his pain was the closest thing he had to love. Perhaps it had been Matthiessen's happiness, the warmth and companionship of sharing his life with Cheney, along with the difficulties, that had imbued the flowers around the house, the old apple trees leading down to the water's edge, and the ocean with such loveliness? Now, with Cheney gone, the ocean looked colder, lonelier, and emptier.

What was Matthiessen like when he cried? Did he wrinkle his brow? Did his chest heave with sobs? Did he ball up his hands into fists in frustration? For Matthiessen, grief more than likely skirted rage. But there were probably fewer tears than might have been expected. Because Matthiessen could not live openly as a gay man, he was unable to grieve in a public way befitting the loss of a spouse. The Cheney family, the couple's friends, and many of

Matthiessen's colleagues and students knew the nature of their relationship, but to the world at large Matthiessen had simply lost his good "friend" and housemate. Not being able to grieve publicly, having to hide it, or at least dissimulate over the depth of his grief, most likely played into Matthiessen's deepening depression. What point was there in living, when the relationship that had been most vital and alive for him was not only gone but also suppressed, as though it had never existed? Notwithstanding the warm consolations of his closest friends and students, Matthiessen slipped into a depression that would last—with only a few bright spots intervening—for the rest of his life.

In the immediate wake of Cheney's death, as Matthiessen had already planned, he took a leave of absence from Harvard for the semester. This was especially fortunate, because bereavement leave for a same-sex partner was inconceivable at the time. Then just as he had also planned, Matthiessen worked and worked and worked. Matthiessen's books from the mid- to late 1940s included a monograph on Cheney's painting and career, *Russell Cheney: A Record of His Work*, and several others. None of these books— even the book on Cheney—was among Matthiessen's best. The grind of Matthiessen's relentless schedule had begun to show itself. But in the years just after Cheney's death, Matthiessen did find a certain degree of emotional and intellectual renewal at the Salzburg Seminar in American Studies, an American-led cultural exchange between West and East in the aftermath of World War II, and then at Charles University in Czechoslovakia, where he also taught.

From the late 1930s and into early 1940s, Matthiessen's political activism had steadily increased, and then after Cheney's death, it increased yet more. In Matthiessen's view, literature fed into political and moral problems. It was the job of literature to ask questions, whereas it was the job of politics to provide answers. As Cheney's health had deteriorated and he withdrew from Matthiessen's life, Matthiessen questioned the limits of art and literature's power. In response, Matthiessen moved further into the realm of political activism. But many of Matthiessen's contemporaries in the academy and the world of letters did not understand how a man who could be so sensitive, discerning, and judicious about literature could be so idealistic and strident about politics. The critic Ernest J. Simmons said that Matthiessen lacked a "clear and compelling political philosophy." And Alfred Kazin maintained that Matthiessen's political attachments "were not founded on any great intellectual passion" and largely served to counteract the "stultifications" of the academy. And this is what Matthiessen's friends said. One of the clearest assessments of Matthiessen's political activism came from his former student, historian Arthur Schlesinger Jr., who said that Matthiessen was wrong about many political matters, but he was wrong for the right reasons. Matthiessen's political activism did have one important consequence: it helped open up his views of what counts as canonical literature.

On numerous occasions Matthiessen maintained that he was not a Communist or even a Marxist but a Christian and Socialist. His reference to his Christianity may well have recalled his connection to his mother's Unitarian faith, as well as his own religious training as a young man. And as for not being a Communist or Marxist, this was true. He wasn't a member of the Communist Party, for all the good it did him, given his association with individuals and organizations having suspected links to Communists. In Matthiessen's support of Henry Wallace's 1948 presidential bid, he became known as a "fellow traveler." And the fevered pitch of those accusations became even more shrill after the publication of Matthiessen's book *From the Heart of Europe* about his experience teaching in Eastern Europe, in which he seriously misjudged the influence of the Communist Party in the 1948 Czechoslovakian coup. But none of it—teaching, books, or political activism—could entirely fend off the loneliness that opened up in Matthiessen's life so much wider and deeper after Cheney's death.

Compounding Matthiessen's sadness during the summer of 1945 was the need to euthanize Pretzel, the old and beloved cat whom he and Cheney shared and cherished. Before taking Pretzel to the veterinarian, Matthiessen held him in his lap for a long while as they looked out to Louisburg Square together. With the loss of Pretzel, Matthiessen said good-bye to yet another part of himself and his life with Cheney.

Matthiessen's first piece of writing published after Cheney's death was a review of a book of Walt Whitman's poetry and prose edited by Mark Van Doren. In the review, Matthiessen touched on homosexuality in a surprisingly candid way. Matthiessen noted that Van Doren "tends to shy away from the more physical aspects of Whitman." He went on to add that Van Doren had originally discounted Whitman's ideas about democracy because many were based on "manly love," and Matthiessen defended Whitman's letters to Peter Doyle, a horsecar conductor in Washington, DC, with whom Whitman enjoyed a romantic friendship. It was remarkable that Matthiessen would even mention "manly love" at all and defend it—albeit in a backhanded sort of way—in conjunction with Whitman. Matthiessen's tacit defense of Whitman's sexuality was a definite advance over his previous characterization of Whitman's sexuality in *American Renaissance* as "pathological."

That summer, Harvard released its survey of and recommendations for education in America entitled *General Education in a Free Society*. Written by a committee of primarily Harvard scholars, the report was three years in the making. Although most of the recommendations were fairly general, a chapter on Harvard made a series of more specific suggestions for the university, including—Matthiessen was probably not surprised to learn—altering and scaling back his beloved tutorial system. Matthiessen's review of the report, which appeared in the *New Republic* in August, just over a month after Cheney's death, reads as if it had become a focal point for his unhappiness.

For if Harvard wants to join America, one can only be grateful. It will be interesting to watch whether this commitment becomes real, whether, for instance, the university will now try to play a functional part in its own immediate community, instead of continuing to be a fenced-in oasis in the midst of the Cambridge jungle. As long as some of the handsome resident Houses look directly across the street at some of the worst slums in the city, built on Harvard-owned land, the violent contrast between "the two worlds" dramatized by Harvard graduate Dos Passos in *U.S.A.* will still remain. It would be a real job of local pioneering if the Harvard administration should decide that the members of a university have an active rather than a passive role in community welfare. Advance in all phases of city planning could then be looked for. And not the least of the results could be the relaxation of the racial tensions that now surge right up to the university's closed gates.

Matthiessen's review must have annoyed and angered some of his colleagues on the committee, not to mention President Conant. But in the context of Cheney's death, these words seem to have been written by a man who, having lost the emotional center of his life, felt he had nothing more to lose: Why not speak truth to power? Matthiessen's disenchantment with Harvard was so profound that he considered leaving for Brandeis in 1946.

But a curious thing happened with this review. To the editors of the conservative *Boston Herald*, it must have been surprising to read a nationally known, distinguished Harvard scholar publicly vent his anger and bitterness about his renowned employer. The *Herald* picked up Matthiessen's review, quoted from it liberally, and ran it as a news story. Matthiessen's words were bold enough that a reference to the *Herald* story found its way into his FBI file, where the agent who summarized the story simply took it as an indication of Matthiessen's Communist leanings.

Later that fall, Matthiessen worked diligently to organize retrospectives of Cheney's work for the following spring. In conjunction with the exhibitions, he wrote the manuscript that would become *Russell Cheney: A Record of His Work*, published first in 1946. The book amounted to a thinly veiled love letter and an undisguised effort to burnish Cheney's reputation and secure his artistic legacy. Matthiessen knew that Cheney was a talented painter, and he was determined that the world was also going to know it. Matthiessen initially paid $1,920 (approximately $28,000 in 2021 dollars) to have five hundred copies of the book printed privately by the Andover Press. He put money of his own into the project and raised additional funds from Cheney's family and friends.

In March 1947, the Ferargil Galleries in New York mounted the first posthumous retrospective of Cheney's work, followed by an exhibition at the Wadsworth Atheneum. The critical response to these shows was warm and laudatory. Frederic Newlin Price, the proprietor of Ferargil, described Cheney as "a New England and American master." By far, the overwhelming first assessment of Cheney's career emphasized the importance of the northern New England coast of Maine and New Hampshire in his paintings. In conjunction with these shows, Oxford University Press published a trade edition of *Russell Cheney: A Record of His Work*, and Matthiessen successfully reached out to a number of critics and reviewers at both mainstream and art publications to drum up interest in the exhibitions and the monograph.

To this day, *Russell Cheney: A Record of His Work* remains the most comprehensive single volume about the painter's career. The groundwork for the book had begun in the earliest days of the two men's relationship, when in a 1925 letter Matthiessen tried to elicit details from Cheney about his painting: "I know that one of the things I look forward to with the greatest anticipation is digging in and going through all of your past work with you. For apart from my love for you, the study of the development of your technique gives me a big intellectual kick. And how else am I going to write your biography in the year 1970?" Cheney's biography arrived twenty-five years earlier than planned. Overall, *Russell Cheney* is a favorable assessment as if written by a friend. And it is less written than curated. Matthiessen selected and reproduced sixty-five images of paintings, all in black and white. Interspersed between reproductions are excerpts from Cheney's letters to Matthiessen and Putnam, mostly regarding the influences on Cheney's painting, his ideas about painting, his work habits, and a running commentary on whatever he was painting at the time. Matthiessen provided some general biographical references and summarized periods in Cheney's life to move the reader along through the book.

The finished product leaves discerning readers with a clear idea of the "open secret" that undergirds it: Matthiessen and Cheney's loving partnership. In selecting Cheney's letters to both himself and Putnam for publication, Matthiessen tried to imply editorially that they were equally close friends with Cheney. Yet for all Matthiessen's dissembling, reviewers seemed to pick up on the especially intimate nature of his and Cheney's relationship. Jerome Mellquist, the art critic and a friend of Matthiessen's, pushed the boundary of publicly acceptable relationships between two men when he referred to Matthiessen as Cheney's "long-time companion" in his review in the *New York Times*. Perhaps even more interesting, Dorothy Adlow, the art critic for the *Christian Science Monitor*, quoted an early Cheney letter to Matthiessen from the book: "I want to establish my life quietly . . . at Kittery, and concentrate on things that mean something." The ellipsis was the result of Matthiessen's editorial hand, and it replaced the simple words "with you." Cheney told Matthiessen that he wanted to establish his life "with you at Kittery." For Cheney, Matthiessen's presence made life in Kittery significant and enabled him to concentrate on those things that mattered most to him. With the instincts of a good journalist and critic, Adlow chose this important passage in *Russell Cheney*, even if history hid from her the full meaning of its significance.

In February 1947, Matthiessen's book *The American Novels and Stories of Henry James* was published, and he learned that Princeton University was awarding him an honorary degree—to add to his degrees from Yale, Oxford, and Harvard. Meanwhile, the FBI's surveillance noose was tightening, which now had a sample of Matthiessen's handwriting in the form of a personal note stolen from or turned over by someone at Little, Brown, the publisher. Journalist Ella Winter had asked Matthiessen to review *Man against Myth* by Barrows Dunham and published by Little, Brown and Company for the *New York Times Book Review*. Matthiessen knew Winter through her husband, screenwriter Donald Ogden Stewart, who had gone to Yale and was in Skull and Bones. In response to Winter's request, Matthiessen sent a note to a contact at Little, Brown acknowledging receipt of *Man against Myth* from the publicity department but regretting that he would not be able to review it. Matthiessen signed his note "As Ever, Matty," suggesting that he knew the person to whom he wrote reasonably well.

In all likelihood, Matthiessen sent his note to Angus Cameron, then editor in chief at Little, Brown. Dunham credited Cameron, together with Winter and Stewart, for their support of *Man against Myth* in the preface to the book. In addition to his position at Little, Brown, Cameron was also head of the Progressive Party in Massachusetts and went on to become the national treasurer of Henry Wallace's 1948 presidential campaign as the Progressive Party candidate. Against the backdrop of increasingly polarized political factions of the Cold War, a number of influential people, including Eleanor Roosevelt, were uneasy about the Progressive Party's willingness to work with Communists. Given this concern, a number of high-ranking officials within the Progressive Party were presumably being watched at the time by the FBI. Without an unredacted copy of Matthiessen's FBI file, there is no way to know who turned over Matthiessen's note to the agency. But given Cameron's association with the Progressive Party, it's quite likely that someone engaged to spy on him at Little, Brown passed it on.

Held at bay for so many years by his loving partnership with Cheney, Matthiessen's search for companionship reappeared in his life after Cheney's death. Relief, however, came from an unexpected quarter over the summer of 1947, the Salzburg Seminar in American Studies in Austria. It proved to be one of the happiest teaching experiences of Matthiessen's life, in large measure because he was living and studying in close quarters with a group of sympathetic students. To a lesser extent, these same qualities informed Matthiessen's experience at Prague, following Salzburg.

In the aftermath of World War II, even in those areas not physically destroyed by the war, much of the social fabric of Europe lay in tatters. Sporadic and insufficient food supplies barely fed the population. Numerous women, and likely not a few men, traded sexual favors for food. Rape, looting, and theft were rampant. Hoping in some small way to help revive war-ravaged Europe, three young Harvard men—Scott Elledge, an English instructor; Clemens Heller, an Austrian-born graduate student; and Richard Campbell, a college senior—inaugurated the Salzburg Seminar in American Studies, and Matthiessen was with them from the first. The seminar grew out of the World Student Relief program and focused for six weeks on American history and literature, social sciences, and fine arts. The US government, for its part, allowed ventures like the Salzburg Seminar to spring up, because in the early days of the Cold War, they were useful tools of cultural diplomacy and American soft power in the battle to win the hearts and minds in a politically divided Europe. In its first year, the seminar brought together ninety-seven students from seventeen countries at the rococo eighteenth-century Schloss Leopoldskron, a mile outside of Salzburg. On a bare-bones budget, the seminar picked up the travel expenses of the students and some of the faculty, but the instructors were expected to donate their teaching services.

The founders initially sought support for the seminar from President Conant, but he told them that it was "too idealistic, too impractical, too premature." Conant's lack of support must only have increased Matthiessen's desire to participate. In its first year, the seminar attracted many scholars, writers, and critics to teach, including Margaret Mead in anthropology, Virgil Thomson in music, and Alfred Kazin and Matthiessen in American literature.

In Mead's assessment, Matthiessen and Kazin's lectures "communicated the sense of a living literature, and of a culture to which self-criticism is a necessary condition of life."

The Salzburg Seminar was in many ways the perfect setting for Matthiessen—the thing that he longed for throughout much of his life, a tight-knit community with an "air of a commune ... transplanted to a dilapidated baroque castle," as one contemporary scholar has written. As Matthiessen wrote to Louis Hyde, Salzburg provided "the most valuable teaching experience of my life so far." The scholar Daniel Aaron, who had been a student of Matthiessen's and later taught at Salzburg himself, described Matthiessen's students at the seminar as an ideal group for him, aesthetically inclined and politically liberal. Alfred Kazin, however, felt that Matthiessen's "lonely passion" attracted his students more than his literary ideas, which Kazin felt were fairly traditional. Still, Kazin conceded that Matthiessen was the "star" of Salzburg during its inaugural year.

Matthiessen's months of teaching in Europe were more than simply a break from dealing with his grief over Cheney and his growing sense of alienation from Harvard. He was perhaps discovering a degree of liberation. Because of Cheney's prolonged absences from their home together, Matthiessen had been acutely lonely in the years leading up to Cheney's death, but at Salzburg, with the sense of isolation temporarily at bay, Matthiessen may have felt a degree of relief and peace about Cheney's death. Cheney had been physically ill and often disengaged for a number of years, and his repeated hospitalizations for long stretches of time took a toll on them both. His cycle of drinking sprees followed by bafflement, remorse, guilt, and yet another hospitalization must have been alternately frustrating, enraging, and agonizing for Matthiessen to watch. Awful as Cheney's death was, it preempted a descent into ever greater ravages of alcoholism that could have played out excruciatingly for several more years. In the warm and genial atmosphere of Salzburg, perhaps Matthiessen even allowed himself the thought that Cheney's death was for the best.

This is not to imply that Matthiessen was any less devoted to Cheney's memory—quite the contrary. Unable to attend another retrospective of Cheney's paintings in Boston in the fall of 1947 because he was in Eastern Europe, Matthiessen asked a friend for an "exact" list of titles, newspaper clippings about the show, and even a diagram of how the paintings had been hung in the gallery.

Maybe it was this admixture of relief and sadness that was behind Matthiessen's reading of *The Waste Land* one evening to a group of students and colleagues in Salzburg:

> April is the cruellest month, breeding
Lilacs out of the dead land, mixing
Memory and desire, stirring
> Dull roots with spring rain.

Kazin described listening to Matthiessen read as "an unforgettable experience of the kind of cultural solidarity that can arise in a group when the lecturer unites it by his conviction and creative emotion." As Matthiessen wrote in *American Renaissance*, experience was the quality that most strongly influenced the human voice. His love for Cheney and his own suffering had imbued his voice with this experience.

After Matthiessen finished at Salzburg in late August and still on leave from Harvard, he spent October and November at Charles University in Prague, teaching another course on American literature. Matthiessen's students in Prague were equally as fond of him as were those at Salzburg. On the feast day of St. Francis, October 4, they honored him because of his first name. Matthiessen described how students took him by the shoulders and feet and tossed him in the air. The young men shook his hand, and the young women kissed him. In his notebooks from his trip, Matthiessen described feeling really "in" after this party, and the ever-receding glow of Skull and Bones initiation rituals probably contributed to Matthiessen's warm associations with this experience.

While in Czechoslovakia, Matthiessen met with the influential foreign minister Jan Masaryk, as well as with many top officials from the ministry of education. Surprisingly, Matthiessen did not record people's names or their titles in his notebooks, and at one point he conceded that "there were so many other meetings that I can't keep them all straight." Matthiessen's discussions with Czechoslovakian officials often seemed to take place in the abstract. Regarding his conversation with Masaryk, Matthiessen wrote nothing about its substance, only that he welcomed its informality. In more formal meetings, Matthiessen seemed to have specialized in big, open-ended questions, along the lines of "What does the Social Democratic Party want?," which he posed to the minister of education. The nitty-gritty of concrete political dynamics in Czechoslovakia eluded Matthiessen, nor did he seem to appreciate the breadth and depth of Cold War intrigue.

In October 1947, while Matthiessen was in Europe, *The James Family: Including Selections from the Writings of Henry James, Senior, William, Henry, and Alice James* was published. As with *Russell Cheney*, *The James Family* is more curated or edited than written, although as one reviewer noted, a not insignificant amount of work went into assembling the writings of the various James family members. Matthiessen highlighted many of his time-honored themes, such as fellowship and fraternity. Gleaned from their letters, Matthiessen offered a portrait of the relationship between William and Henry James, which was remarkably intimate, honest, and forthright. Matthiessen also once again shined a light onto a previously overlooked or underappreciated figure, the diarist Alice James. Matthiessen takes Alice and her writings seriously, crediting her, for example, with a more acute understanding of the "economic make-up of society" than either of her two more famous brothers.

Then just ten days after the publication of *The James Family*, *The Notebooks of Henry James* was published. James's notebooks are not diaries but workbooks in which he recorded his "impressions" and nursed them until they grew into stories and novels. *The Notebooks*, as edited by Matthiessen and Kenneth Murdock, are heavy with their commentary tracing how germs of ideas diverged from the actual finished story or novel, summarizing plots, or providing the details of publication. Matthiessen and Murdock's commentary did not often venture into extracting larger ideas or themes in James's work; rather, they were engaged in the careful editing of *The Notebooks* so that they would be more accessible to readers.

In general, the critics of Matthiessen's day appreciated *The James Family* and *The Notebooks*. The prominent exception was the influential critic Edmund Wilson of the *New Yorker*. Wilson disliked the "copious commentary" throughout *The Notebooks of Henry James* and thought that Matthiessen and Murdock got out in front of their subject a little too much. That Matthiessen and Murdock had access to James's notebooks, when other writers and scholars did not, also irritated Wilson. He went on to add sharply that "Mr. Matthiessen is intelligent and imaginative enough to be able to grasp his subject, but this compilation, too, betrays a certain looseness of method and doughiness of mind."

In the past, reviewers and critics disagreed with Matthiessen on intellectual grounds or quibbled with him over minor points, but Wilson's review questioned the quality of Matthiessen's scholarship. Even discounting some of Wilson's criticism owing to professional jealousy, much of what he wrote was true. Although Matthiessen brought previously unpublished material to a wider reading public, he seemed to have been going through the motions of editing the compilations without absorbing and reflecting on his material. By Matthiessen's own high standard of how best to read, he fell short: he did not internalize the writings of the James family or Henry James's notebooks. The quality of the James books and Wilson's comments raise the question of whether Matthiessen's relentless pace in terms of both his scholarship and his political activities was beginning to wear on him and spread even his formidable talents too thin. In 1947,

Matthiessen published three books, wrote assorted reviews and essays, and spoke at several political events outside his teaching duties. And this was all before spending half of the year in Salzburg and Prague.

Whatever the limitations of *The James Family* and *The Notebooks*, Matthiessen's influence on the reputations of these literary figures extended well into the second half of the twentieth century. In giving standing to Alice James, Matthiessen was once again pushing the boundaries of the literary canon. The biographer Jean Strouse did not begin working on Alice James's life and writings until the 1970s. But Strouse recalled that it was Matthiessen's stature and his serious treatment of Alice James in *The James Family* that gave her the "green light" to pursue her project on the lone James daughter. R. W. B. Lewis, in his book *The Jameses: A Family Narrative* (1991), which was a finalist for the National Book Award, drew heavily on Matthiessen's James family book as well as Henry James's *Notebooks*. Matthiessen and Murdock's edition of the *Notebooks* was the only available version until Lyall H. Powers and Leon Edel, the great scholar of Henry James's life and work, brought out a new edition in 1987. The critic Maxwell Geismar was sarcastic, funny, and admiring of the *Notebooks* especially. In discussing Matthiessen and Murdock's analysis of *The Figure in the Carpet*, Geismar felt they were "more pontifical, orotund and pretentious than the Master himself." But Geismar also acknowledged that the *Notebooks* as edited by Matthiessen and Murdock were a "most useful work of Jamesian scholarship."

President Franklin Delano Roosevelt's death at Warm Springs, Georgia, in April 1945 cast a shadow over the nation, but the country's mood brightened considerably later that summer with the ending of World War II. By this time an estimated 30 percent of the American workforce had joined a union. Sensing its opportunity, big business struck back with the passage of the Taft-Hartley Act in June 1947. Taft-Hartley allowed individual states to pass "right to work" legislation, which provided that union membership could not be required as a condition of employment. The law also outlawed industry-wide boycotts and created provisions for employers to sue unions over secondary boycotts. Importantly, Taft-Hartley excluded foremen and supervisors from union membership. The Foreman's Association of America had allied itself with the Congress of Industrial Organizations (CIO), which had broadened the definition of working class to include managers and undercut notions of unified management.

Taft-Hartley laid the foundation for an internecine battle for the soul of the political Left. Taft-Hartley required union officials to sign an affidavit that they were not Communists. As a result, strident anti-Communists clashed with the more open and inclusive voices on the left. George Meany of the American Federation of Labor called the leadership of the CIO "devoted followers of Moscow." At its 1949 convention, the CIO expelled nine left-leaning unions that had supported Henry Wallace in the 1948 presidential election.

The country's history of racism also figured into these same dynamics within organized labor. Given slavery, sharecropping, and states' rights, the South stood firmly against unionism. In response, unionized northern textile mills began to move south, seeking cheaper operating costs. The CIO tried to organize workers in the South, but with little success. As one CIO organizer claimed, for a region that had fairly recently emerged from deep poverty, nonunionized factory jobs were progress. People in the region weren't going to risk good jobs by aligning themselves with labor unions.

When Matthiessen came back to the United States from Eastern Europe, the first half of 1948 was eventful in ways he could not have begun to imagine. He was inducted into the National Institute of Arts and Letters (which later merged into the American Academy of Arts and Letters); delivered two important lectures at Vassar College and at Yale on the state of arts and culture in late 1940s America; taught at the Kenyon School of

English, a summer literary institute, which he had cofounded; and wrote a review for the *New York Times* about the critic Paul Rosenfeld, and an essay for the *Sewanee Review* about poet John Crowe Ransom and the importance of minor artists in creating a vibrant society. Cheney was almost certainly in the back of Matthiessen's mind on this subject.

Matthiessen was also named as a potential enemy of the United States by the Federal Bureau of Investigation. On February 17, the FBI added Matthiessen's name to its "key figure" list, because Matthiessen was associated with at least eight organizations that Attorney General Tom Clark had identified as subversive a few months earlier. These organizations included the American Committee to Protect the Foreign Born, American Peace Mobilization, American Youth for Democracy, International Labor Defense, Joint Anti-Fascist Refugee Committee, National Federation for Constitutional Liberties, the Samuel Adams School in Boston, and the Massachusetts chapter of the National Council of American-Soviet Friendship.

Later that year, on July 24, 1948, Matthiessen emerged in Philadelphia to second the nomination of Henry Wallace as the Progressive Party candidate for president in a four-way race with Democrat incumbent Harry Truman; Republican Thomas E. Dewey; and a Dixiecrat, a southern Democrat mounting an independent bid, Strom Thurmond. Wallace had been secretary of agriculture, secretary of commerce, and vice president under FDR. In December 1946, after Roosevelt's death, when Wallace had been let go from the Truman cabinet, he became an editor at the *New Republic*, the left-leaning magazine, based in New York, to which Matthiessen frequently contributed. Matthiessen's liberal political sensibility hewed closely to the platform of the Progressive Party, which stood for desegregation, equal rights for women, a national health insurance program, public day care, direct election of presidents, full taxation of capital gains, and public ownership of banks, railroads, and utilities. Wallace and the Progressives also supported the United Nations and peaceful relations with the Soviet Union in the early days of the Cold War. The problem was how to achieve these laudable goals.

Matthiessen's speech at the Progressive Party convention in the Bellevue Stratford Hotel contained many of his time-honored themes, such as his distrust of finance capitalism. Yet Matthiessen also cast Wallace and the Progressive Party platform into a larger cultural context. It was in this sense that his speech was most eloquent. He cited Wallace as the inheritor of Wendell Wilkie's "One World" campaign, Benjamin Franklin's common sense, and the democratic writings of Roger Williams, Emerson, and William James. In his speech, Matthiessen made the important distinction that Wallace had not only read the works of these writers but "his mind had been nourished by them as philosophers of democracy." (Even if Matthiessen himself had on occasion fallen short of his own high ideal in recent years regarding internalizing one's reading, it was still the yardstick by which he judged.) In closing his speech, Matthiessen credited Wallace with having a "mind open to experience and thus capable of growth."

America was scarcely ready for such subtlety and nuance in its political discourse, especially with the growing fear of Communist subversion. With its openness to members regardless of political affiliation, and given that some of its members actually did have ties to the Communists, the Progressive Party found itself turned into a lightning rod during the Red Scare. Prominent anti-Communist liberals distanced themselves from the Progressives and imputed Communist influence to the Progressive Party. Meanwhile, actual leaders within the Communist Party of America tried to exploit their connection to Wallace. By the time of the Philadelphia convention, Wallace and the Progressive Party had been effectively tarred with the Communist brush. Although few people actually believed that Wallace was a card-carrying Communist, many believed that he was a "fellow traveler" or a "pink," who in their gullibility provided cover for Communist front organizations in the United States. These same terms were later applied to Matthiessen. One of Matthiessen's friends at Harvard, the poet and translator John Ciardi, for example, told Matthiessen that he was being used by the Progressive Party. When the nation went to the polls that year, Wallace received only 2.4 percent of the popular vote and not a single vote in the Electoral College.

Part memoir, part travelogue, part essay, Matthiessen's book *From the Heart of Europe* was published in September 1948. Nominally an account of Matthiessen's half year in Salzburg and Prague, the book is personal, informal, and reflective. In many ways, sections of *From the Heart of Europe* were as close to autobiography as Matthiessen came in his public writing. Several years after Matthiessen's death, the editors of a memorial volume about him culled much of their material for their biographical sketch from this book.

Not surprisingly, some of Matthiessen's most beautiful writing in *From the Heart of Europe* centers on Cheney, literature, painting, and Maine. In one particularly lovely evocation of Cheney, Matthiessen wrote:

> At every turn that gives a vista of the medieval Festung [fortress] to the hill or through the poplars to the swiftly rushing gray river, or, more particularly, at every intimate sight that requires an alert eye to pick it out at all: a half-hidden baroque crest over a door or an unexpectedly bright splash of color from a window box of geraniums or petunias at the end of an alley—at any delight of the eye in any place I ever was with Russell Cheney I am pierced with the realization of how much he taught me to see, or how life shared with him took on more vividness than I have ever felt in any other company. When I notice something new or changed here, I find myself speaking it in my mind to him, just as the evening I heard *Così fan tutte* I was hearing it again with him and Hanns. This is the only sense in which immortality has a meaning which I have experienced: these friends are as present to me now as when we were here together. And the evocation of their spirits by so many concrete reminders is, for the most part, not painful, since they bring with them many of the best hours I have known.

For a public document, Matthiessen's writing is strikingly personal and intimate—and very much at odds with the devastation around him in Eastern Europe. Matthiessen recounts the summer of 1931 when he and Cheney went in search of Vermeer's paintings in Holland and Cheney's enthusiasm for Adriaen Isenbrant's painting *Rest on the Flight into Egypt*. He cites the importance of Walt Whitman's poetry, particularly "Calamus" and "The Children of Adam," in helping him learn to trust bodily pleasures. His thoughts go back to Kittery friends such as Howard Lathrop, whom Cheney painted in 1937. A walk in the snow in the Czechoslovakian countryside reminds Matthiessen of similar walks in Maine. Even as Matthiessen questioned the limits of the power of art and literature, there is a marked equivalence among his recollections of personal and aesthetic experiences, which he weaves together effortlessly. Literature and painting enrich the experience of being alive, and in Matthiessen's worldview, aesthetic experience is just as vital to the formation of character as lived experience.

There is also a wistfulness to Matthiessen's writing in *From the Heart of Europe* that seems to have been triggered by his recognition of a slight crack in the world's hostile attitude toward homosexuality—and his inability to follow the world's lead. In discussing the wasted opportunities of secondary education in *From the Heart of Europe*, Matthiessen gives as his example Charles Griffes, who taught at the Hackley School. Matthiessen describes seeing Griffes sitting alone at the end of a corridor at the school reading one literary classic after another: Dostoyevsky, Flaubert, and many others. But it was only on reading Edward Maisel's 1943 biography of Griffes that Matthiessen learned Griffes had been a well-regarded composer. What Matthiessen does not say was that he also learned that Griffes was a gay man, because Maisel wrote very straightforwardly and largely without judgment about Griffes's homosexuality and his longtime relationship with a New York City police officer.

But Matthiessen, now the internationally recognized scholar, could not follow in Maisel's footsteps or those of Alfred C. Kinsey, Wardell B. Pomeroy, and Clyde E. Martin, whose *Sexual Behavior in the Human Male* he also read soon after it had been published in 1948. Matthiessen could not "come out" in the pages of *From the Heart of Europe*, though his tribute to Cheney would have been nearly impossible to miss for anyone skilled at reading between the lines. This tension of not being able to write—or feel free to write—what Matthiessen most wanted to contributes to the sense of missed opportunities that permeates *From the Heart of Europe*.

If Matthiessen was melancholy about his own life in the book, he was uncomfortably naive about the political situation in Czechoslovakia. Matthiessen's lack of experience in the larger political arena was most apparent in his handling of the Communist coup that occurred just three months after his return to the United States and six months before the publication of *From the Heart of Europe*. In February 1948, after months of increasingly open maneuvering and with the obvious support of the Soviet Union, Communists seized control of the government in Czechoslovakia. The premier, a Stalinist named Klement Gottwald, set up "action committees" in plants, shops, offices, universities, and other nonpolitical organizations to "purge" these institutions of people disloyal to the Communist state. Even at Charles University, where Matthiessen had taught, the rector and numerous professors were removed. The Communist minister of education coolly noted that although university professors maintained autonomy, that did "not mean freedom to agitate and organize intrigues." The Communist-controlled police force arrested opponents and suppressed nonparty newspapers. The abrogation of civil liberties unnerved many in the United States, and various American journalists loudly decried the hand of the Soviet Union behind the coup.

In his book, Matthiessen deals with the Czechoslovakian crisis by simply adding a footnote that condemns the Western press for increasing bilateral tensions. He urges his readers to "remember that the new government was brought into existence by the people of Czechoslovakia, not by the Russians." On radio and in print, Matthiessen maintained that the Soviet Union had exerted little military influence in Czechoslovakia, because he had seen so little evidence of it with his own eyes. "The Czechs regard the Soviet Union with gratitude for their liberation," he said at a Harvard forum just days in advance of the coup. Matthiessen was also unwilling to condemn the action committees, claiming that they were more broadly representative than had been depicted in the American press. Later, he blamed "biased" journalists for exaggerating Soviet influence and said that the Iron Curtain existed primarily in the minds of the American people.

Even Masaryk's mysterious death in March 1948, in which he was either thrown or jumped from a window of his apartment at the Czernin Palace in Prague, did not seem to move Matthiessen. Many in Czechoslovakia and the United States believed Masaryk had been killed by the newly installed Communist government. But in a written statement on Masaryk's death, Matthiessen sidestepped the matter almost entirely, simply supporting the United Nations and rejecting the Truman Doctrine, a post–World War II effort of the US government that provided political, military, and economic assistance to democratically elected governments, notably those of Greece and Turkey, in an attempt to block the spread of Communism. It was an oddly impersonal response from a man who valued human relationships so greatly.

History has largely shown that Matthiessen's reading of events in Czechoslovakia was naive. Both American and Soviet foreign ministers entered the country in advance of the coup, and the Soviet foreign minister deliberated with Czech Communists during the coup. In addition, members of the Russian secret police had been flown to Prague from Moscow, and Soviet troops were stationed at the Austrian border. Historians have maintained that Stalin was knowledgeable about the coup in Czechoslovakia and wanted the Czech Communists to ask for Russian assistance. Even though Matthiessen saw few Soviet troops on the ground in Prague during the fall of 1947, history has implicated Soviet influence in the coup.

If Matthiessen had felt alone before the publication of *From the Heart of Europe*, he must surely have felt almost completely isolated after its release into the headwinds of the Cold War and greater polarization both in the general population and on the political left. Several reviewers liked *From the Heart of Europe*, but nearly all acknowledged that Matthiessen's misjudgment of the Soviets and their links to the Communist coup in Czechoslovakia weakened the book.

In the *Nation*, for instance, Franz Hoellering said that Matthiessen's political actions were "less governed by those truths which he has found for himself than by those noble feelings and immature longings which are exploited by demagogues everywhere." The Socialist critic Irving Howe in *Partisan Review* offered the backhanded compliment that Matthiessen was "the most distinguished literary fellow-traveler in this country." Howe also commended Matthiessen for his engagement in politics but then took him to task for his failure to look closely at the substance and facts of Communism, particularly in the Soviet Union under Stalin. That Matthiessen did not report in *From the Heart of Europe* what Stalinist leaders actually said at a rally he attended, rather than how he felt about the experience, infuriated Howe. Howe's critique was trenchant and not without merit.

But at least Howe was wrestling with the intellectual and political substance of Matthiessen's ideas in *From the Heart of Europe*. It was a different story in *Time*, under Henry Luce, Matthiessen's Skull and Bones brother, who was staunchly anti-Communist. This review was downright caustic, dismissing Matthiessen as a "bald, mild-mannered little bachelor" —almost certainly a coded suggestion of homosexuality—who was a prime example of "the gullibility and wishful thinking of pinkish academic intellectuals." In the burgeoning post–World War II prosperity in the United

States, *Time* scoffed at Matthiessen for his questioning of capitalism or willingness to consider alternatives to the American system
of government. In response to the critical reviews, Matthiessen
dug in. He had never been the type to capitulate easily on intellectual matters, and the hostile reviews were no exception. He
remained largely quiet in print, but to friends and later in public
forums he attacked his attackers.

During this time, the loss of friends and family compounded
Matthiessen's isolation. Phelps Putnam died in July 1948 at age
fifty-four. Then Matthiessen's father, Frederick W. Matthiessen Jr.,
died in an automobile accident in Santa Monica in November of
that year. At the time of the elder Matthiessen's death, he held the
controlling interest in Westclox and had become a successful real
estate developer in his own right, having sold tracts of land from
his vast ranches in California. Although still not particularly close
to his father, Matthiessen was named as a beneficiary of a trust set
up by his father that generated about $16,000 per year in income
(approximately $178,000 in 2021 dollars)—roughly 25 percent
more than Matthiessen's yearly salary at Harvard. Matthiessen
had felt like an orphan back in 1923, when his mother died, but
now with the death of his father, his status became official. And
soon into the new year, Theodore Spencer, one of Matthiessen's
few remaining friends on the Harvard faculty, suffered a fatal
heart attack at age forty-five.

Early in 1949, the last full year of his life, Matthiessen once again
found himself embroiled in a largely mean-spirited controversy
in connection with the Cultural and Scientific Conference for
World Peace in New York at the Waldorf Astoria. The House
Un-American Activities Committee branded the conference
and many of its participants as Communists or Communist
sympathizers. Influential intellectuals, led by the staunch anti-
Communist Sidney Hook of New York University, spoke out
against the conference, while an estimated two thousand people,

many from right-wing groups, such as the American Legion, picketed outside in protest. Matthiessen participated in a panel on writing and publishing chaired by W. E. B. Du Bois and attended by over eight hundred people, and he gave a talk in which he highlighted Thoreau's "Essay on Civil Disobedience." During the following question-and-answer session, Mary McCarthy, a writer associated with mid-twentieth-century New York intellectuals and already known for her acerbic and combative stances on literature and politics, challenged Matthiessen sharply: "What would have happened to Thoreau if he made a consistent effort, or even a mild effort, to practice civil disobedience in the Soviet Union today?" "I do not think that Emerson and Thoreau could exist very well in the present Soviet Union," Matthiessen replied. "Nor do I think that great figures like Lenin could have existed very well in twentieth-century America." When the House Un-American Activities Committee released its review of the conference, the *Boston Herald* picked up the story and ran it under the headline, "5 Mass. Educators Held Dupes." Professor F. O. Matthiessen was among the five. (In this context, "dupes" are people who are easily deceived by and unwitting allies of Communists.)

Worse was to come from *Life* magazine—sister publication to *Time*—which then shaped the national discourse to an extent unimaginable today for a magazine. On April 4, 1949, *Life* ran a profile of the conference, which featured a related two-page spread of fifty "dupes" and "fellow travelers," well-known liberal politicians, artists, scholars, writers, clergy, and others. Matthiessen was among those pictured. As J. C. Levenson tells the story, Matthiessen, together with Levenson and his wife, had been at the opera. When they came out of the performance, Matthiessen saw the *Life* story on a newsstand. He was shocked by the story and felt a deep sense of betrayal. It was one thing to be called a Communist sympathizer; it was another thing to be called one in essence by Henry Luce. As Matthiessen had gotten older, his enthusiasm for his Skull and Bones friendships had dimmed, just as Cheney had predicted. But being named a fellow traveler by Luce fueled Matthiessen's growing sense of disillusionment and called into question another of his bedrock principles of reality—fraternity.

Then just a few days later in Boston, Joseph B. Matthews, former research director of the House Un-American Activities Committee, named Matthiessen in a state legislative hearing as being an active supporter of Communist-front organizations in Massachusetts. It has been repeated on several occasions that Matthiessen testified before the House Un-American Activities Committee in Washington, DC, or had been subpoenaed to testify. Writers often cite either Paul Sweezy's profile of Matthiessen's "Labor and Political Activities" in *The Collective Portrait* or Frederick C. Stern's reference in *F. O. Matthiessen: Christian Socialist as Critic* as proof. This is incorrect. Matthiessen did not testify before the House Un-American Activities Committee, nor was he subpoenaed to testify, because no preparatory file had been created about him. In all likelihood, however, after Matthews's public declaration of Matthiessen's supposed Communist ties and sympathies, Matthiessen may well have testified, and perhaps on more than one occasion, before various state-level legislative committees investigating alleged subversive and Communist activity in Massachusetts. At the time of Matthews's claim in Massachusetts, he was no longer serving in his official capacity to the House Un-American Activities Committee but was working as a consultant to state legislatures and corporations concerned about Communism.

After the end of the school year, Matthiessen traveled to California to meet with Sara White Dreiser, Theodore Dreiser's widow, and begin a sabbatical to work on his literary biography of Dreiser. Throughout the fall and into the spring, Matthiessen wrestled with his materials about Dreiser's life and work. He spent much of his time at Kittery, as he worked on the manuscript. He had quiet at Kittery, but without his students or close friends around, he was also isolated practically as well as emotionally. And isolation was not healthy for Matthiessen, given his tendency to work obsessively. As the manuscript that became *Theodore Dreiser* began to emerge, Matthiessen was scheduled to travel to Europe in late May 1950: first to Paris, where he would stay with his former research assistant who had worked with him on *American Renaissance*, Stanley Geist, and his wife, Eileen. From Paris, Matthiessen planned to go on to Italy and then to Austria to teach again at the Salzburg Seminar.

But if happiness beckoned across the Atlantic, subterranean thoughts and emotions simultaneously compelled Matthiessen toward a darker course. Matthiessen had returned to Boston from Maine, and on Friday, March 31, he left his Pinckney Street apartment and checked in at the Manger Hotel on Causeway Street, adjacent to North Station. Matthiessen needed height for what he planned to do. He was shown to Room 1219, facing southwest. Matthiessen had dinner plans at the home of Kenneth and Eleanor Murdock back on Beacon Hill, so he did not settle into his hotel room for the night.

To Murdock, Matthiessen seemed tired and depressed at dinner. Matthiessen presumably didn't say anything to his friends about having checked into the Manger Hotel earlier that day. On parting after dinner, at about thirty minutes before midnight, Matthiessen told the Murdocks to remember that he loved them.

It was a cloudy night but comparatively mild for early spring, with temperatures in the high forties. On getting back to his hotel, Matthiessen continued to prepare his room. On the desk, he placed his Skull and Bones pin and a letter, in which he asked that his friends Kenneth Murdock, Helen Bayne Knapp, and Ruth Putnam, as well as his sister, Lucy Neubrand, be contacted, but not until the morning. In the letter Matthiessen also asked that they go to his apartment and see that several other letters on his desk were mailed. In one of those letters, Matthiessen told Paul Sweezy that he feared that there was "nothing but 'desolate solitude ahead.'" He told Louis Hyde that he could "no longer bear the loneliness with which I am faced."

To his friends generally, Matthiessen wrote: "I am exhausted. I have been subject to so many severe depressions during the past few years that I can no longer believe that I can continue to be of use to my profession and my friends. I hope that my friends will be able to believe that I still love them in spite of this desperate act."

Perhaps another half hour passed. Matthiessen took off his glasses. Perhaps time enough to think about the cottage in Kittery—"the most beautiful house in America." Or to recall the cats, Baby and Pretzel. Time enough to remember riding his bicycle through the English countryside during his Oxford days shouting out with joy, "Rat, Rat, my God feller how I love you." Or the day he stood on the beach in Maine clad only in seaweed, his arms outstretched toward the ocean and sky. Or the "incident of the pear" the night aboard the *Paris* after he and Cheney had met.

At about half past midnight, outside the Manger on Nashua Street, a taxi driver named Jesse Reeves was startled by a tremendous noise. A man had just fallen—or jumped—from a twelfth-floor window. Matthiessen was still breathing when the ambulance crew arrived, but he died before they could reach City Hospital, two and half miles away.

Chapter 10

Aftermath and Afterglow

Matthiessen's funeral took place on Monday, April 3, 1950, at Christ Episcopal Church in Cambridge. Colleagues and former students, including Kenneth Murdock, C. L. Barber, Leo Marx, Harry Levin, and Richard Wilbur served as pallbearers and ushers. More than two hundred people attended the service. Most of Matthiessen's friends, students, and colleagues were shocked by his death. But others, such as Stanley Geist, did not seem surprised. People knew that Matthiessen had been lonely and depressed for several years, ever since Cheney's death. Matthiessen was cremated, and his ashes were taken to the Springfield Cemetery and buried in the Pratt family plot, next to his mother. Wallace Stevens, whose poetry Matthiessen reviewed and liked, remarked that Matthiessen's desire to be buried next to his mother suggested that he was "a man left alone and intensely hurt by it."

In the years following Matthiessen's death, neither his life, his work, nor his politics receded from view. A lengthy legal battle ensued over the disposition of his estate, largely because of his handwritten will. Here, too, Matthiessen's split personality between conservative and progressive choices governed his and—by association—Cheney's legacies. Somewhat paradoxically, Matthiessen's long connection with Harvard and Yale helped preserve the integrity of his estate. As a result, Matthiessen and Cheney's correspondence made its way into the hands of its intended recipient, Louis Hyde. Two of Matthiessen's books, *The Oxford Book of American Verse* and *Theodore Dreiser*, were published posthumously. They give some hint about what his literary pre-occupations might have been in the future. The poignancy of Matthiessen's short life and early death is undeniable. He remains a compelling figure to this day.

The newspapers across the political spectrum relished Matthiessen's suicide. It was page one news in the *Boston Globe* and *Boston Herald*. The *Boston Evening American* quoted Matthiessen's sister, Lucy Neubrand, with whom he had a cordial, but distant relationship: "This is a great shock. The only reason that I can give is that he was discouraged over the setbacks, given his Socialistic principles recently. He was a rabid follower of Harry Bridges and I know that he was grieving over the Bridges trial." (The latest Bridges perjury trial was then churning on into its fifth month.) On the political right, the columnist Bill Cunningham in the *Boston Herald* credited Matthiessen with physical courage for the manner in which he died by suicide—an odd reaction—but then went on to list over thirty of Matthiessen's political affiliations. On the political left, *The Daily Worker* blamed the Cold War for Matthiessen's death.

The story of Matthiessen's suicide did not immediately recede in the press after the funeral, because the newspapers got wind that the FBI was trying to obtain access to his papers in the Pinckney Street apartment. Several informants contacted the Boston bureau offering access to Matthiessen's apartment, claiming that he was a Communist and citing the existence of personal papers that they thought would be of interest to the FBI. One informant offered to go to Matthiessen's apartment with FBI agents to obviate the need to review papers "under court order." Harvard and the free press saved the day. After the FBI learned that their inquiries about Matthiessen's papers had been leaked to the newspapers, the agency, fearing bad publicity given

Matthiessen's association with Harvard, decided not to pursue the matter. Despite Matthiessen's rocky relationship with Harvard, he now benefited from association with the powerful and prestigious institution.

Had the FBI gotten hold of Matthiessen's papers—the letters he and Cheney exchanged in particular—it would have fit neatly into the homosexual panic that was sweeping through the federal government at the time. In March 1950, Senator Joseph McCarthy made charges about a "flagrantly homosexual" employee at the State Department and other gay employees at the Central Intelligence Agency. The US government officially considered homosexuals as security risks, because they were subject to blackmail based on their sexual orientation.

But if fear and loathing of homosexuals gripped one side of American society, hope spread its wings on the other side. Later in the fall of 1950, Harry Hay founded the Mattachine Society, one of the earliest groups in the United States devoted to advocating for the rights of gay men and lesbians. It had taken conceptual shape two years earlier when Hay envisioned forming a group, to be named Bachelors for Wallace, in connection with Henry Wallace's presidential bid. Matthiessen's involvement with Wallace's campaign leads to the intriguing question of what would have happened had Matthiessen met Harry Hay? Matthiessen would have been unfazed by Hay's membership in the Communist Party. But in response to Hay's more self-assertive stance on homosexuality, Matthiessen likely would have retreated. The tragedy of Matthiessen's premature death is that he *could* have lived to see the Stonewall riots of 1969 marking the beginning of gay liberation.

Had Matthiessen lived, the tension in him between conservative and progressive literary choices would have come under still yet greater pressure, as he tried to reconcile his aesthetic standards with his politics. Matthiessen's politics extended his notions about what counts as canonical literature, notably in his last book, a biography of Theodore Dreiser. And an important side benefit of Matthiessen's expanded view of literature was that it led him in the direction of believing that a more self-assertive gay voice was possible. Matthiessen did not go so far as to come out, but he was heading in the right direction.

After Matthiessen's death, books that he had written and edited continued to appear for the next several years, together with a memorial volume devoted to his life and work, and a collection of his essays. Of the final publications, *The Oxford Book of American Verse*, which was published in September 1950, probably gives the best hint of the direction of Matthiessen's future scholarship. Before his death Matthiessen selected the poems and wrote the introduction to this volume. The critic Cleanth Brooks went so far as to call *The Oxford Book of American Verse* "the best one-volume collection of poetry that has ever been made." The *New York Times* also acknowledged the comprehensiveness of the collection, but the reviewer sounded a note of criticism that has been taken up by later critics: Matthiessen defined poetry too narrowly as high art, and he overlooked or dismissed folk songs, spirituals, barroom ballads, and blues that have contributed significantly to American culture. Had Matthiessen included these art forms, he might have recognized poets who were Black, Indigenous, or people of color. Although he fell short in this regard, he did make room in the book for poetry by women, including Anne Bradstreet, Emily Dickinson, Amy Lowell, Elinor Wylie, H.D. (Hilda Doolittle), Marianne Moore, and Edna St. Vincent Millay.

Had Matthiessen lived, his notions about poetry likely would have further opened to include the greater varieties of cultural expression desired by the *New York Times* critic. He might even have written a book about American poetry covering the period of 1910 to 1930. During these twenty years, Matthiessen felt that more good poetry had been written than at any other point in the nation's history and that, as of the late 1940s, poetry was the hallmark of twentieth-century American literature. For Matthiessen, poetry was "the domain in which there has always been the deepest consciousness of the need to resist all official versions" of life. These few hints suggest what might have come next from Matthiessen's pen.

The most substantive book to be published after Matthiessen's death was his literary biography of Theodore Dreiser, released in March 1951. Matthiessen had been at work on the manuscript at the time of his death. Dreiser was not a writer to whom Matthiessen instinctively felt sympathetic, and in letters to friends, he complained of wrestling with the material to shape it into a book: "My annals since you saw me last are sad and simple, as befitting anyone engaged with a book. I have the illusion that I have completed my research, that I have masses and masses of film swarming around me and all that I have to do now is to make my montage. All! Each morning I bend my best efforts to preventing the desk from reeling and heaving and smacking me in the face." Despite his difficulties, Matthiessen ultimately completed the manuscript except for "an unfinished last paragraph," and William Sloan Associates decided to publish the volume.

While Matthiessen worked on *Theodore Dreiser* from 1949 to 1950, Russell Cheney had been dead for nearly five years. But Matthiessen's life with Cheney was so integral to his sense of himself that their relationship continued to show itself in Matthiessen's thinking about Dreiser. Dreiser was not homosexual, but his homosocial relationships with men appealed to Matthiessen, who noted that Dreiser's deepest intellectual connections were with other men. Dreiser wrote about his friend, the newspaper man Arthur Henry, claiming, "If he had been a girl I would have married him, of course. It would have been inevitable." Matthiessen also analyzed his work using visual references. He noted, for instance, that Dreiser was more interested in seeing rather than reading. Matthiessen quoted his early biographer, Dorothy Dudley, who claimed that Dreiser had a "'marvelous eye,' which often went far to offset his inaccurate ear and fumbling sense of touch." Matthiessen equated Dreiser's technique as similar to that of the Ashcan School painters George Luks and John Sloan for his ability to render "homely detail" in convincing ways.

But Dreiser's lapses in style bothered Matthiessen, as he acknowledged in his 1946 review of Dreiser's posthumous novel, *The Bulwark*. Nonetheless, Matthiessen thought that Dreiser deserved careful reading and analysis, because the writer had important things to say about the role of money in American life. Matthiessen even went so far as to say that Dreiser approached being an American Balzac. For Dreiser and for Matthiessen alike, there could be "no real political freedom without the removal of our vast economic inequalities."

This wasn't good enough for the critic Lionel Trilling, who felt that Matthiessen's sympathetic treatment of Dreiser revealed Matthiessen's own liberal bias. Trilling believed that Matthiessen excused Dreiser's shortcomings as a writer in exchange for what he and other liberal critics perceived as Dreiser's ability to portray the cold, hard truths of "reality" in America. But Dreiser did portray a fuller vision of life in America, one that had been largely left out of American letters. As one reviewer wrote, Matthiessen helped elucidate a writer who "moved American literature into a greater, greatly overdue realism."

The bitter reception of *From the Heart of Europe* must also have made Dreiser more of an appealing figure for Matthiessen to study and write about. Dreiser knew what it was like to be on the wrong side of American culture. In this regard, Matthiessen liked Dreiser's sensitivity to the difference between the "official" and the "real." In Matthiessen's view, Dreiser introduced a vocabulary for breaking through the "genteel tradition," a belief that the world of letters should be confined to only the happier, more pleasant aspects of life. Given his political experiences in the last years of life, Matthiessen better appreciated just how thuggish the arbiters of the genteel tradition could be at times. For Matthiessen, the genteel tradition accounted for the suppression of *Sister Carrie* as well as Dreiser's tangles with the Western Society for the Prevention of Vice over its attempts to suppress *The "Genius."* People simply did not want to acknowledge the forces in life that Dreiser depicted, such as "crass chance" and "fierce brutalities," which ran counter to the official version of what life was supposed to be like in America.

Yet Matthiessen, as a gay man, must also have been drawn to these ideas from Dreiser's fiction to move in the direction of greater representation of gay men and women. Matthiessen quoted Dreiser: "My own experience with *Sister Carrie*, as well as the fierce opposition or chilling indifference which, as I saw, overtook all those who attempted anything even partially serious in America, was enough to make me believe that the world took anything even slightly approximating the truth as one of the rankest and most criminal offenses possible. One dared not talk out loud, one dared not report life as it was, as one lived it." For Matthiessen, as a practitioner of "the love that dare not speak its name," Dreiser's words must have resonated deeply. Matthiessen was searching for the intellectual justification, language, and tradition that just might possibly enable him to describe his experience as a gay man, and he found it in Theodore Dreiser, unlikely though it may seem on first impression.

As Matthiessen reached for a language of greater equality, economic and political, in *Theodore Dreiser*, his thinking about homosexuality inched beyond highly coded or negative references to more affirmative, "out" references. In describing Dreiser's literary influences, Matthiessen quotes Dreiser's assessment of Chicago writer Henry B. Fuller's book, *With the Procession*, and then goes on to characterize Fuller's writing more generally, suggesting that Matthiessen was familiar with Fuller's oeuvre: "Fuller was a really fascinating cross between Howells and James. Strongly drawn to the psychological complexity and subtlety of *The Portrait of a Lady*, he nevertheless resolved that he should turn his back on James's Europe and work with the materials of his native city. This conflict—very real for his sensitive nature—produced a quiet intensity which made his contrast between the Chicago of the first settlers and the newer moneyed interests seem genuine to Dreiser in a way that Howells's honest but more external studies of Boston and New York never did." Here Matthiessen gives a hint as to his interest in Fuller's work with his use of the adjective "sensitive." In this context, "sensitive" can be read as a subtle nod to Fuller's homosexuality. In the 1930s and 1940s, to describe someone or something as "sensitive" was one way the mainstream press alluded to homosexuality. For example, a *New York Times* review of *Into an Old Room: A Memoir of Edward Fitzgerald* describes Fitzgerald as a "sensitive, intelligent youth, latently and unconsciously homosexual."

Fuller's work is less known today, but the reviewer in the *New York Herald Tribune* of the first critical biography of Fuller was correct when he called *Bertram Cope's Year* "mildly homosexual." Matthiessen read widely and voraciously; early in their relationship, Cheney noted: "You have the digestion of an ostrich—the books you read per diem." And as suggested earlier, Matthiessen and Cheney learned how to be gay through what they read, so Matthiessen was likely familiar with *Bertram Cope's Year*. Fuller describes Cope as "no squire of dames." Later in the novel, Cope writes to Arthur Lemoyne that "I have had some rather glum hours and miss you more than ever." At the end of the book, Cope and Lemoyne are "'keeping house' together." In sum, the novel depicts a domestic male couple, similar to Matthiessen and Cheney.

As always, the reviews of Matthiessen's biography of Dreiser were wide ranging; some reviewers liked it, others did not. Several of the reviewers read the book in light of Matthiessen's death by suicide. They felt that *Theodore Dreiser* betrayed signs of "weariness." But the main criticism, echoed by more-contemporary scholars, was that Matthiessen missed the power of sex in Dreiser's work. Frederick C. Stern, whose book about Matthiessen was published in 1981, went so far as to call Matthiessen's writing about Dreiser and sex "genteel." Since Matthiessen did not feel at liberty to speak or write publicly about his own sexual likes and dislikes, no wonder his discussion of sex in Dreiser's work seems circumscribed.

Contemporary critics have continued to write about what an odd choice on artistic grounds Theodore Dreiser was for Matthiessen. William E. Cain wrote that Dreiser's style offended Matthiessen, and Leo Marx claimed that Matthiessen willed himself into his appreciation for Dreiser. But other critics who have written biographies and studies of Dreiser's work have been warmer. Ellen Moers, for example, praised Matthiessen for his close attention to the drafts and revisions of Dreiser's manuscripts. *Theodore Dreiser* did not create a new field or shine a critical light on a previously little-known, overlooked, or underappreciated figure, the way Matthiessen had with *American Renaissance*, *Sarah Orne Jewett*, *The Achievement of T. S. Eliot*, and *Henry James: The Major Phase*. But the book found an audience and served as a reliable guide to Dreiser's work, at least through the 1960s and into the 1970s.

It was not simply Matthiessen's posthumously published books or the prospect of trying to nail him as a Communist that kept his memory and name alive in the years following his death. There was also the matter of his "home-made" will and an estate that was originally estimated to be worth $34,000, grew to $63,335, and turned out to be valued at $94,665 (approximately $954,000 in 2021 dollars), when his will was finally probated in 1953—a not insignificant sum, especially for a Socialist.

In October 1945, three months after Cheney's death, Matthiessen had taken steps to ensure the preservation of both his and Cheney's life together, as well as the painter's artistic legacy. But he made alterations to his will in 1947 and 1949. Because Matthiessen did not have the 1949 alteration properly witnessed, his three siblings sought to have the entire will declared invalid, so that Matthiessen's considerable estate would have been divided by them as his only next of kin. The Massachusetts courts ruled against Matthiessen's siblings, allowing the 1947, but not the 1949 alteration, to stand. In the 1947 alteration, Matthiessen solidified his forward thinking on labor rights and racial equality adding a bequest of $1,000 (approximately $12,000 in 2021 dollars) to the Highlander Folk School—now the Highlander Research and Education Center—in Tennessee, a school that became racially integrated the early 1940s and trained workers to take leadership positions in the civil rights and organized labor movements. The Highlander Center counts Rosa Parks as one of its more famous attendees.

Matthiessen planned to leave the bulk of his estate to friends—his family of choice—and to Yale. As the Harvard association helped protect his personal papers, his association with Yale protected his bequests. Yale petitioned the court to allow the 1947 revised will to be probated in keeping with the court's guidance—in opposition to Matthiessen's siblings. In the will, Matthiessen made clear that out of all of his worldly possessions—the house in Kittery, the townhouse on Beacon Hill, his books, his papers, even the letters—he valued Cheney's paintings the most. The opening sentence of his will conveys as much: "Now that I have some property that it is important to dispose of carefully—I refer to Russell Cheney's paintings—I am drafting this will to cancel the one that I made some years ago." Matthiessen wasn't simply expressing his sentimental attachment to his deceased partner's painting. Savvy cultural historian that he was, Matthiessen appreciated how much Cheney and his painting had influenced him, just as he believed that Cheney should find a niche for himself in the annals of American painting. He recognized that the paintings had the power to survive right alongside his own books as a testament to and record of their life together and love for one another deeply rooted in New England and American history.

He also bequeathed private correspondence between him and Cheney to Louis Hyde, his Skull and Bones brother. Even though Matthiessen's energy flagged and his tone became exasperated in some of the later letters, he had never stopped writing. The "Sunday letter" always made its way to Cheney. The letters were peppered with tenderness and love and were therefore the kind of incriminating evidence that one would have instructed a legatee to burn rather than preserve. By entrusting them to Hyde, however, Matthiessen seemed to acknowledge their great importance. Matthiessen wanted what was contained in those letters—the expression of love—to live on despite the fact he couldn't quite envision how that might happen.

Epilogue

Getting Married After All

As part of my research into Matthiessen's and Cheney's lives and work, I stopped in Springfield, Massachusetts, one autumn on my way to Amherst, where one of Cheney's relatives still lived. I had a layover at the local bus station, so I decided to go to the Springfield Cemetery to visit Matthiessen's grave. The Orne-Pratt family plot sits atop a pleasant knoll overlooking the cemetery's grounds. I left a pen on Matthiessen's grave to tell his spirit how much I enjoyed his books and appreciated learning about him and Cheney. The two men gave me a gift, the opportunity to research and write about their life together; leaving a pen was the least that I could do to say thank-you.

That summer back in 2004, after I had discovered *Rat & the Devil: Journal Letters of F. O. Matthiessen and Russell Cheney* and Cheney's paintings at the Portsmouth Public Library, David and I went on to Provincetown as planned, where we had spent many happy summer vacations. Because of a change in Massachusetts law that year, we talked a lot about getting married. Or rather, we talked a lot about having the right to get married if we wanted to. Being able to get married in Massachusetts emboldened us. We had as much right as anybody else to claim our corner of the public square. We felt less self-conscious, for example, about holding hands along Commercial Street, the town's main thoroughfare, during an evening's stroll or out on the breakwater, a mile long dike at the far end of town that protects the salt marshes and prevents the outermost tip of Cape Cod from being separated from the mainland and becoming an island. Provincetown was already a gay-friendly place before marriage equality passed in Massachusetts, but even there, David and I occasionally felt like second-class citizens. Knowing that we could get married if we wanted to changed how we felt about our ourselves and our relationship.

But when it came down to a personal decision as to whether we wanted to get married, that gave us each a bit of pause. Getting married was as big a decision for us as it is for just about any two mature adults. We dated our relationship to a frantic, jubilant run down Broadway in a summer thunderstorm in 1994. That evening had remained chaste, but both of us acknowledged that something shifted that night, and our friendship began to take on a more romantic tinge. Over the months and years that followed, we still lived separately but spent most weekends together and spoke by phone most nights. We even developed a regular, playful sign-off. David, on saying good-night, would wish me "Sweet dreams," and I would answer in my college French: "Tu aussi." We traveled well together. At the five-year mark, we took a trip to Paris and Venice; David called the trip our honeymoon. If we got married, would we be screwing up a good thing?

Despite being undecided about marriage, David and I were about to live the phrase "in sickness and in health" similar to what Matthiessen and Cheney had known, as they wrestled with the physical and emotional trials of tuberculosis, alcoholism, and depression. For me, it began innocuously enough, when I started having trouble walking in January 2005. My left knee began buckling, and it wouldn't bear my weight. Pretty soon, I was using a cane. In February, the monumental public art installation by Christo and Jeanne-Claude, *The Gates*, opened in Central Park. Orange—given my Maine roots, I couldn't bring myself to say "saffron," Christo and Jeanne-Claude's term—banners hung from steel braces and lined the serpentine walking paths throughout the park. Over several weekends, David and I walked the length of the park, going up to Harlem Meer at the park's northern-most boundary. We took our cameras with us, and in one instance asked a friend to snap our photo; this was in the days before selfies. In this photograph, unlike some of the earlier photos of David and me, in which we looked like two brothers standing side by side—close, but not too close—we are clearly together as a couple, relaxed, happy, and smiling. All looks well in the picture, except for the crook of a blond wood cane looped over my forearm.

As I was getting sick, David kept notes and wrote a series of dispatches to our friends and colleagues updating everyone on my worsening illness. From those reports and photos, I've pieced together the story of my cognitive and physical descent and recovery. But given the nature of my sickness, the boundaries between memory and imagination are far from clear.

Through much of the winter and early spring of 2005, I was still working and going to graduate school. And yet mentally and physically, I was closing down. When I started to lose my short-term memory, I eventually left work on disability. During this year David and I continued to live apart, but we still spoke almost every evening by phone. David described how one night we spoke for about twenty minutes, said good-night—"Sweet dreams" followed by "Tu aussi"—and rang off. A few minutes later I called him back with no recollection of the call that had just taken place. My hand-writing deteriorated. My even and mostly regular hand regressed to the jerky, jagged, unsure marks of a child. In our sex life, I could no longer have an orgasm. Then, I had a seizure. When I came out of the seizure, an ambulance had taken me to the hospital, and so began a hospitalization that would last sixty days.

A health care proxy supported David's position as my defender and ally. I had signed the document a couple of years previously, when I got my first will written. That one piece of paper entitled David by law to make medical decisions for me and get medical information about me from my doctors and the hospital. Without that piece of paper, our ten-year relationship may or may not have meant anything in the hospital.

In the depths of it, for example, David reported that I was one day the focus of the chief of service rounds, a weekly meeting between senior doctors and medical residents about a particularly mysterious case in the hospital. David described how I was brought into a classroom in a wheelchair, where an old-school neurologist, a specialist in epilepsy, examined and questioned David and me before his audience of medical residents. As I would learn from my later interactions with this doctor, he was abrupt, dismissive, and, as a foremost expert on seizure disorders, used to getting his way.

He began the examination by questioning David. "And what is your relationship to the patient?"

"I'm Scott's partner," David said.

"We'll say 'friend,'" the doctor replied.

David is a mild-mannered fellow. He favors horn-rimmed glasses and bow ties. But love in a terrifying situation gives people strength they might not know they had.

"No," David said. "We'll say 'partner.'"

Happily, the doctors who were most involved with me, another neurologist and a hematologist, were equally expert in their fields and far more grounded and humane. But before my doctors made a diagnosis, I was examined, poked, prodded, tested, and questioned by just about every type of doctor imaginable, either to try to diagnose my disease or to mitigate the effects of my deepening, mysterious illness. At various points the doctors investigated multiple sclerosis, HIV, testicular cancer, pancreatic cancer, West Nile encephalitis, a brain tumor, and Creutzfeldt-Jakob disease—the human form of mad cow disease—among many other possibilities. A brain biopsy loomed on the horizon.

Yet through it all, parts of me held on. Even as the disease ravaged me and my mind, many of my long-term memories remained intact. I could—and did, as David reported—recite the opening

lines of Chaucer's *Canterbury Tales* in Middle English, which I had
been required to memorize for an undergraduate class:

> Whan that Aprill with his shoures soote
> The droghte of March hath perced to the roote,
> And bathed every veyne in swich licour
> > Of which vertu engendred is the flour[.]

David described how on another night he got into my hospital
bed with me and just held me, drawing imaginary patterns with
his fingers on my bony back to soothe me. By this time I weighed
116 pounds, down from my usual weight of 145 pounds, because
I had such difficulty eating.

But then, after one more surgical biopsy, I tested positive for
Hodgkin's disease, a blood cancer that is often curable. I was given
a diagnosis on May 9, 2005, of encephalitis from Hodgkin's disease, one day before David's fifty-third birthday. My symptoms—
partial paralysis, seizures, and anterograde amnesia—were the
result of antibodies that my body had unleashed to fight an early
stage of the cancer but instead had attacked my central nervous
system. I was having an autoimmune reaction to cancer. Who
knew such things were possible? As David wrote in his daily
updates: "Scott never tires of the good news, in part because he
never remembers it." I started to undergo various treatments to
neutralize and cleanse the antibodies from my body, followed
by the standard treatment for Hodgkin's disease, chemotherapy
followed by radiation.

But the story didn't end there. In January 2006, a month and
half after I finished radiation treatment, David was diagnosed
with colon cancer. When he went for his annual colonoscopy,
the doctor found a tumor that a subsequent surgery and biopsy
revealed had pierced his colon's wall and infected one lymph node.
Because of this infected lymph node, David's cancer was labeled
stage III-A, which wasn't great but wasn't necessarily a death
sentence either. Six months of adjuvant chemotherapy followed

surgery. Every two weeks, David and I headed down to the cancer center in the Chelsea neighborhood. During his treatment, we chatted, or we sat and read.

Mostly, David's chemotherapy proceeded without incident. On infusion days, if David didn't feel nauseated, I would go out at lunchtime to a favorite Italian sandwich counter and get mozza-rella and tomato sandwiches for us. One sunny day, walking back to the cancer center that spring of 2006, I was conscious of being profoundly happy. I have often found that windows of joy open up just this way: Right in the middle of some everyday activity, I'm overtaken by a sense of joy, peace, or contentment. The win-dow often closes up just as quickly as it opened, and I'm back to being my usual self with my typical aggravations and anxieties. But on that day, along West 16th Street, I, of course, wished that David weren't going through cancer treatment, but I was glad that our cancer diagnoses at least had been staggered. It could have been worse. We both could have gotten sick at the same time. But mostly, I was grateful to be alive, to have recovered my cognitive faculties, to have enough money to buy delicious sandwiches from a favorite store, and to be sharing all of it with David.

Several years later, David and I got married in New York. It was a beautiful day that Saturday in May 2012, the type of day that is so rare in New York during the summer: clear, warm, and dry. Throughout planning the wedding, both David and I had won-dered from time to time, Why are we doing this? We had been together for nearly eighteen years at that point. Things were working nicely between us the way they were. Were we going to screw up a good thing? We had put in place what legal safeguards we could. A health care proxy had saved the day when I had first gotten sick in 2005. And then there was all the time and expense of planning and organizing a ceremony and reception for two hundred and fifty people. Why bother? David and I didn't need New York State to affirm our relationship. It was private and personal, something we dated to the 1994 run down Broadway. Still, the phrase "use it or lose it" kept circulating around my mind like an electronic banner.

In deciding to get married, David and I had one overarching idea: to do something that was true to ourselves and not get sucked into other people's expectations about what a wedding, or a gay wedding for that matter, was or was not supposed to be. So: No flowers. No procession. No champagne. No fancy, expensive caterer. A sheet cake and generic ice cream. Recorded music. Paper plates and plastic utensils. David joked that his mother would have drawn the line at the paper plates and plastic utensils. One of David's colleagues suggested that we set up a photo stand, so groups of people could have their photos taken together. We wanted a big but relaxed occasion. We wanted to share the event with many different people from our lives: family, old friends, new friends, colleagues, former colleagues, families with children, neighbors, doormen from our apartment building, and the beloved doctors, nurses, and aides who took care of us in 2005 and 2006.

In planning our wedding, Matthiessen's words must have been doing their work in the back of my mind. How could they not have been? I had spent a decade getting to know him and Cheney. They were a part of me at this point. "We stand in the middle of an uncharted, uninhabited country. That there have been unions like ours is obvious, but we are unable to draw on their experience. We must create everything for ourselves," Matthiessen wrote to Cheney in January 1925. What was a same-sex wedding supposed to look like? No one knew, including David and I. But we trusted in our ability to make it up as we went along.

As the ceremony got under way, David in his welcoming remarks started with the line: "You've had us married for a long time," acknowledging how our families, colleagues, and friends had long treated us as a married couple. In my welcoming remarks, I dated the beginning of our unofficial marriage to our back-to-back cancer diagnoses and treatments. Just about everyone in the church that day knew what an awful ordeal David and I had gone through in 2005 and 2006, when it was a real possibility that death would take one of us. Our respective illnesses colored the day's events and made them seem all the sweeter. It was as though all of us in the sanctuary that day were acknowledging that while life can be awful at times, loving partnerships between two adults affirm life in the face of that abyss. Beyond what our wedding meant to David and me personally, our wedding was a collective, social affirmation of life.

When everyone had arrived for the ceremony, we started with Shakespeare's Sonnet 29, beginning with "When in disgrace with fortune and men's eyes." We next brought Matthiessen and Cheney into the ceremony in a more official way, when a friend read part of an early letter from Matthiessen to Cheney: "Marriage! What a strange word to be applied to two men! Can't you hear the hell-hounds of society baying in full pursuit behind us? But that's just the point. We are beyond society. We've said thank you very much, and stepped outside and closed the door. In the eyes of the unknowing world we are a talented artist of wealth and position and a promising young graduate student. In the eyes of the knowing world we would be pariahs, outlaws, degenerates. This is indeed the price we pay for being born different from the great run of mankind." For the ceremony, I edited out the phrase "of wealth and position." I thought that it distracted from the bigger thought of a marriage between two men. Matthiessen was very good, but he wasn't perfect.

Next another friend read a selection from the New York State Marriage Equality legislation of 2011. "Marriage is a fundamental human right. Same-sex couples should have the same access as others to the protections, responsibilities, rights, obligations, and benefits of civil marriage. Stable family relationships help build a stronger society. For the welfare of the community and in fairness to all New Yorkers, this act formally recognizes otherwise-valid marriages without regard to whether the parties are of the same or different sex. It is the intent of the legislature that the marriages of same-sex and different-sex couples be treated equally in all respects under the law." It tickled me to read from legislation at our wedding ceremony. But the quotation worked well, especially following Matthiessen's inability to conceive of public recognition of a same-sex marriage, even as he privately created one himself. The language and thoughts embodied in the New York State Marriage Equality Act were ennobling.

David and I stood at the altar, facing each other and holding hands. We used traditional vows. But a funny thing happened at the moment to say "I do." A powerful sense seized me that out of all the people in the world, if ever there was a person whom I wanted to marry, it was David. Out of my mouth came, "I *sure* do." I hadn't planned this. But suddenly it seemed like the right thing to say at the right moment. Everyone laughed. David laughed and repeated the phrase, when he made his vow. As the younger and, in the early days of our relationship, the more tentative and ambivalent partner, my unequivocal affirmation surprised us both.

We closed the ceremony with a reading of the poem "Ithaka" by C. P. Cavafy, whom I don't believe either Matthiessen or Cheney had read.

> Keep Ithaka always in your mind.
> Arriving there is what you are destined for.
> But do not hurry the journey at all.
> Better if it lasts for years,
> so you are old by the time you reach the island,
> wealthy with all you've gained on the way,
> not expecting Ithaka to make you rich.
>
> Ithaka gave you the marvelous journey.
> Without her you wouldn't have set out.
> She has nothing left to give you now.

When our friend Diane got to phrase "do not hurry the journey at all," she turned away from the podium, faced David and me, and repeated the line: "do not hurry the journey at all."

There was only one thing about the wedding that David and I would have done differently. We did not take a post-wedding trip. Being eighteen years into our relationship at the time, I couldn't quite bring myself to use the word "honeymoon." We got married on a Saturday, and on Monday both of us went back to our day-to-day lives. This was a mistake. Getting married was exhilarating, and in retrospect it would have been nice to have had a little decompression time. But we didn't know that. We were figuring things out as we went along.

Not helping matters, it poured down rain that Monday morning after the wedding, cascading streams of water, and I was beginning to come down with a head cold. I drifted into a maudlin state. That morning David sent an old photograph of himself as a young man to a friend and copied me on the email. Many years ago, her husband had died prematurely of cancer. The dark rainy Monday morning, not feeling well, seeing David as a young man, and thoughts of early deaths from cancer all set me off; I started to cry. I had been so exhilarated over the weekend, but I was suddenly conscious of life's fragility and its brevity. One of us will likely die first. Although my ill health could hold surprises, based on our ages, David is likely to go first. The warmth, companionship, intimacy, and love, such that I had never known in my adult life, will come to an end. Will I die? Will the end kill me? I stood in the bedroom crying.

By this time David had showered and dressed. He, too, stood in the bedroom, ready to go to work. He wasn't going to descend into this morass of unfounded fears and anxieties with me. He gave me a hug and kiss and then put both hands on my shoulders.

"Yes, it will end," he said. "But we will have experienced something beautiful and timeless, and the world will go on." He looked at me with his steady, calm blue eyes.

David left the apartment. Crying, I waved from the window, so intensely aware of the impermanent and transitory nature of the moment.

In their day, Matthiessen and Cheney kept love alive in the face of some daunting obstacles. And they in turn help me to keep love alive. I suppose it is this cycle, this transfer of spirit and values, that gives me any real sense of immortality as a palpable force in the world. Others will follow David and me, just as we followed Matthiessen and Cheney, and unions like ours will continue to be written.

Notes

Abbreviations

AR	F. O. Matthiessen. *American Renaissance: Art and Expression in the Age of Emerson and Whitman*. New York: Oxford University Press, 1941.
CC	Preliminary catalogue raisonné of Russell Cheney's paintings compiled by Richard Candee and Carol L. Cheney. The catalogue raisonné is not publicly available.
Eliot	F. O. Matthiessen. *The Achievement of T. S. Eliot: An Essay on the Nature of Poetry*, with a chapter on Eliot's later work by C. L. Barber. 3rd ed. New York: Oxford University Press, 1958.
FF	US Federal Bureau of Investigation, Francis Otto Matthiessen, Bureau File 100–569. A copy of the file is in the author's possession, obtained through a Freedom of Information Act request to the agency.
FHE	F. O. Matthiessen. *From the Heart of Europe*. New York: Oxford University Press, 1948.
FOM	Paul M. Sweezy and Leo Huberman, eds. *F. O. Matthiessen: A Collective Portrait*. New York: Henry Schuman, 1950.
HJ	F. O. Matthiessen. *Henry James: The Major Phase*. New York: Oxford University Press, 1944.
JF	F. O. Matthiessen. *The James Family*. New York: Alfred A. Knopf, 1947.
Knapp Papers	Farwell Knapp Papers. Yale Collection of American Literature, Beinecke Rare Book and Manuscript Library, YCAL MSS 256.
Matthiessen Papers	F. O. Matthiessen Papers. Yale Collection of American Literature, Beinecke Rare Book and Manuscript Library, YCAL MSS 495.
Putnam Papers	Phelps Putnam Papers. Yale Collection of American Literature, Beinecke Rare Book and Manuscript Library, YCAL MSS 429.
R&D	Louis Hyde, ed. *Rat & the Devil: Journal Letters of F. O. Matthiessen and Russell Cheney*. Hamden, CT: Archon Books, 1978.
RC	F. O. Matthiessen. *Russell Cheney, 1881–1945: A Record of His Work*. Andover, MA: Andover Press, 1946.
SOJ	F. O. Matthiessen. *Sarah Orne Jewett*. Boston: Houghton Mifflin, 1929.

| Translation | F. O. Matthiessen. *Translation: An Elizabethan Art.* Cambridge, MA: Harvard University Press, 1931. |
| TD | F. O. Matthiessen. *Theodore Dreiser.* New York: William Sloan Associates, 1951. |

PROLOGUE: DO THE DEAD CHOOSE THEIR BIOGRAPHERS?

5   *"Whether we think of Matthiessen":* George Blaustein, *Nightmare Envy, and Other Stories* (New York: Oxford University Press, 2018), 187.

a near-contemporary definition of "gay": The use of the terms "gay" and "homosexual" is elusive in the early half of the twentieth century, because a late twentieth-century/early twenty-first-century definition of "gay" did not exist at the time. The term "gay" as signifying both sexual attraction to members of one's own gender and a sense of personal identity would not fully emerge until after the birth of the gay liberation movement in 1969. Throughout the book, I use "gay" and occasionally "proto-gay" and "homosocial" when they approximate a contemporary understanding of those terms, and I use "homosexual" when I am referring more strictly to sexual contact between members of the same sex. Scholars of lesbian, gay, bisexual, transgender, and queer men, women, and communities can and have teased out these terms and ideas in many different permutations. But given the range and complexity of sexual practices, behaviors, and affinities during Matthiessen's and Cheney's day and times prior, I have adopted "gay" and "homosexual" as the poles of usage primarily for simplicity, clarity, and convenience.

CHAPTER 1: THE SEARCH FOR COMPANIONSHIP

7   *paternal great-uncle:* The elder Francis Otto Matthiessen was born in 1833 in Holstein, Denmark, an area that is now part of Germany. At the time of his immigration to the United States in 1858, he changed his first name to Francis from Franz. A year before he died in 1901, he had retired from the American Sugar Refining Company, the most important firm of the Sugar Trust, a loose network of companies based in New York, which was well on its way to controlling nearly all sugar refining in the United States. At the time of his death, the elder Matthiessen's estate was estimated to be between $10 and $20 million (between approximately $315 and $630 million in 2020 dollars). See "F. O. Matthiessen Dies in His Paris Home," *New York Times,* March 10, 1901, 7.

parents divorced: Frederick W. Matthiessen Jr. and Lucy Orne Matthiessen, Dissolution of Marriage Papers, 1916, Office of the Clerk of the Circuit Court, LaSalle County, Illinois.

"an empty space": F. O. Matthiessen to Russell Cheney, April 18, 1925, *R&D,* 123.

"a distant relative": Dictionary of American Biography, Supplement Four, 1946–1950, ed. John A. Garranty and Edward T. Jones (New York: Charles Scribner's Sons, 1974), s.v. "Matthiessen, Francis Otto"; Gale in Context: Biography, https://www.gale.com/c/in-context-biography.

Sarah Orne Jewett's lineage: Sarah Orne Jewett inherited her Orne family connection through her cherished father, Dr. Theodore H. Jewett. Dr. Jewett's mother was Sarah Orne (1794–1819), the daughter of Captain James Orne (1760–?) and Sarah Odiorne (1762–1807) of Portsmouth, New Hampshire. Beyond this, the trail goes cold. In her 1994 biography of Sarah Orne Jewett, Paula Blanchard also acknowledges that little is known about the Orne side of Sarah Orne Jewett's genealogy. Frederic Clarke Jewett, *History and Genealogy of the Jewetts of America: A Record of Edward Jewett, of Bradford, West Riding of Yorkshire, England, and His Two Emigrant Sons, Deacon Maximilian and Joseph Jewett, Settlers of Rowley, Massachusetts, in 1639; Also of Abraham and John Jewett, Early Settlers of Rowley, and of the Jewetts Who Have Settled in the United States since the Year 1800,* vol. 1 (New York: Grafton Press, 1908), 399; Paula Blanchard, *Sarah Orne Jewett: Her World and Her Work* (Reading, MA: Addison Wesley, 1994), 6.

Ornes in America: The Ornes first spelled their name Horne but dropped the initial *H* after the first generation in America. The family evolved along two distinct branches in Salem and Marblehead, Massachusetts. Matthiessen's family line extended back to William Orne (1751–1815), a mariner and merchant of Salem. Captain Orne's son Samuel (1786–1830), a wealthy lawyer, married Lucinda Dwight Howard (1786–1828), and the couple moved to Springfield. Samuel and Lucinda Orne had two children, a son and a daughter. Matthiessen's Orne family connection proceeded through their son, William Wetmore Orne (1811–52), who was a local businessman and also served as one-time clerk of the Unitarian Society. In 1834 he married Lucy Gassett Dwight (1817–87). William Wetmore and Lucy Dwight Orne's daughter, Lucinda Howard Orne (1840–95) married George Walter Pratt (1840–67). Their daughter, Lucy Orne Pratt, was born in 1866, and she later became Matthiessen's mother. "Death of Mrs. Lucy G. Orne," *Springfield Republican,* April 19, 1887, 6; "One Orne Became Expert in Arab Tongue, Literature," *Springfield Daily News,* August 24, 1970, 15; Charles Wells Chapin, *Sketches of the Old Inhabitants and Other Citizens of Old Springfield of the Present Century; and Its Historic Mansions of "Ye Olden Tyme": With One Hundred Twenty-Four Illustrations and Sixty Autographs* (Springfield, MA: Press of Springfield Print and Binding, 1893), 196, 289, 291, and 289.

8 *Ornes were central to this debate:* In 1815, Samuel and Lucinda Orne, along with fifty-three other parishioners, petitioned the Massachusetts Legislature to grant the incorporation of the Second Society of the First Parish, which was a Congregational church, claiming that they "could no longer profit" from the ministry of the then-current reverend, a strict Trinitarian. This petition was granted in 1819, and about a year later the Second Society changed its name again to the Third Congregational Society, the Unitarians of Springfield, and its house of worship became known as the Church of the Unity. Moses King, ed., *King's Handbook of Springfield, Massachusetts: A Series of Monographs, Historical and Descriptive* (Springfield, MA: James D. Gill, 1884), 176–77; personal email

communication of Cynthia Sommer, archivist, to the Reverend Jason Seymour, Unitarian Universalist Society of Greater Springfield, March 3, 2014.

attended the Howard School for Girls: Springfield Republican, obituary, September 20, 1923, 14.

she had a round face: George H. Van Norman, *Lucy Orne Pratt*, ca. 1893, photograph, 26 x 19 cm, Springfield History Library and Archives, Springfield, MA.

in 1893 they were married: "Still More Weddings," *Springfield Graphic*, October 21, 1893, 7.

gave the newlyweds: "Laurel and Flowers. Church a Bower of Beauty for the Ceremony. Matthiessen-Pratt Wedding Attracted Springfield's Society," *Boston Globe*, October 19, 1893, 6.

2020 dollars: Throughout the book, to determine inflation-adjusted dollar amounts, I have used two inflation calculators: for time periods after 1913, the US Department of Labor, Inflation Calculator, https://www.bls.gov /data/inflation_calculator.htm (1913 is the earliest year from which the Labor Department calculates inflation); for periods before 1913, an inflation calculator created and maintained by Morgan Friedman, https://westegg .com/inflation/. The Department of Labor inflation calculator tabulates equivalent dollar amounts through 2021, whereas the Morgan Friedman calculator tabulates through 2020. Whether an equivalent dollar amount is in 2020 or 2021 dollars is noted parenthetically in the text.

9   *gentleman farmer:* "Real Estate Record," *Los Angeles Times*, July 17, 1896, 5.

no longer going to pay the debts: "Local News," *Bureau County Tribune* (Princeton, IL), April 27, 1906, 12.

her husband would disappear: Frederick W. Matthiessen Jr. and Lucy Orne Matthiessen, Dissolution of Marriage Papers.

live in hotels under assumed names: Matthiessen, "The Oxford Letter," n.d., 2, box 3, Matthiessen Papers.

"divorced," which may have been wishful thinking: 1910 US Federal Census, La Salle Ward 7, La Salle, IL, https://www.ancestry.com.

"'small-town boy'": *Dictionary of American Biography*, s.v. "Matthiessen, Francis Otto"; Gale in Context: Biography.

"a man of extreme vigour": As described below, Matthiessen wrote this description of his paternal grandfather while a student at New College, Oxford University, which partially explains his adoption of the British spelling of "vigour" and "practises" (below).

10   *grandfather came to the United States:* Frederick William Matthiessen Sr. was born in 1835 in Altona, in what is now the city-state of Hamburg in northern Germany, though at the time of his birth Altona was under Danish control. In the younger Matthiessen's later writings, he noted simply that his ancestors were Danish. "F. Matthiessen, LaSalle Zinc Magnate, Dies," *Chicago Tribune*, February 12, 1918, 5.

three terms as LaSalle's mayor: "F. W. Matthiessen of LaSalle Is Dead," *Times* (Streator, IL), February 11, 1918, 1.

if her husband would have taken her back: Frederick W. Matthiessen Jr. and Lucy Orne Matthiessen, Dissolution of Marriage Papers.

listed her as a widow: Tarrytown New York, City Directory, 1914–15, 75, and Tarrytown, New York, City Directory, 1918–19, 75, https://www.ancestrylibrary.com.

baptized at Christ Church: Christ Church, Tarrytown, NY, A New Parish Register, vol. 4, 1901–1950, 60–61, 229.

11   *Hackley offered only a full boarding option*: Hackley School librarian, email to author, October 10, 2013.

"a boy of nineteen was my particular idol": Matthiessen, "Oxford Letter," 3, 5.

short—like his brothers and subsequent quotes: United States, World War I, Frederick William Matthiessen Draft Registration Card, June 1917, and George Dwight Matthiessen, Draft Registration Card, June 15, 1918, October 9, 2013, https://www.ancestry.com.

"extremely well developed" and subsequent quotes: When writing about his sexuality, Matthiessen uses "generic" in the scientific sense of marking one's membership in a genus—above species, but below family—which has characteristics that distinguish it from other groups, that is, homosexuals as distinct from heterosexuals. Matthiessen, "Oxford Letter," 5–6.

several thinkers articulated progressive theories of homosexuality: Jennifer Terry, *An American Obsession: Science, Medicine, and Homosexuality in Modern Society* (Chicago: University of Chicago Press, 1999), 50, 54, 69, 75.

12   *gender identities*: George Chauncey, *Gay New York: Gender, Urban Culture, and the Making of the Gay Male World, 1890–1940* (New York: Basic Books, 1994), 48–50, 65, 83.

13   *used the term "queer" to describe themselves*: Chauncey, *Gay New York*, 100–102, 106, 122.

Gay socializing in public could be dangerous: Chauncey, 140, 172, 184, 186, 189, 339, 349, 360.

14   *"depicting or dealing with sex degeneracy"*: Chauncey, 352.

"suffer or permit such premises": Chauncey, 337.

"began to develop homosexual practises rapidly": Matthiessen, "Oxford Letter," 8.

"What I delighted in most": Matthiessen, "Oxford Letter," 5–6.

met one another at movie theaters: Chauncey, *Gay New York*, 194, 196–97.

15   *Baths, Ira Gershwin*: Chauncey, 217, 221–22.

Matthiessen followed an uncle and several cousins to Yale: *Bulletin of Yale University—Obituary Record of the Undergraduate Schools Deceased during 1949–1950*, 7th ser., January 1, 1951, 110–11, http://mssa.library.yale.edu/obituary_record/1925_1952/1949-50.pdf.

Yale College that Matthiessen entered: Sanford Lakoff, *Max Lerner: Pilgrim in the Promised Land* (Chicago: University of Chicago Press, 1998), 20–24. Max Lerner's dates at Yale overlapped exactly with those of Matthiessen.

16   *member of Skull and Bones*: "Senior Society Elections," *Yale Daily News*, May 28, 1909, 1.

Matthiessen overheard French explain: FHE, 71; "French Dies, Retired Yale

Professor," *Hartford Courant*, August 23, 1954, 4; George Wilson Pierson, *Yale: College and University, 1871–1937*, vol. 2, *Yale: The University College, 1921–1937* (New Haven, CT: Yale University Press, 1955), 159, 405, 336, 458.

broad range of liberal arts courses: Matthiessen's Yale transcripts, 1919–23, box 6, Matthiessen Papers.

role as class deacon: Ralph Henry Gabriel, *Religion and Learning at Yale: The Church of Christ in the College and University, 1757–1957* (New Haven, CT: Yale University Press, 1958), 210.

17 *"Thus functionless property grows":* R. H. Tawney, *The Acquisitive Society* (New York: Harcourt Brace, 1931), 81–82.

"wolfish world": Herman Melville, *Moby Dick* (New York: Harper & Brothers, 1851), reprinted with introduction by Larzer Ziff (New York: Everyman's Library, 1988), 71. Page reference is to the 1988 edition.

18 *"Tawney's ideas about equality":* FHE, 72.

Matthiessen's initial exposure: FOM, ix; "Liberal Club Holds First Annual Banquet at Mory's," *Yale Daily News*, May 22, 1922, 2.

Liberal Club: Edgar L. Furniss, "Prof. Furniss Discusses Objects of Liberal Club, *Yale Daily News*, May 22, 1922, 1–2.

"to extend into industry the brotherhood": Nelson Lichtenstein, *State of the Union: A Century of American Labor* (Princeton, NJ: Princeton University Press, 2002), 6.

The organized labor movement of Matthiessen's day: Philip Dray, *There Is Power in a Union: The Epic Story of Labor in America* (New York: Doubleday, 2010), 353, 368–69, 391, 413.

19 *Matthiessen was tapped for Skull and Bones:* "Senior Society Elections Given to College Juniors," *Yale Daily News*, May 19, 1922, 1.

first family that he ever had: David Levin, "F. O. Matthiessen," in *Exemplary Elders* (Athens: University of Georgia Press, 1990), 54.

Matthiessen's dedication to Skull and Bones: In her bibliography to the book *Secrets of the Tomb: Skull and Bones, the Ivy League, and the Hidden Paths to Power*, Alexandra Robbins cites *Continuation of the History of Our Order for the Century Celebration, 11 June 1933*, written by Little Devil, Class of D'121. Matthiessen's Skull and Bones nickname was Little Devil (described more fully below). As Robbins also helpfully explains, Skull and Bones members denote their class year by subtracting 1,802 and prefacing that number with a D. Since Matthiessen was the class of 1923, subtracting 1,802, made him the Little Devil, Class of D'121. Alexandra Robbins, *Secrets of the Tomb: Skull and Bones, the Ivy League, and the Hidden Paths of Power* (Boston: Little, Brown, 2002), 129, 214.

Matthiessen's initiation: Robbins, *Secrets of the Tomb*, 85, 69, 119, 126, 133, 134–36, 139.

20 *The experience of camaraderie and bonding:* Harry Levin, "The Private Life of F. O. Matthiessen," *New York Review of Books*, July 20, 1978, 43. Many years later, the scholar Harry Levin, a friend and former student of Matthiessen's, cautioned on reading too much into the effect of Skull and Bones rituals on Matthiessen's development. Matthiessen did grow

apart from a number of his Skull and Bones brothers over time. If Skull and Bones was not the end or extent of Matthiessen's notions of camaraderie, it set the tone for much of what was to follow in his later life.
"I had felt in the natural and hearty comradeship": FHE, 73.

20–21 *"Servants of the Devil"*: "DeForest Medal Oration to Take Place To-Night," *Yale Daily News*, January 22, 1924, 1.

21 *"It seems never to have occurred"*: F. O. Matthiessen, "Servants of the Devil," *Yale Alumni Weekly*, February 23, 1923, 642.
Eugene V. Debs: Dray, *There Is Power in a Union*, 228.
"Independent": FHE, 75.
Rhodes Scholarship: "Rhodes Scholarship Awarded to F. Otto Matthiessen 1923," *Yale Daily News*, December 4, 1922, 1.
"overexertion in domestic duties": Matthiessen, "Oxford Letter," 2.

22 *nest egg of $25,000*: Matthiessen to Cheney, November 14, 1924, in *R&D*, 57.
official divorce from Lucy Orne Matthiessen: Cook County, Illinois, Marriages Index, 1871–1920, https://www.ancestry.com.
He left an estate: *Matthiessen v. United States*, 67 Ct. Cl. 571, 574 (1929); "Estate Worth 7 Million Left by Matthiessen," *Chicago Tribune*, February 24, 1918, 8. Although the 1918 newspapers reported the worth of F. W. Matthiessen Sr.'s estate to be $7 million, when finally settled it was worth $9.5 million, as the court notes in *Matthiessen v. United States*, 67 Ct. Cl. 574.

23 *"veritable mountain empire"*: "Manufacturer Finds Cattle Ranching Practical Diversion," *Los Angeles Times*, April 17, 1921, X13; *Matthiessen v. Grand*, 92 Cal.App. 504, 506 (1928). The Court of Appeals of California, First Appellate Division, scaled back this estimate ever so slightly to forty-seven thousand acres.
F. W. Matthiessen Jr.'s second wife claimed: "Wife Seeks to Divorce Millionaire: F. W. Matthiessen, Jr. of Triunfo Is Defendant in Complaint Filed," *Los Angeles Times*, January 8, 1924, B3.
"the greatest present": Edward Whiting Fox, "Political Activism," in *Political Activism and the Academic Conscience: The Harvard Experience, 1936–1941, Hobart and William Smith Colleges, December 5 &6, 1975*, ed. John Lydenberg (Geneva, NY: The Colleges, 1977), 83.
"If, on the contrary": "Applications for Rhodes Scholarships Now Due," *Yale Daily News*, January 22, 1924, 3.

24 *"However shameful"*: Havelock Ellis and John Addington Symonds, *Sexual Inversion* (London: Wilson and Macmillan, 1897; repr., New York: Arno Press, 1975), 153. Page reference is to the 1975 edition.

25 *"I am only five feet six inches,"* and subsequent quotes: "Oxford Letter," 1–1B.

CHAPTER 2: "BETWEEN THE OLD AND THE NEW"

26 *his death in 1907*: "Knight D. Cheney Dies in Maine," *Hartford Courant*, August 14, 1907, 2; "A Well Known Manufacturer Dead," *Portsmouth Herald*, August 14, 1907, 2.
born in South Berwick, Maine: RC, 63. See also "Mrs. Knight D. Cheney;

Widow of Pioneer in Silk Industry Dies," *Hartford Courant*, September 18, 1915, 10, and State of Connecticut, Town of Manchester, Bureau of Vital Statistics, Certificate of Death for Ednah Dow Cheney, September 17, 1915.

27 *among the first to substitute*: Chris Bailey, *Two Hundred Years of American Clocks and Watches* (Englewood Cliffs, NJ: Prentice Hall, 1975), 69. The early clockmaking enterprises of the Cheney family were led by Timothy Cheney (1731–95) and Benjamin Cheney Jr. (1725–1815).

"Americanized" clockmaking: Philip Zea, *Clock Making in New England, 1725–825: An Interpretation of the Old Sturbridge Collection* (Sturbridge, MA: Old Sturbridge Village, 1992), 25.

Cheneys focused their collective gifts: Alice Farley Williams, *Silk and Guns: The Life of Connecticut Yankee, Frank Cheney, 1817–1904* (Manchester, CT: Manchester Historical Society, 1996), 45; William E. Buckley, *A New England Pattern: The History of Manchester, Connecticut* (Chester, CT: Pequot Press, 1973), 88–89, 91.

28 *Frank Woodbridge Cheney*: Antoinette Cheney Crocker, *Frank Woodbridge Cheney: Two Years in China and Japan, 1859–1861* (Worcester, MA.: Davis Press, 1970), 16, 107; Margreta Swenson Cheney, *If All the Great Men: The Cheneys of Manchester* (Manchester, CT: privately printed, 1975), 9.

his brother Clifford: Clifford Dudley Cheney (1878–1948) became a director of Cheney Brothers in 1918. In 1904, he a married his second cousin, Alice Elizabeth Cheney, known as Cass. Unless otherwise noted, all dates for births, deaths, and marriages of Cheney family members come from Edward H. Little, Descendants of George Cheney of Manchester, Connecticut, sponsored by the Cheney Cemetery Association, 1993, https://www.cheneycemetery.org.

Cheney Brothers produced dress and millinery silks: Buckley, *New England Pattern*, 142, 147, 244; Williams, *Silk and Guns*, 37, 72; Cheney Brothers Silk Manufacturing Company, *The Miracle Workers* (1916; repr., Manchester, CT: Manchester Historical Society, 2012), 15; Cheney, *If All the Great Men*, 42.

29 *"deep responsibility to the community"*: Buckley, *New England Pattern*, 148.

"business and community rose and declined together": Buckley, 150; Cheney, *If All the Great Men*, 44.

"The Cheneys occupy": Farwell Knapp Journal, February 14, 1921, pp. 367–68, box 10, folder 154, Knapp Papers.

a number of ancillary businesses: Buckley, *New England Pattern*, 145–46; Cheney, *If All the Great Men*, 31–32, 39; Williams, *Silk and Guns*, 110; John F. Sutherland, "Of Mills and Memories: Labor-Management Interdependence in the Cheney Silk Mills," *Oral History Review* 11 (1983): 39–40.

30 *"We will not submit"*: John F. Sutherland, "'One Loom or No Looms!': The 1902 Cheney Weavers' Strike," *Journal Inquirer* (Manchester, CT), September 17, 1993, 34.

Two more strikes occurred: Sutherland, "'One Loom'": Sutherland, "Of Mills and Memories," 25.

"searing bitterness" and subsequent quote: Sutherland, "Of Mills and Memories," 26.

workers were well paid: Cheney Brothers, *Miracle Workers*, 41; "Peace in Weavers' Strike Seen in Cheney Offer," *Hartford Courant*, April 19, 1923, 1.

A survey of the workers: Mathias Spiess and Percy W. Bidwell, *History of Manchester* (Manchester, CT: Centennial Committee of the Town of Manchester, 1924), 140.

Thanksgiving: Buckley, *New England Pattern*, 155; Emily Neville Cheney, *Traveler from a Small Kingdom* (New York: Harper & Row, 1968), 147; Williams, *Silk and Guns*, 165.

31 *posters "advertising" the theatricals:* The curators at the Cheney Homestead have attributed these posters to Russell Cheney, even though he did not sign them. David K. Smith, curator, Manchester Historical Society, email to author, January 2, 2012. The similarities with Cheney's later style bear out this attribution.

Walter Griffin and William Merritt Chase: "High School and Art Society," *Hartford Courant*, May 8, 1899, 8.

paintings of trees: Colin Sargent, "In the Studio of Walter Griffin," *Portland Monthly Magazine*, September 1994, 25.

"great colorist": Royal Cortissoz, *Walter Griffin* (New York: Ferargil, 1935), xiii.

32 *"One evening":* Cortissoz, *Walter Griffin*, xiii.

followed his four brothers: "Senior Society Elections," *Yale Daily News*, May 22, 1891, 1 (Knight Dexter Jr.); "Senior Elections," *Yale Daily News*, May 28, 1897, 1 (Clifford Dudley); "Senior Elections," *Yale Daily News*, May 25, 1900, 1 (Philip and Thomas Langdon); and "Senior Elections," *Yale Daily News*, May 22, 1903, 1 (Russell).

being very quiet: "Sons of Rich Men at Yale College," *Pittsburgh Weekly Gazette*, November 15, 1903, 13.

becoming an architect: RC, 5.

33 *tolerated it:* Louis Hyde, introduction to *R&D*, 6.

John Cheney and Seth Wells Cheney: These two were brothers of the seventh generation of Cheneys, who did not join their siblings in the founding of Cheney Brothers Silk Manufacturing Company. Instead, John Cheney (1801–85) did portraits of prominent literary and political men and women of his day, including William Cullen Bryant, Henry Wadsworth Longfellow, and Daniel Webster. Seth Wells Cheney (1810–56) was married to Ednah Dow Littlehale Cheney (1824–1904), who was an aunt to Russell's mother. Ednah Cheney was a prolific author, supporter of education for freed formerly enslaved people, and a promoter of women's rights. Both she and her husband were interested in Transcendentalism, and she wrote books about both her husband and his brother John. Ednah Dow Littlehale Cheney, *Memoir of John Cheney* (Boston: Lee and Shepard, 1889), and *Memoir of Seth W. Cheney* (Boston: Lee and Shepard, 1881).

Cheney gave a talk: "Russell Cheney Will Tell about Engravers," *Hartford Courant*, May 6, 1926, 13.

"rich vibrant Connecticut voice": RC, 6.

Officially listed as "hazel": 1921 US Passport Applications, Russell Cheney, National Archives and Records Administration, Washington, DC; Roll no. 1629; vol. no. Roll 1629—certificates 42376–42749, May 26–27, 1921, Ancestry Library, https://www.ancestrylibrary.com.

"unusually large brown eyes": C. L. Barber, "Statements by Friends and Associates," in *F. O. Matthiessen: A Collective Portrait*, ed. Paul M. Sweezy and Leo Huberman (New York: Henry Schuman, 1950), 100.

"lively mind": RC, 6.

"imbibe culture": Knapp quoted by Louis Hyde, introduction to *R&D*, 7.

35   *his brother Thomas*: Thomas Langdon Cheney (1879–1916) became general manager of the New York City sales offices of Cheney Brothers after the death of Knight Dexter Jr., Russell's eldest brother, from tuberculosis. He married Judith Stager Calkins in 1916. "Thomas L. Cheney Dies in Colorado," *Hartford Courant*, October 24, 1916, 10.

Cheney studied with: New York Art Students League, Class Records for Russell Cheney, 1912, 1914–15.

Académie Julian: There are some discrepancies in the dates that Cheney was at the Art Students League of New York and the Académie Julian. In *Russell Cheney: A Record of His Work*, Matthiessen claimed that Cheney was at the Art Students League from 1904 to 1907 followed by three years at the Académie Julian. In *The Julian Academy, Paris, 1868–1939*, Catherine Fehrer records that Cheney was a student of Jean-Paul Laurens at the Académie Julian from 1906 to 1909. See *RC*, 5, and Catherine Fehrer, *The Julian Academy, Paris, 1868–1939* (New York: Shepard Gallery, 1989), n.p.

Several of Cheney's teachers: Walter Griffin, Kenyon Cox, and Charles H. Woodbury, as well as his cousin Charles Adams Platt, and his friend Henry Varnum Poor, who was a painter, also studied at the Académie Julian. Fehrer, *Julian Academy*, n.p.

studied at the New York Art Students League: In *Russell Cheney: A Record of His Work (RC, 5)*, Matthiessen claimed that Cheney was president of the Art Students League in 1912. Matthiessen probably took this date from Cheney's own handwritten curriculum vitae (n.d., collection of Richard Candee), which also claims that he had been president in 1912. In the *Sexennial Record of the Class of 1904* of Yale College published in 1911, Cheney noted that he resigned his position as president in 1910. Although Cheney had many talents and charms, being detail oriented was not among them. By the league's own records, Cheney was president from 1909 to 1910. Marchal E. Landgren, *Years of Art: The Story of the Art Students League of New York* (New York: Robert M. McBride, 1940), 110.

36   *"decorative"*: References over the years to Cheney's work as "decorative" include "Russell Cheney Paintings Simply Defy Classification," *Portland Sunday Telegram*, January 25, 1920, 7; Edwin Alden Jewell, "Five Artists," *New York Times*, April 9, 1939, X9; and "Native Art on Parade," *New York Sun*, October 31, 1941, 32.

Chase pushed his students' work: Ronald Pisano, *The Students of William*

Merritt Chase (Huntington, NY: Heckscher Museum, 1973), 3, 25–26; Ronald G. Pisano, "The Teaching of William Merritt Chase," *American Artist*, March 1976, 33, 64.

Charles H. Woodbury: Woodbury was born in Lynn, Massachusetts, in 1864. He is credited with turning Ogunquit into a summer arts colony. Woodbury opened his Ogunquit Summer School of Drawing and Painting in 1898 and enrolled between sixty and one hundred students each summer. Later, in 1923, he renamed his school The Art of Seeing— Woodbury Course in Observation. Joan Loria and Warren A. Seamens, *Earth, Sea and Sky: Charles H. Woodbury—Artist and Teacher, 1864–1940* (Cambridge, MA: MIT Museum, 1988), 29, 32.

37 *Cheney had a painting studio:* Elizabeth Cheney Blackburn Photograph Album, "Uncle Russell—Studio at York Harbor," photo no. 117, Connecticut Historical Society Museum and Library, Hartford.

stayed frequently at Kincroft: Olive Floyd and Samuel Thorne, *Joy Is the Banner: The Life of Ethel M. Cheney* (Rye, NY: privately printed, 1950), 93.

"older, quieter": George M Young, *Force through Delicacy: The Life and Art of Charles H. Woodbury* (Portsmouth, NH: Peter E. Randell, 1998), 28.

"Art is not based": Loria and Seamens, *Earth, Sea and Sky*, 32–33.

paint outside: Young, *Force through Delicacy*, 24.

"taught him how to paint": "The Mission at Santa Barbara," *Boston Sunday*, March 4, 1934, A-8.

38 *independently rich:* Town of Manchester, CT, Probate Records, Knight Dexter Cheney, will dated May 17, 1880, vol. 25, pp. 280–83, proved Knight Dexter Cheney Estate-Application, December 7, 1915, vol. 32, pp. 523–526.7, Connecticut Probate Court (Manchester District), www.ancestrylibrary .com.

lengthy stay of several years: The precise dates of Cheney's stay at Cragmor are not clear. In his note in the 1919 Yale Vicennial, Cheney claimed to have been at Cragmor for three years from 1916 to 1918. Cheney definitely arrived there in October 1916. But judging from his correspondence with friends throughout these years, the date that he left Cragmor is less clear. During late 1917, he traveled back to the East Coast for two or three months, perhaps for the holidays. Then in 1918, he spent several months during the beginning of the year with his sister Harriet and her family in Santa Barbara. Yale University, Class of 1904, *Vicennial Record of the Class of Nineteen Hundred and Four*, Yale College, ed. Elton Parks (New Haven, CT: Published under the Direction of the Class Secretaries Bureau, 1924), 131, https://archive.org/stream/vicennialrecordooounse /vicennialrecordooounse_djvu.txt.

lost his sister: RC, 16; "Thomas L. Cheney Dies in Colorado," *Hartford Courant*, October 24, 1916, 10.

Before antibiotics: Thomas M. Daniel, *Captain of Death: The Story of Tuberculosis* (Rochester, NY: University of Rochester Press, 1997), 184.

39 *"Sun Palace":* Douglas R. McKay, *Asylum of the Gilded Pill* (Denver: State Historical Society of Colorado, 1983), 54, 17, 14–15, 76, 100, 9–10.

40   *He read constantly, widely*: I have supplemented Matthiessen's reference
to Cheney's reading at Cragmor with a listing of the books inscribed and
dated by Cheney in 1916. I compiled this list at Matthiessen and Cheney's
Kittery home during the summer of 2009 with Richard Candee, professor emeritus, American and New England studies, Boston University;
Carol L. Cheney, Russell Cheney's great niece; and Jay Grossman, associate professor of English at Northwestern University. *RC*, 17.

he bought himself a new Ford: "Cars Delivered during May," Vollmer Bros.,
Colorado Springs Gazette, June 10, 1917, 15.

he often bought a new car: Farwell Knapp Journal, May 21, 1922, p. 170, box
11, folder 158, Knapp Papers.

Cheney had his Fords specially outfitted: Patricia L. Heard and Richard M.
Candee, "Russell Cheney: Artist of the Piscataqua," 11, www.russellcheney
.com/biography/; Horace Mitchell, "Proof of the Hour," *Christian Science
Monitor*, March 24, 1955, 12.

"assimilated" Cézanne: *RC*, 16.

Cézanne's importance to Cheney dated back: *RC*, 12; Yale University, *1910
Sexennial Record for the Class of 1904 at Yale College* (New Haven, CT: Yale
University Press, 1911), 75; John Rewald, in collaboration with Walter
Feilchenfeldt and Jayne Warman, *The Paintings of Cézanne: A Catalogue
Raisonné* (London: Thames and London, 1996), 1:98–99.

42   *paid for*: Farwell Knapp Journal, October 6, 1917, n.p., box 8, folder 145,
Knapp Papers.

also in Skull and Bones: Alexandra Robbins, *Secrets of the Tomb: Skull and
Bones, the Ivy League, and the Hidden Paths of Power* (Boston: Little, Brown,
2002), 148.

ambiguous territory: Although Cheney and Putnam's friendship had homoerotic overtones, I can find no definitive proof in their correspondence
that they were romantically or sexually involved with each other as
William J. Mann asserts in *Kate*. Putnam would go on to marry twice: to
Ruth Peters in 1920, and after they divorced in 1930, to Una Fairweather in
1933. Heterosexual marriage notwithstanding, Putnam did have a number of remarkably close relationships with other men who were either
gay, such as Cheney, or whose sexuality has been questioned over the
years. See William J. Mann, *Kate: The Woman Who Was Hepburn* (New York:
Henry Holt, 2006), 106; Putnam and Peters marriage, Massachusetts
Marriage Index, 1901–1955 and 1966–1970, and Putnam and Fairweather
marriage, New Hampshire Marriage and Divorce Records, 1659–1947,
https://www.ancestry.com.

affinity for younger people: Farwell Knapp Journal, December 4, 1921, p.
338, box 10, folder 156, Knapp Papers.

prevented him from serving: United States, World War I Draft Registration
Card for Russell Cheney, September 14, 1918, https://www.ancestry.com.

43   *"Jehovah Skies"*: *RC*, 17.

"enforced idleness" and subsequent quote: *RC*, 16.

first major exhibition: To date, the most complete published record of

Russell Cheney's work remains Matthiessen's book *Russell Cheney: A Record of His Work*, 1947, with black-and-white images of Cheney's paintings. In discussing Cheney's exhibitions and paintings, I have also relied on the Herculean efforts of Richard Candee and Carol L. Cheney, who have compiled a preliminary catalogue raisonné and timeline of Cheney's exhibitions and gave me access to the database. A more thorough, contemporary art historical assessment of Cheney's work, complete with color photographs, has yet to be undertaken and published.

Cheney sold at least four: Russell Cheney to Phelps Putnam, January 17, 1917, box 1, Putnam Papers; Exhibition of Paintings by Russell Cheney, Wadsworth Atheneum Annex, January 15 to 20, 1917, catalogue annotated in Cheney's hand, private collection.

"to convey through the canvas": "Connecticut as a Field for the Artist's Brush," *Hartford Courant*, December 7, 1919, pt. 5, 8.

44   *Welles purchased:* The Cheneys were staunch abolitionists. Charles Cheney's home in Ohio, for example, where Russell Cheney's father was born, had even served as an outpost of the Underground Railroad. The Spencer repeating rifle represented a tactical advantage for the North, because it could fire ammunition more quickly than the muzzle-loader rifles in use at the time. Christopher Spencer, the inventor of the Spencer repeating rifle, was an employee at Cheney Brothers, and the company supported him in the development of his rifle. Later, the Cheneys invested in the Spencer Repeating Rifle Company, with Russell Cheney's grandfather and great-uncles, Rush and Ward, serving on its board of directors. The Cheney Brothers investment in the Spencer Repeating Rifle Company also helped Cheney Brothers stay afloat through the Civil War. Joseph G. Bilby, *A Revolution in Arms: A History of the First Repeating Rifles* (Yardley, PA: Westholme, 2006), 74–75; Cheney, *If All the Great Men*, 7; Williams, *Silk and Guns*, 90–92, 97.

Cheney had begun "to employ color": Babcock Galleries and Rhode Island School of Design, *Paintings by Russell Cheney, with a foreword by Christian Brinton* (New York, 1921–22), n.p.

44–45 *created an environment, arranging "old furniture":* Lula Merrick, "In the World of Art," *Morning Telegraph* (New York), December 18, 1921, 6.

45   Woodstock: Prior to going to Cragmor in 1916, Cheney spent the summer in Woodstock, New York, where the New York Art Students League maintained its summer school. Landgren, *Years of Art*, 85; Cheney to Putnam, August 20, 1916, box 1, folder 1, Putnam Papers.

"the struggle going on within Mr. Cheney": "Versatility Shown by Russell Cheney," *American Art News*, December 17, 1921, 1.

"Of the new people": Henry McBride, "New Landscapes by Russell Cheney," *New York Herald*, December 18, 1921, 3.

"the flower paintings": "Art: The December Exhibits: Paintings by Russell Cheney," *New York Times*, December 18, 1921, X-8.

"feels surfaces well" and subsequent quote: Hamilton Easter Field, "Works of Various Shows," *Brooklyn Daily Eagle*, December 18, 1921, sec. C-7.

46 *"needs only to be"*: Royal Cortissoz, "Random Impressions in Current Exhibitions," *New York Tribune*, December 18, 1921, sec. C-6.
Vitrine: RC, 18, 26.
Cheney sold thirteen paintings: Knapp Journal, December 3, 1922, p. 70, box 11, folder 160, Knapp Papers.
the trustees agreed to acquire: "Atheneum Accepts Cheney Painting," *Hartford Daily Courant*, December 4, 1922, 7. Although the *Hartford Courant* reported that the museum had acquired *Skungimaug—Afternoon*, the museum bought *Skungimaug—Morning*, which it still owns.

47 *"The thing is"*: RC, 58.

CHAPTER 3: FALLING IN LOVE

48 *Ellen Lambert and her husband, Alex*: In 1895 Ellen Waitstill Cheney (1863–1938), Russell's eldest sister, married Yale graduate and Skull and Bones member Alexander Lambert. Lambert served as the personal physician to President Theodore Roosevelt, whom he counted as a friend. For many years Lambert was a director of medical services at Bellevue Hospital in New York City; he was also a noted expert on alcoholism and drug addiction. During World War I, when Lambert went to France to work for the American Red Cross, his wife joined him, working in the personnel bureau of the agency. "Mrs. Alexander Lambert," *New York Times*, January 14, 1938, 23; "Dr. Lambert Dies; Narcotics Expert," *New York Times*, May 10, 1939: 23; "The Senior Society Elections," *Yale Daily News*, May 25, 1883, 1.
wedding of his Skull and Bones brother: "Penelope Overton Weds L. K. Hyde, Jr.," *New York Times*, September 10, 1924, 21; "Senior Society Elections Given to College Juniors," *Yale Daily News*, May 22, 1922, 1.

49 *an elite crowd*: United Kingdom Incoming Passenger Lists, 1878–1960, Paris, https://www.ancestry.com.
"fell into easy intimacy" and subsequent quotes in next two paragraphs: R&D, 17–18.

50 *talking about their respective sexual histories*: R&D, 18
"That was all": R&D, 18.

51 *"I carried Walt Whitman"*: Matthiessen to Cheney, September 21, 1924, R&D, 26.
As historian George Chauncey: George Chauncey, *Gay New York: Gender, Urban Culture, and the Making of the Gay Male World, 1890–1940* (New York: Basic Books, 1994), 180.
"Hard faces": Matthiessen to Cheney, September 24, 1924, R&D, 33.
"Marriage!": Matthiessen to Cheney, September 23, 1924, R&D, 29.

52 *"even painted whores"*: Matthiessen to Cheney, October 10, 1924, R&D, 35.
"more about life": Cheney to Matthiessen, October 13, 1924, R&D, 37.
San Marco . . . and Colleone: RC, 34, 36.
Cheney modeled Colleone: In 1911 Cheney had studied privately with Chase after his return to New York from Paris. If Cheney hadn't seen *Old Venetian Houses* (1913) (or *Old Houses, Venice*) in Chase's studio, then

he saw the painting in the 1914 *Ten American Painters* show in New York. Also included in this show was Chase's painting *Asters* (ca. 1913), which inspired several other Cheney canvases, including *Canterbury Bells*, (1918?) and *Chrysanthemums and Elephant* (n.d.). *Ten American Painters* (New York: Montross Gallery, March 18, 1914–April 7, 1914), n.p.; Ronald G. Pisano, completed by D. Frederick Baker and Carolyn K. Lane, *William Merritt Chase: The Complete Catalogue of Known and Documented Work—Landscapes in Oil*, vol. 3 (New Haven, CT: Yale University Press, 2009), 151, plate no. L317.

53   *"hentracks across eternity"*: RC, 6.

photographer Wilhelm von Gloeden: Robert Aldrich, *The Seduction of the Mediterranean: Writing, Art and Homosexual Fantasy* (New York: Routledge, 1993), 143–44, 146, 149.

54   *"My union with you"*: Matthiessen to Cheney, February 8, 1925, *R&D*, 90.
"unions like ours": Matthiessen to Cheney, January 29, 1925, *R&D*, 71.

55   *"The base of our love"*: Cheney to Matthiessen, February 5, 1925, *R&D*, 80.
Summoning Walt Whitman's poem: Matthiessen to Cheney, February 7, 1925, *R&D*, 86.
"'if the body is'": Matthiessen recalls Whitman's line from "I Sing the Body Electric" as "if the body is not the soul, what then is the soul?" His memory was close, but not exact. Line 8 of the poem reads: "And if the body were not the soul, what is the soul?" See https://www.poetryfoundation.org/poems/45472/i-sing-the-body-electric.
"For it is obvious": Matthiessen to Cheney, February 9, 1925, *R&D*, 93.
"It is a much smaller thing": Cheney to Matthiessen, February 11, 1925, *R&D*, 95.

56   *Russell Davenport*: "Senior Society Elections Given to College Juniors," 1.
"Thank God you found it!": Matthiessen to Cheney, April 10, 1925, *R&D*, 119–20. Matthiessen quotes Davenport in his letter to Cheney.
Cheney sold eighteen paintings: Exhibition of Paintings by Russell Cheney, Babcock Galleries, New York, April 27–May 9, 1925, and Exhibition of Paintings by Russell Cheney, Wadsworth Atheneum Annex, Hartford, CT, May 13–23, 1925. Both catalogues are annotated in what appears to by Cheney's handwriting.

57   *"tenth cognac"*: Matthiessen to Cheney, January 28, 1925, *R&D*, 69.
"The remark about sneaking": Matthiessen to Cheney, February 8, 1925, *R&D*, 92.

58   *"Being alone"*: Matthiessen to Cheney, April 7, 1925, *R&D*, 116.
"perfect Chaucerian yeoman" and subsequent quotes: Matthiessen to Cheney, April 18, 1925, *R&D*, 124.
"I get the whole scene": Cheney to Matthiessen, April 30, 1925, *R&D*, 137.

59   *"I'm afraid Mr. Matthiessen"*: Cheney to Matthiessen, March 23, 1926, box 17, folder 14, Matthiessen Papers.
Cheney's new brother-in-law: Knapp Journal, July 7, 1930, pp. 83, 85, 87, 89, box 15, folder 174, Knapp Papers.

60   *architects*: Marge Flynn, "Learned House Rich in Cheney Memorabilia," *Manchester Evening Herald*, January 28, 1961, 5.

The main room of the studio: Marge Flynn, "Learned House Rich in Cheney Memorabilia"; Susan Plese, "Home Sweet Barn," *Manchester Evening Herald, Weekend Plus*, August 16, 1986, 20; "Exhibition of Paintings by Russell Cheney and Varnum Poor at the Atheneum All This Week," *Hartford Courant*, December 5, 1920, X7.

he planted violets: Antoinette Cheney Crocker, *Great Oaks: Memoirs of the Cheney Family* (Concord, MA: privately printed, 1977), 104–5.

"The lion throws": Wolfram Eberhard, *A Dictionary of Chinese Symbols*, trans. G. L. Campbell (London: Routledge, 1986), 164.

61   *"a sea green":* Cheney to Matthiessen, February 14, 1926, box 17, folder 13, Matthiessen Papers.

KDs decided to sell the house: Charles Adams Platt designed and oversaw the renovation of the KD House. It had been four stories; Platt made it three. Platt covered the clapboard exterior in brick and remodeled everything except the living room. He also designed the house of Russell's brother Clifford, who lived next door to the KD House. Knapp Journal, April 1926, pp. 174–76, box 15, folder 166, Knapp Papers; Elizabeth C. Chase and Margarete E. Rhodes, interview with Elizabeth C. Chase, April 21, 1976, transcript, p. 6, published in Manchester, CT, by the Institute of Local History, Manchester Community College, 1976. Elizabeth C. Chase was Clifford and Alice Cheney's housekeeper.

"He is so steeped": Knapp Journal, September 21, 1925, p. 69, box 13, folder 166, Knapp Papers.

62   *"I have not been blind":* Matthiessen to Cheney, April 26, 1926, box 19, folder 13, Matthiessen Papers.

"get out": Matthiessen to Cheney, April 29, 1926, box 19, folder 13, Matthiessen Papers.

a transition is apparent: In *Russell Cheney: A Record of His Work*, Matthiessen dates the development of Cheney's mature style to a few years earlier, 1923–24, when the two men met, but Matthiessen does not explain how or why he arrives at this opinion. See *RC*, 31.

"God, feller": Cheney to Matthiessen, March 31, 1925, *R&D*, 111.

63   *The change was not lost:* "He is obviously on an auspicious path," in "Random Impression in Current Exhibitions," *New York Herald Tribune*, March 20, 1927, sec. VI-10; "He has come to feel the persuasions of the modernist," in Ralph Flint, "The Independents and Others Exhibit," *Christian Science Monitor*, March 17, 1927, 11.

Hotel Royal Grande Bretagne: I'm grateful to David W. Dunlap for his architectural sleuthing on this point.

CHAPTER 4: A STAR IS BORN

65   *"filled with an increasing desire":* RC, 63.

"the sailorman locks": "Cutting Costs in Our Navy Yards," *Marine Review* 46, no. 11 (November 1916): 374.

67   *"whale of a cut":* Russell Cheney to Phelps Putnam, August 13, 1927, box

1, folder 5, Putnam Papers; Minutes, Directors Meeting, September 14, 1926, and Minutes, Directors Meeting, June 5, 1928, Cheney Brothers Silk Manufacturing Company records, 1734–1979, Archives & Special Collections, University of Connecticut Library, https://archivessearch .lib.uconn.edu/repositories/2/resources/304.

Two photographs: In a letter from March 1928, Matthiessen sent Cheney these two photographs of himself. He did not label them, but Louis Hyde, who much later edited the published collection of Matthiessen and Cheney's correspondence, *Rat & the Devil*, queried in his notes for the book whether these photographs might have dated from the summer of 1927 at Kittery Point. If Hyde's speculation is accurate, the photographs were likely taken at Seapoint Beach in Kittery Point, where Matthiessen and Cheney liked to swim. F. O. Matthiessen to Cheney, March 9, 1928, box 19, folder 25, Matthiessen Papers.

"seldom overflowed": John Rackliffe, "Notes for a Character Study," in *FOM*, 84.

Cheney returned to South Manchester: The 1928 town directory of Manchester was the first year in which Russell Cheney's studio at 30 Forest Street was officially listed as his home address. Later, when Cheney moved to Kittery permanently, he rented out his studio home to Horace Learned, his first cousin, once removed, and his wife, Eileen. Town of Manchester, CT, Warranty of Deeds, book 93, 93–94, Town Clerk, Land Records; Town of Manchester Directory, 1928, 116; Marge Flynn, "Learned House Rich in Cheney Memorabilia," *Manchester Evening Herald*, January 28, 1961, 3.

68 *"'Bayne had you and Matty watched'":* Cheney to Matthiessen, November 8, 1927, box 17, folder 29, Matthiessen Papers. Hugh Aiken Bayne and Helen Cheney divorced after World War I in 1919. A lawyer, Bayne had served in World War I and at its end was stationed in Berne, Switzerland, to negotiate an agreement on the treatment of prisoners of war. He noted in his memoirs that Berne, because it was situated in Switzerland and bordered by Germany, France, and Italy, was a hotbed of spy activity. Given these contacts as well as his fluency in French, he likely had easy access to arranging for the services of a private detective. See Alexander Blackburn, *Meeting the Professor: Growing Up in the William Blackburn Family* (Winston-Salem, NC: John F. Blair, 2004), 47–50; "H. A. Bayne in France during WWI," Bayne and Gayle Family Papers no. 1101, reel 4, pp. 83, 150, Southern Historical Collection, Wilson Library, University of North Carolina at Chapel Hill.

"sick of Manchester": Farwell Knapp Journal, February 1928, p. 90, box 14, folder 170, Knapp Papers.

well-known houses of worship: These paintings included *Meeting Street, Charleston, SC* (1928); *Timrod's Square, Charleston, SC* (1928); *St. Philips Church, Charleston, SC* (1928); *Charleston Church in Spring* (1928); and *Old Coffee House, Charleston, SC* (1928 or earlier), among others. CC.

69 *"paint less":* RC, 76.

"half day masterpieces": Matthiessen to Cheney, March 10, 1926, box 19, folder 12, Matthiessen Papers.

"He has all the technical skill": Farwell Knapp Journal, March 7, 1928, p. 92, box 14, folder 177, Knapp Papers.

working in the mornings: Helen B. Knapp, "Statements by Friends and Associates," in *FOM*, 116.

70   *switched from Babcock*: Matthiessen to Cheney, September 28, 1928, box 19, folder 16, Matthiessen Papers; "Visiting the Art Galleries," *Brooklyn Union Times*, June 2, 1929, 28.

"full richness": "About Town," *New York Times*, December 2, 1928, 151.

In focusing on New England: Donna M. Cassidy, "'On the Subject of Nativeness': Marsden Hartley and New England Regionalism," *Winterthur Portfolio* 29, no. 4 (Winter 1994): 227–45; Michael C. Stein, "Regionalism in the Great Depression," *Geographical Review* 73 (October 1983): 430–46; Barbara Rose, "The Thirties: Reaction and Rebellion," chap. 5 in *American Art since 1900*, rev. and expanded ed. (New York: Praeger, 1975), 93–129.

"cheap": Russell Cheney, review of *The Birth of the American Tradition in Art*, by Oskar Hagen, *New England Quarterly* 13, no. 2 (June 1940): 343.

"Painter from Maine": Donna M. Cassidy, *Marsden Hartley: Race, Region, and Nation* (Hanover, NH: University Press of New England, 2005), 17.

71   *Katharine Hepburn*: William J. Mann, *Kate: The Woman Who Was Hepburn* (New York: Henry Holt, 2006), 144. The *Hartford Daily Times* reported that "Russell Cheney of South Manchester, who has been spending the winter in New York, has been painting the portrait of Mrs. Ludlow Ogden Smith, formerly Miss Katherine [*sic*] Hepburn, daughter of Dr. and Mrs. Thomas Hepburn of Bloomfield Avenue." *Hartford Daily Times*, Society, March 16, 1929, 13.

Elizabeth Foster . . . Virginia Biddle; and Marcia Clarke: These portraits were entitled *Mrs. Maxwell E. Foster* (1928 or earlier); *Mrs. Nicholas Biddle* (1928); and *Mrs. Marcia Clarke* 1928–29, respectively. Maxwell Foster was a classmate of Matthiessen's who went on to practice law. Virginia Biddle (née Morris) cannot be identified with absolute certainty, because Cheney offered no clues in his correspondence as to how he came to paint her portrait. A native of New York, she married Nicholas Biddle in September 1928. Cynthia Cheney, another of Russell Cheney's first cousins, once removed, was a bridesmaid at the Biddle ceremony, so he may have come by this job through a family connection. Marcia Clarke married Russell "Mitch" Davenport on May 13, 1929. At the time Cheney painted this portrait, Clarke and Davenport also had an apartment on Beekman Place near Cheney's. "Senior Society Elections Given to College Juniors," *Yale Daily News*, May 19, 1922, 1; "Marriage Announcement," *New York Times*, September 16, 1928, 28; "Mrs. M. G. Clarke Becomes a Bride," *New York Times*, May 14, 1929, 37; Mann, *Kate*, 115.

72   *"Well, all of a sudden"*: Cheney to Matthiessen, January 16, 1929, box 17, folder 38, Matthiessen Papers.

73   *"whoring"*: Cheney to Matthiessen, February 14, 1929, box 17, folder 38, Matthiessen Papers.

"He [the doctor] has a friend": Cheney to Matthiessen, February 14, 1929, box 17, folder 38, Matthiessen Papers.

"This time, after the freshness": Matthiessen to Cheney, January 10, 1929, box 19, folder 30, Matthiessen Papers.

74 *"New York always stimulated him"*: RC, 76.

"Matthiessen and Cheney constructed": David Bergman, "F. O. Matthiessen: The Critic as Homosexual," *Raritan* 9, no. 4 (Spring 1990): 67.

75 *"My friend"*: SOJ, 155.

Cheney contributed: A great deal of variety exists in the titles of Cheney's paintings. For example, *Miss Jewett's Staircase* has been known as *Stairway, Jewett House* and *Hall of the South Berwick House*, as Matthiessen referred to the painting in *Russell Cheney: A Record of His Work*. The most complete record of Russell Cheney's paintings to date is the preliminary catalogue raisonné compiled by Richard Candee and Carol L. Cheney, thus I have used their titles when a discrepancy exists. CC.

his painting entitled The Hall: Given his affection for Sarah Orne Jewett's work and his ties to Charles H. Woodbury, Cheney must have seen a copy of Jewett's collection *Deephaven* published in 1894 and illustrated by Woodbury and his wife, Susan Marcia Oaks. Cheney's painting *Miss Jewett's Staircase* is very similar in composition to *The Hall* by Woodbury and Oaks, which appeared in that edition of the book. Woodbury and Oaks also went on to illustrate *The Tory Lover*, another Jewett collection. In one of the many roads that lead back to this particular corner of New England, Susan Marcia Oaks was originally from South Berwick. George M. Young, *Force through Delicacy: The Life and Art of Charles H. Woodbury* (Portsmouth, NH: Peter E. Randell, 1998), 12, 13–14.

76 *"covert celebration"*: Bergman, "F. O. Matthiessen," 72.

Boston marriage: Is a long-term, loving relationship between two women, which may or may not have been sexual. Lillian Faderman, *Odd Girls and Twilight Lovers: A History of Lesbian Life in Twentieth-Century America* (New York: Penguin Books, 1992), 15.

77 *"Pinny" for Jewett and "Fuffy" for Fields*: F. O. Matthiessen, *Sarah Orne Jewett* manuscript, 53, F. O. Matthiessen Papers, 1929–1950, Houghton Library, Harvard University, b MS AM 1433; Kate Kennedy, "Sarah Orne Jewett: Writer of 'Country of the Pointed Firs,'" in *More Than Petticoats: Remarkable Maine Women* (Guildford, CT: Globe Pequot Press, 2005), 46.

"daily letters": SOJ, 73.

"Nan is": SOJ, 72.

"deserves to be read": Dorothy Van Doren, "A Distinguished Book," review of *Sarah Orne Jewett* by F. O. Matthiessen, *New York Herald Tribune*, April 14, 1929, K4.

One of Jewett's later biographers: Paula Blanchard, *Sarah Orne Jewett: Her World and Her Work* (Reading, MA: Addison Wesley, 1994), 232.

78 *Matthiessen had a tendency to empathize*: Giles Gunn, *F. O. Matthiessen: The Critical Achievement* (Seattle: University of Washington Press, 1975), 44.

he points out and subsequent quotes: *SOJ*, 144, 149, 145.

78–79　*"Not at all"* . . . *"Personality"*: Horace Mitchell, "Artist's Picture of Kittery Point Put Spirit of Old Town on Canvas," *Portland Sunday Telegram and Sunday Press Herald*, October 14, 1928, 7.

79　*artistic conscience*: Matthiessen to Putnam, September 18, 1945, box 6, Putnam Papers.

80　*"Much as he loves him"*: Farwell Knapp Journal, April 21, 1930, p. 17, box 15, folder 175, Knapp Papers.

　　Madame Sosostris: Cheney to Putnam, September 18, 1928(?), box 1, folder 1, Putnam Papers.

　　"Baby Doll": Cheney to Putnam, December 12, 1932, box 2, folder 7, Putnam Papers.

　　"Old Fairies Lane": Cheney to Putnam, December 12, 1932, box 2, folder 7, Putnam Papers.

　　"I feel the need": Cheney to Putnam, November 5, 1941, box 2, folder 8, Putnam Papers.

　　Bronson Cutting: Richard Lowitt, *Bronson M. Cutting: Progressive Politician* (Albuquerque: University of New Mexico Press, 1992), 17–18.

81　*Larry Tighe*: "Senior Society Elections Given to College Juniors," *Yale Daily News*, May 21, 1915, 1; "L. G. Tighe, 60, Dies; Yale Ex-Official," *New York Times*, December 4, 1954, 17.

　　"Cheney and his little boys": Cheney to Matthiessen, December 26, 1929, *R&D*, 180. The *Dictionary of Sexual Slang* cites the term "boy" as a euphemism for a homosexual man. William J. Mann, in his discussion of Putnam and his circle of friends in Santa Fe in *Kate*, notes that "little boys" referred to homosexual men. Manning points out that Katharine Hepburn used this expression disparagingly to refer to the circle around gay director George Cukor. Alan Richter, *Dictionary of Sexual Slang: Words, Phrases, and Idioms from AC/DC to Zig-Zig* (New York: John Wiley & Sons, 1993), 28; Mann, *Kate*, 108, 384–85.

　　"I wrote 'inexcusable'": Cheney to Matthiessen, December 26, 1929, *R&D*, 181.

　　"that crowd that he traveled with": Lowitt, *Bronson M. Cutting*, 310.

　　Cheney befriended Paul Hoen: RC, 83, 86–87.

82　*"I am certain this picture of Paul Hoen"*: Cheney to Matthiessen, April 19, 1930, *R&D*, 213.

　　"a damn bourgeois": RC, 52.

83　*"Your extraordinary poignant letter"*: Matthiessen to Cheney, April 21, 1930, *R&D*, 215.

　　Harvard College of the early 1930s: Morton Keller and Phyllis Keller, *Making Harvard Modern: The Rise of America's University* (New York: Oxford University Press, 2001), 14, 32, 47.

　　History and Literature Program: Leo Marx, "The Teacher," *FOM*, 40; F. O. Matthiessen, "A Teacher Takes His Stand: The President of the Teachers' Union Contributes a Harvard Credo," *Harvard Progressive*, September 1940, 12–14.

84　*lived at Eliot house*: Eliot House was named for Charles Eliot, who served as president of Harvard from 1869 to 1909 and famously compiled and edited the Harvard Classics, a series of classic works from world literature.

"essentially a teacher": Richard M. Cook, *Alfred Kazin: A Biography* (New Haven, CT: Yale University Press, 2007), 122.

Matthiessen's main courses: *Dictionary of American Biography, Supplement Four, 1946–1950*, ed. John A. Garranty and Edward T. Jones (New York: Charles Scribner's Sons, 1974), s.v. "Matthiessen, Francis Otto"; Gale in Context: Biography, https://www.gale.com/c/in-context-biography.

Matthiessen was not a slick lecturer: Daniel Aaron, scholar and former student of F. O. Matthiessen, in discussion with the author, October 4, 2010.

"knew more students": Shaun O'Connell, "F. O. Matthiessen's Stature Reinforced," review of *Rat & the Devil: Journal Letters of F.O. Matthiessen and Russell Cheney, Boston Globe*, August 20, 1978, B24.

Kinoy: Paul Lewis, "Arthur Kinoy Is Dead at 82, Lawyers for Chicago Seven," *New York Times*, September 20, 2003, A-11.

85   *surrogate father*: Given Matthiessen's friendships with his students, it is worth noting that there is no record of him crossing the line into sexual activity with any of them. Matthiessen's student Joseph Summers and his wife, U. T. Summers, in their entry on Matthiessen in the *Dictionary of American Biography*, noted that Matthiessen was "unusually hostile to homosexual colleagues who mixed their academic and sexual relations." In colleges and universities, sexual relations between faculty and students are hardly the domain of gay people, but Matthiessen's sensitivity to the subject may account for the suggestion of self-hatred conveyed in Summers's account. *Dictionary of American Biography*, s.v. "Matthiessen, Francis Otto"; Gale in Context: Biography.

fourteen hundred copies: Matthiessen to Cheney, November 2, 1929, *R&D*, 168.

favorable note: Matthiessen to Cheney, October 21, 1929, *R&D*, 165.

"It is time for the history": F. O. Matthiessen, "New Standards in American Criticism," *Yale Review*, 1929, reprinted in *The Responsibilities of the Critic: Essays and Reviews by F. O. Matthiessen, selected by John Rackliffe* (New York: Oxford University Press, 1952), 181.

86   *"a natural fighter"*: John Rackliffe, "Notes for a Character Study," *FOM*, 85.

"I have been lost in loneliness": Matthiessen to Cheney, November 29, 1929, *R&D*, 173.

87   *"just like any fairy"*: Matthiessen to Cheney, January 21, 1930, *R&D*, 197.

"My sex bothers me": Matthiessen to Cheney, January 30, 1930, *R&D*, 200.

"Dear feller": Matthiessen to Cheney, December 2, 1929, *R&D*, 174.

"contemptible manuscript": Matthiessen to Cheney, January 13, 1930, *R&D*, 194.

made a great impression: Matthiessen to Cheney May 14, 1930, *R&D*, 217.

88   *"There are other equally disturbing contrasts"*: "Russell Cheney, Montross Galleries," *Art News*, May 10, 1930, 15.

"drinks because he is unhappy": Farwell Knapp Journal, May 30, 1930, p. 47, box 15, folder 174, Knapp Papers.

A Star Is Born: The original version of *A Star Is Born* was released in 1937 and starred Janet Gaynor and Fredric March. But given Judy Garland's near-iconic status in the gay community, her remake of the film in 1954 under gay director George Cukor seems a more fitting comparison for Matthiessen and Cheney's story.

CHAPTER 5: MAKING A HOME IN KITTERY

89   *economic downturn:* Irving Bernstein, *The Lean Years: A History of the American Worker, 1920–1933* (Boston: Houghton Mifflin, 1960), 255.

gross national product fell: Nelson Lichtenstein, *State of the Union: A Century of American Labor* (Princeton, NJ: Princeton University Press, 2002), 24.

fire's glow: Bernstein, *Lean Years*, 454.

labor devised public policy solutions: Bernstein, *Lean Years*, 492–93, 427; Philip Dray, *There Is Power in a Union: The Epic Story of Labor in America* (New York: Doubleday, 2010), 422–23.

90   *Kittery . . . population:* Kittery Booklet Committee, *Kittery: Ancient and Modern* (Kittery, ME, 1931), 4.

12 Old Ferry Lane: The house formerly owned by Matthiessen and Cheney sits at the intersection of Old Ferry Lane and Bowen Road in Kittery. During Matthiessen and Cheney's day, the address of the house was 12 Old Ferry Lane. Later, the Town of Kittery switched its numbering of houses in the area and listed Matthiessen and Cheney's house as 23 Bowen Road.

91   *"most beautiful house in America":* Bernard Bowron, "The Making of an American Scholar," in *FOM*, 47.

Cheney Brothers announced: Farwell Knapp Journal, August 1930, p. 124, box 15, folder 174, Knapp Papers; Russell Cheney to Phelps Putnam, September 21, 1930, box 1, folder 6, Putnam Papers.

Matthiessen purchased the Kittery house: Farwell Knapp Journal, August 22, 1930, p. 140, box 15, folder 174, Knapp Papers; Deed of Sale from Alice Parker Hoyt Shurtleff to Russell Cheney and Francis O. Matthiessen, August 19, 1930, book 890, p. 119, York County Registry of Deeds, Alfred, ME.

Cheney became financially dependent: On Matthiessen's selective service registration during World War II, he claimed that beginning in 1931, he began to contribute $1,000 (approximately $17,000 in 2021 dollars) per year to Cheney for living expenses. In late 1932, Cheney's brother Clifford began providing an allowance of $1,500 (approximately $31,000 in 2021 dollars) per year for him. Although Clifford was also affected by Cheney Brothers' decision to stop paying dividends, as an executive with the company, he continued to draw a salary. Report, Francis Otto Matthiessen, Boston, MA, FBI, October 28, 1943, p. 2, FF; Farwell Knapp Journal, December 28, 1932, pp. 279–80, box 15, folder 176, Knapp Papers.

92   *"Matty has no experience":* Farwell Knapp Journal, May 30, 1930, p. 47, box 15, folder 174, Knapp Papers.

"only real home": Bowron, "American Scholar," 47.

Cheney brought furniture: C. L. Barber, "Statements by Friends and Associates" *FOM*, 99.

books from family members: Specifically, Cheney-family books included *The Country Doctor* by Sarah Orne Jewett, inscribed by K. D. Cheney (Russell's father); *How to Do It* by Edward Everett Hale, inscribed by K. D. Cheney, 1871; *Poetry and Prose* by Michelangelo, inscribed by Ednah D. Cheney (Russell's mother), 1854, and Russell Cheney, 1908; *Concord Days* by A. Bronson Alcott, inscribed by Ednah D. Cheney, September 24, 1872; *Rules and Exercises of Holy Living*, inscribed by Ednah D. Cheney; *Letters* by Celia Thaxter, inscribed by Ednah D. Cheney; *The Life of Charlotte Bronte* by Elizabeth Gaskell, inscribed by E. D. Smith (Russell's mother before her marriage to Knight Dexter Cheney); *Pilgrim's Progress* by John Bunyan, inscribed as a gift from Ednah Dow Littlehale Cheney (Russell's great aunt) to her sister Elizabeth, January 1, 1838; *Walden* by Henry David Thoreau, inscribed by Charles Cheney (Russell's grandfather) and K. D. Cheney, 1869; and *L'Allegro, Il Penseroso, Comus, and Lycidas* by John Milton, inscribed by Thomas Langdon Cheney (Russell's brother).

93   *"was not a family":* Barber, "Statements by Friends and Associates," 101.

94   *"Deezie":* Matthiessen to Cheney, December 26, 1929, *R&D*, 180.

"Weeds," "Creature," and "Branchy": Matthiessen to Cheney, October 7, 1928, box 19, folder 30; Matthiessen to Cheney, January 11, 1931, box 19, folder 47; and Cheney to Matthiessen, April 13, 1932, box 18, folder 65, all in Matthiessen Papers; Cheney to Matthiessen, December 14, 1929, *R&D*, 178.

Miss Pansy Littlefield: Matthiessen to Cheney, March 6, 1932, box 19, folder 60; Matthiessen to Cheney, January 12, 1941, box 19, folder 60; and Matthiessen to Cheney, May 13, 1945, box 19, folder 64, all in Matthiessen Papers; Matthiessen to Cheney, December 15, 1944, *R&D*, 305.

Matthiessen sitting with various cats: Paintings of Matthiessen with one of his and Cheney's cats include *F. O. Matthiessen with Cat* (1927–29) and *F. O. Matthiessen with Pawsey* (1928), CC.

"special language": *R&D*, 146.

"I only hope": Matthiessen to Cheney, May 1, 1938, box 19, folder 59, Matthiessen Papers.

sexual or drinking indiscretion: Cheney to Matthiessen, November 12, 1927, box 19, folder 29, Matthiessen Papers.

95   *a degree of privacy and freedom:* George Chauncey, *Gay New York: Gender, Urban Culture, and the Making of the Gay Male World, 1890–1940* (New York: Basic Books, 1994), 274–75.

"non-residents": Town Reports, 1930–43, 1945–50, Town of Kittery, ME, Rice Public Library, Kittery, ME.

Translation: An Elizabethan Art: The book focuses on the 1561 Sir Thomas Hoby translation of *The Courtier* by the Italian Renaissance writer Baldassare Castiglione; Thomas North's 1579 translation of Plutarch's *Lives*; John Florio's 1603 translation of Montaigne's *Essays*; and Philemon Holland's translations in the early 1600s of the works of Livy and Suetonius. *See Translation.*

Matthiessen introduces many of the themes: Translation, 4, 42, 83, 198, 223, 86, 147, 181, 128, 216.

96 *value . . . placed on reading* and subsequent quote: *Translation*, 27, 164, 181.
books shaped Matthiessen's and Cheney's budding gay identities: Matthiessen kept much of his professional, literary library at Eliot House at Harvard. But he and Cheney kept all of their proto-gay–related books at Kittery. As above, concerning Cheney's reading at Cragmor during his 1916 stay and Cheney family books that Russell Cheney brought to Kittery, I compiled these listings of books on a visit to Matthiessen and Cheney's Kittery home during the summer of 2009 with Richard Candee, professor emeritus, American and New England studies, Boston University; Carol L. Cheney, Russell Cheney's great niece; and Jay Grossman, associate professor of English at Northwestern University.
Matthiessen and Cheney construct gay identities: Chauncey, *Gay New York*, 283.
connection between literature and society and subsequent quotes: *Translation*, 4, 44, 42, 82, 221, 229–30.

97 *"sat there a long while":* RC, 101.
"fixed here for life": RC, 103.

98 *"Make hay while the snow lasts":* RC, 103.
"skeptic": Farwell Knapp Journal, March 7, 1928, p. 92, box 14, folder 177, Knapp Papers.

99 *"These wintry landscapes":* "Large Show by Cheney," *New York Evening Post*, February 17, 1934, 8.

100 *"Those who know New England":* Dorothy Adlow, "The Art of Russell Cheney," *Christian Science Monitor*, September 29, 1934, 8.
Hope Smith: Peter Hastings Falk, ed., *Who Was Who in American Art, 1564–1975: 400 Years of Artists in America*, vol. 3 (Madison, CT: Sound View Press, 1999), 3080.
Smith "yearned" after him: Farwell Knapp Journal, March 5, 1931, p. 207, box 15, folder 175, Knapp Papers.
"in the early morning light": Cheney to Russell Wheeler Davenport, March 7, 1931, box 5, Russell Wheeler Davenport Papers, Library of Congress.
"I wish I could describe": Matthiessen to Cheney, January 11, 1931, box 19, folder 47, Matthiessen Papers.

101 Common Sense of Drinking: *The Common Sense of Drinking* was among Matthiessen and Cheney's books at Kittery catalogued over the summer of 2009.
characteristics of the alcoholic: Given the era in which Peabody was writing, it's not entirely surprising that his book focuses mostly—but not exclusively—on men. Richard Rogers Peabody, *The Common Sense of Drinking* (Boston: Little Brown, 1931), 17, 50, 59, 77, 96.
Their vacation ended in England: Farwell Knapp Journal, August 21, 1931, p. 29, box 15, folder 175, Knapp Papers.
"infuriate" Cheney: Matthiessen to Cheney, January 23, 1931, box 19, folder 47, Matthiessen Papers.

102 *"Russell Cheney's painting progress continues"*: "Exhibitions in New York," *Art News*, March 5, 1932, 9.

"*I walked home*": Cheney to Matthiessen, March 5, 1932, box 18, folder 65, Matthiessen Papers.

the young man came back: Cheney to Matthiessen, March 21, 1932, and March 24, 1932, box 18, folder 65, Matthiessen Papers.

103 *"mince meat" out of another*: Cheney to Matthiessen, May 1, 1933, box 18, folder 73, Matthiessen Papers.

"no special amicis [sic]" there: Cheney to Matthiessen, March 22, 1932, box 18, folder 65, Matthiessen Papers.

"a couple of drinks" and subsequent $1,000 fine: The accuracy of the $1,000 fine is somewhat dubious, since it's nearly $21,000 in 2021 dollars, which is unusually high. Nonetheless, this is the figure that Farwell Knapp reported in his diary. Farwell Knapp Journal, December 28, 1932, pp. 277–79, box 15, folder 176, Knapp Papers.

104 *"I wholly disapprove of the Ph.D."*: Matthiessen to Cheney, January 7, 1931, box 19, folder 47, Matthiessen Papers.

"One little piddling article": Matthiessen to Cheney, January 21, 1930, *R&D*, 197.

105 *"our most powerful individuals"*: F. O. Matthiessen, review of *The Liberation of American Literature*, by V. F. Calverton, *New England Quarterly* 6, no. 1 (March 1933): 194.

"Yesterday was the culmination": Matthiessen to Cheney, February 28, 1932, box 19, folder 53, Matthiessen Papers. The "Roger" mentioned in the quotation is the historian Roger Merriman, who served as master at Eliot House.

woke up out of a nightmare: Matthiessen to Cheney, September 28, 1932, box 19, folder 55, Matthiessen Papers. Editor Louis Hyde gives this letter a different date: October 4, 1932; see *R&D*, 223.

106 *hearing Eliot read*: Matthiessen to Cheney, March 14, 1933, box 19, folder 57, Matthiessen Papers.

"darn good guest": Cheney to Putnam, June 1, 1933, box 2, folder 7, Putnam Papers.

Eliot taking a canoe trip: *Harvard Crimson*, September 28, 1933, https://www.thecrimson.com/article/1933/9/28/portraits-of-harvard-figures-pprofessor-francis/.

implicitly accepted them as a couple: In researching Matthiessen's and Cheney's lives and work, I have had the good fortune and pleasure to interview several of Matthiessen's students, who are or were still alive, including the scholars Leo Marx and J. C. Levenson and the writer and editor Justin Kaplan, among others. They told me that everyone knew the romantic nature of Matthiessen and Cheney's relationship. But in the days before the gay rights movement, homosexuality was a taboo subject. No one talked about such things. At the very least, it would have been considered impolite. Whatever people's exact level of knowledge about Matthiessen and Cheney's relationship, it was not enough

to keep them away from Kittery when invited for Thanksgiving dinner
or for a summer weekend. Leo Marx, in discussion with author, digitally
recorded, October 1, 2010; Justin Kaplan, in discussion with author,
digitally recorded, January 5, 2011; J. C. Levenson, in discussion with
author, digitally recorded, February 23, 2011.

"genius of the place": Barber, "Statements of Friends and Associates," 99.

CHAPTER 6: SHINING IN A DARK TIME

107 *1,856 work stoppages:* Irving Bernstein, *Turbulent Years: A History of the American Worker, 1933–1941* (Boston: Houghton Mifflin, 1970), 217.

five million new members: Nelson Lichtenstein, *State of the Union: A Century of American Labor* (Princeton, NJ: Princeton University Press, 2002), 52.

108 *association went out on strike:* Bernstein, *Turbulent Years,* 255; Philip Dray, *There Is Power in a Union: The Epic Story of Labor in America* (New York: Doubleday, 2010), 430, 432; Associated Press, "Labor Dispute Board Meets," *New York Times,* July 5, 1934, 15; "Radicals in Full Sway," *New York Times,* July 15, 1934, 1; "Hiring Halls' Rule Chief Strike Issue," *New York Times,* July 15, 1934, 20.

vomiting on the strikers: Vomiting gas was reported by the *New York Times.* It may well have been Adamsite, a chemical warfare agent developed and used in World War I that induced vomiting, sneezing, and other respiratory irritation and discomfort. Associated Press, "Labor Dispute Board Meets."

109 *the two men drove to New Mexico:* Matthiessen kept a diary of this trip, entitling it the "Unofficial Guide of the Road between Santa Barbara, Calif. and Santa Fe, N.M." This document recalls the record that Matthiessen kept of his 1919 road trip across the United States after graduating from the Hackley School. *R&D,* 227.

"blue-eyed, square jawed": "Unofficial Guide of the Road between Santa Barbara, Calif. and Santa Fe, N.M.," p. 9, Matthiessen Papers.

gave a ride to two men: Santa Fe New Mexican, November 25, 1935, 8.

Nordfeldt House: "Russell Cheney Revisits Santa Fe," *Santa Fe New Mexican,* December 19, 1934, 1.

Cheney set about painting: Some of the paintings from Cheney's time in Santa Fe include portraits *Lee Lucero* (1935 or earlier) and *Jose of Buena Vista* (1935); architectural painting *Abandoned Adobes* (1935); and landscapes *Santa Fe Mountains* (1935) and *Study for New Mexico Scene* (1935). CC.

the coal industry . . . had collapsed: Bernstein, *Lean Years,* 360, 362, 363, 380.

110 *National Miners' Union:* Katherine Gay, "Background of the Gallup Riot," *Nation,* May 1, 1935, 511–12; Harry R. Rubenstein, "Political Repression in New Mexico: The Destruction of the National Miners' Union in Gallup," in *Labor in New Mexico: Unions, Strikes, and Social History since 1881,* ed. Robert Kern (Albuquerque: University of New Mexico Press, 1983), 93–95, 105, 109–11, 113–15.

first leaseholder, Exiquio Navarro, arrested: In one of the many complications of the Gallup riot, Victor Campos was evicted from the property, but Exiquio Navarro was arrested. Campos was a subtenant of Navarro, who as the leaseholder bore ultimate responsibility for not paying the rent. Rubenstein, "Political Repression in New Mexico," 109.

111 *Matthiessen joined a crew of reporters:* The group included Clarence Lynch, a lawyer for the International Labor Defense, the legal defense arm of the Communist Party USA, Ann Webster, a former Washington, DC, lawyer; and Katherine Gay, a former newsperson from Springfield, Massachusetts, who had come to Santa Fe to recover from tuberculosis. Rubenstein, "Political Repression in New Mexico," 117, 121; Gay, "Background of the Gallup Riot," 511; Matthiessen to Laurette Murdock, July 17, 1941, box 3, Matthiessen Papers. *"strong-armed frontier refusal"* and subsequent quote: F. O. Matthiessen, "The New Mexican Workers' Case," *New Republic*, May 8, 1935, 361–62.

112 *garden party fundraiser:* "Gallup Miners' Garden Party Brings Out Society in Force," *Santa Fe New Mexican*, July 6, 1935, 3.
"best known visiting artists": Ina Sizer Cassidy, "Art and Artists of New Mexico: Russell Cheney," *New Mexico Magazine*, March 1935, 26, 39.

113 *"collapsed on viewing":* "Senator Cutting Is Killed in Air Crash, Fatal to 4," *New York Times*, May 7, 1935, 14.
Cheney painting his portrait: Richard Lowitt, *Bronson M. Cutting: Progressive Politician* (Albuquerque: University of New Mexico Press, 1992), 234.
Senator Cutting purchased: "Cheney's Show," *Kittery Press*, January 24, 1936, 8.
very generous: Lowitt, *Bronson M. Cutting*, 315.
Kenneth and Laurette Murdock: Peter B. Flint, "Kenneth B. Murdock of Harvard Is Dead," *New York Times*, November 16, 1975, 75; "Kenneth B. Murdock, 80," Obituaries, *Boston Globe*, November 18, 1975, 39.

114 *emphasizing the main ideas: Eliot*, 16, 56, 58, 68, 98, 102, 143, 173, 193.
"objective correlative": In "Hamlet and His Problems," T. S. Eliot defines the "objective correlative": "The only way of expressing emotion in the form of art is by finding an 'objective correlative'; in other words, a set of objects, a situation, a chain of events which shall be the formula of that particular emotion; such that when the external facts, which must terminate in sensory experience, are given, the emotion is immediately evoked." T. S. Eliot, "Hamlet and His Problems," in *Select Essays* (New York: Harcourt, Brace), 124–25; *Eliot*, 58.
"the working out": Matthiessen, *Eliot*, 173, quoting Granville-Barker, *The Exemplary Theater* (London: Chatto and Windus, 1922), 49.
"When a poet's": Matthiessen, *Eliot*, 14, quoting from T. S. Eliot, "The Metaphysical Poets," in *Select Essays*, 247.

115 *Matthiessen did not have:* C. L. Barber, "Statements by Friends and Associates," in *FOM*, 98.
"would so utterly disapprove": Matthiessen to Cheney, January 30, 1930, *R&D*, 200.
He is credited: John Xiros Cooper, *The Cambridge Introduction to T. S. Eliot* (Cambridge: Cambridge University Press, 2006), 111.

116 *contemporary scholars:* William E. Cain, *F. O. Matthiessen and the Politics of Criticism* (Madison: University of Wisconsin Press, 1988), 56.

"probably remain . . . the best": Russell Kirk, *Eliot and His Age: T. S. Eliot's Moral Imagination* (New York: Random House, 1971), 191.

pick up lobsters: Helen Bayne Knapp, "Statements by Friends and Associates," in *FOM*, 116.

Matthiessen boasted endlessly: Leo Marx, email to author, November 22, 2010.

deck tennis: Deck tennis was a cross between tennis and quoits, a ring toss game, in which players toss a rubber ring back and forth over a net similar to those used in badminton. It was popularized by steamship companies during the 1920s, because it could be played in confined spaces with minimal equipment and required little training or practice. Matthiessen and Cheney presumably began playing deck tennis on their transatlantic voyages.

In the evenings and subsequent quote: Barber, "Statements by Friends and Associates," 101; *R&D*, 225, 228–29.

117   *"Matty's attitude"*: Helen Knapp, "Statements by Friends and Associates," in *FOM*, 116.

"Matty enters into all games": Farwell Knapp Journal, September 1928, p. 208, box 13, folder 166, Knapp Papers.

"partners": "Cheney's Show," *Kittery Press*, January 24, 1936, 8.

"In the main room": Royal Cortissoz, "The Abstractionists of Foreign Origin," *New York Herald Tribune*, March 8, 1936, E10.

"taken this vicinity": "Cheney's Show," *Kittery Press*, January 24, 1936, 1.

118   *They went to boxing matches together*: Cheney to Matthiessen, November 14, 1937, box 18, folder 78, Matthiessen Papers.

Matthiessen donated the painting: "Cheney Painting Given to Portsmouth Library," *Portsmouth (NH) Herald*, September 8, 1948, 8.

119   *"talent emerges"*: William Germain Dooley, "Colorful and Versatile Ways Abound amid Our Realism," *Boston Evening Transcript*, February 13, 1937, 7.

Cheney painted a number of strong landscapes: See CC; *RC*, 112, 114.

120   *then-distinctive Memorial Bridge*: The Memorial Bridge was demolished in 2012. "River Closed as Memorial Bridge Demolition Begins," *Portland Press Herald*, February 6, 2012, https://www.pressherald.com/2012/02/06/river-closed-as-memorial-bridge-demolition-begins/.

Charles "Chili" McCaffery: *Portsmouth Herald*, obituary, June 2001, 7, A15.

"openness to life": Barber, "Statements by Friends and Associates," 100.

"Trotsky and toast": Matthiessen to Cheney, September 23, 1935; see also Matthiessen to Cheney, September 25, 1935, and Matthiessen to Cheney, February 28, 1936, all in box 19, folder 58, Matthiessen Papers.

121   *Matthiessen was primarily attracted*: Barber, "Statements of Friends and Associates," 100.

one of the boys: Leo Marx. in conversation with the author, digitally recorded, October 1, 2010; Daniel Aaron, in conversation with the author, digitally recorded, October 4, 2010.

"spotty, irregular": John Rackliffe, "Notes for a Character Study," *FOM*, 85.

moving lilac bushes: Cheney to Matthiessen, April 20, 1933, box 18, folder 73, Matthiessen Papers.

Teacher's Oath: M. J. Heale, *McCarthy's Americans: Red Scare Politics in State and Nation, 1935–1965* (London: Macmillan Press, 1998), 158–59, 161, 170; "Oath for Teachers Opposed by Labor," *Daily Boston Globe,* March 1, 1935, 19.

122 *Harvard Teachers' Union:* "Look Forward, Young Teachers," *Harvard Crimson,* November 12, 1935, https://www.thecrimson.com/article/1935/11/12/look-forward-young-teachers-pthe-newly-formed/; "Cambridge Teachers Union Gathers Today," October 7, 1936, https://www.thecrimson.com/article/1936/10/7/cambridge-teachers-union-gathers-today-pcontinuing/; Paul M. Sweezy, "Labor and Political Activities," in *FOM,* 61; F. O. Matthiessen, "A Teacher Takes His Stand: The President of the Teachers' Union Contributes a Harvard Credo," *Harvard Progressive,* September 1940, 12–14; Henry Nash Smith, "A Texan Perspective," in *Political Activism and Academic Conscience: The Harvard Experience, 1936–1941, Hobart and William Smith Colleges, December 5 & 6, 1975,* ed. John Lydenberg (Geneva, NY: The Colleges, 1977), 51.

a way to break down barriers: Matthiessen to Kenneth Murdock, 15 November 1935, box 3, Matthiessen Papers; Matthiessen, "Teacher Takes His Stand," 12.

"I simply cannot take": Matthiessen to Kenneth Murdock, November 15, 1935, box 3, Matthiessen Papers.

two young economists: Harry Levin, "A View from Within," in Lydenberg, *Political Activism and the Academic Conscience,* 4; "Labor Union at Harvard," *Daily Boston Globe,* October 24, 1935, 1.

123 *"solely on grounds":* Special Committee Appointed by the President of Harvard University, *Report on the Terminating Appointments of Dr. J. R. Walsh and Dr. A. R. Sweezy* (Cambridge, MA: Harvard University Press, 1938), Appendix D, Harvard Press Release, April 6, 1937, 84, box 21, Matthiessen Papers.

attention of major newspapers: "Leaders in Teachers Union Face End of Harvard Career," *Baltimore Sun,* April 7, 1937; "Labor Unionist Leaders Stir Harvard Row," *Chicago Tribune,* April 7, 1937; "Harvard Teachers Union Leaders to Lose Jobs," *St. Louis Post-Dispatch,* April 6, 1937; "Harvard Agitators to Lose Jobs," *Los Angeles Times,* April 7, 1937. These articles, among others, are cited in Special Committee, *Report on the Terminating Appointments,"* 65. "Kittery Man Objects to Management of Harvard Affairs," *Kittery Press,* June 10, 1938, 1.

"would be both unwise and impractical": "Harvard Refuses to Reinstate Two," *New York Times,* June 2, 1938, 14; "Professors Hit Conant's Action," *Daily Boston Globe,* June 6, 1938, 1.

"how far short": F. O. Matthiessen and David Prall, "The Case of Dr. Conant," *New Republic,* June 22, 1937, 190.

124 *substantial changes at Cheney Brothers:* William E. Buckley, *A New England Pattern: The History of Manchester, Connecticut* (Chester, CT: Pequot Press, 1973), 246–47, 249; "Cheney Brothers Ask for Debt Moratorium," *Manchester*

Evening Herald, April 26, 1935, 1, 2; "Cheney Workers Accept Wage Cut," *Manchester Evening Herald*, November 18, 1935, 7; "RFC Grants Cheneys Loan of $1,081,000," *Manchester Evening Herald*, January 25, 1937, 2; "Cheney Bros. Petition to Reorganize," *Hartford Courant*, April 27, 1935, 17; "Cheney Mills to Lay Off 500 Workers," *Hartford Courant*, June 25, 1935, 1.

spoke about the changes: "Final Cheney Plan Action on Monday," *Manchester Evening Herald*, April 9, 1937, 10.

125 *Cheney Brothers got out of the business:* "Cheneys May Sell Most of Holdings in House Property," *Manchester Evening Herald*, August 10, 1937, 1; "Cheneys Announce Property Auction," August 18, 1937; "Cheney Auction Brings $831,725, 77 P.C. of Loan," September 27, 1937, 1; "Three-Day Auction of 245 Dwellings Is Planned for Public by Cheneys," *Hartford Courant*, September 12, 1937, B5.

"collection d'art chinois": RC, 100.

collection of Asian art objects: Antoinette Cheney Crocker, *Great Oaks: Memoirs of the Cheney Family* (Concord, MA: privately printed, 1977), 51.

"treasure room": Margreta Swenson Cheney, *If All the Great Men: The Cheneys of Manchester* (Manchester, CT: privately printed, 1975), 13; Antoinette Cheney Crocker, *Frank Woodbridge Cheney: Two Years in China and Japan, 1859–1861* (Worcester, MA: Davis Press, 1970), 15.

126 *paintings as Nicotiana:* Other paintings with images of the Far East from this time included *Banquet* (1937?) and *Epergne* (1937). CC.

CHAPTER 7: IN SICKNESS AND IN HEALTH

127 *Doctors played a key role:* George Chauncey, *Gay New York: Gender, Urban Culture, and the Making of the Gay Male World, 1890–1940* (New York: Basic Books, 1994), 124; Jennifer Terry, *An American Obsession: Science, Medicine, and Homosexuality in Modern Society* (Chicago: University of Chicago Press, 1999), 82, 288, 293, 295.

attraction to drink and flesh: RC, 62.

crossed the line into alcoholism: Louis Hyde, in *R&D*, 270.

129 *fate handed him a double tragedy:* "Mrs. Alexander Lambert," obituary, *New York Times*, April 11, 1938, 15; "Publisher's Wife Dies at Montecito," obituary, *Los Angeles Times*, April 11, 1938, 14; "Mrs. Cowles, 71, Dies in California," obituary, *Hartford Courant*, April 11, 1938, 4; *R&D*, 231.

drinking at Kittery grew so toxic: Russell Cheney to F. O. Matthiessen, May 5, 1938, box 18, folder 79, Matthiessen Papers; Hyde, *R&D*, 231.

checked himself into the Hartford Retreat: At the time of Cheney's stay in 1938, the Hartford Retreat was in the process of changing its name to the Institute of Living. As early as 1935, Charlotte Kellogg did an article about the institute for the *Atlantic*. The hospital also used the Institute of Living name internally on its annual reports during the time that Cheney was a patient there. But Matthiessen and Cheney referred to the hospital as the Hartford Retreat, and the sanatorium did not officially change its name until 1943. Steven Lytle, archivist, Hartford Hospital, email to author, November 9, 2010.

NOTES

130 *Hartford Retreat:* Charlotte Kellogg, "An Institute of Living," *Atlantic*, March 1935, 326, 328–31, 333; *Myths, Minds and Medicine: Two Centuries of Mental Health Care*, A Permanent Exhibition on the History of the Institute of Living and the Treatment of Psychiatric Illnesses, Institute of Living, 2010.

McLean: Alex Beam, *Gracefully Insane: The Rise and Fall of America's Premier Mental Hospital* (New York: Public Affairs, 2001), 9, 11, 50–51, 64, 66, 70.

Cheney became an avid bowler: Cheney to Matthiessen, February 16, 1941, and Cheney to Matthiessen, March 11, 1941, both in box 18, folder 83, Matthiessen Papers.

"Philippine Pete and Katchina Kate": Although the provenance of "Philippine Pete" is a bit of mystery, "Katchina Kate" likely referred to *Autumn Thoughts* (1936), which features an image of a small kachina doll. The kachinas are small wooden dolls important to Hopi spiritual beliefs. Cheney learned about the dolls on his visits to the Southwest. As was often the case, he liked incorporating images of art objects from other cultures into his paintings. Phelps Putnam to Russell Cheney, February 11, 1937, box 4, folder 16, Putnam Papers.

Cheney's doctor at the Retreat: Cheney to Matthiessen, May 2, 1938, box 18, folder 79, Matthiessen Papers.

Dr. Burlingame: C. Charles Burlingame was hired by Cheney Brothers in 1916 in an effort to better match workers with their jobs. That year Cheney Brothers published a promotional pamphlet entitled *The Miracle Workers* to attract new workers to the company, which stated: "The object is to place the employee at once at the task for which he is best qualified and in which he can make most rapid advance." The pamphlet went on to add: "The firm is always seeking to discover persons who have natural ability and endeavors to surround such persons with every facility for its development." Dr. Burlingame was behind much of this thinking at Cheney Brothers. C. Charles Burlingame, *A Psychiatrist Speaks: The Writings and Lectures of Doctor C. Charles Burlingame, 1885–1950* (Hartford, CT: Connecticut Printers, 1959), 20; Cheney Brothers Silk Manufacturing Company, *The Miracle Workers* (1916; repr., Manchester, CT: Manchester Historical Society, 2012), 34–35.

131 *before coming to Cheney Brothers:* Burlingame, *Psychiatrist Speaks*, 20; Dorothy Cheney, *Memories* (Hartford, CT: Finlay Brothers, 1929), 20.

Retreat's board of directors: In addition to Howell Cheney, B. Austin Cheney and Colonel Louis R. Cheney served on the board of the Retreat during Russell's stay at the sanatorium. Howell was Russell Cheney's cousin, whom he had met up with in Venice in 1924, soon after meeting Matthiessen. Howell had been forced into retirement from Cheney Brothers in the fall of 1934. He went on to serve as chairman of the board of the Retreat for several years during the 1940s. Francis J. Braceland, *The Institute of Living, 1822–1972* (Hartford, CT: Connecticut Printers, 1972), 164; Institute of Living, 117th Annual Report, April 1, 1941, Institute of Living Medical Library, Hartford, CT.

"a place for education": Kellogg, "An Institute of Living," 326.

"assure me it was mostly shock" and subsequent quote: Cheney to Matthiessen, April 16, 1938, box 18, folder 79, Matthiessen Papers.

"the individual takes alcohol": Robert Fleming, "Psychiatric Aspects of Alcoholism," Social Forces 21, no. 1 (October 1942–May 1943): 74; "Robert Fleming," obituary, Boston Globe, August 12, 1977, 38.

He got much rest: Cheney to Matthiessen, April 26, 1938, box 18, folder 79, Matthiessen Papers.

"Do you ever cross the street": Cheney to Matthiessen, May 4, 1938, box 18, folder 79, Matthiessen Papers.

132   "light baths": Putnam to Cheney, February 11, 1937, box 4, folder 16, Putnam Papers; Beam, Gracefully Insane, 76.

"At least half the doctor's battle": Burlingame, Psychiatrist Speaks, 14.

"milieu therapy": Cheney to Matthiessen, May 4, 1938, box 18, folder 79, Matthiessen Papers.

Burlingame counseled him not to stop: Cheney to Matthiessen, May 2, 1938, box 18, folder 79, Matthiessen Papers.

"Dear Matty": Cheney to Matthiessen, April 15, 1938; Cheney to Matthiessen, April 18, 1938; and Cheney to Matthiessen, May 2, 1938, all in box 18 folder 79, Matthiessen Papers.

133   walking trip in Ireland: Henry H. Stebbins Jr., ed., Thirty-Fifth Anniversary Record of the Class of 1904, Yale College ([New Haven, CT?]: E. L. Hildreth, with the assistance of the Class Secretaries Bureau, 1940), 88.

"experiment": Hyde, R&D, 232.

show trials: Robert W. Thurston, Life and Terror in Stalin's Russia, 1934–1941 (New Haven, CT: Yale University Press, 1996), 25, 42.

aboard the Europa: S.S. Europa Passenger List, http://www.ancestry library.com/.

After the hurricane: "Storm Damage Mounts in New England," Portsmouth Herald, September 22, 1938, 1, 7; "Cleaning Up Job in Manchester Begun," Hartford Courant, September 22, 1938, 6; R&D, 232; Cheney to Putnam, October 9, 1938, box 4, folder 3, Putnam Papers.

134   binge: Matthiessen, January 4, 1939, R&D, 247.

"his hands still shaking desperately" and subsequent quote: Matthiessen, January 4, 1939, R&D, 247.

Newton Arvin: Barry Werth, The Scarlet Professor: Newton Arvin, a Literary Life Shattered by Scandal (New York: Nan A. Talese, 2001), 296.

135   Daniel Aaron: conversation with the author, digitally recorded, October 4, 2010.

"hauled out of sleep": Matthiessen, January 4, 1939, R&D, 245.

136   He exercised and listened to music: Matthiessen to Cheney, January 3, 1939, and Matthiessen to Cheney, January 8, 1939, both box 19, folder 59, Matthiessen Papers; Matthiessen, January 4, 1939, R&D, 246.

confided in a tearful revelation: Matthiessen, January 4, 1939, R&D, 248.

"He [Murdock] also reasoned with me": Matthiessen, January 4, 1939, R&D, 248.

137   dismissed on "moral grounds" for being gay: David Bergman, "F. O. Matthiessen: The Critic as Homosexual," in Gaiety Transfigured: Gay Self-Representation in American Literature (Madison: University of Wisconsin Press, 1999), 92.

"assumed my relationship with Russell": Matthiessen, January 8, 1939, *R&D*, 252.

Hanns Caspar Kollar: In the text of his diary entry written at McLean, Matthiessen refers to "Bruno," which was Hanns Caspar Kollar's nickname. Hyde, Cast of Characters, *R&D*, 384.

absence of "paternal affection": F. O. Matthiessen, "Oxford Letter," n.d., p. 7, box 3, Matthiessen Papers.

Matthiessen continued seeing Dr. Barrett: F. O. Matthiessen Agendas, January 27, 1939, February 9, 1939, May 10, 1939, May 15, 1939, May 16, 1939, in August 1938–August 1939 Agenda, box 7, Matthiessen Papers; City of Boston Directories, Professional—Physicians Listings, 1938, p. 379; City of Boston Directories, Professional—Physicians Listings, 1939, p. 2122, Central Library, Boston Public Library, Boston, MA.

"I have hated imaginary illnesses": Matthiessen, January 8, 1939, *R&D*, 253.

"I have every reason": Matthiessen, January 8, 1939, *R&D*, 254.

manic-depressive psychiatric illness: Frederick K. Goodwin, MD, and Kay Redfield Jamison, PhD, *Manic-Depressive Illness* (New York: Oxford University Press, 1990), 22, 36, 61.

138 *"I fight my own devil"*: Cheney to Matthiessen, December 31, 1938, *R&D*, 243.

"It's one of the real beauties": Matthiessen to Cheney, January 3, 1939, box 19, folder 59, Matthiessen Papers.

139 *"Would you like to have the cap?"*: Although this photograph is together with Cheney's letter to Matthiessen dated January 8–10, 1939, in the Beinecke's collection of Matthiessen and Cheney's correspondence, it appears to have been misfiled. Matthiessen refers specifically to this photograph of Cheney at the beach in his letter/diary entry, dated January 10, 1939, written from McLean, noting that the photograph was given to him by his student, Dick Schlatter. Moreover, the note written on the back of the photograph is clearly Matthiessen's handwriting and not Cheney's. Cheney to Matthiessen, January 8–10, 1939, box 18, folder 79, Matthiessen Papers; Matthiessen, January 10, 1939, *R&D*, 259.

"live, hold on to": Matthiessen to Cheney, December 29, 1938, *R&D*, 241.

Louisburg Square on Beacon Hill: Louisburg Square was named in honor of the battle of Louisbourg of 1745, in which forces from the Massachusetts Bay Colony led by William Pepperrell of Kittery fought the French for control of Cape Breton Island in Nova Scotia. Matthiessen and Cheney likely knew about the connection between William Pepperrell and Louisburg Square, if not through local history then through John Mead Howells's book *The Architectural Heritage of the Piscataqua: Houses and Gardens of the Portsmouth District of Maine and New Hampshire*, 1937, which they owned. John Mead Howells, an architect, was the son of William Dean Howells, who served as editor of the *Atlantic Monthly* and *Harper's Monthly* and was Kittery's most famous nineteenth-century literary resident. Cheney did a number of paintings of landscapes, houses, and interiors related to the Pepperrell family in Kittery. These included *Lady Pepperrell House* (1928 or earlier); *Pepperrell's Lane/Frisbee's Wharf* (1928); *Pepperrell's Wharf* (1932 or earlier); *Pepperrell's Cove* (1933); *Cove in Winter* (1933); *Interior—Pepperrell*

House, Kittery (ca. 1935); and *Kittery Village* (1939). Richard Candee and Carol L. Cheney speculate that *Cove in Winter* may be the same painting as *Pepperrell's Wharf*, despite their different titles and dates. As Cheney had done with other paintings, he sometimes changed their names over time. John Mead Howells, *The Architectural Heritage of the Piscataqua: Houses and Gardens of the Portsmouth District of Maine and New Hampshire* (New York: Architectural Book Publishing, 1937), 7; CC.

Pinckney Street apartment: Paul M. Sweezy, "A Biographical Sketch," *FOM*, x; John Rackliffe, "Notes for a Character Study," *CP*, 87; Hyde, *R&D*, 273; *Dictionary of American Biography, Supplement Four, 1946–1950*, ed. John A. Garranty and Edward T. Jones (New York: Charles Scribner's Sons, 1974), s.v. "Matthiessen, Francis Otto"; Gale in Context: Biography, https://www.gale.com/c/in-context-biography.

140 *"lively, fluent, agreeable":* "Ferargil Has Two Shows," *New York World Telegram*, April 8, 1939, 12.

referred to Cheney throughout as . . . Sheldon Cheney: In his review in the *Boston Evening Transcript* of Cheney's show at the Grace Horne Galleries in late January to early February 1938, William Germain Dooley referred to Russell as Sheldon Cheney throughout the review. Going back to at least the eighteenth century, I find no relation between the two men. Edward H. Little, *Descendants of George Cheney of Manchester, Connecticut*, sponsored by the Cheney Cemetery Association, 1993. William Germain Dooley, "Novelty Sculpture Features Local Gallery Exhibitions," *Boston Evening Transcript*, January 29, 1938, IV-4.

"couple of weeks": Matthiessen to Farwell Knapp, November 17, 1940, collection of Richard Candee; Matthiessen to Cheney, November 7, 1943, box 19, folder 61, Matthiessen Papers.

Dr. Harry Cesar Solomon: Dr. Harry Cesar Solomon was a psychiatrist at Harvard Medical School, medical director and superintendent of Boston Psychopathic Hospital, and president of the American Neurological Association in 1941. He also later became the Massachusetts Commissioner of Mental Health. "Heads Neurological Group," *New York Times*, June 11, 1941, 15; "Harvard Psychiatrist to Retire," *New York Times*, May 27, 1956, 69; "Dr. H. C. Solomon Dies at Age of 92," obituary, *New York Times*, May 25, 1982, D23; Maida Solomon, *Carrying the Banner for Psychiatric Social Work: Essays, Perspectives, and Maida Herman Solomon's Oral Memoir*, ed. John B. Gussman (Oakland, CA: Old Heidelberg, 2004), 62.

141 *early proponent of halfway houses:* Lawrence E. Davis, "Mental Hospital Called Outmoded," *New York Times*, May 13, 1958, 31.

ward with five or six men: Cheney to Putnam, November 5, 1941, box 2, folder 8, Putnam Papers.

Kenneth J. Tillotson: Dr. Tillotson was medical director of McLean until he became embroiled in a scandal involving a nurse, Ann Marie Salot, with whom Dr. Tillotson had an affair. When the affair ended, Salot filed a claim against Dr. Tillotson with the Massachusetts Department of Mental Health in October 1948. Both were arraigned on morals charges, including committing an "unnatural act," which likely referred to either oral or anal sex. How this information came out at the arraignment and become public is not clear. But as a result of the scandal, Dr. Tillotson resigned from both McLean and Harvard Medical School. After McLean, Dr. Tillotson practiced at the Valleyhead Hospital in Carlisle, Massachusetts, where he oversaw several electroshock therapy treatments of one of his more famous patients, Sylvia Plath. Matthiessen to Cheney, January 3, 1939, box 19, folder 59, Matthiessen Papers; "Nurse, Belmont Doctor Held for Trial on Morals Charge," *Boston Evening American*, November 20, 1948, 20; "Pleads Innocent to Morals Charge," *Washington Post*, November 21, 1948, M20; Beam, *Gracefully Insane*, 118.

had written an article: Kenneth J. Tillotson and Robert Fleming, "Personality and Sociological Factors in the Prognosis and Treatment of Chronic Alcoholism," *New England Journal of Medicine* 217, no. 16 (October 14, 1937): 611–15.

142   *"their lack of masculine security and aggression"*: James Hardin Wall, "A Study of Alcoholism in Men," *American Journal of Psychiatry* 92 (May 1936): 1391.

"intricacy & beauty": Cheney to Putnam, January 21, 1941, box 2, folder 8, Putnam Papers.

"dominance of a few Easterners": F. O. Matthiessen, "Our First National Style," review of *Greek Revival Architecture in America*, by Talbot Hamlin, *New Republic*, March 13, 1944. Reprinted in John Rackliffe, ed., *The Responsibilities of the Critic: Essays and Reviews by F. O. Matthiessen* (New York: Oxford University Press, 1952), 63.

143   *Nelson Cantave*: Hyde, *R&D*, 388.

Chase also liked to paint images of reflective surfaces: Ronald G. Pisano, completed by D. Frederick Baker and Carolyn K. Lane, *William Merritt Chase: The Complete Catalogue of Known and Documented Work—Still Lifes, Interiors, Figures, Copies of Old Masters, and Drawings* (New Haven, CT: Yale University Press, 2010), 4:3.

turning down an invitation from the Ferargil Galleries: Cheney to Matthiessen, February 16, 1941, *R&D*, 267.

CHAPTER 8: THE GREEN LIGHT ACROSS THE PISCATAQUA

145   *"incident of the pear"*: *R&D*, 17–18.

146   *contemplated the questions*: BLSA, "Who Killed F. O. Matthiessen," review of *F.O. Matthiessen: Christian Socialist as Critic*, by Frederick C. Stern, *American Studies* 23, no. 1 (Spring 1982): 102, https://www.jstor.org/stable/40641695?refreqid=excelsior%3Aa5d6030dbd2a8699ed0a14c9cf624236.

American Renaissance more like an artistic work: Giles Gunn, *F. O. Matthiessen: The Critical Achievement* (Seattle: University of Washington Press, 1975), 134. Gunn cited a private conversation with Henry Nash Smith.

"fine intricacy of pattern": Louis Hyde, in *R&D*, 266.

"the spirit of protest and revolution": F. O. Matthiessen, "The Great Tradition: A Counterstatement," review of *The Great Tradition: An Interpretation of*

American Literature Since the Civil War, by Granville Hicks, *New England Quarterly* 7, no. 2 (June 1934): 233.

"who have taught me most": Harry Dorman functioned in *American Renaissance* as an uncanny stand-in for Cheney; the similarities between the two men are striking. Dorman lived in Santa Fe, where he arrived in 1901 suffering from tuberculosis. Cheney and Matthiessen met him in 1929 or 1930. And on their return to Santa Fe in 1935, Cheney painted Matthiessen and Dorman sitting together and sharing a bottle of whiskey, entitled *Good Irish* (1935). Like Matthiessen, Dorman was politically active and progressive. And like Cheney, architecture interested him. Dorman helped promote traditional architecture of the Southwest, including Spanish Pueblo Revival and California Mission, and sought out styles that were independent of a European past. In 1913, he became president of the Chamber of Commerce of Santa Fe, promoting the city to tuberculosis specialists, who in turn recommended it to their patients for the climate. Hanns Caspar Kollar was Austrian, had studied medicine and archaeology, had been a drama critic, and traveled around the United States as manager of an exhibition of Austrian children's art. Kollar impressed Matthiessen as seeming to know more about America than Matthiessen did. Kollar fit well into that category of people whom Matthiessen admired and wrote about in *American Renaissance*, "jack of many trades and master of several." Dedication, AR, n.p., and 642; Corinne P. Sze, "The Harry Dorman House, 707 Old Santa Fe Trail," *Bulletin of the Historic Santa Fe Foundation* 28, no. 1 (November 2001): 1, 6–7, 13; FHE, 15.

147 *"friends"*: SOJ, 155; RC, 6.

thrilled him to be living Whitman's words: Matthiessen to Cheney, September 21, 1924, R&D, 26.

"man cannot use words": AR, 518.

Thoreau, for example: George Minkin, Notebook for English 7, cotaught by F. O. Matthiessen and Perry Miller, 1939–1940, Harvard University Archives.

"wooden" and subsequent quote: AR, 86, 428.

"fasten words again to visible things" and subsequent quotes: AR, 33, 35, 517, 526.

148 *Emerson valued the American tradition of oratory* and subsequent quotes: AR, 15, 18, 554.

Matthiessen's love of Cheney's voice: RC, 6.

Emerson's influence on Thoreau and Whitman: AR, 30, 248, 293, 305.

149 *"assimilate his reading"*: AR, 119.

enthralled by Melville's reading of Shakespeare: AR, 412, 423–24, 429.

Swimming: Although Matthiessen used the title *The Swimming Hole* in *American Renaissance*, I have elected to use the title *Swimming* for the painting, which is what the Amon Carter Museum, the current owner of the painting, uses. AR, 399.

Swimming (1885) depicts: AR, 610; Adam Gopnik, "Eakins in the Wilderness," New Yorker, December 26, 1994/January 2, 1995), 87; Martin A. Berger, Thomas Eakins and the Construction of Gilded Age Manhood (Berkeley: University of California Press, 2000), 92; Doreen Bolger and Sarah Cash, eds., Thomas Eakins and the Swimming Picture (Fort Worth, TX: Amon Carter Museum, 1996), 49.

151   "The beards of the young men": Whitman, "Song of Myself," sec. 11, lines 210–13.

uncredited picture: In The Miracle Workers, Cheney Brothers highlighted its working conditions, housing, medical care, and recreational facilities. One such facility was Globe Hollow Reservoir, one of the man-made lakes that the company used to supply water to its mills. During the Depression, Globe Hollow Reservoir was a popular swimming spot with male workers from Cheney Brothers. At the time, women would have swum separately. John E. Majkowski, Interview with James Tierney, November 20, 1987 (Manchester, CT: Institute of Local History, Manchester Community College, 1987), 9, held by the Manchester Public Library (James Tierney's father worked for Cheney Brothers Silk Manufacturing Company for thirty-five years); Cheney Brothers Silk Manufacturing Company, The Miracle Workers (1916; repr., Manchester, CT: Manchester Historical Society, 2012), 29; William E. Buckley, A New England Pattern: The History of Manchester, Connecticut (Chester, CT: Pequot Press, 1973), 145.

153   "something defective or abnormal" and subsequent quote: Herman Melville, Billy Budd, Sailor (1924; repr., New York: Penguin Books, 1986), 314, 322; AR, 504, 506.

"sexual element in Claggart's ambivalence": AR, 506.

interpreted Billy Budd using a queer lens: Eve Kosofsky Sedgwick, Epistemology of the Closet (Berkeley: University of California Press, 1990), 92.

154   critical reception, and subsequent quotes: Clifton Fadiman, Books, New Yorker, June 7, 1941, 74; George S. Hellman, "They Are the Mountains in Our Range of Letters," New York Times, June 15, 1941, BR4; Robert E. Spiller, "Emerson & Co.," Saturday Review of Literature, June 14, 1941, 6; Stanley Williams, "In the Age of Emerson and Whitman," Yale Review 31, no. 1 (September 1941): 200.

"The whole book": Granville Hicks, review of American Renaissance, New England Quarterly 14, no. 3 (September 1941): 562. When The Responsibilities of the Critic, the posthumous collection of Matthiessen's short essays and reviews, was published, the Scottish poet and translator Edwin Muir reviewed the book in the Observer. He felt similarly to Kazin and Hicks, noting that Matthiessen's shorter reviews betrayed "timidity" and "excessive carefulness." But Muir was willing to grant that Matthiessen wrote one book of "outstanding merit": American Renaissance. Edwin Muir, "Contrasted Critics," review of The Responsibilities of the Critics: Essays and Reviews by F. O. Matthiessen, Observer (London), January 25, 1953, 9.

intensely honest: Alfred Kazin, "Statements by Friends and Associates," in *FOM*, 114; Helen Merrell Lynd, "Statements by Friends and Associates," in *FOM*, 126.

appreciated Henry James: Matthiessen to Cheney, *R&D*, March 21, 1943, 277.

155 *"American Renaissance (1941) has given its name":* Jonathan Arac, "F. O. Matthiessen: Authorizing an American Renaissance," in *American Renaissance Reconsidered,* ed. Walter Benn Michaels and Donald Pease (Baltimore, MD: Johns Hopkins University Press, 1985), 90.

"spontaneous eruption of affection": Leo Marx, conversation with the author, digitally recorded, October 1, 2010.

"apogee of his career": Harry Levin, "A View from Within," in *Political Activism and the Academic Conscience: The Harvard Experience, 1936–1941, Hobart and William Smith Colleges, December 5 & 6, 1975,* ed. John Lydenberg (Geneva, NY: The Colleges, 1977), 6.

155–156 *Cheney was not involved in Matthiessen's academic career:* Leo Marx, conversation with the author, digitally recorded, November 26, 2010.

156 *Federal Bureau of Investigation opened a file:* Opened on May 23, 1941, Matthiessen's FBI file ran to 155 pages, consisting primarily of memoranda written by agents working out of the Boston FBI office. The memos, in the version of the file that is made available to the public, are heavily redacted and describe Matthiessen's political affiliations, public statements, and appearances in connection with the many liberal and progressive organizations with which he became involved—organizations which were deemed Communist and Communist-infiltrated by the FBI. Much, but not all, information in the file was obtained from public sources. The file was closed on April 27, 1950, several weeks after Matthiessen's death. See FF.

Cheney had simplified his canvases: "Native Art on Parade," *New York Sun,* October 31, 1941, 32; *Brooklyn Eagle,* Sunday, November 2, 1941, 5–6.

"Mr. Cheney is a prolific painter": Margaret Breuning, "In the World of Art," *New York Journal American,* November 2, 1941, 7.

157 *"I'm sure that you can live":* Matthiessen to Russell Cheney, November 2, 1941, box 19, folder 60, Matthiessen Papers.

"I do wish": Matthiessen to Cheney, May 25, 1942, box 19, folder 60, Matthiessen Papers.

"For I still believe": Matthiessen to Cheney, August 14, 1943, box 19, folder 61, Matthiessen Papers.

doctors were beginning to recognize AA: Early in his career, Dr. Robert Fleming, one of Cheney's doctors at Baldpate, maintained that alcoholics should be institutionalized. By 1945, however, a few years after the worst of Cheney's drinking travails, Dr. Fleming went on the record as a supporter of Alcoholics Anonymous, writing: "Alcoholics Anonymous is, as I say, an important and useful group in this country." Robert Fleming, "Medical Treatment of the Inebriate," in *Alcohol, Science and Society: Twenty-Nine Lectures with Discussions as Given at the Yale Summer School of Alcohol Studies* (New Haven, CT: Quarterly Journal of Studies on Alcohol, 1945), 395.

"déclassé": Eric Solomon, conversation with the author, digitally recorded, December 2, 2010.

158 stories began to appear: In addition to the Saturday Evening Post piece, the Cleveland Plain Dealer ran a series by Elrick B. Davis on Alcoholics Anonymous from October 21 through October 26, 1939, describing the organization and its work. In the first piece, Davis alluded to the impor-tance of avoiding the first drink: "The alcoholic is allergic to alcohol. One drink sets up the poisonous craving that only more of the poison can assuage. That is why after the first drink the alcoholic cannot stop." Elrick B. Davis, "Alcoholics Anonymous Makes Its Stand Here," Cleveland Plain Dealer, October 21, 1939, 8.

"After a while": Jack Alexander, "Alcoholics Anonymous: Freed Slaves of Drink Now Free Others," Saturday Evening Post, March 1, 1941, 90.

"shots": Cheney to Matthiessen, May 5, 1942, box 19, folder 84, Matthiessen Papers.

PTZ (also known as metrazol): Without access to Cheney's medical records, his decision to undergo pentylenetetrazol-induced shock therapy is not an ironclad assertion, but the circumstantial evidence in support of PTZ shock therapy, as opposed to other kinds of shock therapy, is persuasive. In his correspondence with Matthiessen, Cheney specifically referred to the prospect of receiving "shots," hence electroshock therapy can be ruled out. Although tuberculosis was contraindicated for PTZ therapy, because Cheney's tuberculosis had been cured over a decade ago, his doctors may have been willing to continue with the treatment. Cheney could have received insulin shock therapy, which was also administered by shots. But his treatment in the spring of 1942 lasted approximately one month, whereas insulin shock therapy typically lasted two and a half to three months. In addition, patients undergoing insulin shock therapy often had "considerable" weight gain. Cheney did not mention any weight gain in his 1942 correspondence with either Matthiessen or Putnam, nor do photographs from this point in his life reflect an appreciable weight gain. Lucie Jessner, MD, PhD, and V. Gerard Ryan, MD, Shock Treatment in Psychiatry (New York: Grune and Stratton, 1941), 119, 48, 37, 75, 102; A. Kennedy, "A Critical Review: Treatment of Mental Disorders by Induced Convulsions," Journal of Neurology & Psychiatry 3, no. 1 (January 1940): 77. As Jennifer Terry has pointed out: Jennifer Terry, An American Obsession: Science, Medicine, and Homosexuality in Modern Society (Chicago: University of Chicago Press, 1999), 295.

"the drastic step": Cheney to Matthiessen, May 4, 1942, box 19, folder 84, Matthiessen Papers.

159 Cheney's term of treatment: Regarding Cheney's first treatment, see Cheney to Matthiessen, May 5, 1942, box 19, folder 84, Matthiessen Papers; regard-ing Cheney's resumption of drinking, see Matthiessen to Cheney, May 25, 1942, box 19, folder 60, Matthiessen Papers.

average course of PTZ therapy: Jessner and Ryan, Shock Treatment in Psychiatry, 72, 71, 67–68, 75.

"*alcohol has been out of your system*": Matthiessen to Cheney, May 25, 1942, box 19, folder 60, Matthiessen Papers.

"*More and more I realize*": Cheney to Matthiessen, June 1, 1942, box 19, folder 84, Matthiessen Papers.

160 "*it strikes me*": Matthiessen to Cheney, December 13, 1942, box 19, folder 60, Matthiessen Papers.

 least productive years of his career: The number of paintings that Russell Cheney completed in 1942 is based on the preliminary catalogue raisonné compiled by Richard Candee and Carol L. Cheney; see CC. Because many of Cheney's paintings are currently identifiable by a date range, it's possible that a more accurate number of paintings completed in 1942 may be later determined. Closely related to the falloff in production is the "unevenness" and "uncertainty" in Cheney's work in the later years of his career, as one critic noted. See, for example, Patricia Bennett, "Mature Connecticut Painter," *Hartford Courant Sunday Magazine*, April 20, 1947, 13.

"*regular 'family' life*": Cheney to Matthiessen, February 15, 1943, *R&D*, 276.

161 *He landed back at Baldpate:* Cheney to Matthiessen, May 8, 1943, *R&D*, 277.

"*There's nothing whatsoever*": Matthiessen to Cheney, July 21, 1943, box 19, folder 61, Matthiessen Papers.

 "*So please try to work out a defense*": Although Matthiessen probably picked up the notion of avoiding the first drink from stories about Alcoholics Anonymous in the popular press at the time, it's quite likely that he read about the need for an alcoholic to develop a mental defense against drinking from Richard Roger Peabody's *The Common Sense of Drinking*, which Cheney had read sometime after 1931. Peabody urged the alcoholic to "work out in advance mental preparation to guard against drinking." Richard Rogers Peabody, *The Common Sense of Drinking* (Boston: Little Brown, 1931), 103; Matthiessen to Cheney, August 14, 1943, box 19, folder 61, Matthiessen Papers.

the lonely disease: In 1965, Elizabeth D. Whitney published a book about alcoholism entitled *The Lonely Sickness* (Boston: Beacon Press, 1965). Cheney's doctor, Robert Fleming, wrote the preface to the book.

demanding, rude, and even belligerent: Leo Marx, "The Teacher," in *FOM*, 41; May Sarton, *Faithful Are the Wounds* (New York: W. W. Norton, 1955), 233; William E. Cain, *F. O. Matthiessen and the Politics of Criticism* (Madison: University of Wisconsin Press, 1988), 102.

Matthiessen's stress: If Matthiessen did suffer from some form of manic-depressive illness, that, too, could have contributed significantly to his personality change noted by friends and acquaintances during the early 1940s.

162 "*The wife or husband*": Alexander, "Alcoholics Anonymous," 90.

"*some illness*": Sarton, *Faithful Are the Wounds*, 56; Cain, *Matthiessen and the Politics of Criticism*, 102.

"*Russell's drinking*": Donald Pitkin, conversation with the author, digitally recorded, November 19, 2010.

"The Humanities in War Time": "The Humanities in War Time," 1943 *Harvard Album* (Cambridge, MA, 1943), 33–37.

Eliot's essay "Poetry in Wartime": Eliot's "Poetry in Wartime" had been published in the October 1942 issue of the journal *Common Sense*. Matthiessen later alluded to Eliot's essay in the 1947 edition *The Achievement of T. S. Eliot*. *Eliot*, 188.

163   *increasing intellectual distance*: John Rackliffe, "Notes for a Character Study," in *FOM*, 79; Giles Gunn, *F. O. Matthiessen: The Critical Achievement* (Seattle: University of Washington Press, 1975), 138.

Harvard president James Bryant Conant: Hyde, *R&D*, 271; James Hershberg, *James B. Conant* (New York: Alfred A. Knopf, 1993), 81, 160–71; M. A. Farber, "James B. Conant Dies at 84," obituary, *New York Times*, February 13, 1978, D9.

George Abbott White wrote: George Abbott White, "Have I Any Right in a Community That Would So Utterly Disapprove of Me If It Knew the Facts," *Harvard Magazine*, September–October 1978, 62.

"possess the slick competitive knacks": Matthiessen to Cheney, December 13, 1942, box 19, folder 60, Matthiessen Papers.

"I've got a fairly low view": Matthiessen to Cheney, April 1, 1945, *R&D*, 341.

164   *too short and two years too old*: The height requirement for service in the US Marines during World War II for men over nineteen years of age was between 66 and 74 inches. This would suggest that Matthiessen was 5 foot 5 ½ inches tall, as was reported in his Selective Service file. But it is below Matthiessen's self-reported height of 5 foot 6 inches tall on his 1943 State of Maine driver's license. In a profile in the *Harvard Crimson* on September 28, 1933, Matthiessen grew another two and a half inches and reported his height as 5 foot 8 inches. In addition to being too short, Matthiessen was too old and received IV-H classification, which was used for men from thirty-eight to forty-five years. As historian Beth Crumley, Historical Reference Branch, Marine Corps-History Division, described in a telephone conversation with me, Matthiessen could have been rejected from the Marines for being a half inch too short as well as his IV-H deferment. State of Maine Driver's License, Francis Otto Matthiessen, January 1, 1943, box 21, Matthiessen Papers; Report, Francis Otto Matthiessen, Boston, MA, FBI, August 14, 1943, pp. 1, 3, FF; Robert V. Aquilina, US Marines, Historical Reference Branch, letter to author, January 7, 2011; "Selective Service System Classifications for WWI, WWII, and PWWII through 1976," e-mail to author and follow-up conversation, February 3, 2011, from historian Beth Crumley, Historical Reference Branch, Marine Corps.

"unable to make a living for himself": Report, Francis Otto Matthiessen, Boston, MA, FBI, October 28, 1943, p. 2, FF.

Harry Bridges: Matthiessen likely came into contact with Harry Bridges through Paul M. Sweezy and Leo Huberman, who went on to found the *Monthly Review*, a Socialist magazine. Paul Sweezy followed in the footsteps of his older brother, Alan R. Sweezy, in becoming a left-leaning

economist at Harvard during the late 1930s and early 1940s, whom
Matthiessen befriended. Both Paul Sweezy and Leo Huberman had
studied at the London School of Economics, where R. H. Tawney taught,
and Huberman even studied with Tawney. Huberman wrote at length
about Harry Bridges's trials. "Leo Huberman, Publisher, 65, Dead," *New
York Times*, November 10, 1968, 88; Louis Uchitelle, "Paul Sweezy, 93,
Marxist Publisher and Economist Dies," March 2, 2004, B9.
Matthiessen joined: "Orson Welles Forms Group to Aid Bridges," *Pittsburgh
Press*, April 29, 1941, 10.

165 *enthusiasm for Harry Bridges:* Irving Bernstein, *Turbulent Years: A History
of the American Worker, 1933–1941* (Boston: Houghton Mifflin, 1970), 252,
257–58; Leo Huberman, *Storm over Bridges* (San Francisco: Charles L.
Conlan Printers, 1941), 8, 16; Wolfgang Saxon, "Harry Bridges, Docks
Leader, Dies at 88," obituary, *New York Times*, March 31, 1990, 11; Theodore
Dreiser, "The Story of Harry Bridges," *Friday*, October 4, 1940, 1, 2; Harvey
Schwartz, "Harry Bridges and the Scholars: Looking at History's Verdict,"
California History 59, no. 1 (Spring 1980): 68; *FHE*, 86.
"*How's your mandolin player getting along?*": Frances Perkins, *The Roosevelt
I Knew* (New York: Viking Press, 1946), 318.
loneliness: Harry Levin, "Statements by Friends and Associates," in *FOM*,
125; Lynd, "Statements by Friends and Associates," *FOM*, 126; Ernest J.
Simmons, "Statements by Friends and Associates," in *FOM*, 137.
"*I feel pretty lonely*" and subsequent quote: Matthiessen to Cheney, January
15, 1943, box 19, folder 61, Matthiessen Papers.

166 "*I needn't pretend*": Matthiessen to Cheney, August 14, 1943, box 19, folder
61, Matthiessen Papers.
"*I had a funny sense*": Matthiessen to Cheney, December 26, 1943, box 19,
folder 61, Matthiessen Papers.
acquired taste: Matthiessen to Cheney, February 10, 1943, *R&D*, 274.
spark interest in James's work: Pearl Kazin Bell, "Mentors," *American Scholar*
72, no. 1 (Winter 2003): 101–2; *HJ*, xvi.

167 *Matthiessen denounced:* "Harvard Prof. Denounces Ban on 'Strange Fruit,'"
Daily Worker (New York City), March 25, 1944, 2.
"*it is thoroughly shameful*": F. O. Matthiessen, letter to the editor, *Harvard
Crimson*, March 24, 1944, https://www.thecrimson.com/article/1944/3/24/
the-mail-pto-the-editor-pas/.
stress on sight and subsequent quote: *HJ*, 32, 36.
convey imagery: *HJ*, 60, 65.

168 "*Reading the opening sections*": Cheney to Matthiessen, November 24, 1944,
R&D, 297–98.
they were real people: René Wellek, *American Criticism, 1900–1950*, vol. 6 of
History of Modern Criticism, 1750–1950 (New Haven, CT: Yale University
Press, 1986), 81.
"*indomitable energy*" and subsequent quotes: *HJ*, 177, 178, 179.
increasingly political tone: William E. Cain views the coming together of
Matthiessen's literary and political judgments in *Henry James: The Major*

Phase as a positive development. Whatever the literary assessment of such, the difficulties in Matthiessen's personal life with Cheney help shed light on at least some of the motivation for Matthiessen's increasingly political tone in his scholarship. Cain, *Matthiessen and the Politics of Criticism*, 84.

"The Golden Bowl is morally deficient": Philip Rahv, "Modernizing James," review of *Henry James: The Major Phase*, by F. O. Matthiessen, *Kenyon Review* 77, no. 2 (Spring 1945): 313.

"religion of consciousness" and subsequent quotes: Robert B. Heilman, review of *Henry James: The Major Phase*, by F. O. Matthiessen, *New England Quarterly* 18, no. 2 (June, 1945): 269–70.

169 *"sentimental, uneasy, apologetic, and evasive"*: Maxwell Geismar, *Henry James and the Jacobites* (Boston: Houghton Mifflin, 1963), 115, 130, 225, 259, 281, 301.

"Harvard Professor F. O. Matthiessen": Geismar, *Henry James and the Jacobites*, 268.

similarly praised Matthiessen's assessment: R. W. B. Lewis, *The Jameses: A Family Narrative* (New York: Farrar, Straus and Giroux, 1991), 516.

170 *"I don't know whether the relief"*: Cheney to Matthiessen, May 25, 1944, *R&D*, 281.

171 *"You and I know"*: Cheney to Matthiessen, November 24, 1944, *R&D*, 298; Cheney to Matthiessen, January 7, 1945, *R&D*, 312.

"It's been very exciting": Cheney to Matthiessen, December 17, 1944, *R&D*, 304.

The Lost Cause: Cheney borrowed the bulto from his new art dealer in Santa Fe, Willard Hougland. Santos bultos are painted and sculpted icons indigenous to the Southwest. Although based on religious figures, bultos can have broader associations outside the realm of religion. Cheney's figure, St. James the Greater, was often depicted as bearded, on horseback, in a soldier's uniform, and carrying a sword or spear. Hougland speculated that the flag held by St. James in Cheney's painting had been substituted for the original sword or spear. Cheney to Matthiessen, December 17, 1944, *R&D*, 304; *Santos: A Primitive American Art: Collection of Jan Kleijkamp and Ellis Monroe*, with introduction and text by Willard Hougland and foreword by Donald Bear (New York: Jan Kleijkamp and Ellis Monroe, 1946), 3, 32; Sheldon Cheney and Martha Candler, "Santos: An Enigma of American Native Art," *Parnassus* 7, no. 4 (May 1935): 22–23.

172 *"how much you have taught me"*: Matthiessen to Cheney, March 5, 1945, *R&D*, 333.

"Here I lie": Matthiessen to Cheney, May 13, 1945, *R&D*, 350.

"I'm counting on": Matthiessen to Cheney, May 13, 1945, box 19, folder 64, Matthiessen Papers.

"good steady time all summer": Cheney to Matthiessen, May 20, 1945, box 19, folder 93, Matthiessen Papers.

"When the moon is full": Cheney to Matthiessen, May 6, 1945, *R&D*, 348.

173 *everything can be made right:* Although the analysis of Cheney's reference to the green light is my own, I am grateful to Leo Marx for the broader cultural significance of the green light in *The Great Gatsby* in his book *The Machine in the Garden*. It seems only fitting that the work of a scholar who studied with Matthiessen should prove helpful in interpreting a key image in understanding Matthiessen and Cheney's life together. Leo Marx, *The Machine in the Garden: Technology and the Pastoral Ideal in America* (New York: Oxford University Press, 1970), 360.

CHAPTER 9: LOSING TOUCH

174 *Matthiessen described:* I am curious to know whether this was genuinely Cheney's bedroom or Matthiessen simply referred to the room that way for the purpose of speaking with the newspaper reporter. In earlier correspondence from late 1938 when Matthiessen was at McLean Hospital and Cheney had forgotten his key, Cheney referred in a letter to trying to unlatch "our bedroom window." In all likelihood, Matthiessen and Cheney shared a bedroom on the first floor of the house. The bedroom to which Matthiessen referred to in the news story may have been a spare room that Cheney used from time to time. Alternatively, the two men could have taken separate bedrooms at this point in their relationship. Whatever the exact configuration of their sleeping arrangements, the discrepancy between Matthiessen's public statements and Cheney's private correspondence suggest how careful Matthiessen needed to be regarding the facts of their lives, notwithstanding the tremendous grief and stress he must felt after Cheney died. Matthiessen to Cheney, December 27, 1938, *R&D*, 239.

died later that day: "Russell Cheney, Noted Artist, Dies Suddenly," obituary, *Portsmouth Herald*, July 13, 1945, 1; "Russell Cheney," obituary, *Kittery Press*, July 20, 1945, 1; Helen Bayne Knapp, *A Death* (Kittery Point, ME: privately printed, 1968), 1, 2.

Lavender, gladiolas, lilies, and red roses: Although Cheney was buried on July 14, 1945, Matthiessen's entry in his daybook was for July 12, 1945, the date of Cheney's death. It may have been that he discussed the flowers with one of Cheney's family members on July 12. F. O. Matthiessen, 1945 Daybook, July 12, 1945, box 7, Matthiessen Papers.

175 *the family resented:* Knapp, "A Death," 2–3.

Cheney bequeathed: Russell Cheney, will dated August 19, 1942, proved November 30, 1945, book 1049, p. 87, State of Maine, Probate Court, County of York, Alfred, ME.

closest thing he had to love: F. O. Matthiessen to Harry Levin, July 19, 1945, box 14, Harry Levin Papers, 1920–1995, MS Am 2461, Houghton Library, Harvard University.

176 *suppressed, as though it had never existed:* Contemporary psychologists who have researched grief in same-sex relationships, point out that when a partner dies, the surviving partner often experiences greater stress because of the mainstream culture's unwillingness to acknowledge the

validity of the relationship in the first place. Societal homophobia complicates the grieving process. In Matthiessen's day, it was even worse. In a rough survey of books on death, bereavement, loss, and grief in the 1930s and 1940s, there were—not surprisingly—no references to same-sex relationships. Nor were there any references to widowers, only widows. Men were not supposed to grieve over the loss of their partners, much less same-sex partners. Many books of the era on death carry cheerful titles that ring hollow to contemporary ears, such as *Conquest of Grief* (1933), *The Joy of Sorrow* (1936), *Beyond Sorrow* (1938), *Silver Lining* (1941), *Victory over Suffering* (1941), *Rainbows through Sorrow* (1947), *Solace in Shadowlands* (1948), *Not Death at All* (1949), and *Widows Can Be Happy* (1950). In other words, the strain of American culture that wanted to acknowledge only the happy and smiling side of life—"genteel culture"—exerted a strong influence in shaping the discourse around death. Matthiessen grew increasingly opposed to genteel culture in the late 1940s, and Cheney's death set the stage for this development. Michael Shernoff, *Gay Widowers: Life after the Death of a Partner* (New York: Hayworth Press, 1997), 144; Carolyn Ambler Walter, *The Loss of a Life Partner: Narratives of the Bereaved* (New York: Columbia University Press, 2003), 25, 28.

fed into political and moral problems: R. M. Goodwin, "Statements by Friends and Associates," in *FOM*, 111.

job of politics to provide answers: Rufus W. Matthewson Jr., "Statements by Friends and Associates," in *FOM*, 128.

177   *"clear and compelling political philosophy":* Ernest J. Simmons, "Statements by Friends and Associates," in *FOM*, 136.

political attachments "were not founded": Alfred Kazin, "Statements by Friends and Associates," in *FOM*, 114.

wrong for the right reasons: Arthur M. Schlesinger Jr., *A Life in the Twentieth Century: Innocent Beginnings, 1917–1950* (Boston: Houghton Mifflin, 2000), 129.

Christian and Socialist: John Rackliffe, "Notes for a Character Study," in *FOM*, 92; "Note Professor Left in Suicide Is Studied," *Boston Evening Globe*, April 1, 1950, 2.

178   *Matthiessen held him in his lap:* Louis Hyde, in *R&D*, 357.

"tends to shy away": F. O. Matthiessen, "Whitman: His Poetry and Prose," book review, *New York Times*, July 29, 1945, BR1.

"pathological": *AR*, 535.

focal point for his unhappiness: It's not certain that Matthiessen wrote this review after Cheney's death. Matthiessen may well have written a draft of it before Cheney's death. But whatever the exact timing, Matthiessen let it and others go forward for publication with a sharper tone than in much of his earlier writing.

179   *"For if Harvard wants to join America":* F. O. Matthiessen, "Harvard Wants to Join America," *New Republic*, August 20, 1945, 221.

considered leaving for Brandeis in 1946: J. H. Summers, "Statements by Friends and Associates," in *FOM*, 143.

The Herald picked up Matthiessen's review: "'Harvard Wants to Join U.S.'

Writes Professor," *Boston Herald*, August 26, 1945, B9; Report, Francis Otto Matthiessen, Boston, MA, FBI, July 17, 1947, p. 4, FF.

180   *printed privately by the Andover Press:* Andover Press to Matthiessen, June 14, 1946, box 1, Matthiessen Papers; Ella Winter, "Statements by Friends and Associates," in *FOM*, 147.

raised additional funds: Matthiessen to Clifford Cheney, November 1, 1945, box 1, Matthiessen Papers.

"a New England and American master": Ferargil Galleries, *Russell Cheney—1881–1945*, Retrospective Memorial Exhibition, March 17–29, 1947, 2.

Matthiessen successfully reached out: "Cheney Mailing List Additions," box 9, Matthiessen Papers.

"one of the things I look forward to": Matthiessen to Cheney, April 5, 1925, *R&D*, 112.

181   *"long-time companion":* Jerome Mellquist, "A Painter's Personality as It Emerges in His Letters," book review, *New York Times*, April 27, 1947, BR7.

"I want to establish my life quietly": *RC*, 95; Dorothy Adlow, *Christian Science Monitor*, April 3, 1947, 12; Cheney to Matthiessen, April 25, 1931, *R&D*, 222.

sample of Matthiessen's handwriting: Report, Francis Otto Matthiessen, Boston, MA, FBI, July 17, 1947, p. 7, FF; Schlesinger, *Life in the Twentieth Century*, 402, 456; Curtis D. MacDougall, *Gideon's Army* (New York: Marzani & Munsell, 1965), 248, 301; Douglas Martin, "Angus Cameron, 93, Editor Forced Out in McCarthy Era," *New York Times*, November 23, 2002, A17.

182   *Salzburg Seminar in American Studies:* It was through Heller that the Salzburg Seminar began meeting at Schloss Leopoldskron, which was then owned by the Austrian-born theater and film director Max Reinhardt and his wife, Helene Thimig. Heller was the son of a distinguished publisher in Vienna and had been involved with Reinhardt's theater school during his boyhood. The Salzburg Seminar was initially known by the name Salzburg Seminar in American Civilization but then officially registered as the Salzburg Seminar in American Studies. I use this latter name, except when the former name has been preserved in a title. Later, the seminar adopted a more international focus and renamed itself the Salzburg Global Seminar. F. O. Matthiessen, "Statement on Salzburg," p. 1, box 7, folder: Statements on Seminar Arrangement—Mead and F.O.M., Matthiessen Papers; Margaret Mead, "The Salzburg Seminar in American Civilization 1947, p. 2, https://www.salzburgglobal.org/fileadmin/user_upload/Documents/General_SGS_Documents/1947_MeadArticle.pdf; George Blaustein, "'Other' American Studies: The Salzburg Seminar, American Intellectuals, and Postwar Europe," in *E Pluribus Unum or E Pluribus Plura: Unity and Diversity in American Culture*, ed. Hans-Jürgen Grabbe, David Mauk, and Ole Moen (Heidelberg, Germany: Universitätsverlag Winter GmbH Heidelberg, 2011), 264; Dr. Timothy W. Ryback, "The Salzburg Seminar—A Community of Fellows," https://www.salzburgglobal.org/about/history/articles/a-community-of-fellows; Mead, "Salzburg Seminar," 2.

183 *focused for six weeks on American history*: The organizers of the Salzburg Seminar decided to focus on American history and literature, because they felt that it was the one area in which American scholars and writers were confident that they knew more than their European counterparts. As it so happened, those subjects also fit well with the cultural diplomatic goals of the US government at the time. From the Salzburg Seminar's earliest days, it was international—albeit Western—by default. The inaugural class included students from England, France, Italy, Austria, West Germany, Belgium, the Netherlands, Denmark, Finland, Hungary, Greece, Czechoslovakia, Sweden, Poland, Switzerland, Yugoslavia, and Australia. J. C. Levenson, conversation with the author, digitally recorded, Feburary 23, 2011; Alfred Kazin, "Salzburg: Seminar in the Ruins," *Commentary* 6, no. 1 (July 1948): 56.

useful tools of cultural diplomacy: Blaustein, "'Other' American Studies," 264.

"too idealistic, too impractical, too premature": Dr. Timothy W. Ryback, "The Salzburg Seminar—A Community of Fellows," https://www.salzburg-global.org/about/history/articles/a-community-of-fellows.

Kazin and Matthiessen in American literature: Together, Matthiessen and Kazin lectured on Emerson, Thoreau, Hawthorne, Whitman, Melville, Henry James, Twain, Henry Adams, Dreiser, Hemingway, Dos Passos, Eliot, and E. E. Cummings.—Kazin, "Salzburg," 57.

184 *"communicated the sense of a living literature"*: Mead, "Salzburg Seminar," 6.

"air of a commune": Blaustein, "'Other' American Studies," 272.

"most valuable teaching experience": Matthiessen to Louis Hyde, September 12, 1947, *R&D*, 361.

aesthetically inclined and politically liberal: Daniel Aaron, conversation with the author, digitally recorded, October 4, 2010.

"lonely passion": Alfred Kazin, *New York Jew* (New York: Alfred A. Knopf, 1978), 168–69.

185 *"exact" list of titles*: Matthiessen to Laurette Murdock, September 12, 1947, box 3, Matthiessen Papers.

"April is the cruellest month": T. S. Eliot, *The Waste Land*, lines 1–4.

"an unforgettable experience": Kazin, "Salzburg," 58.

human voice: AR, 554.

course on American literature: This course covered Emerson, Whitman, Hawthorne, and Melville, as well as Sherwood Anderson, Faulkner, Eliot, and Hart Crane among others. F. O. Matthiessen, Notebook V, Charles University syllabus, box 7, F. O. Matthiessen Papers, 1929–1950, MS Am 1433, Houghton Library, Harvard University.

feeling really "in": F. O. Matthiessen, Notebook V, Prague, p. 30, box 7, F. O. Matthiessen Papers, 1929–1950, MS Am 1433, Houghton Library, Harvard University.

186 *Jan Masaryk*: Jan Masaryk was perhaps the most influential person Matthiessen met with during his time in Czechoslovakia. Matthiessen

likely got to know Masaryk either through networks of friends or academic connections. The son of Czechoslovakia's first president, Tomáš Garrigue Masaryk, and Charlotte Garrigue, an American, Jan Masaryk spent a great deal of time in the United States and married Frances Crane Leatherbee, the daughter of industrialist Charles Crane, Masaryk's first employer. Later, Masaryk lectured at American universities. After his divorce from Leatherbee in 1931, Masaryk began dating Marcia Davenport, the former of wife of Russell Davenport, Matthiessen's friend from Yale and Skull and Bones.

Masaryk was known for his humanity and warmth and as a fighter on behalf of persecuted men and women—a man entirely in keeping with Matthiessen's sensibility. He hated the protocols and formalities of government and had a gift for colorful speech. At a news conference a reporter once addressed him as "Excellency," to which Masaryk responded with, "Don't be a blasted fool." During World War II, Masaryk gave a weekly radio address on the Czechoslovakian cause from London, which helped lead to American recognition of the exiled Czechoslovakian government after the country had been invaded by the Nazis. On his return to Czechoslovakia after the war, Masaryk became foreign minister. A man with a decidedly western sensibility, Masaryk attempted to form a bridge between East and West in the early days of the Cold War—another notion that appealed greatly to Matthiessen. Marcia Davenport, *Too Strong for Fantasy* (New York: Charles Scribner's Sons, 1967), 291, 313; Claire Sterling, *The Masaryk Case: The Murder of Democracy in Czechoslovakia* (Boston: David R. Godine, 1982), 122, 124, 126; "Masaryk Devoted Life to Country," *New York Times*, March 11, 1948, 4 (quotation); International, *Time*, March 8, 1948, 29.

"there were so many other meetings": F. O. Matthiessen, Notebook VI, n.d., box 7, F. O. Matthiessen Papers, 1929–1950, MS Am 1433, Houghton Library, Harvard University.

"What does the Social Democratic Party want?": FHE, 152.

not insignificant amount of work: Jean Lehman, review of *The James Family*, by F. O. Matthiessen, *Philadelphia Inquirer*, November 2, 1947, 165.

"economic make-up of society": JF, 650.

"impressions": Henry James, *The Notebooks of Henry James*, ed. F. O. Matthiessen and Kenneth B. Murdock (New York: Oxford University Press, 1947), 33–34.

187 *access to James's notebooks*: Wilson's criticism highlights the high degree of access that Matthiessen's association with Harvard afforded him. Matthiessen and Murdock had use of Henry James's notebooks before anyone else, because James's nephew, also named Henry, had donated them to the Houghton Library at Harvard. Whatever Matthiessen's frustrations with Harvard, he derived concrete benefits from his long association with the prestigious, influential institution. "Henry James, Head of Annuity Board," obituary, *New York Times*, December 15, 1947, 25.

"Mr. Matthiessen is intelligent" and Wilson quote just above: Edmund Wilson, "New Documents on the Jameses," *New Yorker*, December 13, 1947, 119–20.

188 *"green light"*: Jennifer Allen, "The Woman Who Understood Alice James," *Daily News* (New York, NY), January 19, 1981, 101.

"more pontifical": Maxwell Geismar, *Henry James and the Jacobites* (Boston: Houghton Mifflin, 1963), 139.

"most useful": Geismar, *Henry James*, 54.

Taft-Hartley Act in June 1947: Nelson Lichtenstein, *State of the Union: A Century of American Labor* (Princeton, NJ: Princeton University Press, 2002), 100, 110, 115–16, 118–19; Philip Dray, *There Is Power in a Union: The Epic Story of Labor in America* (New York: Doubleday, 2010), 496–97, 502, 504–6; Barbara S. Griffith, *The Crisis of American Labor: Operation Dixie and the Defeat of the CIO* (Philadelphia: Temple University Press, 1988), 38.

189 *"devoted followers of Moscow"*: Dray, *There Is Power in a Union*, 504; Griffith, *Crisis of American Labor*, 24–25.

1948 was eventful: "Arts Institute Names Members," *Washington Post*, January 4, 1948, L6; A Documentary Chronicle of Vassar College, February 27–29, 1948, http://chronology.vassar.edu/records/1940-1949/; "Dr. Matthiessen to Speak Friday," *Yale Daily News*, May 19, 1948, 1; Grant Webster, *The Republic of Letters: A History of Postwar American Literary Opinion* (Baltimore, MD: Johns Hopkins University Press, 1979), 105–6; F. O. Matthiessen, "Primarily Language," *Sewanee Review*, Summer 1948, 391–401.

190 *"key figure"*: Memorandum, SAC (Special Agent in Charge) to Director, Boston, FBI, February 17, 1948, FF.

eight organizations: 13 Fed. Reg., Appendix A, List of Organizations Designated by the Attorney General Pursuant to Executive Order No. 9835, 1473 (March 20, 1947); Lewis Wood, "90 Groups, Schools Named on U.S. List as Being Disloyal," *New York Times*, December 5, 1947, 1; Lewis Wood, "Subversion Laid to 32 More Groups in a Supplemental Listing by Clark," *New York Times*, May 29, 1948, 1.

platform of the Progressive Party: Progressive Citizens of America, *Peace, Freedom and Abundance: The Platform of the Progressive Party as Adopted at the Founding Convention, Philadelphia, July 23–25, 1948* (New York, 1948), 16; John C. Culver and John Hyde, *American Dreamer: The Life and Times of Henry A. Wallace* (New York: W. W. Norton, 2000), 501, 107, 373, 218, 480, 481n.

191 *Matthiessen's speech* and subsequent quotes: F. O. Matthiessen, seconding speech for Henry Wallace, Progressive Party Founding Convention, Philadelphia, PA, NBC radio broadcast, Philadelphia, July 24, 1948, recording available at the Library of Congress.

lightning rod during the Red Scare: Late in 1946, the Progressive Party grew out of the merger of the National Citizens Political Action Committee and the Independent Citizens Committee for the Arts, Science, and Professionals. The Progressive Party would admit anyone regardless of "race, creed, color, national origin, or political affiliation," which meant that the Progressive Citizens of America would admit Communists.

Complicating matters further, some prominent members of the Progressive Party did actually have ties to the Communist Party. Lee Pressman had been general counsel for the Congress of Industrial Organizations (CIO) and was later platform committee secretary for the 1948 Progressive Party Convention. He acknowledged membership in the Communist Party but later broke with it. John Abt, a lawyer, was general counsel for Wallace for President Committee. Abt's wife, Jessica Smith, had been editor of the journal *Soviet Russia Today*, and Marion Bachrach, his sister, had been public relations director for the Communist Party. Charles Kramer, who later served as Henry Wallace's speechwriter, had become a Communist Party member in 1934. Although Kramer had contact with Soviet intelligence, it appears that he did not pass along particularly sensitive information but rather materials on American politicians that were available through the public record. Matthiessen's former student, historian Arthur Schlesinger Jr., cited Pressman's and Abt's involvement with the Communist Party of America in his indictment of the Progressive Party, but later historians have felt that the Communist Party influence in the Progressive Party was overblown. Culver and Hyde, *American Dreamer*, 434 (quotation), 464; MacDougall, *Gideon's Army*, 20, 117, 119, 277, 279; Mary Sperling McAuliffe, *Crisis on the Left: Cold War Politics and American Liberals, 1947–1954* (Amherst: University of Massachusetts Press, 1978), 39; Schlesinger, *Life in the Twentieth Century*, 455; Allen Weinstein and Alexander Vassiliev, *The Haunted Wood: Soviet Espionage in America—The Stalin Era* (New York: Random House, 1999), 39, 233–34; William R. Conklin, "Wallace Charts Policies for 1948 in Liberal Merger," *New York Times*, December 30, 1946, 1.

anti-Communist liberals: Given the Progressive Party's openness to Communists, a split quickly developed on the political left between the Progressives and a group of influential New Deal Democrats, who were outspoken opponents of Communism and maintained a confrontational stance toward the Soviet Union. This group of Democrats went on to become Americans for Democratic Action and included such influential people as theologian Reinhold Niebuhr; Minneapolis mayor Hubert Humphrey; and Harvard economist John Kenneth Galbraith, among many others. But as John C. Culver and John Hyde, Wallace biographers, have noted, Americans for Democratic Action's "patron saint" was Eleanor Roosevelt. Culver and Hyde, *American Dreamer*, 435 (quotation); McAuliffe, *Crisis on the Left*, 7.

actual leaders within the Communist Party: Culver and Hyde, *American Dreamer*, 464–65.

192   *John Ciardi . . . told Matthiessen:* Leo Marx, conversation with the author, digitally recorded, October 1, 2010.

2.4 percent of the popular vote: Culver and Hyde, *American Dreamer*, 501.

"At every turn": FHE, 22. "Hanns" is Hanns Caspar Kollar, one of the men to whom Matthiessen dedicated *American Renaissance*.

193   *strikingly personal and intimate:* FHE, 23, 39, 150, 184.

Griffes . . . well-regarded composer: FHE, 74.

What Matthiessen does not say: Matthiessen owned a copy of Edward Maisel's biography entitled *Charles T. Griffes: The Life of an American Composer* (1943). This book is currently in the collection of Matthiessen's books in the F. O. Matthiessen Room, Eliot House, Harvard University. For a discussion of Griffes's sexuality, see Edward Maisel, *Charles T. Griffes: The Life of an American Composer* (New York: Alfred A. Knopf, 1943), 157.

194   Sexual Behavior in the Human Male: Matthiessen owned a copy of *Sexual Behavior in the Human Male*, 1948, by Alfred C. Kinsey, Wardell B. Pomeroy, and Clyde E Martin. This book is currently in the collection of Matthiessen's books in the F. O. Matthiessen Room, Eliot House, Harvard University. The book's statistics on homosexuality arrested Matthiessen's attention: According to Kinsey, 37 percent of all men had experienced some kind of homosexual sex activity during their lifetimes; 10 percent of men were more or less exclusively homosexual during their adult lives; and 4 percent of men were exclusively homosexual throughout their entire lives. These numbers have since been criticized as overestimating homosexual contact, but Matthiessen had no way of knowing that at the time. The other observation that must have registered poignantly with Matthiessen was that "long-time relationships between two males are notably few." Against the odds, he and Cheney had forged just such a union, at least until death intervened. Alfred C. Kinsey, Wardell B. Pomeroy, and Clyde E. Martin, *Sexual Behavior in the Human Male* (Philadelphia: W. B. Saunders, 1948), 633 (quotation), 650–51; George Chauncey, *Gay New York: Gender, Urban Culture, and the Making of the Gay Male World, 1890–1940* (New York: Basic Books, 1994), 70.

Communist coup: "The Space for Freedom Grows Smaller," Foreign Affairs, *Newsweek*, March 8, 1948, 27–28, 30; Michel Gordey, "Gottwald Wastes No Time," *New Republic*, April 19, 1948, 19–20; International, *Time*, March 8, 1948, 27; Richard H. S. Crossman, "Prague's February Revolution," *Nation*, March 27, 1948, 350; "U.S. Foreign Policy Takes a Licking," *Life*, March 8, 1948, 27.

did "not mean freedom to agitate": Michel Gordey, "Gottwald Wastes No Time," *New Republic*, April 19, 1948, 20.

195   *"remember that the new government":* FHE, 143.

On radio: F. O. Matthiessen, interview by Paul Badgers, *Your Opinion Please!*, WBMS, Boston, February 9, 1948, box 7, Matthiessen Papers.

"The Czechs regard the Soviet Union": "Matthiessen Says Czechs Are Not Run from Soviet Union," *Harvard Crimson*, February 14, 1948, http://www.thecrimson.com/article/1948/2/14/matthiessen-says-czechs-are-not-run/.

"biased" journalists: In *From the Heart of Europe*, Matthiessen took special umbrage at a column by Joseph Alsop entitled "The Creeping Terror in Prague" that appeared on November 9, 1947, in the European edition of the *New York Herald Tribune*. In the column, filed from Prague, Alsop more or less got it right regarding the political situation in Czechoslovakia—three months before the Communist coup. But in Matthiessen's

notebooks from his trip, he simply dismissed Alsop, having known him as a right-leaning undergraduate during his days at Harvard. Alsop's closeted homosexuality may also have fueled Matthiessen's taking offense. F. O. Matthiessen, Czechoslovakia Journals V, n.d., pp. 228–29, 240, box 7, F. O. Matthiessen Papers, 1929–1950, MS Am 1433, Houghton Library, Harvard University; Joseph Alsop, "The Creeping Terror in Prague," *New York Herald Tribune*, European ed., Paris, Sunday, November 9, 1947, 4.

Iron Curtain . . . in the minds of the American people: "Matthiessen Reports No Czech 'Iron Curtain' as Result of Red Intrusion," *Harvard Crimson*, March 5, 1948, http://www.thecrimson.com/article/1948/3/5/matthiessen-reports-no-czech-iron-curtain/.

Masaryk's mysterious death: On March 10, 1948, Jan Masaryk was either thrown or jumped from a bathroom window in his apartment at the Czernin Palace in Prague. The Communist government maintained that Masaryk committed suicide. But many Czechs at the time believed that Masaryk had been murdered by the Communists on orders from the Soviets. Masaryk's girlfriend, Marcia Davenport, and the American press generally supported this belief as well. Although many contemporary historians concur that Masaryk was killed, his death is still officially considered a suicide. Davenport, *Too Strong for Fantasy*, 431; Sterling, *Masaryk Case*, 2, 195, 338; International, *Time*, March 8, 1948, 28; "Holds Masaryk Was Slain," *New York Times*, March 11, 1948, 3.

in a written statement: "Masaryk's Suicide Seen," *Harvard Crimson*, March 11, 1948, http://www.thecrimson.com/article/1948/3/11/masaryks-suicide-seen-pthe-suicide-of/.

History has largely shown: Josef Korbel, *The Communist Subversion of Czechoslovakia, 1938–1948: The Failure of Coexistence* (Princeton, NJ: Princeton University Press, 1959), 208; Sterling, *Masaryk Case*, 101.

196   *"less governed by those truths":* Franz Hoellering, "The Head and the Heart," *Nation*, September 11, 1948, 293–94.

"the most distinguished literary fellow-traveler": Irving Howe, *Partisan Review* 15, no. 10 (October 1948): 1125.

infuriated Howe: The passage in *From the Heart of Europe* that Howe refers to begins with, "If I lived in France, I don't quite see how I could help being a Communist." This was not exactly the best way to win friends in the early days of the Cold War in America. Matthiessen, *FHE*, 79.

Henry Luce . . . Skull and Bones brother: "Senior Society Elections Given to College Juniors," *Yale Daily News*, May 16, 1919, 1.

"bald, mild-mannered little bachelor" and subsequent quote: "Innocent Abroad," *Time*, September 20, 1948, 112–14.

197   *he attacked his attackers:* Thomas B. Ross, "Matthiessen Hits Political Apathy," *Yale Daily News*, January 13, 1949, 1; Matthiessen to Alfred Kazin, October 12, 1948, box 2, Matthiessen Papers.

Phelps Putnam died: Daily Boston Globe, obituary, July 5, 1948, 31.

Frederick W. Matthiessen Jr., died: "F. W. Matthiessen Dead," obituary, *New York Times*, November 13, 1948, 18.

$16,000 per year in income: "Teacher's Opinion of Reds Related in Suit over Will," *Daily Boston Globe*, January 18, 1951, 5.

Theodore Spencer: "Theodore Spencer," obituary, *Daily Boston Globe*, January 19, 1949, 22.

Cultural and Scientific Conference for World Peace: Comm. on Un-American Activities, H.R. Rep. No. 82–378, *Report on the Communist "Peace" Offensive*, at 104–8 (April 1, 1951); "Red Visitors Cause Rumpus," *Life*, April 4, 1949, 39; "5 Mass. Educators Held Dupes," *Boston Herald*, April 19, 1949, 1; Sidney Hook, *Out of Step: An Unquiet Life in the Twentieth Century* (New York: Harper & Row, 1987), 385.

198   *panel on writing and publishing:* Daniel S. Gillmor, ed., *Speaking of Peace: An Edited Report of the Cultural, Scientific Conference for World Peace, New York, March 25, 26 and 27 under the Auspices of National Council of Arts, Sciences, and Professions* (New York: National Council of Arts, Sciences and Professions, 1949), 3; "Panel Discussions of the Cultural Conference Delegates Cover a Wide Range of Subjects," *New York Times*, March 27, 1949, 44.

he gave a talk: Report, Francis Otto Matthiessen, Boston, MA, FBI, November 19, 1949, pp. 10–11, FF.

"What would have happened to Thoreau": Gillmor, *Speaking of Peace*, 86; Panel Discussions of the Cultural Conference, 44.

Boston Herald picked up the story: "5 Mass. Educators Held Dupes," *Boston Herald*, April 19, 1949, 1.

fifty "dupes" and "fellow-travelers": Matthiessen could take comfort that *Life* included a veritable *Who's Who* of twentieth-century politicians, intellectuals, scientists, and artists in its list of supposed Communist sympathizers: Dorothy Parker, Adam Clayton Powell Jr., Langston Hughes, Albert Einstein, Aaron Copland, Leonard Bernstein, Thomas Mann, and Norman Mailer among many others. "Red Visitors Cause Rumpus," *Life*, April 4, 1949, 42–43.

Life story: J. C. Levenson, conversation with the author, digitally recorded, February 23, 2011.

199   *Matthiessen did not testify:* As Rodney A. Ross, an archivist at the Center for Legislative Archives, which houses and administers HUAC's archives, explained in email correspondence with the author on August 25, 2011, typically HUAC staff assembled a preparatory file on an individual in advance of someone being subpoenaed. No such file was ever prepared for Matthiessen. Frederick C. Stern, *F. O. Matthiessen: Christian Socialist as Critic* (Chapel Hill: University of North Carolina Press, 1981), 28; Paul M. Sweezy, "Labor and Political Activities," in *FOM*, 74–75; Arthur Redding, "Closet, Coup, and Cold War: F. O. Matthiessen's *From the Heart of Europe*," *Boundary 2* 33, no. 1 (Spring 2006): 172; "6 Harvard Men, 1 at M.I.T. Named Red Front Backers," *Daily Boston Globe*, April 7, 1949, 2.

Because Massachusetts requires that testimony be kept only for legislation that becomes law, Matthiessen's testimony is probably lost to history, because many of the pending bills on which he would have been called to testify were ultimately defeated. Commonwealth of

Massachusetts, *The Journal of the House, 1948–1950* (Boston: Wright & Potter, 1948–50); Commonwealth of Massachusetts, *The Journal of the Senate, 1948–1950* (Boston: Wright & Potter, 1948–50).

Matthiessen wrestled with his materials: See Matthiessen to Joe Summers, December 14, 1949, box 4, Matthiessen Papers.

he was also isolated practically: Helen Merrell Lynd, "Statements by Friends and Associates," in *FOM*, 126; Rufus W. Mathewson, "Statements by Friends and Associates," in *FOM*, 128; Ernest J. Simmons, "Statements by Friends and Associates," in *FOM*, 137.

200 *Matthiessen planned to go on to Italy:* "Tributes Paid Matthiessen, Suicide Here," *Daily Boston Globe,* April 2, 1950, C36.

Manger Hotel: Rackliffe, "Notes for a Character Study," 90; "Professor Plunges to Death," *Boston Post,* April 1, 1950, 1.

Matthiessen told the Murdocks: Rackliffe, "Notes for a Character Study," 90.

Skull and Bones pin and a letter: A 1955 article in *Esquire* reported that Matthiessen had been wearing his pin when he jumped to his death, and that it was found beside his body by a policeman who arrived on the scene. This is the position taken by David Alan Richards in his 2017 book about Yale's senior societies. Sweezy, "Labor and Political Activities," 72; Rackliffe, "Notes for a Character Study," 91; George Frazier, "Yale's Secret Societies," *Esquire,* September 1955, 106; David Alan Richards, *Skull and Keys: The Hidden Histories of Yale's Secret Societies* (New York: Pegasus Books, 2017), 75; Putnam v. Neubrand, 329 Mass. 453, 455 (1952).

"nothing but 'desolate solitude ahead'": Sweezy, "Labor and Political Activities," 72.

"no longer bear the loneliness": Hyde, *R&D,* 3.

201 *"I am exhausted":* Rackliffe, "Notes for a Character Study," 91.

took off his glasses: "What I Have to Do," *Time,* April 10, 1950, 43.

"the most beautiful house in America": Bernard Bowron, "The Making of an American Scholar," in *FOM,* 47.

"Rat, Rat, my God feller": Matthiessen to Cheney, April 7, 1925, *R&D,* 116.

he died before they could reach City Hospital: "Note Professor Left in Suicide Is Studied," *Boston Evening Globe,* April 1, 1950, 1, 2; Rackliffe, "Notes for a Character Study," 89, 91.

CHAPTER 10: AFTERMATH AND AFTERGLOW

202 *Matthiessen's funeral:* "F. O. Matthiessen," Deaths and Funerals, *Boston Daily Globe,* April 4, 1950, 25.

Stanley Geist, did not seem surprised: Barbara Wasserman, conversation with the author, digitally recorded, November 9, 2010.

"a man left alone": Wallace Stevens to Norman Holmes Pearson, May 18, 1950, in *Letters of Wallace Stevens,* ed. Holly Stevens (New York: Alfred A. Knopf, 1966), 679.

203 *"This is a great shock":* "Harvard Professor Leaps to Death," *Boston Evening American,* April 1, 1950, 2.

On the political right, the columnist: Bill Cunningham, "Matthiessen's End a Warning," *Boston Herald*, April 3, 1950, 20; "Prof. Matthiessen Called Victim of Cold War and Witchhunts," *Daily Worker*, April 3, 1950, 3; "They Murdered Him," *Daily Worker*, April 3, 1950, 7.

"under court order": Memorandum, SAC (Special Agent in Charge) to Director, Boston, FBI, April 13, 1950, pp. 1–2, FF; "Professor Leaves His Biography of Dreiser to Harvard," *Boston Morning Globe*, April 6, 1950, 1; "FBI Seeks Suicide Prof's Private Data," *Boston Evening American*, April 5, 1950, 2.

204 *"flagrantly homosexual":* William S. White, "McCarthy Says Miss Kenyon Helped 28 Red Front Groups," *New York Times*, March 9, 1950, 5; William S. White, "Miss Kenyon Cites Patriotic Record to Refute Charges," *New York Times*, March 15, 1950, 3.

Bachelors for Wallace: Will Roscoe, "The Radicalism of Harry Hay," *Gay & Lesbian Review*, November–December 2013, reprinted in Richard Schneider Jr., ed., *In Search of Stonewall: The Riots at 50; The Gay & Lesbian Review at 25; Best Essays, 1994–2018* (Boston: G&LR Books, 2019), 60.

205 *books that he had written and edited:* In addition to the *Oxford Book of American Verse* discussed below, these books included a memorial volume edited by Paul M. Sweezy and Leo Huberman, entitled *F. O. Matthiessen (1902–1950): A Collective Portrait*, which was published in November 1950. It contained the heartfelt recollections of Matthiessen's friends and some of his colleagues, as well as a preliminary catalogue and assessment of his work. The last book, *The Responsibilities of the Critic*, was edited by Matthiessen's former student John Rackliffe and published in October 1952. It collected a wide-ranging sample of Matthiessen's essays and reviews. "Books Published Today," *New York Times*, November 21, 1950, 45 (FOM); "Books Published Today," *New York Times*, October 16, 1952, 27 (*The Responsibilities of the Critic*).

"the best one-volume collection": Cleanth Brooks, "Matthiessen's Anthology," review of *The Oxford Book of American Verse*, ed. F. O. Matthiessen, *Poetry* 79, no. 1 (October 1951): 36.

Matthiessen defined poetry too narrowly: Selden Rodman, "A Poetic Mirror of America's Growth," review of *The Oxford Book of American Verse*, ed. F. O. Matthiessen, *New York Times*, October 8, 1950, BR2.

poetry was the hallmark: F. O. Matthiessen, "The Pattern of Literature," in *Changing Patterns in American Civilization*, ed. Robert E. Spiller (Philadelphia: University of Pennsylvania Press, 1949), 43.

"the domain": Matthiessen, "The Pattern of Literature," 42.

206 *"My annals since you saw me last are sad"* and subsequent quote: Matthiessen to Joe Summers, December 14, 1949, box 4, Matthiessen Papers.

"unfinished last paragraph": "Matthiessen Leaves His Biography of Dreiser to Harvard," *Daily Boston Globe*, April 6, 1950, 1.

"If he had been a girl": TD, 34.

"marvelous eye": TD, 49.

207 *"homely detail":* TD, 53.

Dreiser's lapses in style: F. O. Matthiessen, "God, Mammon, and Mr. Dreiser," review of *The Bulwark*, by Theodore Dreiser, *New York Times*, March 24, 1946, 122.

American Balzac: Henry James, *The American Novels and Short Stories of Henry James*, ed. F. O. Matthiessen (New York: Alfred A. Knopf, 1947), 27.

"no real political freedom": TD, 223.

wasn't good enough for the critic Lionel Trilling: Lionel Trilling, "Dreiser and the Liberal Mind," *Nation*, April 20, 1946, 466–69.

"overdue realism": E. L. Holland Jr., "A Lucid Study of Dreiser," review of *Theodore Dreiser*, by F. O. Matthiessen, *Birmingham (AL) News*, March 11, 1951, 60.

208 *"crass chance" and "fierce brutalities"*: TD, 31.

"My own experience": TD, 107–8.

"Fuller was a really fascinating cross": TD, 58.

209 *"sensitive . . . unconsciously homosexual"*: Charles Weir Jr., "Victorian Aristocrat," review of *Into an Old Room: A Memoir of Edward Fitzgerald*, by Peter de Polnay, *New York Times*, April 17, 1949, BR7. Other pairings of homosexuality and sensitivity often occurred in reviews of books that either directly touched on homosexuality or were written by authors thought to be homosexual, such as Proust. See, for example, David C. Tilden, "A Gallant Social Document," review of *Strange Brother*, by Blair Niles, *New York Herald Tribune*, August 23, 1931, J10; "Recent Novels for Early Autumn Reading," review of *The Great Gulf*, by Erich Ebermayer, *New York Herald Tribune*, October 9, 1932, I10; Ruth Lechlitner, "Rimbaud in Verse," review of *Dream and Action*, by Leonard Bacon, *New York Herald Tribune*, August 19, 1934, F13; and Lloyd Morris, "Marcel Proust, Sick Man and Great Artist," review of *The Two Worlds of Marcel Proust*, by Harold March, *New York Herald Tribune*, July 4, 1948, E1.

"mildly homosexual": Ernest Sutherland Bates, "A Chevalier in Chicago," review of *Henry Blake Fuller: A Critical Biography*, by Constance M. Griffin, *New York Herald Tribune*, October 15, 1931, H19.

"digestion of an ostrich": Cheney to Matthiessen, March 5, 1925, R&D, 104.

"no squire of dames" and subsequent quotes: Henry Blake Fuller, *Bertram Cope's Year* (Chicago: Ralph Fletcher Seymour—The Alderbrink Press, 1919), 10, 152–53, 313.

"weariness": "Re-examination of Dreiser," review of *Theodore Dreiser*, by F. O. Matthiessen, *Times Literary Supplement*, December 21, 1951, 814.

Matthiessen missed the power of sex and subsequent quote: Maxwell Geismar, "Social and Sexual Revolutionary," review of *Theodore Dreiser*, by F. O. Matthiessen, *Saturday Review of Literature*, March 17, 1951, 16; Frederick C. Stern, *F. O. Matthiessen: Christian Socialist as Critic* (Chapel Hill: University of North Carolina Press, 1981), 202; William E. Cain, *F. O. Matthiessen and the Politics of Criticism* (Madison: University of Wisconsin Press, 1988), 97.

210 *Dreiser's style offended Matthiessen*: Cain, *Matthiessen and the Politics of Criticism*, 93; Leo Marx, conversation with the author, digitally recorded, October 1, 2010.

close attention to the drafts and revisions: Ellen Moers, *Two Dreisers* (New York: Viking Press, 1969), 62–63.

"home-made" will and an estate: "Matthiessen's 'Home-Made' Will Cuts Two Subversive Groups," *Boston Evening Globe*, April 5, 1950, 1; "Area Residents Benefit by Will of Harvard Professor," *Portsmouth Herald*, June 22, 1951, 1; "2 'Subversive' Groups Named in Matthiessen Will," *Daily Boston Globe*, June 22, 1951, 2; Francis Otto Matthiessen, will dated 7 June 1947, allowed and verified, 20 May 1953, vol. 2103, p. 238, Commonwealth of Massachusetts, Probate Court, County of Suffolk, Boston.

211 *Rosa Parks:* Aimee Isgrig Horton, *The Highlander Folk School: A History of Its Major Programs, 1932–1961* (Brooklyn, NY: Carlson Publishing, 1989), 208.
Yale petitioned the court: "Area Residents Benefit by Will," 1, 3.
"Now that I have some property": Francis Otto Matthiessen will.
bequeathed private correspondence: Francis Otto Matthiessen will.
"Sunday letter": Louis Hyde, "Rat & the Devil," *Christopher Street*, July 1978, 29.

EPILOGUE: GETTING MARRIED AFTER ALL

217 *"Whan that Aprill":* Chaucer, General Prologue, *The Canterbury Tales*, lines 1–4.

219 *"We stand in the middle":* F. O. Matthiessen to Russell Cheney, January 29, 1925, *R&D*, 71.

220 *"Marriage! What a strange word":* Matthiessen to Cheney, September 23, 1924, *R&D*, 29.
"Marriage is a fundamental human right": New York State Marriage Equality Act, Chapter 95 of the Laws of 2011, sec. 2.

221 *"Keep Ithaka always in your mind":* C. P. Cavafy, *Collected Poems*, ed. George Savidis, trans. Edmund Keeley and Philip Sherrard (Princeton, NJ: Princeton University Press, 1975), lines 25–34.

Index

Page references in *italics* refer to figures and photos.

Aaron, Daniel, 135, 184

Abandoned Adobes (1935, Cheney), 250n

Abt, John, 274n

Académie Julian (Paris), 35, 41, 234n

The Achievement of T. S. Eliot (Matthiessen), 75, 113–16, 136, 210

The Acquisitive Society (Tawney), 16–18

Adlow, Dorothy, 100, 181

À la Recherche du Temps Perdu/Remembrance of Things Past (Proust), 96

alcoholism: Alcoholics Anonymous (AA), 157–58, 162, 262n, 263n; Cheney's early problems with, 57, 73–74, 80, 100–104, 249n; Cheney's hospitalizations for, 128–33, 140–44, 157–61, 166; *The Common Sense of Drinking* on, 101, 248n, 264n; *New England Journal of Medicine* on alcoholism and homosexuality, 141

Alexander, Jack, 158, 162

Alsop, Joseph, 275–76n

The Ambassadors (H. James), 139, 167, 169

American Art News, Cheney's work in, 45, 46

American Civil Liberties Union, 111

American Committee for the Protection of the Foreign Born, 165

American Federation of Labor, 189

American Federation of Teachers (AFT), 122

American literature field: inception of American studies field, 85; Matthiessen on aesthetic vibrancy in literature generally, 78–79, 96–97; Matthiessen on poetry, 205; Matthiessen's gay sensibility to, 74–75; Matthiessen's legacy to canon of, 3–4, 145, 154–55, 204–5; Matthiessen's theories developed about, 95–97, 104–5; Matthiessen's undergraduate education in relationship to, 17–18. See also *American Renaissance*

The American Novels and Stories of Henry James (Matthiessen), 181

American Renaissance (Matthiessen): book dedication, 137, 146–47; Harvard celebration dinner of, 155–56; homosexual/homosocial references in, 75, 178; legacy of book, 108–9, 145, 154–55, 210; legacy of Cheney/Matthiessen relationship to, 1–3; research and early drafts of, 116, 128, 133, 135, 144; reviews of, 152, 154–55; Stanley Geist's contribution to, 200; themes of, 146–53, 150, 153, 185

The American Scene (H. James), 167

Americans for Democratic Action, 274n

American Studies (Merlis), 5

Anderson, Sherwood, 40, 110

antigay laws. *See* LGBTQ rights
The Architectural Heritage of the Pisca-taqua (J. M. Howells), 257–58n
The Artist's Father, Reading "L'Événe-ment"/ "Portrait du Père de Cézanne" (Cézanne), 40–41, 72
Art Journal (1911), and Cézanne, 41
Art News, on Cheney, 88
The Art of Seeing—Woodbury Course in Observation, 235n
Art Students League: New York City location, 34–36, 42–43, 234n; Wood-stock (New York) location, 237n
Arvin, Newton, 85, 134–35
Atlantic Gypsum Company (1934, Cheney), 119
Autumn Thoughts (1936, Cheney), 255n

Babcock Galleries (New York City), 44–46, 56–57, 70, 239n
Baby (Zuzu, cat), 94, 143, 172, 201
Baca, Jesus, 113
Bachelors for Wallace, 204
Bachrach, Marion, 274n
Baldpate Hospital, 128, 130, 140–44, 157–61, 166
Bane, Scott: decision to write about Matthiessen and Cheney, 1–6; health issues of, 214–19; marriage of, 213–14, 218–23
Barber, C. L. "Joe," 85, 93, 106, 115, 116, 163, 202
Barrett, William, 137
Bayne, Hugh Aiken, 68, 241n
Baynes, Lillian, 32
Bell, Pearl Kazin, 85
Benito Cereno (Melville), 152
Benton, Thomas Hart, 70
Bergman, David, 74, 76
Bernstein, Irving, 89
Berthoff, Warner, 85
Bertram Cope's Year (Fuller), 209
Biddle, Nicholas, 242n
Biddle, Virginia, 71, 242n
Billy Budd, Sailor (Melville), 75, 152–53
Blanchard, Paula, 227n
Bolt Hill Road (Eliot, Maine) (1933, Cheney), 99

Boorstin, Daniel J., 85
Boston: apartment of Cheney and Matthiessen, 139; Louisburg Square (Beacon Hill), 139, 257–58n
Boston Evening American, on Matthies-sen's death, 203
Boston Evening Transcript, on Cheney, 258n
Boston Globe, on Matthiessen's death, 203
Boston Herald: on Cultural and Scien-tific Conference for World Peace, 197; on Harvard and Matthiessen, 179; on Matthiessen's death, 203
Bowron, Bernard, 85, 91, 92
Bradstreet, Anne, 205
Breuning, Margaret, 156–57
Bridges, Harry, 107–8, 164–65, 203, 265–66n
Bridgman, George, 35
Brinton, Christian, 44
Brooklyn Daily Eagle, on Cheney, 45
Brooks, Cleanth, 115, 205
Brown Brothers & Company, 81
Brown v. Board of Education (1954), 167
Buckley, William E., 29
bultos, 171, 267n
The Bulwark (T. Dreiser), 207
Burlingame, C. Charles, 130–32, 134, 255n
Bynner, Witter, 81

Cain, William E., 4, 152, 155, 210, 266–67n
"Calamus" (Whitman), 193
Calkins, Judith Stager, 234n
Calla Lilies (1926, Cheney), 61
Calverton, V. F., 105
Cameron, Angus, 182
Campbell, Richard, 183
Campos, Victor, 110, 250–51n
Canadian Royal Air Force, 15
Candee, Richard, 243n, 248n
Cantave, Nelson, 143
Canterbury Tales (Chaucer), 217
Carmichael, Mack R., 110–12
Carpenter, Edward, 51, 96
Cassidy, Ina Sizer, 112

Cather, Willa, 77

Cavafy, C. P., 221

Cézanne, Paul, 36, 40–41, 72, 102

Charles T. Griffes (Maisel), 275n

Charleston Museum, 68

Charles University (Czechoslovakia), 176, 185, 194

Chase, William Merritt: influence on Cheney, 31, 36, 47, 60, 79, 100, 125, 143; *Old Venetian Houses*, 52, 238–39n

Chaucer, Geoffrey, 16, 217

Chauncey, George, 51

Cheney, Alice Elizabeth "Cass" (sister-in-law), 68, 232n

Cheney, Anne (cousin's spouse), 52

Cheney, B. Austin (cousin), 255n

Cheney, Benjamin, Jr. (clockmaker), 232n

Cheney, Carol (great-niece), 243n, 248n

Cheney, Charles (grandfather), 27, 43–44

Cheney, Clifford (brother): brother's estate and, 175; Cheney Brothers and, 28, 124, 232n, 246n; home of, 61, 134, 240n; Matthiessen and, 68; visits to brother in hospital, 132; World War I service of, 42

Cheney, Cynthia (cousin), 242n

Cheney, Ednah Dow Littlehale (great-aunt), 233n, 247n

Cheney, Ednah Dow Smith (mother), 26, 37–38, 247n

Cheney, Elizabeth (sister), 38

Cheney, Frank (great-uncle), 27–28

Cheney, Frank Woodbridge (uncle), 28, 30, 125

Cheney, Harriet (sister), 42, 61, 109, 129, 235n

Cheney, Helen (sister), 61, 241n

Cheney, Howell (cousin), 52, 131, 255n

Cheney, John (great-uncle), 33, 233n

Cheney, Knight Dexter (father), 26, 38, 125

Cheney, Knight Dexter, Jr. (brother), 38, 234n

Cheney, Louis R. (great-uncle), 255n

Cheney, Philip (brother), 42, 61, 132, 174

Cheney, Rush (great-uncle), 237n

Cheney, Russell, 26–47; aesthetic theory of, 43–45; art collection of, 125–26; art study by, 31–38, 40–43, 238–39n; career problems of (1929–30), 82, 87–88; cars of, 40, 81; Cheney's painting during Great Depression, 112–13, 116–21; childhood and family wealth of, 26–31 (*see also* Cheney Brothers Silk Manufacturing Company); in *The Crimson Letter*, 1–2; death of, 174–76, 184–85, 264n, 268n, 268–69n; early homosexuality of, 34; *en plein air* practice of, 37, 98, 149; exhibitions by, 43–47, 56–57, 64, 99–100, 102, 112–13, 119, 156–57, 239n; family Thanksgiving posters by, 30–31, 233n; financial dependence on Matthiessen, 90–92, 101–2, 164; *From the Heart of Europe* reference to, 192–93; influence on *American Renaissance*, 145–49, 152, 154–56; inheritance of, 38; interest in boxing/boxers, 54, 102–3, 109, 118, 120, 121; literature interest of, 39–40, 92, 114–15, 236n, 247n, 248n; paintings in *Sarah Orne Jewett*, 75–76; paintings of, in Matthiessen's will, 211; paintings sold by, 43, 56–57, 238n, 239n; personality characteristics of, 33, 36, 57, 67, 120, 121; physical characteristics of, 33; posthumous retrospective (Boston, 1947), 185; Putnam's friendship with, 41–43, 236n; "Rat" nickname of, 32; *Russell Cheney: A Record of His Work* on, 2, 6, 176, 179–81, 240n, 243n; teaching by, 71; work style of, 69; at Yale, 32, 34, 34, 42, 43. *See also* alcoholism; Cheney, Russell, works of; health issues; Kittery, Maine; relationship of Cheney and Matthiessen; Skull and Bones

Cheney, Russell, painting styles and themes of, 63, 66–67, 70, 75–76, 95, 97–100; landscapes, 70, 119–20, 156; portraits, 70–72, 117–19, 242n; still lifes, 46, 70, 88, 140, 142–43, 156

Cheney, Russell, works of: *Abandoned Adobes* (1935), 250n; about titles of paintings, 243n; *Atlantic Gypsum Company* (1934), 119; *Autumn Thoughts* (1936), 255n; *Bolt Hill Road (Eliot, Maine)* (1933), 99; *Calla Lilies* (1926), 61; *Colleone* (1924), 52; *Depot Square* (1927), 66–67, 66; *Desert Pool* (1926), 61; *Facing East, Kittery, Maine* (1944), 93; *Flowers in Venice* (1926), 63, 72; *F. O. Matthiessen at Vieux-Port* (1925), 59; *F. O. Matthiessen on Balcony* (1926), 63–64, 64; *Fred Reading* (1929), 82; *Garden of the Gods* (1918), 40; Gideon Welles home, painting of, 43–44; *Good Irish* (1935), 260n; *Hauled Up* (1937), 119–20; *Howard Lathrop* (1937), 2, 117–20, 118; *Jewett Doorway* (1927?), 75; *Jose of Buena Vista* (1935), 250n; *Kenneth Hill* (1937), 119, 120; *Lee Lucero* (ca. 1935), 250n; *Lilies and Salute* (1926), 63; *The Lost Cause* (1944), 171; *Meeting House Hill* (1940), 142; *Miss Jewett's Staircase/ Stairway, Jewett House/Hall of the South Berwick House* (1927), 75–76, 78, 243n; *Mrs. Marcia Clarke* (1928–29), 71–72, 242n; *Mrs. Maxwell E. Foster* (ca. 1928), 242n; *Mrs. Nicholas Biddle* (1928), 242n; *Nelson Cantave* (1940), 143; *Nicotiana* (1937), 126; *Paul Hoen* (1930), 81–83; *Pepperell's Cove* (1933), 99; "Philippine Pete and Katchina Kate," 130, 255n; *Piscataqua Lane* (ca. 1933–36), 98–99, 99; *Portsmouth Factory* (1935), 119; *Portsmouth Waterfront,* two paintings entitled (1933? and 1937), 119; preliminary catalogue raisonné (Candee and Carol Cheney), 243n, 264n; *Professor A. Canolle* (1911), 40; *San Marco/St. Mark's* (1924), 52; *Santa Fe Mountains* (1935), 250n; *Skungimaug—Morning* (ca. 1922), 47, 47, 57; *Study for New Mexico Scene* (1935), 250n; *Taormina* (1924–25), 53; *Vitrine* (1921), 46; *Water Front,* 98; *Woodstock* (1916), 45

Cheney, Seth Wells (great-uncle), 33, 233n

Cheney, Sheldon (no relation to Russell Cheney), 140, 258n

Cheney, Thomas (brother), 35, 38, 234n

Cheney, Ward (great-uncle), 28, 237n

Cheney Brothers Silk Manufacturing Company: ancillary businesses of, 29–30, 125; Cheney family's wealth from, 26–31, 38; Cheney family traditions, 30–31, 233n; Great Depression and effect on, 91–92, 101–2, 124–26, 129, 246n; Hartford Retreat connection of, 129, 131; labor issues of, 30–31; during late 1920s and Great Depression, 67, 71; Manhattan office of, 35, 234n; *The Miracle Workers,* 151–52, 153, 255n, 261n; Russell Cheney's brothers in business of, 32, 33; size and sales of (1923–33), 28, 124–25; Spencer repeating rifle and, 43–44, 237n

Cheney family: birth/death/marriage dates for, 232n; books of, 92, 247n; disapproval of Matthiessen/ Cheney relationship, 68, 174–75; Hartford Retreat connection of, 129–31, 255n; KD House of, 26–28, 61–62, 174, 240n; siblings known as "KDs," 26–27, 36–37; Thanksgiving tradition of, 30–31, 233n. *See also* Cheney Brothers Silk Manufacturing Company; *individual names of family members*

"The Children of Adam" (Whitman), 193

Christ Church (Tarrytown, New York), 10

Christian Science Monitor, on Cheney's work, 99–100

Christo, 214–15

Church of the Unity (Springfield, Massachusetts), 227n

Ciardi, John, 192

Citizens Victory Committee for Harry Bridges, 164–65

Civil War: Cheney family and, 43–44, 237n; slavery omitted from *American Renaissance,* 152

Clark, Tom, 190

Clarke, Marcia, 71, 72, 242n

Clayton Antitrust Act (1914), 18

Cleveland Plain Dealer, on Alcoholics Anonymous, 263n

clockmaking, Cheney family and, 27, 232n

coal industry strikes, 109–12, 250–51n

Cold War: Communist Party and, 90, 110, 133, 273–74n; Czechoslovakia coup, 194–97; FBI investigation of Matthiessen, 156, 164, 181–82, 189, 203–4, 262n; House Un-American Activities Committee, 197–99, 204, 277n; Matthiessen's Socialist identity and, 177; Matthiessen's work in Eastern Europe and, 177, 182–86, 189; *Monthly Review* founding, 265–66n; Progressive Party, 182, 190–92, 273–74n

The Collective Portrait (Matthiessen), 199

Colleone (1924, Cheney), 52

The Common Sense of Drinking (Peabody), 101, 248n, 264n

Communist Party: National Miners' Union and, 110; National Unemployment Day (March 6, 1930), 90; Progressive Party and, 273–74n; show trials by Stalin, 133

Compagnie Générale Transatlantique, 48

Complete Works (Rimbaud), 96

Conant, James Bryant, 123–24, 163, 179, 183

Concerning Painting (Cox), 35

Congregationalism, 7–8

Congress of Industrial Organizations (CIO), 189, 274n

Copley, John Singleton, 57

Cortissoz, Royal, 45–46, 117

A Country Doctor (S. O. Jewett), 77

The Country of the Pointed Firs (S. O. Jewett), 76

Cox, Kenyon, 35–37

Cragmor Sanatorium ("Sun Palace," Colorado Springs), 38–43, 74, 75, 78, 79, 87, 128, 235n

Crane, Charles, 272n

Crane, Hart, 134

The Crimson Letter (Shand-Tucci), 1–2

Cukor, George, 244n, 246n

Cultural and Scientific Conference for World Peace (1949), 197

Cunningham, Bill, 203

Curry, John Steuart, 70

Cutting, Bronson, 80–81, 113

Czechoslovakia: Charles University, 176, 185, 194; coup in, 194–97; Jan Masaryk and, 186, 195, 271–72n, 276n

Dasburg, Andrew Michael, 81

Davenport, Marcia, 272n, 276n

Davenport, Russell "Mitch," 56, 242n, 272n

Davis, Elrick B., 263n

Debs, Eugene V., 21

Deephaven (S. O. Jewett), 75, 172, 243n

DeLacey, Al, 85–86

Department of Labor, US, 228n

de Polnay, Peter, 209, 280n

Depot Square (1927, Cheney), 66–67, 66

Desert Pool (1926, Cheney), 61

DeVoto, Bernard, 167

Dewey, Thomas E., 190

Dickinson, Emily, 205

Dictionary of American Biography (Summers & Summers), 245n

doctors. *See* health issues

Dooley, William Germain, 258n

Dorey, Halstead, 160

Dorey, Theodora, 160

Dorman, Harry, 137, 146–47, 260n

Dos Passos, John, 110, 179

Doyle, Peter, 178

Dreiser, Sara White, 199

Dreiser, Theodore: *The Bulwark*, 207; on coal industry strikes, 110, 111; *The "Genius*," 207–8; *Harlan Miners Speak*, 110; Matthiessen's political activism and written work about, 5; *Sister Carrie*, 207–8; *Theodore Dreiser* (Matthiessen), 75, 199–200, 203, 205–10

Du Bois, W. E. B., 198

Dudley, Dorothy, 206

DuMond, Frank Vincent, 35

Dunham, Barrows, 182
Dunlap, David W.: author's and Dunlap's health issues, 214–19; author's research and, 1–3; marriage of, 213–14, 218–23
Dunster House Bookshop (Cambridge, Massachusetts), 85–86
Dwight, Lucy Gassett, 227n

Eakins, Thomas, 149–52, 150, 154
Edel, Leon, 188
Eliot, Charles, 244–45n
Eliot, T. S.: The Achievement of T. S. Eliot (Matthiessen), 75, 113–16, 136, 210; American Renaissance (Matthiessen), on, 149; Cheney's literary interest in, 40; "Hamlet and His Problems," 251n; at Harvard, 106; Matthiessen's role in fame of, 4, 74, 76, 116; "Poetry in Wartime," 162; The Waste Land, 80, 185
Eliot House, 244–45n
Elledge, Scott, 183
Ellis, Havelock: influence on Matthiessen, 49, 115, 149; Sexual Inversion, 12; Studies in the Psychology of Sex, 24, 96
Elm Crest Manor, 160
Emerson, Ralph Waldo, 3, 147–49, 191. See also American Renaissance
Esquire magazine, on Matthiessen, 278n
"Essay on Civil Disobedience" (Thoreau), 198
eugenics, 127
Europa (ocean liner), 133

Facing East, Kittery, Maine (1944, Cheney), 93
Fadiman, Clifton, 154
Fairweather, Una, 236n
Faithful Are the Wounds (Sarton), 5, 162
Fantasia (film), 142
Federal Bureau of Investigation (FBI), 156, 164, 181–82, 189, 203–4, 262n
Ferargil Galleries (New York), 117, 140, 143, 156, 180
Field, Hamilton Easter, 37, 45

Fields, Annie, 76–77
Fields, James T., 77
The Figure in the Carpet (H. James), 188
Fitzgerald, Edward, 209
Fitzgerald, F. Scott, 172–73, 268n
Fleming, Robert, 131, 141–42, 158–59, 262n
Florio, John, 95–96, 104
Flowers in Venice (1926, Cheney), 63, 72
Foerster, Norman, 85
F. O. Matthiessen: Christian Socialist as Critic (Stern), 4, 199
F. O. Matthiessen: The Critical Achievement (Gunn), 4
F. O. Matthiessen (1902–1950): A Collective Portrait (P. Sweezy, ed.), 199, 279n
F. O. Matthiessen and the Politics of Criticism (Cain), 4
F. O. Matthiessen at Vieux-Port (1925, Cheney), 59
F. O. Matthiessen on Balcony (1926, Cheney), 63–64, 64
Forbes, Malcolm, 72–73
forced sterilization, 127
Fortune, R. Davenport as editor of, 56
Foster, Elizabeth, 71, 242n
Foster, Maxwell, 242n
Foster, William, 90
Franklin, Benjamin, 191
Fred Reading (1929, Cheney), 82
Fremont-Smith, Maurice, 137
French, Robert "Bob" Dudley, 15–16, 21, 95
Friedman, Morgan, 228n
From the Heart of Europe (Matthiessen), 177, 192–97, 207
Frost, Robert, 40
Fuller, Henry B., 121, 208–9
"functionless property," 17, 91–92

Galerie Vollard (Paris), 41
Gallup American Coal Company, 110–12, 250–51n
Garden of the Gods (1918, Cheney), 40
Garland, Judy, 246n
The Gates (Christo & Jeanne-Claude), 214–15

Gay, Katherine, 251n
gay, terminology for, 226n. *See also* homosexuality; LGBTQ rights
Gaynor, Janet, 246n
Geismar, Maxwell, 169, 188
Geist, Eileen, 200
Geist, Stanley, 200, 202
General Education in a Free Society (Harvard study), 178–79
The "Genius" (T. Dreiser), 207–8
Gershwin, Ira, 15
Gideon Welles home, painting of (Cheney), 43–44
Globe Hollow Reservoir, 261n
Gloeden, Wilhelm von, 53
The Golden Bowl (H. James), 167, 168
Good Irish (1935, Cheney), 260n
Gottwald, Klement, 194
Grace Horne Galleries, 258n
Granville-Barker, Harley, 114
Great Depression, 107–26; *The Achievement of T. S. Eliot* publication during, 113–16; Cheney Brothers and effect of, 124–26; Cheney's financial dependence on Matthiessen and, 90–92, 101–2, 164; Cheney's painting during, 112–13, 116–21; hitchhikers'/wanderers' search for work during, 89, 102, 109–10; organized labor and Matthiessen's activism during, 107–12, 121–24, 250n; social disruption of, 89–90; as *Water Front* subject, 98
The Great Gatsby (F. S. Fitzgerald), 172–73, 268n
Greek Revival Architecture in America (Hamlin), 142
Griffes, Charles, 15, 193
Griffin, Walter, 31–32, 69
Grossman, Jay, 248n
Gunn, Giles, 4, 78, 115, 155

Hackley School, 10–15, 19, 25, 58
The Hall (Woodbury & Oaks), 75, 243n
"Hamlet and His Problems" (T. S. Eliot), 251n
Hamlin, Talbot, 142
Hammond, John Henry, 164

Harlan Miners Speak (T. Dreiser, Dos Passos, & Anderson), 110
Harris, Frank, 96
Hartford Art Society, 31
Hartford Courant, on Cheney, 43, 64
Hartford Retreat, 128–33, 254n, 255n
Hartford Times, on Cheney, 43
Hartley, Marsden, 70
Harvard Classics (C. Eliot), 245n
Harvard University: Eliot House, 84, 104–6, 139, 244–45n; *Harvard Crimson* and Matthiessen, 167, 265n; Harvard Teachers' Union, 121–24; History and Literature Program, 83–84; homosexuality shunned by, 86, 136–37, 151; Matthiessen on Czechoslovakia coup, 194–97; Matthiessen's book collection housed at, 275n; Matthiessen's criticism of, 104–5, 163–64; Matthiessen's estate and, 211–12; Matthiessen's graduate studies at, 59, 62, 64; Matthiessen's promotions by, 87, 104, 154; Matthiessen's sabbaticals from, 108, 134–35, 199; Matthiessen's salary, 197; Matthiessen's work in Eastern Europe and, 176, 183; Tillotson and, 258–59n; tutorial system of, 84, 178–79
Hauled Up (1937, Cheney), 119–20
Hawthorne (Arvin), 85
Hawthorne, Nathaniel, 3, 114, 148–49
Hay, Harry, 204
H.D. (Hilda Doolittle), 205
Heale, M. J., 122
health issues, 127–44; of author and author's husband, 214–19; Cheney at Baldpate Hospital, 128, 130, 140–44, 157–61, 166; Cheney at Cragmor Sanatorium, 33, 38–43, 74, 75, 78, 79, 87, 100–101, 105–6, 128, 235n; Cheney at Hartford Retreat, 128–33; Cheney's shock therapy treatment, 140–41, 158–60, 263n; early medical views of Alcoholic Anonymous, 157–58, 162, 262n, 263n; health proxies as legal safeguard, 215–16, 218; Matthiessen at McLean Hospital, 128–30, 134–39; Matthiessen's

health issues (*continued*)
outpatient treatment, 137–38; theories about alcoholism and homosexuality (early twentieth century), 127–28, 131, 141–42; tuberculosis treatment, 260n. *See also* alcoholism

Heilman, Robert, 168–69

heliotropy (sun treatment), 39

Heller, Clemens, 183, 270n

Hellman, George, 154

Henry, Arthur, 206

Henry James: The Major Phase (Matthiessen), 75, 145, 162, 166–70, 210, 266–67n

Hepburn, Katharine, 71, 242n, 244n

Hicks, Granville, 154–55

Highlander Folk School (Tennessee), 211

Hill, Kenneth, 119, 120

Hirschfeld, Magnus, 12

Hoby, Thomas, 95–97, 247n

Hoellering, Franz, 196

Hoen, Fred, 81

Hoen, Paul, 81–83, 121

holiday traditions: Christmas in Boston, 139, 166; Thanksgiving and Cheney family, 30–31, 233n; Thanksgiving in Kittery, 93–94, 139, 166, 249–50n

Holland, Philemon, 95–97

homosexuality: *American Renaissance* and homosocial themes, 149–53, 150, 153; "Boston marriage" between women, 76, 243n; Cheney's and Matthiessen's acceptance in Kittery, 93–95, 100, 106, 117, 249–50n; Cheney's/Matthiessen's disclosure to each other about ("incident of the pear"), 49–50, 145, 201; Cheney's/Matthiessen's disclosure to friends about, 54–56; grief of partners in same-sex relationships, 268–69n; Harvard's disapproval of, 86, 136–37, 151; homosexual identity as middle-class phenomenon (early twentieth century), 13; House Un-American Activities Committee on, 204; "little boys" reference, 81, 244n; Matthiessen's early sexual identity

and encounters, 11, 13–15, 19–21, 23–25, 51; "Oxford Letter" on, 24–25, 229n; references to, in Matthiessen's publications, 178, 192–93, 204–10; sexual inversion theory ("fairy" persona), 12, 24–25, 86–87; suggestive themes in Cheney's paintings, 118–19, 118; terminology for, 226n. *See also* LGBTQ rights; marriage

Hook, Sidney, 197

Hoover, Herbert, 89

Hoover, J. Edgar, 156

Hotel Royal Grande Bretagne (Florence), 63, 64

Houghton Mifflin, 75

House Un-American Activities Committee, 197–99, 204, 277n

Howard, Lucinda Dwight, 227

Howard Lathrop (1937, Cheney), 2, 117–20, 118

Howe, Irving, 196

Howells, John Mead, 257–58n

Howells, William Dean, 208–9, 257–58n

"The Humanities in War Time" (Matthiessen), 162

Hungarian Club (New Haven, Connecticut), 20

Huntington, John Watkinson, 60

hurricane of 1938, 133–34, 137

Hyde, Louis: on Cheney's and Matthiessen's "special language," 94; Cheney's/Matthiessen's correspondence preserved by, 203, 211–12; Cheney's portrait of, 70; Matthiessen's correspondence about Salzburg, 184; on Matthiessen's politics, 133; Matthiessen's suicide note to, 200; *Rat & the Devil*, 2, 3, 213, 241n; wedding of, 48

"incident of the pear," 49–50, 145, 201

Independent Citizens Committee for the Arts, Science, and Professionals, 273–74n

Industrial Association (San Francisco), 107–8

inflation calculators, about, 228n

Institute of Living, 254n. *See also* Hartford Retreat

International Labor Defense, 251n

International Longshoremen's Association, 107–8, 164

Into an Old Room (de Polnay), 209, 280n

Isenbrant, Adriaen, 193

"I Sing the Body Electric" (Whitman), 55, 239n

"Ithaka" (Cavafy), 221

The Ivory Tower (H. James), 167

James, Alice, 186, 188

James, Henry: *The Ambassadors*, 139, 167, 169; *The American Novels and Stories of Henry James* (Matthiessen) on, 181; *American Renaissance* (Matthiessen) on, 148–49, 154; *The American Scene*, 167; *The Figure in the Carpet*, 188; *The Golden Bowl*, 167, 168; *Henry James: The Major Phase* (Matthiessen) on, 75, 145, 162, 166–70, 210, 266–67n; *The Ivory Tower*, 167; *The James Family* and *The Notebooks of Henry James* (Matthiessen) on, 186–88, 272n; Matthiessen's literary interest in, 4, 74, 78, 114; *The Portrait of a Lady*, 167–68, 208; *The Wings of the Dove*, 167–68

James, William, 186, 191

The Jameses: A Family Narrative (Lewis), 188

The James Family (Matthiessen), 186–88, 272n

James the Greater (Saint), 171, 267n

Jeanne-Claude, 214–15

Jessner, Lucie, 159

Jewett, Mary Rice, 75

Jewett, Sarah Orne: *A Country Doctor*, 77; *The Country of the Pointed Firs*, 76; *Deephaven*, 75, 172, 243n; Matthiessen's literary interest in, 4, 7; romantic life of, 77; *Sarah Orne Jewett* (Matthiessen) on, 69, 70, 73–79, 85, 114, 115, 147, 210; *The Tory Lover*, 243n

Jewett, Theodore H., 227n

Jewett Doorway (1927?, Cheney), 75

Jones, Howard Mumford, 105

Jose of Buena Vista (1935, Cheney), 250n

Joyce, James, 40

Kaplan, Justin, 85

Kate (Mann), 236n

Kazin, Alfred, 84, 154–55, 177, 183–85

Kellogg, Charlotte, 254n

Kenneth Hill (1937, Cheney), 119, 120

Kinoy, Arthur, 84

Kinsey, Alfred C., 194, 275n

Kittery, Maine, 89–106; author's connection to, 1–3; Cheney's and Matthiessen's books on homophile topics at, 96, 248n; Cheney's and Matthiessen's lifestyle and acceptance in, 93–95, 100, 106, 116, 249–50n, 252n; Cheney's and Matthiessen's Old Ferry Lane home purchase, 89–93, 93, 246n; Cheney's career while living in, 95, 97–100, 99, 102; Cheney's Depression-themed paintings in, 116–17; Cheney's encounters with other men in, 102–3; Cheney's final return to (1945), 171–73; Ditty Box cottage in Kittery Point, 65; early summer stays in Kittery, 61; Ednah Dow Smith Cheney's early life near, 26; Louisburg Square connection to, 257–58n; Matthiessen's career while living in, 95–97, 104–6; Matthiessen's return, after Cheney's death, 175–76, 193, 199–200; Piscataqua River and, 91, 172–73, 174; Thanksgiving tradition, 93–94, 139, 166, 249–50n

Kittery Press, on Harvard, 1

Knapp, Farwell: on Cheney family, 29, 61; on Cheney's drinking, 103, 249n; on Cheney's painting, 69, 72, 88; Cheney's painting of, 70; Kittery, summers at, 116, 117; on Putnam, 80, 82

Knapp, Helen Bayne: on Cheney's personality, 33; Kittery home of, 69; Kittery visits of, 116, 117; on Matthiessen's death, 175; Matthiessen's suicide note to, 200; relationship to Cheney, 29, 68

Knopf, Alfred A., Sr., 170
Kollar, Hanns Caspar, 137, 146–47, 260n

labor unions. *See* organized labor
Lacoste, René, 49
Ladd, Cecil, 120
Lady Chatterley's Lover (Lawrence), 86
"Lady Clara Vere de Vere" (Tennyson), 139
Lafayette (ocean liner), 100
Lafayette Baths, 15
Lambert, Alexander "Alex," 48, 131, 238n
Lambert, Ellen Cheney, 48, 129, 238n
Lanier's Tea Garden (Eliot, Maine, arts colony), 156
Lardner, Ring, 49
Lathrop, Howard, 117–20, *118*, 193
Laurens, Jean-Paul, 35, 234n
Lawrence, D. H., 86
Learned, Horace and Eileen, 241n
Leatherbee, Frances Crane, 272n
Leaves of Grass (Whitman), 96, 146
Lee Lucero (ca. 1935, Cheney), 250n
legal issues. *See* LGBTQ rights; organized labor; race issues; *individual names of laws*
Lenin, V., 198
Levenson, J. C., 85, 198
Levin, Harry, 85, 155, 202, 230n
Lewis, R. W. B., 169, 188
LGBTQ rights: antigay laws (1920s and 1930s), 13–14, 56, 127; antigay laws (1960), 135; health proxies, 215–16, 218; legalized same-sex marriage, 213–14, 218–23; legal ramifications of homosexuality (1923), 14; Mattachine Society, 204; Matthiessen's vision of sexuality as public identity, 5; New York State Marriage Equality legislation (2011), 220–21; separation of personal vs. professional lives before, 115
The Liberation of American Literature (Calverton), 105
Life magazine, and Cold War, 198–99

light bath therapy, 132
Lilies and Salute (1926, Cheney), 63
Lincoln, Abraham, 43–44
Lloyd, Henry Demarest, 18
London, Jack, 165
longshoremen's strikes (San Francisco), 107–8, 164, 250n
Los Angeles Times, on F. W. Matthiessen Jr., 23
Louisburg Square (Beacon Hill, Boston), 139, 257–58n
Love's Coming of Age, Towards Democracy (Carpenter), 96
Loving v. Virginia (1967), 167
Lowell, Abbott Lawrence, 84
Lowell, Amy, 205
Lowry, Howard, 121
Luce, Henry, 196–97, 198–99
Luks, George, 207
Lusk, Bill, 68
Lynch, Clarence, 251n

Macdonald, Charles, 42
Macdonald, Evelyn, 42–43
Maisel, Edward, 193
Man against Myth (Dunham), 182
"Man in the Open Air" (Matthiessen), 67
Mann, William J., 236n, 244n
Manning, Frederick, 81
March, Fredric, 246n
marriage: "Boston marriage" between women, 76, 243n; Cheney's and Matthiessen's marriage-like solidity (early 1930s), 100; heterosexual marriage expectation by Matthiessen, 14; Massachusetts legalized same-sex marriage in, 213–14; Matthiessen on, 51; Matthiessen on race issues in connection with, 166–67; New York State Marriage Equality legislation (2011), 220–21
Martin, Clyde E., 194, 275n
Marx, Leo, 85, 155, 202, 210
Masaryk, Charlotte, 272n
Masaryk, Jan, 186, 195, 271–72n, 276n
Masaryk, Tomáš Garrigue, 272n
Massachusetts: Department of

Mental Health, 258–59n; legalized same-sex marriage in, 213–14; Matthiessen's estate probated by, 210–12; Teacher's Oath, 121–22; testimony on pending legislation saved by, 277n. *See also* Boston

Massachusetts Institute of Technology, 122

Mathewson, Rufus W., Jr., 85

Mattachine Society, 204

Matthews, Joseph B., 199

Matthiessen, F. O. (Francis Otto): burial place of, 202, 213; in Canadian Royal Air Force, 15; Cheney's alcoholism and effect on, 100, 157–62 (*see also* alcoholism); on Cheney's union with, 219; choices of writing subjects for, 74–75; death of, 5, 200–201, 202–4, 278n; early book sales of, 85; early sexual identity and encounters, 11, 13–15, 19–21, 23–25, 51; in Eastern Europe, 177, 182–86, 189; estate of, 202, 210–12; family wealth and inheritances of, 7–10, 21–25, 197; grief from Cheney's death, 174–76, 184–85, 264n, 268–69n; at Hackley School, 10–15, 19, 25, 58; mental health issues of, 86–87, 128–30, 134–39, 162, 175–76, 200–201; *The Notebooks of Henry James*, 186–88; personality characteristics of, 57–58, 67, 69, 73, 120–21; posthumous publications of, 204–10, 261n; religious views of, 7–8, 10–11, 16–17, 177; as Rhodes Scholar, 21–25, 50, 53, 54, 57; *Sarah Orne Jewett* as first book published by, 75; Sarton character based on, 162. *See also* American literature field; Harvard University; Kittery, Maine; Matthiessen, F. O. (Francis Otto), works of; political activism of Matthiessen; relationship of Cheney and Matthiessen; Skull and Bones; Yale University

Matthiessen, F. O. (Francis Otto), works of: *The Achievement of T. S. Eliot*, 75, 113–16, 136, 210; *The American Novels and Stories of Henry James*,

181; *American Renaissance*, 1–3, 75, 108–9, 116, 128, 133, 135, 137, 144, 145–56, 178, 185, 200, 210; *The Collective Portrait*, 199; *From the Heart of Europe*, 177, 192–97, 207; *Henry James: The Major Phase*, 75, 145, 166–70, 210, 266–67n; "The Humanities in War Time," 162; *The James Family*, 186–88, 272n; "Man in the Open Air," 67; *The Notebooks of Henry James*, 186–88, 272n; "Our First National Style" (book review), 142; *The Oxford Book of American Verse*, 203, 205; "Oxford Letter," 24–25, 229n; *The Responsibilities of the Critic*, 261n, 279n; *Russell Cheney: A Record of His Work*, 2, 6, 176, 179–81, 240n, 243n; *Sarah Orne Jewett*, 69, 70, 73–79, 85, 114, 115, 147, 210; *Theodore Dreiser*, 75, 199–200, 203, 205–10; *Translation*, 74, 95–97, 115, 149, 247n

Matthiessen, Francis Otto (paternal great-uncle), 7, 226n

Matthiessen, Frederick William, Jr. (father), 7–10, 22–23, 197

Matthiessen, Frederick William, Sr. (grandfather), 8–10, 22, 228n, 231n

Matthiessen, Frederick William, III (brother), 7, 8–9

Matthiessen, George Dwight (brother), 7, 9

Matthiessen, Lucy Orne Pratt (mother), 7–11, 21–22, 23, 76, 202, 227n

McCaffery, Charles "Chili," 120

McCarthy, Clifford, 81, 113

McCarthy, Joseph, 204

McCarthy, Mary, 198

McCarthyism (House Un-American Activities Committee), 197–99, 204, 277n

McLean Hospital, 128–30, 134–39, 258–59n

Mead, Margaret, 183–84

Meany, George, 189

medical community. *See* health issues

Meeting House Hill (1940, Cheney), 142

Mellquist, Jerome, 181

Melville, Herman: *American Renais-sance* (Matthiessen) on, 147–49, 154; *Benito Cereno*, 152; *Billy Budd, Sailor*, 75, 152–53; Matthiessen on canon of American classics, 3, 74; Matthiessen's book contract plans, 169; Matthiessen's edited collection of poems by, 166; *Moby Dick*, 17, 146

Memorial Bridge (Kittery, Maine), 103, 120, 252n

Merlis, Mark, 5

Merriman, Roger, 105, 249n

metrazol (pentylenetetrazol-induced shock therapy treatment), 140–41, 158–60, 263n

Metropolitan Museum of Art, 102, 171–72

milieu therapy, 132

Miller, Perry, 83

Milton, John, 148

The Miracle Workers (Cheney Brothers pamphlet), 151–52, 153, 255n, 261n

Miss Jewett's Staircase/Stairway, Jewett House/Hall of the South Berwick House (1927, Cheney), 75–76, 78, 243n

Moby Dick (Melville), 17, 146

Moers, Ellen, 210

Montaigne, Michel de, 96

Monthly Review, founding of, 265–66n

Montross Gallery (New York), 70, 87–88, 102

Moore, Marianne, 205

Mount, William Sidney, 172

Mrs. Marcia Clarke (1928–29, Cheney), 71–72, 242n

Mrs. Maxwell E. Foster (ca. 1928, Cheney), 242n

Mrs. Nicholas Biddle (1928, Cheney), 242n

Muir, Edwin, 261n

Murdock, Eleanor, 200

Murdock, Kenneth: *The Achievement of T. S. Eliot* (Matthiessen) dedication to, 113–14; Matthiessen's collab-oration with, 170; Matthiessen's correspondence from McLean, 136–37, 202; on Matthiessen's first year at Harvard, 87; Matthiessen's

labor activism and, 122, 124; Mat-thiessen's suicide note to, 200, 202; Matthiessen's World War II plans and, 164; *The Notebooks of Henry James*, 186–88, 272n

Murdock, Laurette, 113–14

Museum of Fine Arts School (Boston), 32

Museum of New Mexico (Sante Fe), 112

National Citizens Political Action Committee, 273–74n

National Industrial Recovery Act (1933), 30, 90, 107–8

National Labor Relations Board, 90

National Miners' Union, 110

National Unemployment Day (March 6, 1930), 90

Navarro, Exiquio, 110–11, 251n

Nelson Cantave (1940, Cheney), 143

Neubrand, Lucy Orne Matthiessen, 7, 9, 10, 200, 203

New England: Cheney's painting themes of, 66–67; criticism of Matthiessen's portrayal of, 78; regionalism, 70. *See also* Kittery, Maine; Ogunquit, Maine; South Manchester, Connecticut

New England Journal of Medicine, on alcoholism and homosexuality, 141

New England Quarterly, on *American Renaissance*, 154

New Mexico Magazine, on Cheney, 112–13

New Republic: Matthiessen's articles/reviews in, 1, 111–12, 134–35, 178–79; Wilson and, 85

New York City: legal ramifications of homosexuality (1923), 14; National Unemployment Day (March 6, 1930), 90

New Yorker, on *American Renaissance*, 154

New York Evening Post, on Cheney's work, 99–100

New York Herald, on Cheney, 45

New York Herald Tribune: Alsop in, 275–76n; on *American Renaissance*, 154

New York Journal American, on Cheney, 156

New York State: FDR as governor of, 90; legal ramifications of homosexuality (1923), 13–14; Marriage Equality legislation (2011), 220–21

New York Times: on *American Renaissance*, 154; author's husband employed by, 1; Cheney reviewed by, 45; *The Crimson Letter* reviewed in, 1; on *Into an Old Room*, 209; Matthiessen's speech for, 170; on *The Oxford Book of American Verse*, 205

New York Tribune, on Cheney, 45–46

New York World Telegram, on Cheney, 140

Nicotiana (1937, Cheney), 126

North, Thomas, 95, 97

The Notebooks of Henry James (Matthiessen & K. Murdock), 187–88, 272n

Oaks, Susan Marcia, 75, 243n

Observer, Matthiessen reviewed in, 261n

Odiorne, Sarah, 227n

Ogunquit, Maine: Cheney's art training in, 36–37, 235n; Summer School of Drawing and Painting, 235n

Old Ferry Lane home of Cheney/Matthiessen. *See* Kittery, Maine

Old Venetian Houses (Chase), 52, 238–39n

Olmstead, Frederick Law, 130

organized labor: American Federation of Labor, 189; Cheney Brothers workers' strikes (1902, 1923, 1934), 30; CIO, 189, 274n; coal industry strikes, 109–12, 250–51n; Great Depression and public policy, 89–90; Harvard Teachers' Union, 121–24; longshoremen's strikes, 107–8, 164, 250n; Matthiessen's exposure to, at Yale, 18–19; National Industrial Recovery Act (1934), 30; Taft-Hartley Act (1947), 188–89

Orne, James, 227n

Orne, Lucinda Dwight Howard, 227n

Orne, Lucinda Howard, 227n

Orne, Samuel, 227n

Orne, William, 227n

Orne, William Wetmore, 227n

Orne family, 7–8, 227n

Oscar Wilde: His Life and Confessions (Harris), 96

"Our First National Style" (book review, Matthiessen), 142

Overton, Penelope, 48

The Oxford Book of American Verse (Matthiessen), 203, 205

"Oxford Letter" (Matthiessen), 24–25, 229n

Oxford University, Matthiessen as Rhodes Scholar, 21–25, 50, 53, 54, 57

Oxford University Press, 121, 169, 180

Paris (ocean liner), 2, 26, 48–50

Paul Hoen (1930, Cheney), 81–83

Peabody, Richard Rogers, 101, 248n, 264n

pentylenetetrazol-induced shock therapy treatment (PTZ), 140–41, 158–60, 263n

Pepperrell, William, 257–58n

Pepperell's Cove (1933, Cheney), 99

Perkins, Frances, 165

Peters, Ruth, 236n

"Philippine Pete and Katchina Kate" (Cheney), 130, 255n

Pike's Peak paintings (Cheney), 41

Piscataqua Lane (ca. 1933–36, Cheney), 98–99, 99

Piscataqua River, Kittery location on, 91, 172–73, 174

Pitkin, Donald, 162

Pitkin, Emily Knapp, 162

Platt, Charles Adams, 33, 35, 60, 240n

"Poetry in Wartime" (T. S Eliot), 162

political activism of Matthiessen: Bridges's naturalization campaign, 164–65, 203; Dunster House Bookshop censorship case, 85–86; FBI investigation of Matthiessen, 156, 164, 181–82, 189, 203–4, 262n; following Cheney's death, 176–77, 190–92; increased activism during Cheney's illnesses, 145; Matthiessen

political activism of Matthiessen (*continued*)
as Socialist, 21; Matthiessen on literature and political/moral problems, 176–77; Matthiessen's interest in, as Yale undergraduate, 15–17, 20–21; political tone of *Henry James*, 168–70; Progressive Party speech, 190–92, 273–74n; race issues, 166–67. *See also* Cold War; World War II
Pomeroy, Wardell B., 194, 275n
Portland Press Herald, on Cheney, 78
"Portrait du Père de Cézanne"/*The Artist's Father, Reading "L'Événement"* (Cézanne), 40–41, 72
The Portrait of a Lady (H. James), 167–68, 208
A Portrait of an Artist as a Young Man (Joyce), 40
Portsmouth Factory (1935, Cheney), 119
Portsmouth Herald, Cheney's obituary in, 2, 174
Portsmouth Waterfront, two paintings entitled (1933? and 1937, Cheney), 119
Pound, Ezra, 149
Powers, Lyall H., 188
Prall, David, 123
Pratt, George Walter, 227n
Pratt, Lucy. *See* Matthiessen, Lucy Orne Pratt (mother)
preliminary catalogue raisonné (Candee & Carol Cheney), 243n, 264n
Pretzel (cat), 94, 138, 139, 143, 178, 201
Price, Frederic Newlin, 180
Professor A. Canolle (1911, Cheney), 40
Progressive Party, 182, 190–92, 273–74n
Proust, Marcel, 96
Putnam, Howard Phelps "Put": with Cheney and Matthiessen in Europe, 101; Cheney's drinking and, 100; correspondence published in *Russell Cheney* (Matthiessen), 181; at Cragmor Sanitorium, 41–43; Cutting's bequest to, 113; death of, 197; on disclosure of relationship between Matthiessen and Cheney,

56; at Hartford Retreat, 132, 142; Hepburn and, 71; marriages and sexual orientation of, 236n; poetry of, 80; in Santa Fe, 79–81
Putnam, Ruth, 200

race issues: *Brown v. Board of Education* (1954), 167; integration by Highlander Folk School (Tennessee) and, 211; Matthiessen on poetry and, 205; slavery omitted from *American Renaissance*, 152
Rackliffe, John, 121, 261n, 279n
Rahv, Philip, 168
Ransom, John Crowe, 190
Rat & the Devil (Hyde, ed.), 2, 3, 213, 241n
Reconstruction Finance Corporation, 125
Reeves, Jesse, 201
regionalism, 70
Reinhardt, Max, 270n
relationship of Cheney and Matthiessen, 48–64, 65–88; Boston apartment of Cheney and Matthiessen, 139; cats of, 94, 138, 139, 143, 178, 201; Cheney family's disapproval of, 68; Cheney family's sale of KD House, 61–62; Cheney's return to New York (1925), 56–57; Cheney's sexual encounters with other men, 72–74; correspondence, preservation of, 202–3, 211–12; disclosure to friends about, 54–56; early correspondence, 50–53; early meetings in Europe, 53, 56, 59, 63, 64; early visits to Kittery, 61, 65–67, 69, 80 (*see also* Kittery, Maine); holiday traditions, 93–94, 139, 166, 249–50n; "incident of the pear," 49–50, 145, 201; intimacy of, 53–54, 57–59, 62, 82–83; legacy of, 223; literature and role in, 114–15, 248n; Matthiessen's career and self-imposed censorship of, 155–56; nicknames for each other, 32, 59, 94, 148; *Paris* ship crossing and initial meeting, 2, 26, 48–50; Putnam, disclosure to,

56; *Rat & the Devil*, 2, 3, 213, 241n; Santa Fe stays of, 79–83, 108–13, 170, 260n; *Sarah Orne Jewett* and Cheney's paintings, 75–76, 78, 243n; separation due to alcoholism and, 160–71; stays at Cheney's Connecticut studio, 59–61. *See also* alcoholism; health issues; Kittery, Maine; marriage; Skull and Bones

Remembrance of Things Past/À la Recherche du Temps Perdu (Proust), 96

The Responsibilities of the Critic (Matthiessen), 261n, 279n

Rest on the Flight into Egypt (Isenbrant), 193

Reynolds, Joshua, 57

Rimbaud, Arthur, 96

Robbins, Alexandra, 230n

Roberts, Dee, 111

Roosevelt, Eleanor, 182

Roosevelt, Franklin Delano, 81, 90, 165, 188, 190

Roosevelt, Theodore, 81, 238n

Rosenfeld, Paul, 190

Ross, Rodney A., 277–78n

Royal Photographic Society of Great Britain, 53

Ruland, Richard, 115

Russell Cheney: A Record of His Work (Matthiessen), 2, 6, 176, 179–81, 240n, 243n

Ryan, V. Gerard, 141, 159, 160

Salot, Ann Marie, 258–59n

Salzburg Seminar in American Studies (American Civilization), 176, 182–84, 200, 270n, 271n

San Marco/St. Mark's (1924, Cheney), 52

Santa Barbara Arts Club, 61

Santa Fe, Cheney's/Matthiessen's visits to, 79–83, 108–13, 170, 260n

Santa Fe Mountains (1935, Cheney), 250n

Santa Fe New Mexican, owner of, 81

Santos bultos, 171, 267n

Sarah Orne Jewett (Matthiessen), 69, 70, 73–79, 85, 114, 115, 147, 210

Sarton, May, 5, 162

Saturday Evening Post, on Alcoholics Anonymous, 158, 162

Saturday Review of Literature, on American Renaissance, 154

Schlesinger, Arthur, Jr., 85, 177, 274n

Sea Wolf (London), 165

Second Society of the First Parish, 227n

Secrets of the Tomb (Robbins), 230n

Sexual Behavior in the Human Male (Kinsey, Pomeroy, & Martin), 194, 275n

Sexual Inversion (Ellis), 12

Shakespeare, William, 96, 149, 154, 220

Shand-Tucci, Douglas, 1–2

"shape-up" (labor practice), 108

shock therapy treatment, 140–41, 158–60, 263n

Shock Treatment in Psychiatry (Jessner), 159

Shurtleff, Alice, 91

Shurtleff, Harold, 91

silk manufacturing. *See* Cheney Brothers Silk Manufacturing Company

Simmons, Ernest J., 177

Singer, William Henry, Jr., 32

Sister Carrie (T. Dreiser), 207–8

Skull and Bones: Cheney as member of, 32, 42; Cheney's/Matthiessen's shared bond through membership in, 48–50, 54; male camaraderie of, 19–20, 230–31n; Matthiessen as "Little Devil" of, 19, 58–59, 230n; Matthiessen's disillusionment about, 196–99, 200, 278n; Matthiessen's membership in, 16, 19–20, 24; Putnam as member of, 42; Tighe and, 81

Skungimaug—Morning (ca. 1922, Cheney), 47, 47, 57

Sloan, John, 207

Smith, E. D. *See* Cheney, Ednah Dow Smith (mother)

Smith, Henry Nash, 146

Smith, Hope, 100

Smith, Jessica, 274n

Smith, Lillian, 166–67

Smith, Mrs. Ludlow Ogden. *See* Hepburn, Katharine
Solly, Edwin, 39
Solomon, Harry Cesar, 140–41, 258n
"Song of Myself" (Whitman), 150–51
Sonnet 29 (Shakespeare), 220
Southern Pacific Railroad, 89
South Manchester, Connecticut: Cheney Brothers presence in, 26–29, 31 (*see also* Cheney Brothers Silk Manufacturing Company); Cheney's studio/garden in, 59–61, 67–68, 92, 126, 133–34, 241n; hurricane of 1938, 133–34; KD House of Cheney family, 26–28, 61–62, 65, 174, 240n; South Manchester Railroad, 29; South Manchester Water Company, 29
Soviet Russia Today, editor of, 274n
Spencer, Christopher, 237n
Spencer, Theodore, 197
Spencer repeating rifles, 43–44, 237n
Spiller, Robert E., 154
Spinoza, Baruch, 114
Stalin, Joseph, 133, 195–96
A Star Is Born (films), 246n
sterilization, forced, 127
Stern, Frederick C., 4, 155, 199, 209
Stevens, Wallace, 202
Stewart, Donald Ogden, 182
Stowe, Harriet Beecher, 152
Strange Fruit (L. Smith), 166–67
strikes. *See* organized labor
Strouse, Jean, 188
Studies in the Psychology of Sex (Ellis), 24, 96
Studies of Greek Poets (Symonds), 96
Study for New Mexico Scene (1935, Cheney), 250n
St. Vincent Millay, Edna, 205
Summers, Joseph and U. T., 245n
Sutherland, John, 30
Sweezy, Alan R., 123–24, 265–66n
Sweezy, Paul, 163, 199, 200, 265–66n, 279n
Swimming (1885, Eakins), 149–52, *150*, 154
Symonds, John Addington, 24, 96, 149

Taft-Hartley Act (1947), 188–89
Taormina (1924–25, Cheney), 53
Tawney, R. H., 16–18, 91–92, 165
Teacher's Oath (Massachusetts), 121–22
Ten American Painters (New York exhibition, 1914), 239n
Tennyson, Alfred, 139
Terry, Jennifer, 158
Theodore Dreiser (Matthiessen), 75, 199–200, 203, 205–10
Thimig, Helen, 270n
Third Congregational Society (Springfield, Massachusetts), 227n
Thomson, Virgil, 183
Thoreau, Henry David, 3, 147–49, 198
Thorne, Ethel Cheney, 37
Thurmond, Strom, 190
Tighe, Larry, 81
Tillotson, Kenneth J., 141–42, 258–59n
Todd, Eli, 130
The Tory Lover (S. O. Jewett), 243n
"To Think of Time" (Whitman), 151
Translation (Matthiessen), 74, 95–97, 115, 149, 247n
Trilling, Lionel, 207
Truman, Harry, 190
tuberculosis sanitoria (early twentieth century), 38–43
Tufts University, 122
Tyler, Moses Coit, 105

Unitarianism: Congregationalism and inception of, 7–8; Matthiessen family's religious practice, 7–8, 10–11, 16–17; Matthiessen's identification with Christianity, 177; Unitarians of Springfield, 227n
An Unknown People (Carpenter), 96

Vanderbilt, Reginald C., 49
Van Doren, Mark, 178
Vanguard Press, 169
Vermeer, Johannes, 101, 193
Vitrine (1921, Cheney), 46
Vogel, Clarence F., 110, 112

Wadsworth Atheneum Museum (Hartford), 33, 43, 46, 56–57, 64, 180, 239n
Wall, James Hardin, 142
Wallace, Henry, 177, 182, 189–92, 204
Walsh, J. Raymond, 123–24
Walt Whitman (Arvin), 134
Walt Whitman (Symonds), 96
The Waste Land (T. S. Eliot), 80, 185
Watch and Ward Society, 85–86, 166–67
Water Front (Cheney), 98
Webb, Gerald, 39–40, 41
Webster, Ann, 251n
Welles, Gideon, 43–44
Welles, Orson, 164
Westclox, 7, 8, 10, 197
White, George Abbott, 163
Whitman, Walt: *American Renaissance* (Matthiessen) on, 146–51, 154, 178; "Calamus," 193; "The Children of Adam," 193; Griffin and, 32; "I Sing the Body Electric," 55, 239n; *Leaves of Grass*, 96, 146; Matthiessen on canon of American classics, 3; Matthiessen on literature of, 51; "Song of Myself," 150–51; "To Think of Time," 151; *Walt Whitman* (Arvin), 134; *Walt Whitman* (Symonds), 96. See also *American Renaissance*
Wilbur, Richard, 84, 85, 202
Wilde, Oscar, 53, 96
Wilkie, Wendell, 191

Williams, Roger, 191
Williams, Stanley, 154
William Sloan Associates, 206
Wilson, Edmund, 85, 187, 272n
The Wings of the Dove (H. James), 167–68
Winter, Ella, 182
With the Procession (Fuller), 208–9
Wood, Grant, 70
Woodbury, Charles H., 36–37, 45, 47, 75, 79, 100, 235n, 243n
Woodstock (1916, Cheney), 45
World War II: Matthiessen on, 164, 166, 265n; Matthiessen's work in Eastern Europe during, 177, 182–86, 189; Salzburg Seminar in American Studies (American Civilization), 176, 182–84, 200, 270n, 271n; Taft-Hartley Act (1947) at end of, 188–89
Wylie, Elinor, 205

Yale University: Cheney as undergraduate at, 32, 34, 34, 42, 43; Matthiessen as undergraduate at, 11, 15–21, 22; Matthiessen's estate and, 211–12; Matthiessen's teaching position at, 67, 73; *Yale Daily News* and Matthiessen, 16, 23; Yale Liberal Club, 18–19; *Yale Review* and Matthiessen, 85, 154, 155. See also Skull and Bones

Zuzu (Baby, cat), 94, 143, 172, 201

SCOTT BANE was born in Portsmouth, New Hampshire, and grew up in Maine, not ten miles from where F. O. Matthiessen and Russell Cheney made their home. After reading about the two men in the *New York Times*, Bane began researching their life together, leading him to libraries, archives, and historical societies throughout New England and the Northeast. Bane is a proud product of the City University of New York system, obtaining a BA, summa cum laude, from Hunter College; an MPA from Baruch College; and a JD from CUNY School of Law. He has worked in philanthropy for fifteen years, largely focused on helping vulnerable people obtain health care, housing, and employment. *A Union Like Ours* is his first book. He lives in New York City with his husband, David W. Dunlap.